FERENC ERDEI
SELECTED WRITINGS

FERENC ERDEI
SELECTED WRITINGS

EDITED BY

TIBOR HUSZÁR

AKADÉMIAI KIADÓ, BUDAPEST 1988

Translated by Pál Félix and Sándor Eszenyi
Translation revised by Dávid Bíró

ISBN 963 05 4779 1

Printed in Hungary
by Szegedi Nyomda, Szeged

CONTENTS

I
HUNGARIAN SOCIETY BETWEEN
THE TWO WORLD WARS*

* The Hungarian original is to be found in Ferenc Erdei's *Összegyűjtött művei* (Collected Works) *A magyar társadalomról* (Writings on Hungarian Society), *A magyar társadalom a két világháború között* (Hungarian Society between the two World Wars), Akadémiai Kiadó, Budapest, 1980, pp. 292—346. Originally this essay was published in *Valóság* 1976, No. 4. pp. 23–53, No. 5. pp. 36–58.

I. THE STRUCTURE OF HUNGARIAN SOCIETY

1. CLASSES AND SOCIETY IN HUNGARIAN DEVELOPMENT

In the original capitalist society the technology of production, the capitalist relations of production and the bourgeois structure of class society developed simultaneously on the foundations which had been developed in the course of medieval evolution. Within this development economic structure and social structure had been the mutual products of each other and, at the same time, these societal structures replaced feudal society based on estates. These societies were thus reconstructed from below concurrently and transformed into a capitalist economic system and bourgeois society by the industrial revolution and the bourgeois socio-political revolution. Though this original capitalist-bourgeois development shows caharacteristically differing types such as the French, British or American type of transformation, they have some common features as well: both the capitalist order of their production and the bourgeois structure of their society have emerged owing to their own specific development.

On he other hand, in the societies of Eastern Europe, modern development has followed a different trajectory. Here medieval transformation had not brought about the technological and social conditions for bourgeois society already during feudalism, or even if it had produced such conditions on a primitive level, these conditions were prevented from developing further in modern times. Neither the technological nor the socio-political revolution have taken place in these societies, and therefore the feudal forms of the social structure have survived to a great degree in later times, too. Nevertheless, from the middle of the 19th century the capitalism of Western societies penetrated this region and acquired considerable influence over this region. Capitalism penetrated these societies from outside and above; these societies did not succeed in developing along their indigeneous way into a capitalist economic system and bourgeois social structure. In spite of this, however, production and exchange of goods took on a capitalist character here, too, and as a result, sooner or later the constraints of the feudal economy disintegrated here, too; both agricultural production and industry as well as trade have been restructured fundamentally according to the conditions of capitalism. At the same time, the structure of society has not been transformed simultaneously and at one sweep in accordance with this economic change. This is not surprising since

9

no bourgeois stratum existed in these societies which could have carried out such a social revolution. As a result, the feudal forms of social structure survived despite the capitalist development of the economy. These forms adapted themselves to the new economic order and/or they became integrated with the adequate situations of the capitalist production relations. Thus agricultural production, too, underwent a capitalist transformation, however, the capitalists and workers of agriculture had not been transformed into bourgeois social classes but remained stuck in their feudal social structure, i. e., they remained landowning gents and peasants.

Nevertheless, in these societies which underwent a capitalist transformation it was not exclusively the historical feudal social structure which continued on a changed economic basis, but capitalist production gave rise to new social elements as well. However, these, too, differed considerably from similar strate of the original capitalist bourgeois societies. Here these were new formations as opposed to the further development of the historical bourgeois society. That is to say that here the bourgeoisie and working classes of capitalism also emerged, but these were entirely new formations which had no historical-social antecedents or at least only very rudimentary ones. Here the genuine bourgeois society equal to capitalism was not only a new formation devoid of historical roots but at the same time it represented an isolated, separate piece as well in addition to the "indigeneous" historical feudal social structure. This bourgeois society was made up of the freer elements of feudal society and to a great extent of aliens organizing as a separate, modern social structure in addition to the surviving historical social structure. Thus it became a colonial type formation as well as a "foreign body" in the general structure of society.

In the long run this peculiar organization was the consequence of the delayed development of these societies which could not be easily corrected in the course of modern capitalist development. Naturally such a disturbed development can forge ahead and there can take place a belated bourgeois revolution which subsequently can liquidate the feudal social structure and generally transform society as a whole into a bourgeois structure. But this does not occur under any circumstances. And it did not take place in the majority of the Eastern European societies and thus in most regions until recently this heterogeneous structure of society and/or the discrepance between the social structure and the system of production has survived.

Thus in the East European societies which have taken the road of capitalism the economy being of basically capitalist character is one question and the social structure which is partly a feudal formation, and partly a colonial-like formation is another. These societies are also capitalist class societies. However, they are not real and clear-cut bourgeois social structures but historical formations of feudal character or bourgeois formations without any historical antecedents. Thus there is an essential divergence in these societies between the organization of production and the structure of society, i. e., the actual class relations and social conditions are not identical. The two have developed along different historical lines with the result that they have retained their different natures all through modern development.

The specific social development embodied by the capitalistic societies of Eastern Europe naturally does not invalidate the general laws and regularities of the interconnections between productive relations and social structure. The point in question is that in the course of this specific development a time-lag evolved between productive relations and social forms. Further development shows a tendency of absolute validity: this time-lage decreased, the structural conditions of society adapted themselves to the changed conditions of production. Such a process is generally characteristic of these societies and their more recent development is the most characteristic feature of their slower or faster progress. This process should be termed in the broadest sense of the word bourgeois development meaning that historical forms of society adapt themselves to and fall in step with the productive relations at all stages. Thus, the historical landowning upper classes have been increasingly transformed into a capitalist entre-preneur bourgeois class, while peasant smallholders have more and more developed into a small-scale entrepreneur agrarian petit bourgeoisie, whereas the cotters and poor peasants have become the agrarian proletariat. No matter how fast this process had advanced, it still had not made so great progress that this duality had ceased to exist. It is still not the fulfilment of this process, i. e., the levelling off of the time-lag but the levelling process itself which reflects the reality of these societies. And this transitory state has proved to be very lasting. As a rule the societies of Eastern Europe have started out on the capitalist road around the middle of the past century and bourgeois transformation is still more or less unaccomplished.

Hungarian society is a characteristic example of East-European societies where capitalist transformation has been achieved from outside; therefore, also the development of Hungarian society significantly reflects the peculiar dualism of production relations and the structure of society. Hungarian society is organized and stratified according to the production relations of capitalism, yet the social structure is not the direct result of the capitalist mode of production but it is a further development of the structural elements which have survived from the times of feudalism. Moreover, Hungarian society, too, is characterized by the process of equalization of the time-lag, i. e., bourgeois development, as well as by the fact that besides the historical social structure also a modern bourgeois society has been built up in the course of modern development according to the capitalist relations of production.

If Hungarian society is analyzed only in terms of the relations of production and class stratification, we get a rather abstract and by far not typical picture of it. Though our above characterization is sound because our society is characterized by such an organization of the conditions of production, nevertheless actual Hungarian society differs from it. The empirically observable class positions are not occupied by the formations of genuine bourgeois societies but by other social forms which have emerged in the course of Hungarian history. Thus, the actual reality of Hungarian society becomes evident only if it is thoroughly examined what kinds of historically evolved social forms do subsist in certain class situations. Such a special attention to the specific development of social structure is important, so much the more as the process of bourgeois transformation has not made considerable progress in our society.

Thus Hungarian society between the two World Wars ought to be examined according to the above viewpoints if our aim is to comprehend empirical reality. The class stratification of our society should be defined unambiguously according to the production relations; at the same time, the specific development of social structure, which has to a great extent developed separately, has to be thoroughly analyzed as well. From such an approach it follows first of all that in that period – as generally in the course of development following 1867 – Hungarian society had an extremely complex structure. Generally and as a whole it was not bourgeois society but the compound of a bourgeois society developed together with the capitalist transformation and a feudal social structure which continued to exist in the course of capitalist evolution as well. Under such circumstances entirely independent structures became interlinked with each other within the framework of Hungarian society. Although these occupy the class positions of the very same economic structure, they are still parallel and separately viable social forms which are interconnected, interrelated and associated, nevertheless they have not merged into homogeneous bourgeois society even at that time. The topmost and dominating social structure was the modernized historical national society which has developed as a continuation of the feudal society of the nobility. In that period, it still filled the same roles and positions in production as it did in the feudal society, however, it adapted itself to the conditions of capitalist production. And underneath it we find a historical folk social structure which has developed and become to a certain extent modernized as the continuation of the serfdom of feudal society and/or the folk society which had survived underneath all the feudal classes. In that period, too, this social structure prevailed maintaining the class situations and roles of feudal society though adapted by and large to the conditions of capitalist production. In addition to these historical structures, there developed within Hungarian society, too, the specific structure of capitalism as a modern bourgeois society being, however, but one of the factors of Hungarian society in the positions and roles of production in industrial production, trade and modern urban-intellectual life.

Thus class stratification and social structure have become a complex fabric in Hungarian society, and the period between the two World Wars was characterized by that intricate social structure. These structures have become assimilated to each other and therefore the process of bourgeois development – which is generally a progressive one in such societies – gained different meanings, and to a certain extent was disturbed. Due to such structural conditions in the period of our society mentioned above clear types did not emerge but an infinite number of transitional social forms were established which co-existed with each other. Nevertheless these multiple forms were integrated in a single social mechanism by capitalist production and the intertwining community of life within the framework of the Hungarian borders resulting in an orientally multiple stratification and blending of various social and cultural forms in the Hungarian villages and towns.

2. THE HISTORICAL NATIONAL SOCIETY

Fully developed national societies are at the same time genuine bourgeois societies as well. In such societies feudal domination has been destroyed by bourgeois revolution which has transformed the nation into a bourgeois society to which all members of the nation belong. Thus national society has become the unity of the whole people as a bourgeois production organization and social structure, and, within that, the whole society became involved according to its civic situation. The bourgeoisie has become a national bourgeoisie, and similarly the working class has become a national working class.

Since no bourgeois transformation has taken place in Hungarian development, Hungarian national society could not become a full-fledged bourgeois nation. The Hungarian bourgeois revolution was carried out by the lesser nobility, whereas the national-bourgeois transformation of the state and the economy was accomplished by the top and middle strata of feudal nobility, or more precisely it was these strata which headed that process and therefore, such transformation could not achieve results like a bourgeois revolution. Since society as a whole was not transformed into a bourgeois structure, the nation itself could not become the society of the whole people either. Though, owing to capitalist development, the nation has been transformed into a bourgeois production community, the structure of society still retained its feudal nature. And thus the modern nation, too, has emerged within the framework of feudal structures instead of including all members and layers of society. Thus the new concept of "nation" was the direct descendant and continuation of the social organization of the nation of the nobility, i. e., it was made up of strata and social forms which developed in feudal society.

As a result of such a historical development "national society", also in the period between the two World Wars, was but a superimposed structure and controlling-organizing supreme power in the life of the people and the community as a whole. National society in this period, too, contained only those strata and activities which it comprised in an earlier period of history while it imposed itself on the other strata of the community only from above and for the purposes of control. It can be pointed out precisely what roles of production and social life were organized within the bounds of national society: the very same ones which were developed and had been organized already in feudal society, i. e. big estate farming and the entire state and church life. All other activities such as industry and commerce as a whole, actual agricultural productive work as well as certain domains of intellectual life were excluded and had never been part of the formation of the "national society". All these developed within the framework of separate social structures according to their own historical and economic conditions, and were controlled by the "national society" from a distance and above.

The character of national society as a superimposed mechanism of social domination is stressed by the very fact that big estate farming still existed in that period. Bourgeois development and capitalist economy would have demanded in that period that the big estates of feudal origin should disintegrate into bourgeois production enterprises, i. e., mainly into small farms and to a lesser extent into capitalist medium-sized farms. This, however, did not happen for the very reason that "national society" essentially did not become transformed along the lines of bourgeois evolution but retained the feudal basis of its development. And it followed necessarily that big estate farming was preserved and with lesser or greater modifications it survived in that period, too. As a result, a considerable part of social production had been forced into the rigid, historically conservative forms of big estate farming. Between the two World Wars the smaller part of Hungary's agricultural production came from big estates preserving conservative farms and the system of big estates had provided a great support for the whole conservative social structure.

Similarly, in that period, too, state and church life retained those historical social forms which had developed in the course of preceding feudal development. Thus almost all the administrative-leadership-educational roles of society had been organized in the same conservative social structure that provided the framework for big estate farming. State organization and the churches underwent the same gradual transformation in the course of modern development as big landlord farming by entering the road of capitalism, however, neither of them changed fundamentally their underlying nature.

National culture in the period between the two World Wars has also been a clearly delimited entity in the Hungarian society not only as regards its intellectual contents but also due to the whole social process, i. e. external forms, organs and institutions of intellectual life. Following World War I, this conservative national culture became particularly separated, and

14

represented in literature, science and the arts the intellectual culture of the conservative high society. All the state and church organizations supported this intellectual workshop and as the state expanded over ever increasing areas during that period, the national culture, too, extended its domain. The organs of that culture had been first and foremost all the public and church institutions, i. e. schools, scientific, art and literary associations but all these social groups controlled a multitude and, at later times, ever proliferating number of newspapers, magazines and publishing houses as well.

This social organization assuming ever more a separated character was exactly reflected by the intellectual trends. In all the domains of intellectual culture the conservative national schools of thought drew the line sharply between themselves and the more modern intellectual tendencies rooted in other social traditions. So much so that the Christian-national press, national literature, national science and national arts had all become unambiguously identified with conservative trends, with intellectual endeavours which were not the work of the intellectual forces of society as a whole but were only intellectual reflections of the conservative high society. The restricted nature of the social basis of this intellectual culture is clearly demonstrated by the fact that throughout this era this culture was unable to boast of any truly outstanding, major intellectual achievement. The genuine and popular forces of the nation could not find a place in this intellectual life and the few manifestations of national forces lost their originality in the course of adaptation to conservative discipline. At any rate, it is a fact that the oustanding achievements of this period did not spring from the sources of conservative intellectual life.

In any genuine bourgeois national society the idea might not even arise that the upper institutions of society are not the representatives of the same nationhood as the lower organizations of society. In such societies the people as a whole is integrated and structured within the very same national social organization and the different amount of participation is but the function of class relations and background. Hungarian society, however, is a complex, stratified system of social structures and these structures differ from each other in terms of their popular-national content.

The historical antecedents of the historical classes and the entire structure of the conservative historical national society is the Hungarian nobility. In the era of feudalism this nobility used to be overwhelmingly Hungarian also in the ethnic sense of the word, and it communicated with the classes below the estates according to the rules of feudal society. But even at that time there was a wider gap between the Hungarian nobility and the people on the lower scales of social structure than in Western Europe, in the same period. An alien state organization interfered with Hungarian development succeeding in various ways in separating the Hungarian nobility from the Hungarian people. First of all it elevated foreigners into the ranks of the

Hungarian nobility by means of land-grants and the endowment of court and state offices, and it furthered also by other ways and means the influx of alien nationalities into Hungarian nobility. Moreover, by its overall policy it tried to transform the upper strata of the nobility into a transnational estate of the (Hapsburg) Empire. However, despite such influences the Hungarian nobility was predominantly of Hungarian ethnic origin at the middle of the nineteenth century, and thus it had an ethnic character common with the Hungarian people. However, this situation underwent a radical change because modern development, too, proceeded within the bounds of the Hapsburg Empire and, as a consequence, a further inflow of alien elements took place into the historical classes which preserved themselves as the heirs of the nobility. In the period of absolutism a considerable number of Austrian-Czech officials were absorbed by the feudal upper middle class whereas later on it was particularly the lower social strata of German nationality that became assimilated to the higher positioned historical classes. Thus, in the period between the two World Wars the ethnic background of the historical classes had become a diversely blended Hungarian origin, and these classes had not only ceased to communicate socially but practically lost all contacts with the lower strata of the Hungarian people.

The capitalist development of the Hungarian national economy ran parallel with the conservation of the historical social structure, and this had a serious effect on the development of the society. The historical social order had undoubtedly succeeded in preserving itself, nevertheless some modifications, changes were brought about in this structure by the capitalist transformation of the economy. Both in the period between the two World Wars and earlier, in the era following 1867, this process of bourgeois transformation progressed under two influences. First, big landlord farming and the state organization as well as church life had to face a new situation, in order to solve new problems resulting from the capitalist transformation of the economy and thus, these historical formations, too, adapted themselves to the requirements of capitalism. Second, capitalism had called into life under Hungarian conditions a modern bourgeois society, i. e., this separately developed bourgeois society, too, exerted influence on the conservative national society. As a result of this dual influence the methods of both big landlord farming and the church as well as public administration had been modernized, had assumed a bourgeois character, and together with them other forms and institutions of the historical national society had also developed on a similar line. This influence was strong both as regards the functioning of the state and the intellectual culture of society. However, this bourgeois transformation was merely an adaption to changed circumstances and it did not result in a structural reorganization in compliance with the new conditions; on the contrary it aimed at preserving the traditional order. In the period between the two World Wars one may find

16

several examples which show that this conservative society had been able to adapt in a variety of ways to the new conditions without essentially changing, however, its historical nature.

3. MODERN BOURGEOIS SOCIETY

The social structure in the era of Hungarian feudalism was not of a kind where the subordinate organizations of society could have developed and grown. Thus, neither the bourgeoisie could develop as far as its production technologies, social organizations or political power are concerned nor the peasantry could take appropriate steps aimed at bourgeois development. When the capitalist mode of production forced its way into Hungarian society from outside there were no such elements in the society's structure which could have contributed to this development from below. There was no considerable middle-class stratum which could have developed the bourgeois society of capitalism on the basis of its own previous development, whereas the nobility and peasantry were even less able to undergo a transformation into bourgeois society as required by capitalism.

Capitalism itself had built up the modern Hungarian bourgeois society alongside the historical social structure. This was accomplished partly by alien elements and partly by more mobile elements of the Hungarian society, i. e., first with the help of Jews and second with Germans. Capitalist production and trade expanded with such an overwhelming dynamism and colonial business mentality that already existing bourgeois elements were not fostered and raised but crushed and absorbed by it. As a matter of fact, there did exist a rudimentary bourgeoisie in Hungarian society which fulfilled the functions of industrial production and commodity trade by adopting primitive capitalist methods under the conditions of feudal society. However, just because of its underdeveloped nature and because capitalism was well prepared and penetrated Hungarian society with developed methods, this bourgeoisie was unable to switch over to the new ways and, as a result, was worn out in the course of competition. Under such circumstances modern Hungarian bourgeois society built up not on the foundations of a previous historical development but as an entirely new formation.

This course of development rendered it self-evident that Hungarian bourgeois society was essentially different from bourgeois societies of genuine development. Actually Western bourgeois society is a historically specific formation shaped by a long development. There all the elements of bourgeois society, including production technologies and bourgeois social organizations had been built up within the framework of the feudal society under the feudal superiority of the nobility. Finally they shook off feudal superiority and by means of a bourgeois revolution the whole of society was transformed into a bourgeois structure. As a result of that lengthy historical development, the people as a whole became organized within the framework of bourgeois society in these societies and the history of the entire community proceeded on the road of bourgeois development.

Bourgeois society became something quite different in Hungarian history. It was first of all a colonial formation. It was built up under the circumstances of external dependency by borrowing ready-made foreign examples: the enterprises of the developed capitalist bourgeois societies simply established themselves in Hungarian society. But Hungarian bourgeois society differed from its Western counterparts also in the sense that here capitalist production did not make use of historical social methods but functioned on the basis of brusque business mentality and unrestrained profit incentives. In the genuine bourgeois societies both capitalist enterprises and the workers in capitalist factories had a certain amount of social "resources": the former ones had qualifications for the development of production and production technologies, the latter ones were to a certain degree protected against the full exploitation of their labour. Hungarian development lacked all these elements, and Hungarian bourgeois society therefore took the form of an unrestrained business organization.

Nevertheless, even under such conditions there emerged a full-fledged bourgeois society based on those functions of production which had not been organized in the course of feudal development or had been created by capitalism. Thus the whole of industrial production, commercial activity and credit system had been organized within the framework of modern bourgeois forms, and similar was the case of the business enterprises of intellectual and political life. All these activities had been stratified therefore not only according to the capitalist mode of production but had established a genuine bourgeois social structure reflecting the class positions as they were formed by the system of production. By the inter-war period this bourgeois society had become fully developed, yet even in this period it did not go beyond the roles assumed at the beginning of capitalist development. Thus also at that time industrial production, the trade and the credit system were organized within the bounds of bourgeois society. In these fields, however, bourgeois society prevailed completely. The capitalists of this mode of production became genuine bourgeois citizens, the small capitalists became real petty bourgeois citizens and the workers real proletarians. In this way, the whole structure of modern bourgeois society took shape, but even in that age bourgeois society was alien to the simultaneously existing historical national society.

The rise of this modern bourgeois society manifested itself first and foremost in urbanization. The enormous simultaneous increase in industrial production, trade and entrepreneurial spirit was reflected by the development of the capital, and the provincial towns, and it demonstrated the expansion of bourgeois social structure by the side of the historical formations. This development made progress in the inter-war period, too. As the bourgeois society expanded it exerted an increasingly bourgeois influence on the upper national society and the lower popular society of the peasantry, too, but it did not develop far enough to make bourgeois society the prevailing structure of the Hungarian community. Even at the end of that period bourgeois society was only one of the social structures; more precisely, it was the other upper structure of Hungarian society.

Modern bourgeois society has been representing modern urban civilization in Hungarian society both on a higher middle-class level and also among the petite bourgeoisie and the working class. Although the petit bourgeois and proletarian class relations were common and similar among the lower urban strata and the peasantry, the social forms of everyday life showed some marked differences. These differences were reflected by the fact that while industrial and commercial urban society had reached a certain level of civilization, the peasantry had been excluded from this development. However, this difference in development levels does not truly characterize the middle-class way of life brought about by bourgeois society since this itself is of a colonial nature. In other words, it had been created on the basis of foreign examples, it had adapted itself to these examples all the time, and had not been the product of an indigenous evolution built up from the roots. The way of life of the nobility originated from history and was opposed to the world of lower classes. Similarly, the urban bourgeois way of life had been created on the basis of European patterns and appeared like a higher world floating above the real existence of the peasantry.

The intellectual culture of modern bourgeois society is an abstract high-brow culture in the same way as that of the historical national society. However, it has much fewer restrictions and a much broader social base. For this very reason it is able to make greater intellectual efforts and to exert a greater influence. It was not a mere chance that in the modern heroic age of Hungarian literature the institutions and organs of bourgeois society provided career opportunities to talents of other social background as well. After World War I, this situation changed for the worse, however, for highly talented persons it was still a more feasible course than that of the historical national society. This is the reason why, irrespective of quality, the products of bourgeois intellectual culture had a much greater influence on the whole of society than those of conservative national society. On the other hand, also bourgeois culture had its inherent restrictions and limits. Its sources are rather ready-made Western patterns than the grass-root energies of a whole bourgeois-national community. As a result, both bourgeois culture and the intellectual life of national society failed to unite all intellectual forces of society. The guiding principle of bourgeois society was Western style progress, and in this respect there was no difference between the bourgeoisie and the working-class. This guiding principle is just the opposite of the national conservatism of the historical classes. This

19

explains the deep-rooted antagonism between the two and the abstract character of both, too. The conservative national conception goes far back to history and it represents a conservative reaction to existing reality, whereas the idea of Western style progress is linked to Western development and thus loses touch with the reality of Hungarian society.

Hence both ideas are hampered by more or less similar restrictions and abstractions, and therefore neither of them is able to become the generally valid guiding conception of Hungarian society. The conservative national conception is restricted since it is conservative and therefore not truly national, while the idea of progress is limited since it was formed as the simple negation of the conservative national society and therefore it is not national either. However, as a considerable result of the social development between the two World Wars, the working class discovered the national road of development, i. e. it understood the requirement that Hungarian society has to transform itself into a truly national productive organization and social structure. The working class therefore, represents in its political ideas both the principle of progress and the general conception of the nation.

In the period between the two World Wars the alien character of the bourgeois society had become an acrimonious political problem. Subsequently the two revolutions were condemned as revolutions of the Jews by the historical national society branding both the democratic liberal aspirations of the bourgeoisie and the socialist movement of the working class as Jewish revolts. As a matter of fact, in the leading strata of both the radical movement of the bourgeoisie and the socialist labour movement Jews had a majority. This, however, was the result of the fact that Hungarian bourgeois society developed above the lower strata of the Hungarian society and alongside the conservative historical classes, and those Hungarian strata which had become rigid within the historical framework were practically excluded from this evolution in the course of development. In spite of this, the significance of the movements of the bourgeoisie and the working class in terms of the social development of the Hungarian people as a whole was the same as anywhere of the elements furthering bourgeois progress independent of nationality. The bourgeois and labour movements headed by Jews were condemned as destructive only in the formulations of the conservative national society since they actually aimed at the destruction of the conservative social order.

The great Hungarian poet, Endre Ady once wrote about the weakness of Hungarian bourgeois development: "... in our country there grew a scattered, spineless bourgeoisie inclined to playing the gentry". And it had been like this not only at his times but also in the inter-war period. The conservative national society put up such a strong resistance to bourgeois development on the one hand and represented such an irresistible upperclass superiority on the other, that the upstart and "spineless" bourgeoisie proved highly susceptible to assimilation. Thus, instead of realizing a bourgeois conquest waging a gradual fight for bourgeois revolution it adapted itself and became assimilated to the conservative upper-class superiority. This assimilation became a markedly strong trend within the highest stratum of the capitalist bourgeoisie but it is also observable among the petite bourgeoisie. Only the working class resisted assimilation since its class interests would not have made possible such a transformation. However, the process of assimilation came to a standstill in the second half of that period and as the national society expanded towards middle-class professions amidst the clamour of antisemitic propaganda, the middle class itself gradually withdrew within its bourgeois framework.

II. HISTORICAL NATIONAL SOCIETY

1. THE CHURCH

The two main Churches of Hungary—the Catholic and the Calvinist Churches—differ essentially not only as regards their dogmas and organizations but in their historical development as well. Both their internal development and their social roles are rendered different by this difference. The Catholic Church is a hierarchic world organization which became a Hungarian national Church in the course of development by its having been for centuries the imperial Church of the Hapsburg Empire. The Calvinist Church, however, followed another way: it had been the persecuted Church of the Hungarian people in the period of Hapsburg rule, and in this way it became the other national Church of Hungarian society. Today both of them have become national Churches of Hungarian society and therefore their evolution, too, has taken by and large a similar course.

The two Churches pursued closely parallel courses in the period between the two World Wars both as regards religious life and pastoral work. The consequences of modern life made themselves felt in Hungarian society, too: organized religion has considerably decreased and the number of faithful diminished in all denominations. It was particularly the bourgeois development within the ranks of the peasantry which resulted in the reduction of the number of believers. At the same time, a new religious trend evolved in response to the crisis of modern life and this, too, manifested itself in Hungarian society. Under the changed circumstances of religious life both Churches embarked on the road of vigourously propagating the faith and established appropriate organizations. In both Churches increased religious work was the result of the recognition that the historical organization and methods of the Church were insufficient to retain and lead the congregations amidst the complex and increasingly materialist conditions of modern life. For this reason they established religious organizations in all spheres of life and introduced more direct and effective methods of disseminating the faith.

In the case of the development of both Churches the most important and most characteristic element in the period following World War I was the establishment of these novel organizations and methods. To a lesser extent they regenerated the old organizational frameworks but more frequently they established new organizations where they fostered religious life on a

22

broader basis. By these methods the two Churches penetrated particularly the ranks of youth, and both university and high-school students became targets of intensive religious education, whereas those youngsters who did not attend high-school were organized with the same purpose into girls' and young men's associations. The religious life of the adults was organized with similar zeal by the Churches: the Catholic Church endeavoured to protect and strengthen Christian ideology and religious faith within the framework of *Actio Catholica,* and the same goal was pursued by the Calvinist Church in the various organizations of domestic missions. This missionary work used new methods as well, and gradually it actually took the form of religious propaganda activity. That is, it assumed a more rational and worldly form interpreting religious faith as an ideology which answered also the questions of modern life. A so to speak new image of the religious man took shape as a result of this innovation which nevertheless did not blur the old historical forms of religiousness altogether, retaining the historical style of worship at the Catholics and that of piety at the Presbyterians. This kind of modernized mission work proved fruitful, the more so, as in both Churches a new type of priest emerged who was able to approach people living under modern conditions more successfully than his predecessor. Among Catholics there appeared agitator-type missionary individuals penetrating into the whole pagan fabric of secular life and argued with strong, realistic words in the interest of a religious Christian world outlook. In the Calvinist Church, the new type of ministers expressed *intellectualism*; for religious persuasion they relied on sophisticated reasoning and they combined this with personal intimacy. As a result—more or less to the same extent in both of the denominations—by the end of the period a certain religious renewal ensued, and though big masses could not be won back by the Church, it could rest assured to have a faithful minority. And the religious feelings of this minority actually grew into a world outlook manifesting itself both in political views and the practical views on the way of life.

However, all through history the Church has achieved a significant role more by means of its actual administrative-organizing work than by its missionary activity and dogmas. This role and power of the Church made themselves felt in the society of the period between the two World Wars, too. The regime which became consolidated in the wake of the counter-revolution called itself Christian-nationalist reflecting not only the restoration of the Christian ethico-religious ideal, not only antisemitism aimed against Jews having taken part in the revolutions, but first and foremost conservativism. This term meant therefore a programme of the full restoration of the historical social order and beyond the political power of the historical classes the renewal of the influence of the Church. In the course of that restoration the Church not only regained its pre-war positions but succeeded in achieving an ever greater and more influential role than before. One of the emigrated leaders of the bourgeois revolution has bitterly characterized the counter-revolution as the resurrection of the "feudal church state".

Naturally this did not take place, however, the church succeeded in actually regaining all her historical roles. The representatives of the church carried enormous weight in political life and the authority of the clergy and the church was reestablished completely. The church reconquered her positions in the educational system and the press, and parallel to the implementation of a conservative policy the church, too, reorganized her conservative educational activities. However, the two churches did not participate in the reestablishment of the old order in the same sense of the word.

Catholics used to complain that the process of consolidation was accomplished with the predominance of the Calvinists. This has been true not only to the effect that the majority of the outstanding personalities of the restoration were Calvinists but also the Calvinist Church identified herself more sincerely with the reestablishment of the conservative liberal system. Moreover the Calvinist Church has reacted in a different way to the collapse of the Monarchy and the dethronement of the Hapsburg king. These were the results of historical differences between the two Churches. In the same way as in political life it was the Protestant aristocrats of Transylvania who followed a realistic course and by their very nature were to a greater extent able to adapt themselves to the actual situation than the pro-Hapsburg Catholic peers. The Calvinist Church, due to her historical nature, associated herself without reservations with that policy. The Hungarian Calvinist Church represented the tradition of liberalism and the anti-Hapsburg wing of the national society, so inevitably it took this position. On the other hand, Hapsburg traditions were cultivated to a much greater extent by the Catholic Church the big landlord interests of which had much in common with the feudal conservative policy, and therefore she could not follow without qualms Bethlen, the non-legitimist prime minister who relied on the smallholders. Thus the Catholic Church took an oppositionist position through its party while the clergy doggedly stood by the ideology of legitimism.

Nevertheless, these political differences did not prevent the two Churches from becoming equally important elements of the reconstructed historical national society. The representatives of the churches had a decisive word in public life as a whole, and both churches were permitted complete liberty to develop their church life, moreover they received equal subsidies from the state. The only reason of a certain rivalry or jealousy was that they felt this liberty and subsidies were not always proportionate. Now and again the "denominational question" flared up inevitably because of these power and/or predominance differences. It was often felt by both Churches that the other one had been granted a wider field of activities and had received a greater amount of subsidies. Neither did the frequently referred to

24

bridge-building between Pannonhalma and Debrecen succeed in coordinating the religious activities or educational and organizing work of the two Churches; its only aim was the reconcilement of their political interests. In the second half of that period such denominational strife died down for the most as it became sufficiently clear that the state does not restrict the activities of either denomination and also that these activities do not jeopardize each other. The two great churches were equally acknowledged as influential factors of the historical national society and in that capacity of theirs they were prudently granted absolutely proportionate scope for their self-assertion.

In the same way as the conservative national society as a whole adapted itself to the changing times and ideas, the Churches also had to adjust. New demands which the church had to satisfy arose not only in religious life, but also the whole of social educational work had to face new tasks. The consciousness of people had been undermined to such an extent by the crisis and the political trends fighting against the conservative social order that both the conservative society and the church—in defence of their own existence—were forced to strengthen their educational work and political influence. The Churches actually did take this course. Both the great Churches became likewise political-minded; they took a stand as regards the new political tasks and answered the great questions of society by appropriate political ideas and political organizing work. However, once again here the historical differences between the two Churches became evident, and both as regards political ideas and political approaches they chose different ways.

True to its nature of being a mighty world institution of two thousand years, and aware of the fact that in Hungarian society she was not a people's institution built from below but was the successor of an imperial church superimposed on the people, the Catholic Church treated the crisis and the dominant political ideas not as Hungarian problems but as a universal problem of the age. Thus, also the social problems of Hungarian society were regarded as major dilemmas of materialism and idealism, capitalism and communism, tradition and revolution, Christianity and paganism, and were answered on the basis of the universal principles of the church. The Catholic Church revived therefore the papal social encyclics and framed her conservative reformist ideas in accordance with them. The Catholic Church faced these problems as a universal social Church, and rising above the specific problems of Hungarian society she gave voice here, too, to the universal social principles of the Churches. The conservative Catholic reform programme took shape most explicitly in the idea of vocational order, and a rather strong organization was built around this ideology by some extremely active and politically-minded clerics. In terms of the same political conception the church and/or certain organizations supported by the church-organized people's colleges, too, and here young peasants were

25

educated in this very spirit. Moreover, this conservative reformist policy was upheld by the church not only by means of such proclaimed political ideas and organized movements but was explained in the press, too, both among the intellectuals and the lower strata of society. Though the representatives of the Church or the laymen supporting the Church took a stand according to the innumerable varieties of actual problems, the same political idea lurked behind all and every variety: the espousal of such great humanistic ideas as liberty, natural law, social justice, the recognition of the justified human demands of the working class, the defense of the traditions of European cultural development, loyalty to constitutionalism, to the Christian-national pattern of Hungarian history. The standpoint taken by these organs as regards the various political aspirations was also characteristic. With unflagging and unrelaxing zeal they opposed materialist socialism, vigorously though less unambiguously approved of democratic efforts and distrustfully faced the movement of people's democracy.

The ever more vigorous political attitude of the Calvinist Church was of a markedly different nature. Since the Hungarian Calvinist Church has been the Hungarian people's church in its history, it regarded the social problems of the new era again as the major issues of the fate of the Hungarian people. Accordingly the symptoms of the crisis were viewed primarily not as the great all-embracing struggle between the different social systems and ideologies but were perceived as dangers menacing the Hungarian people. On the part of the Calvinist Church there evolved the idea of a popular Hungarian radicalism not only as defence against the crisis and the threatening hostile political tendencies but also as a definite demand for reforms aimed against the prevailing conservative order which has not been the indigenous organization of the Hungarian people. Though the Church herself did not support any regular, organized movement based on these ideas, some popular movements emerging outside the Church were viewed with sympathy and approval by the most progressive representatives of the Church. Only a few papers served that popular radicalism popularized and spread by various organizations of the church. At the same time, a number of people's colleges were organized by the various branches of the church where peasant youths were educated in the spirit of popular reformism. Incidentally, all manifestations of popular radicalism both in literature and science met with approval in Calvinish church circles.

However, neither of the great Churches as a whole only some of their affiliates and their more progressive and younger representatives became more politically conscious and active. These elements represented the social Church, and they had to—and actually did—emphasize this fact in relation to their own Churches, too, since both Churches as a whole remained conservative bodies. Thus, though they kept up with modern times both as regards their pastoral work and the socio-political education of the believers, and called into being new organizations and methods, in their main bodies they remained the supporting-pillars of the conservative social order. The trunks of the two great Churches sprouted only side-shoots in the direction of social reforms but as a whole they did not bend under the impact of the times. As a consequence, a kind of duality developed within the organizations of the Churches.

Two types of priests emerged in that period as a consequence of the two kinds of educational and social organizing roles. These two types corresponded to the conservative and modern models of priesthood. The majority, the higher clergy and the older ones continued to represent the conservative clerical quality in both Churches according to the historical past of the Churches and priesthood. In compliance with the nature of conservative society, this part remained an upper class clergy the members of which were eminent and influential elements of the social structure. There was, however, a difference between such kinds of Catholic and Calvinist clergy. The minister of the Calvinist Church was a gentleman of rebellious inclinations close to the people (it is by no means a mere chance that such outstanding Hungarian literary figures as Endre Ady or Zsigmond Móricz had such a family background) cherishing liberal and democratic ideas and representing from the early beginnings a more popular variant of gentleman mentality. On the other hand, even in that period the Catholic clergy has not shed the superior attitudes of the imperial church and has remained the "more feudal" variant of upper-class intelligentsia. The majority of it adhered to the House of Hapsburgs, its whole way of life and social outlook being more conservative but, at the same time, that clergy had a more general education and qualification.

The updated activities of the Church had brought about a novel type of priesthood, too, within the younger generation and within the ranks of the lower clergy. This transformation had been similar to the changes within the upper middle classes as a whole. Here, too, we experience a less detached and descending stratum of intellectuals just as has been the case in most professions and fields with the younger middle-class generation. Thus the Calvinist minister was an intellectual with a popular background, the priest of the people looking for cultural community and social connection with the lower strata of society, whereas the Catholic priest was a more general social character relaxing around himself the more traditional restrictions of the conservative society and clergy and communicating more freely with the secular society.

The development of the other churches differed very much from that of the two major churches. Most similar to that of the Calvinist Church might be considered the course taken by the Unitarian Church, whereas the development of the Lutheran Church shows markedly different features. The same can be said of the relation between the Roman Catholic and Greek Catholic churches. However, these minor Churches represented a much smaller percentage of the population and were of much smaller influence within Hungarian society, and therefore their significance fell far behind that of the two major churches.

2. THE STATE

In the period following the Compromise of 1867, the Hungarian state developed into a liberal constitutional state. This means that its legislation was organized on the basis of representative parliamentarism; the administration of justice and public administration were organized as separate organizations, municipal and county administration was built up on the basis of representative autonomy, national defense was transformed into a people's army based on general and compulsory military service—in brief, the Hungarian state was transformed all over into a liberal democratic constitutional state. Nevertheless, this state which has been entirely converted as regards both its basic principles and organizations did not transform the feudal state of the nobility in a radical, revolutionary way with respect of its actual social reality. First of all Hungary's constitutional links with Austria were not radically altered though these, too, underwent essential changes. In this respect radical change would have been created if Hungary had become independent of Austria and left the Monarchy. Since this had not been achieved, the country continued to be shackled by restrictions which did not permit a genuine transformation of its internal state organization.

In spite of representative parliamentarism, legislation remained in the hands of the upper strata of society, i. e. of the heirs of nobility and showed but little changes as compared to feudal legislation. The narrow framework and limitations of suffrage, the actual arrangement and organization of the elections, the laws defending the greatest tax-payers of the communities, the House of Lords—all these were elements in legislation and county and municipal autonomy which prevented the realization of a genuine people's sovereignty. And similarly, public administration was not transformed radically either, despite certain theoretical and organizational changes. It adopted entirely modern organizational forms. However, in its actual activities, it continued to function partly along the lines of the administrative traditions of the Hapsburg Empire and partly of the system of the public administration of the Hungarian nobility. Thus it remained some kind of superior legal administration instead of being transformed into a system of specialized administration. Its functions were ensured by the most refined guarantees of legality. However, the special forces functioning within it, remained similar to those of the times prior to its reorganization. And not surprisingly so, since social development as a whole proceeded in a way in that period that no actual transformation could take place, not even by

28

means of the most consistent theoretical radicalism. The entire historical social structure was preserved in such a way that the state organization was bound to be preserved, too, in its actual functioning.

This line of development continued in the period between the two World Wars, too, as the pre-war social pattern was restored by the process of consolidation. In all fields of the state organization only such reforms were carried out by which state life was not transformed essentially. The organization of legislation was not altered radically: franchise, the House of Lords, the actual proceedings of elections all retained their pre-war character. At the same time, county and communal self-government did not strengthen but rather declined. At two points, however, radical changes ensued in actual state life. First, the country became independent of Austria, i. e. it developed into a sovereign state and second, the state organization expanded enormously. Nevertheless, in the pattern of state organization no far-reaching transformation was brought about even by these actual changes. The same applies to the functioning of state organs. The independence of the country was ensured in a way—by exercising the rights of the head of state by the regent—that nothing was changed as regards historical legality, whereas the extension of the system of public administration was brought about without changing either the structure of public administration or the rules of procedure of administration.

As the political consequence of the preservation of the state organization, the state was superimposed on the lower strata of society in the form of an omnipotent power organization and did not permit any changes which could have infringed upon the interests of the conservative upper society. But at the same time this also meant that in this way, the state organization became an almost independent conservative power in addition to the socio-economic forces of the big estates and big capital. The power character of the state organization became markedly manifest particularly at times of crisis when it acted politically almost independently of its two power partners. By means of guiding economic life and by shouldering social tasks as a consequence of the crisis, public administration wielded so strong an operative power that not even the most powerful vested interests were strong enough to resist it. Against the ever more preponderant state organization opposition parties demanded democracy, secret ballot, the development of local government as well as the reform of public administration, however, under the prevailing political balance of power to no avail.

A phenomenon not only politically but more generally criticized was also brought about by this situation: the proliferation of bureaucracy. Bureaucracy meaning in verbatim translation the domination of office, in actual life, too, realizes always the intervention of office into the life of individuals, and therefore there can be complaints against it at all times. The bureaucracy of this period, however, was not only one which had huge jurisdictions but it was also a cumbersome and inefficient public administration. Though its activities extended to all the fields of the community, it solved but very few problems by purposeful and successful intervention. For this very reason, the demand for a more businesslike, rationalized public administration was voiced even independent of any political implications.

Actually the public tasks of the state grew to such an extent, the size of the organization of public administration assumed such dimensions that its operation could not be efficient by adopting conservative methods of administration. The state has become an immense operative organization which was bound to solve tasks demanding expertise in all fields of social life. Public administration actually approached all these tasks at that time, however, it operated with the very same methods and organs which had developed in the course of previous evolution. Thus, the state tried to cope with the new tasks but by retaining its old character. True to the nature of a constitutional state, it created an immense tangle of legal rules the majority of which could neither be enforced or clearly understood. Moreover, true to the nature of a conservative society, that public administration was operated by forces which did not rely on administrative expertise but one based on power. In addition to ensuring the rule of conservative forces, this public administration could not realize its goals.

Thus, in a modern age, the state organization built up an abstract and superimposed organization of power, i. e. it preserved its former character in the course of new developments, too. Even in the period between the two World Wars it guided and ruled over the lower strata of society by means of the upper-class legal methods of conservative national society, with the result of strong political rule and performing the tasks of a modern state with moderate success. Legal methods also manifested themselves in the fact that even in emergency situations and amidst the extremely fierce competition of 20th-century ideas, the state succeeded in more or less preserving its conservative character, and did not become transformed into a totalitarian state. In other words, the state organization remained constitutional and conservative yielding only as much to the influence of emergencies and fashionable ideas as the historical national social structure had changed under these influences. In the long run, the state remained the organization of the conservative national society in that period, too, just as it had been in the previous eras, and whatever changes and transformations were brought about, it did not develop as opposed to that society but together with it.

The development of state administration meant that government jobs remained open to and were held by members of the feudal class just like in earlier times. In that period, the civil servant stratum of state government and public administration did not become an efficient public servant class of a middle-class character but retained its nature of feudal upper middle-class. Above all, similarly to the previous stages of Hungarian statehood, the legal profession invariably retained its dominant role. It did not develop administrative efficiency in that period either but continued to be the same bossy, legislative, dominating procedure which had developed out of the nobiliary-juristic policy. This implied high-handed, dominant attitudes towards affairs and people instead of a businesslike approach to issues and the mutual respect and the equality of the parties involved. On the basis of such a procedure the job held in public administration did not become a professional position or an objective administrative role but it retained its nature of official dignity, social rank and privilege serving the representation of high-ranking state organization and of the upper strata of national society. This brought about the Oriental profusion and strict compulsory character of titles and addresses. An office job became almost identical with a letters patent of nobility defining not only assignment and administrative role but laying the foundations of social status, too. All this has been the unavoidable consequence of defining the roles of administration in terms of feudal middle and upper class dominance.

This bossy, feudal legislative management had been characteristic of all walks of state life, i. e. of public administration, police, national defense, the administration of justice as well as the public life of counties and communities. Indeed, in the counties the superior upper class attitudes manifested themselves even more strikingly, owing to the fact that in county administration a continuous line of development led from the county of the nobility to that of modern times. The situation did not differ considerably in the administration of communities though their development took another historical course. At the time of the feudal society, communal administration had only partly been a means of county and landlord superiority; it had also been the peculiar organizational form of village society aimed at self-administration and its own representation. In the course of more recent development, however, the lower class and popular roles in communal administration withered away since the upper-class state administration subordinated communal administration to itself and in this capacity it assumed the role of the county and landlord authority. The village mayor and all the other organs of popular representation have been entirely subordinated to administrative bodies trained from above and thus, community administration, too, as a whole had adapted itself to the character of upper-class administration. Accordingly, the village notary was by no means "the quill of the village" as he used to be, but the lowest-ranking member of the higher state and county administration, and as the representative of this administration he became a gentleman—only at a lower level—just as the representatives of the higher offices. However, even at this lower level he held just as a high and isolated position opposed to the lower strata of the village as the lords of the county.

Modern state development affected social life even beyond the power functions of the state, and succeeded in building up its administrative activities in almost all the fields of life. Thus state activity has become organized not only in transport and communications, in economic life as a whole as well as in education and intellectual life, but in public health and general social policy as well. The state organized not only administration in these fields but in many respects it made all activities the task of the state. This expansion has become especially enormous in the period between the two World Wars aiming particularly at the economy. Nevertheless, this did not bring about either methodological or structural changes in the political structure, these new developments took place within the same social structure as the previous expansions of state activities. In the same way as previously the state had organized transport and communications or schools or the control and administration of economic life by methods developed in the course of exerting its power functions, by and large the very same methods and organization were applied in the domains of economy, public health and the more active social policy of modern times. Thus, the introduction of new spheres of regulation resulted in scarcely any change in state life. By drawing new fields of activity into the orbit of state life new social elements were incorporated into administration and state activities as a whole; no new methods or technical skills were mobilized; on the contrary, the new spheres were drawn into the orbit of the organization and method developed in the state life of previous times. So it happened that in these spheres, too, the historical national society extended its control entrenching the feudal upper middle-class and its highly developed efficiency in domination. As a result, the intelligentsia of the newly annected spheres did not develop further on the basis of the up-to-date technical skills of the professions in question, but came under the influence of upper middle-class attitudes and became assimilated to the conservative society. These professions, too, were engulfed by gentlefolk attitudes and thus, even technical positions became official dignities. As a matter of fact, the same things occurred to state, economic policy, health and social political activities which were organized in this period as what had happened in the course of the organization of state schools or state transport system in an earlier epoch. In the same way as teachers, railway and post officials had become a technically competent intelligentsia as members of the feudal upper middle-class, the technical, economic and medical professions drawn into the orbit of state organization in the course of the latest developments have likewise become "gentlemen's vocations".

Naturally, the activities of experts show more objective competence even in the organization of public administration, nevertheless competence could not dethrone the feudal upper middle-class mentality. In the course of historical development, the professional vocations evolved in such a way that intellectual qualification was regarded as being of full value only by assuming feudal upper middle-class forms, moreover it could become consummate only in the official positions of the state organization. Though the upper middle-class forms of the professionals might be able to establish themselves even without official authority, there was one thing missing: the superior sphere of authority which could only be attributed to jobs in public administration. This is the reason why qualified intellectuals were attracted by public administration also in this period. Both the security of the guaranteed pensions, and an absolutely gentleman-like style of living demanded that doctors, technicians or economic experts all should strive at obtaining positions in public administration or state-owned enterprises and institutions. Also in this period doctors, technical or economic experts represented a colourless and insignificant quality in carrying not enough weight to become honoured professions no matter how successful they were in terms of income. Even if somebody achieved outstanding results in one or another intellectual profession it was regarded an exception that he was respected for this. No material success could make up for the worth of an administrative position. Even statistical questionnaires carried questions on profession and the person's work place and the answers physician, veterinary surgeon or chemical engineer seemed rather bashful as compared to chief medical officer, chief inspector of the veterinary service or chief technical counsellor. The little weight carried by intellectual professions became in the terms of addressing or greeting so much so that nobody could be addressed by names of occupations indicating only the qualification. It was impolite to address somebody as "physician" or "chemist", one had to add "Mr Doctor" or "Mr Engineer" or "Mr Professor". The obvious reason for this was that all these ways of addressing somebody had some sort of social relevance to the gentleman's status—at least in Hungarian history. Doctors and engineers had been assimilated to Hungarian society indicating some kind of gentleman's status even without actual administrative positions, whereas a professorship was by all means a job which also became a gentleman's profession—even if not a high-ranking one—within the historical social structure.

Changes having taken place around the middle of the past century are characterized by historiography as the emergence of a national state out of a feudal state of the nobility. Although the transformation was actually of that nature, the development of a national society did not bring about the same results in Hungarian development as in the original bourgeois societies, and likewise the emergence of a national state did not result in a similar state either. In the period between the two World Wars the Hungarian state was not a completely capitalistic one and its functioning could not be fitted into the structure of a generally bourgeois society. Even at that time Hungarian state life was not imbued entirely with either bourgeois society or capitalism and these were not assimilated to public life. Capitalism influenced and to a certain degree organized the state within the functioning of the economy, however, it did not succeed in adapting it entirely to bourgeois society. This is demonstrated by the fact that the state was able to resist to some extent capitalist interests all through the period, moreover—relying on other power factors—it could strongly intervene, too.

The development of capitalism in that period, however, was not without any influence on both state organization and that section of the society which functioned as an organ of the state. In Hungarian society, too, that period was one of the mature development of capitalism in the first stage of which the state developed—though retaining its relatively liberal character—into a more or less dominant factor of Hungarian society. Neither did the further development of capitalism come to a deadlock; it was only the state which more energetically joined into this process. All through that period another process also unfolded: the capitalistic development of state and the society organized within the framework of the state. Thus the functioning of the state organization became more expedient; this functioning came nearer to the conditions of society controlled by economic interests. It relinquished some of its superior position and juristic-power status exclusivity without, however, carrying into effect a radical transformation in this respect. Thus it remained an essentially abstract conservative organization governing and administrating by means of general and higher aspects, and did not become such an easily changing and responsive pattern as for instance the Eastern European societies which have started on the road of capitalist development more recently and have taken a course of even more colonial character. Corruption and the influencing or dismissal of public servants according to direct interests remained phenomena in state life which were opposed by both the higher forums of state theory and conservative national society.

Incidentally the theory of state of that period was characterized by a firm social elaboration and conservative conformity and this could not be altered by strong external influences either. This reliable, firm and rather moderately flexible organization was protected by the historical national society as a whole, and at all times it succeeded in opposing radical transforming efforts deriving either from emergencies or individual idealistic aspirations.

How efficiently did the historical state organization—which proved amazingly stable under extremely varied conditions—function under the changed and strained conditions of that period? Different achievements and failures can be pointed out. In those fields where the power aspects of state life were the decisive factors, Hungarian state organization functioned with one-hundred-per-cent efficiency. Under extremely difficult conditions it achieved a kind of consolidation which succeeded in getting rid of the consequences of the war and the revolutions but was also able to reconstruct in the dismembered country a historical Hungary proportioned to the historical national territory. A similar governmental success was achieved when following the crisis, under the impact of highly contradictory and strong influences the state was able to uphold the continuity of Hungarian constitutionalism, the validity of legality and the independence of the country. And all this had been achieved not by efforts of policial geniuses but by means of a wide-ranging and traditionally elaborated governmental

34

culture of state life and the historical national society, and last but not least through the institution of the Hungarian state organization and con-stitutionalism. It was not through the efforts of epoch-marking, outstanding politicians that government functioned in that way but through a host or rather a whole class of highly erudite governing individuals trained in the course of long historical practice.

The state life of this period can boast of similar achievements in the lower functional spheres of governmental power, i.e. in the ranges of police and judicature. Hungarian gendarmerie and police developed into perfect professional institutions guaranteeing the highest degree of security of the political system.

On the other hand, Hungarian state organization achieved outstanding results even in those fields where power aspects did not make themselves felt at all. Records and registrations necessary for the administration of modern life were exemplary in Hungary, the same applies to the functioning of the public institutions in the fields of transport and communication, i.e. of the railway and the postal services. The situation was rather different, however, in such fields of administrating modern life where both power aspects and factual expertise exerted their influence. In these relations, i.e. more or less in the whole range of public administration the achievements of the state organization were of considerably less value in that period. The same is true of those fields of education and vocational training which offered not purely professional training but asserted also certain ideological elements by means of education. Power and political, ideological and objective professional elements were merged disproportionately in these branches of activity and eventually always the political elements dominated. As a consequence, professional competence was subordinated to power-political aspects. This hindered the development of the professional side. As a result, in most spheres of public administration but also in the field of education even results which could have been accomplished under the given circumstances were not achieved. The very structure of society and the objective methods of state life were of a quality which rather exercised power instead of permitting objective professional skills to prevail. And this could be criticized not only by the lower strata of society but was a constant complaint of all experts as well of those who worked in any position of the state organization and were not conservative gentlemen but rather experts with a university training.

3. LANDED PROPERTY

In terms of their material character great farms can be capitalist large-scale enterprises just as any industrial factory. Certain elements of agricultural production differ essentially from industrial production, however, these do not prevent agriculture from becoming organized as capitalist large-scale enterprises. True, agrarian production is overwhelmingly a natural process linked to time and space, moreover capital and labour invested are returned in an entirely different way as in industrial production. However, none of these differences are of a nature which could become material obstacles to organizing agricultural production along the lines of large-scale capitalist enterprises. Yet, it is only a fraction of world agricultural production which is operated in such a form. Possibly only production at the large-scale American farms could be regarded as properly capitalist. This might be explained by the fact that agricultural production has developed in the course of an entirely different historical evolution and, as a consequence, the social conditions of production are also radically different from those of industrial production. For this reason, large-scale capitalist production units are but exceptional phenomena in agriculture, and on the farms of big estates production proceeds to a much greater extent within traditional forms than in the industrial factories.

In Hungarian history, big-estate farming had by no means become a real large-scale capitalist enterprise. There were some rare exceptions in Hungary, too, when big farms could be regarded as large-scale capitalist enterprises because of the volume of their commodity production, their production technique and work organization. These, however, were exceptional formations and as a rule Hungarian large-estate farming was of a different nature. The character of farming at large estates was clearly reflected by the colloquial term of large estates—big manors. They were actually big manors meaning that although their production basically adapted itself to capitalist production, quite a few feudal elements were retained in their organization.

In the inter-war period the feudal character of large estates was abolished almost entirely legally, nevertheless even then some significant remnants continued to be valid even at that time. No independent farmsteads, i.e. manors which had been at the same time bodies of public law outside the communal, village organization did exist at that time, but there still were such big manors where the administrations of the village and the large estate actually coincided. The Table of Magnates ceased to exist, too. The members of this organization had been the historical big landlord families by their established rights. But there was a House of Lords whose members were the directly elected delegates of the big landlord families. And similarly there existed the rights of the great tax-payers guaranteeing prerogatives to the historical big landowner families both in the legislature and in the life of the self-governing communities. Hunting rights, too, gave privileges to the big estates. However, more importantly a significant part of the latifundia were entailed estates, i.e. they were either family estate tails or church, state and/or community lands the free marketability and usability of which were restricted.

Apart from legal prerogatives or restrictions, a great number of feudal

36

elements could be still found in the actual economic organization of the great estates. Even by law the labour conditions and relations at the landed properties were regulated differently from those of the industrial enterprises. Regulated worktime or any legally settled minimum wages did not exist. Moreover different rules were valid as regards labour discipline at the big estates. Actual work conditions here were considerably more restricted and more burdensome for workers than in industrial factories. The overwhelming majority of the labourers at the big manors lived within the limits of the estate and had to make their worktime available to the estate without any restraints whatsoever. Living quarters were provided by the estate, and workers had but little influence on their housing conditions. Wages were mainly paid in produce the greater part of which were victuals and therefore their provision was highly dependent on the procedure of the estate management. As a matter of fact, labour discipline meant not only professional supervision and guidance as regards work performance but used to be the imposing of discipline on life as a whole of the work force at big estates. Thus, peasant workers employed at the big estates were not even nominally workers but were called farm hands or contract labourers. In both cases they actually were not workers like generally those under capitalism, but their whole situation rather reminded one of the farm hands or serf cotters under feudal work conditions.

Thus, taken as a whole, the great landed estates had not become entirely capitalistic as regards either their legal conditions or their actual work conditions and work organization but remained even in that period a traditional economic formation which differed essentially from the industrial form of great capitalist enterprises. Although the big manor too, was substantially a capitalist enterprise and the overwhelming majority of Hungarian great estates came into being like any other capitalist great estates, their order of production had been organized at the time of feudalism, and this order of production was retained with only a few modifications in the course of modern history. Neither the abolition of serfdom nor the various land reforms changed radically the farming system of the great estates, while, on the other hand, capitalism and bourgeois society did not gain so much ground in Hungarian history as to achieve radical changes also in the economic organization of the big manors. The events of political history indicated that on the part of politics no serious intervention took place into the conditions of big manors. Under such circumstances, the manorial farming system succeeded in preserving its existence to a great extent which was reflected not only in its ownership conditions and economic organization but in its whole production process as well.

In the first stage of manorial type farming production continued by methods developed in the course of the productive activities of the serfs. At this stage, farming on the great estates simply pooled the procedures of

37

peasant farming and raised them to mass-scale production just as the big state's labour force was mainly provided by the sum total of serf labour. It was only towards the end of the 19th century that, following the English pattern, the modernization of big estate farming started by introducing new breeds, new production methods and procedures as well as by the use of agricultural machines. Only at that time did great manorial farming depart from peasant methods becoming thereby more up-to-date and rational than peasant farming. However, this transformation became a general feature but very lately and though Hungarian great estate farming was affected repeatedly by ever new waves of rationalization and mechanization, even in the period between the two World Wars this process did not reach a level where the techniques of its production would have been entirely of a rational character and as regards the utilization of machine power it would have achieved anything of an up-to-date standard.

The most striking feature was that manorial farming made use to a much smaller extent of the machines than one would have taken for granted on the basis of the capital and machine park available to great estates. The overwhelming majority of the big estates at that period still had work done mostly manually though perfect or at least satisfactory mechanical means were already available at the great estates. Thrashing and milking remained manual work in most of the big manors. The use of machines was at the same time much less common at the big estates than could have been assumed at the given standard of technological development and under the circumstances of manorial commodity production. At that period, draught animals still had such a dominating part in great estate farming that the utilization of mechanical energy was of an exceptional and subordinate character. But most conspicuously, even at that time, big estates made almost no use of sophisticated machines and labour-saving devices although such equipment had assumed great significance in modern agriculture. Neither sowing and hoeing machines nor more specific kinds of mechanical equipment of harvesting were adopted and thus, all these work processes were performed almost entirely by manual labour. This is clearly explained by the fact that on the one hand manual work was cheaper and on the other hand much more qualified and better trained workers would have been necessary for running such machines than the farm-hands and seasonal contract labourers of the big manors.

Though manorial farming was much more rational than the peasant farms, even in this respect it did not exhaust its potentialities. Great estate farming had by and large reached the standard of rational extensive production at that period, i.e. it continued to operate the general production branches and production methods of peasant farming in a rational way. However, it was unable to develop beyond that stage. In other words, it did not develop new production branches or basically novel production methods.

38

Compared with both industry and more developed agricultural production, the role of skilled labour and specialized work in manorial production was particularly rudimentary. Underdevelopment of specialization was reflected by the fact that, although the majority of big estates had one or a few rather advanced branches of production, farming as a whole did not follow a single production trend. Nor did it occur that manors should have specialized in a few complementary production branches thus achieving in these branches a standard higher than the average. However, lacking such kind of specialization no advanced agriculture could be attained. This phenomenon can be explained by the fact that skilled labour remained on a very low level in the manors. Actually there existed two kinds of skilled labour in manorial farming: that of the farm managers and of the manorial farm hands. The first was high-standard intellectual skill, the second almost brute peasant mass labour force. Between these two there was a rather thin stratum of skilled workers who found employment in the big manors but were more or less excluded from the homogeneous agricultural enterprise. Mostly the marginal industrial activities were performed by these skilled workers, i.e. work in iron, in wood and construction works, whereas there were very few skilled workers employed in agricultural production itself. Gardeners, dairymen, etc. were exceptional personalities at the big manors, and even if there worked some highly qualified specialists at the estates, their activities covered not the whole estate but only a single specialized production line. Without qualified skilled workers, however, no kind of large-scale production could reach a high standard.

The working labour force of manorial farming had a very restricted technical competence. Neither the farm hand nor the seasonal contract labourers could be termed skilled workers. If these labourers still had some competence this did not exceed the general level of peasant work skill but this, too, was of a considerably lower standard than that of agricultural labourers employed by working farmers or small farms. In the case of peasants toiling at the manors this work skill was simply an immense working capacity, the patient endurance of monotonous mass work and at the same time superficiality and unconcern as regards craftsmanship involved in labour. Such work could be adapted forcefully to the professional demands of production only by alert supervision and brutal disciplining, and even that did not guarantee unfailing results. Such conditions were a regression as compared to the former craftsmanship of the manorial farm hands. At the time when manorial production used to be simply the gigantically inflated form of peasant farming, a wide variety of different peasant craftsmanships collaborated within the framework of the manorial estate. The various sorts of herdsmen, the tenders of stable animals and those employed in the tilling of arable land were not only technical performers of the different kinds of work but were also in their own traditional peasant way experts of these occupations. However, as in the

39

course of an evolution started from above the manor had become a rationally controlled enterprise, the manorial farm hands degenerated to the status of peasant mass-workers who were henceforward but semi-skilled labourers performing single operations.

The professional competence of farm managers, particularly of the younger generations was undoubtedly of a very high standard. Though quite a few of them were outstanding plant breeders and stockmen or developers of one or another production process, they did not represent pure professional skill at the manorial estates. The same holds for the landed proprietors if they themselves were working as agricultural experts on their estates. They were commanders of their estates rather than professional leaders, had work done on their lands rather by means of superimposed regimentation and orders than leading by actual involvement in work. Under the given social conditions, their own craftsmanship and professional qualifications could not become fully effective and neither could the work of their farm-labourers be developed into skilled labour.

On the basis of these conditions of production, the society within the manors was not a bourgeois world but a conservative order of society where the landowners and the farm managers kept aloof from the world of the manorial farm hands. The upper stratum was the most characteristic inherent element of the historical national society, whereas the manorial farm hands and the seasonal contract labourers were the lowest stratum of the peasant society.

The great landowner was the most perfect representative of the upper-class way of living, "the lord of the manor" as called by the lower strata of the people; enjoying absolute prestige not only on his estate and in his direct surrounding but in general terms as well. If somebody wanted to get to the topmost grades of society he had to be a squire. Such an upper-class authority did not require the landowner to belong to the aristocracy since the landowning status had become such an upper-class privilege in the course of history which automatically and objectively transformed him into a squire. Thus the term landowner was equal to that of a lord of the manor. The landowner did not have to be an expert farmer since at that time neither qualifications nor even traditional leading role but propriety rights themselves were the essential features of the upper-class status. The habitual concomitant of the status of a landowning squire was rather the political and corporative activity, and the great landowners actually did participate in such activities at that time.

The farm manager was the purest type of the feudal upper middle-class being the most characteristic representative of the historical gentlemanly intellectual occupations. In the course of history the job of a farm manager was equal to the ownership of a medium-size landed property; it was generally an occupation held by impoverished noblemen or those having but small estates. This occupation had become a gentleman's profession the authority and upper-class forms of which did not lag behind those of public administration jobs. In this respect the manor was an equal employer to the state; intellectual professions in the service of the big estates had the same weight and dignity as those in the service of the state or the church, i.e. they enjoyed much higher prestige and esteem than being employed by a capitalist enterprise. The term "manorial farm manager" had by and large the same meaning as that of a county economic supervisor, whereas the term "estate manager" was rather similar in meaning to that of a county Lord Lieutenant.

It was very characteristic of the social nature of a manor that within that structure a stratum of intermediaries could be found which was very much similar to the attendants in office of public administration. Those belonging to this stratum were therefore not workmasters and foremen as in industrial production, even if they represented some kind of craftsmanship, but represented rather the lower spheres of the higher command. Professional qualifications were therefore not general at this stage. The element of commanding, of exerting power in a competent way was considerably more important in the work of the overseers and supervisors than proficiency in farming.

In that period the great estates occupied the smaller part of the cultivable land and about one third of the arable land of the country. This means that one-third of Hungarian agricultural production took place within the bounds of the socio-economic enterprise of the big manors. Thus it is a serious question what national economic achievements can be claimed by great estate farming of that period. The yields of arable lands were by about twenty per cent higher than those of the small holdings. Animal husbandry at the great estates yielded quantitatively less than the small farms; however, it represented undoubtedly a considerably higher quality. Taken all the products of agricultural production, the production of big estates was of a relatively smaller volume though it was of a higher value regarding all its products. Considering the technological development of agricultural production, the achievements of the big estates can be assessed from two aspects. On the one hand, the significance of production in the great manors in the fields of plant improvement and qualitative stock-breeding was beyond argument. It is also indisputable that by setting an example it had a certain influence on the production of the small farms. On the other hand, as regards implements, machines and work methods, the big estates did not develop the productive forces to an extent that could have been expected on the basis of their capital, more favourable farming conditions and social privileges. In the area of smaller tools, smaller machines and the methods of intensive production, i.e. in all the fields where small farms could operate at all, the achievements of the peasantry constrained in its social structure in many ways were much more significant. Great estates also lagged behind— and considerably in that respect!—as regards the spread of agricultural skills. Manorial production did achieve great results and, as a rule, production at the big estates used to be of a much higher standard than at the peasant farms, however, a relatively considerably greater number of agronomists and gardeners were trained on small holdings and the farms of tenants than at the great manors. Manorial estates employed only experts graduated from state schools and from the ranks of smallholders or landless producers, while small farms themselves trained and broadened the ranks of qualified and competent producers.

Finally, great manorial production was beaten beyond all proportions as regards its role in producing food for the population. Though big estates of the same acreage brought more produce to the market than similar areas of small farms, the population living there was disproportionately small. And taking into account the standard of living of the majority of the population at the great estates, the result is unambiguous: big estates were rather a hindrance than a furthering element both in terms of social and economic progress.

4. THE HISTORICAL ARISTOCRACY

At that time the aristocracy by birth—the bearers of aristocratic titles and members of *de genere* families being aristocrats without a title included— was in numerical minority as regards ownership of the historical capital, i.e. landed property, and also concerning the historical positions of social leadership, i.e. taken the leading positions of the state and church all together. Their influence and prestige on the other hand was almost unbroken in social leadership and they represented the numerical majority of the owners of large estates, too. Thus the "count" was a fixed star in the development of Hungarian society and not only his prestige did not become tarnished in the course of recent evolution but neither did his actual leading role. Only at the time of attempted reforms during the Great Depression, had the historical aristocracy been ousted from political leadership. Later, however, it more or less succeeded in reconquering its shaken positions. And similarly, it regained its historical leading role following the short-lived bourgeois—petit bourgeois period of the counter-revolution. Only at the time of the counter-revolution and the Great Depression were there governments without any counts, in all other cabinets they held more or less dominant positions.

Even in the bourgeois democracies of the West the prestige of the historical aristocracy prevailed, however, there aristocracy by itself did not mean an actual leading role having been a rather nostalgically tinged vestige. Aristocrats participated in actual leadership only by means of additional civic work, venture and political activity started from scrap on. Birth could facilitate careers in civilian life, yet hard work was by no means rendered unnecessary by it. In contrast to that, in Hungarian society the

42

historical aristocracy has been the owner of a continuous political leading role, this being its traditional position. To achieve this position it had not to compete under identical conditions with those of a middle-class background. Together with the ownership of great estates this leading role used to be an historical heritage, and up to that time no lower ranking social force ousted the aristocrats from that position. This leading role together with the ownership of great estates, was an historical heritage which had not been snatched by any lower social force. Though the enriched capitalists of capitalistic ventures succeeded in acquiring properties out of the historical great estates, and it was the historical aristocracy which had lost the bulk of their estates at disannexed territories, and finally, land reform, too, somewhat decreased the sum total of their holdings—even this threefold loss was not of a magnitude which could have shaken fundamentally their positions based on landed property. Their political leading role, too, was jeopardized by the dominance of other classes, yet in the long run even that did not result in the ousting of the aristocracy from political leadership. Both following the counter-revolution and the Great Depression, the aristocracy succeeded in retaining its significant influence; yet after the Depression the role of the middle-classes in state management increased to the detriment of the aristocracy.

Neither had the leading role of the historical aristocracy been radically transformed in a way that the members of this class should have extended their activities to other areas of the society or should have achieved leading positions in economic life beyond large estate farming or in intellectual life beyond political leadership. They acted only as the representative figureheads in these fields, thus upholding their historical character in that period, too. They seized only leading positions traditionally due to them, whereas they gained actual authority in other fields but quite exceptionally by means of special pursuits.

Hence aristocracy by birth was an absolute historical leading class in the period between the two World Wars, though its history had been by no means an ancient one. There was only one family which gained its peerage prior to the Hapsburg era, all the others attained their titles but later. The overwhelming majority of these families had gained both their estates and peerage as well as their political leading role at the time of the Hapsburg Empire. The only exceptions were the Transylvanian grandees and the distinguished ancient noble families having no peerage of the home-country. The Transylvanian families founded their aristocratic existence on Transylvanian history, and characteristically the majority of them became or remained Protestants. The *de genere* noble families, on the other hand, preserved their estates and their leading role among the Hungarian nobility despite the Hapsburg rule. However, they were compelled to withdraw exclusively to county-level public life. Only in the Reform Era and after the Austro-Hungarian compromise of 1867 did they gain national importance once again.

The aristocratic families of different origins did not intermix considerably. The Transylvanian grandees and the distinguished families of ancient lineage remained more or less Hungarian nobility marrying mainly among themselves and playing a political role rather in the ranks of the resistance of the nobility and in the movements of the Reform Era. On the other hand, the families elevated by the Hapsburg monarchs became rather aristocrats of the Empire than of Hungary, and took leading political positions not only in the government of the empire but had intermarried to a great extent with the aristocracy of other nations as well, first and foremost with Austrian and German families.

This aristocracy which had been of a more historic descent at both of its lines intermixed even less with the official and soldier barons who have emerged after the compromise of 1867 and who were mostly of Austrian origin. Nevertheless, Hungarian aristocracy had become more numerous becoming to an ever greater extent the aristocracy of the Hapsburg monarchy.

As a result of this development, only the minority of the Hungarian aristocracy was of a national character, while its majority was the product of an imperial development and was opposed both to the Hungarian people and the Hungarian nobility. This, too, was a reason why the majority of the Hungarian aristocracy as well as the leading stratum of the Catholic Church were the main props first of the Hapsburg Empire and later of the monarchy.

Following World War I, the various elements of the aristocracy played different roles in the new independent Hungary. Consolidation and the restauration of the old order mainly resulted from the activities of the more Hungarian aristocracy, the Transylvanian grandees and the leading distinguished families of ancient lineage of the home-country. The Hapsburg aristocracy, most influential at the time of the monarchy, has lost its footing — though it succeeded in keeping most of its estates — in the course of the disintegration of the monarchy and the dethronization of the Hapsburg king. Political leadership was taken over by the Hungarian feudal aristocracy. Thus the pro-Hapsburg aristocracy was pushed to the background for quite a long time, and as a result the leading aristocracy was more national than that of the monarchy.

Whatever the historical origins of the Hungarian aristocracy and whatever various elements it had been composed of, in the period between the two World Wars it was the leading stratum of the historical national society, and outwardly it seemed a very homogeneous class at that. It held this position not by means of an intellectual leadership or competent activity covering the whole range of life but by reconquering and maintaining its traditional political role based on its latifundia. At that time, too, an aristocrat who was a scientist or entrepreneur, or even an agricultural expert was considered a rare exception. In general, the aristocrats constituted first and foremost a political class in that era, too, and in this capacity they were the leading

44

stratum of the conservative national society. Thus, they took active part almost exclusively in the political life and corporate movements. In that field, however, they represented political competence and efficiency developed throughout history. This competence was not the juristic competence of the lesser nobility and upper middle-classes rooted in public administration and practical law but a competence reflected by the power and diplomatic aspects of government, a qualification which made it possible to move in a superior way in the balancing acts of power. In this respect, the political activity of the aristocry of that period reflected mostly the heritage of Transylvanian political traditions. The two most characteristic premiers of the era were Transylvanian counts.

At that time, too, the historical aristocracy was a political leading class to such an extent that even those of its members who became enemies of the conservative line did this as political key-figures. Democratic counts were just as well politicians as the conservative ones: the Hungarian bourgeois revolution was headed by a democratic count, and politically-minded counts took an active part in the movements of the extreme right and in the democratic efforts which had become quite significant towards the end of the era.

5. THE FEUDAL MIDDLE-CLASS

The two pillars of the middle-class existence in European development had been material independence and a sophisticated culture. Such were the characteristics of the prosperous landed gentry at the time of feudalism and also of the independent bourgeoisie of medium wealth in the bourgeois society. The stratum, however, called middle-class in Hungarian society was not such a class formation. Under our conditions middle-class status meant rather an intellectual career than financial independence or a sophisticated culture developed by the liberal professions. Thus, under Hungarian circumstances the members of the middle-class rarely had an independent existence of medium wealth and they were mainly salaried intellectuals, i.e. officials. Even in this respect distinctions should be made. To be exact, only the intellectual employees of the state, the church and the manor were regarded as belonging to the middle-class, i.e. the historical intelligentsia and/or the officialdom. The intellectual officials of the liberal professions of the industrial and commercial enterprises, though belonging statistically and as regards their class position to the middle-class, constituted a highly different social formation and they were quite distinct from the historical, feudal middle-class. A clear-cut difference was made both in people's minds and in public opinion: the intelligentsia of the state, the church and the manors constituted a historical class, the feudal middle-class, whereas the intelligentsia of industrial and commercial enterprises were private employees, bourgeois middle-class or urban bourgeoisie or Jewish intelligentsia in common parlance.

According to the census of 1930, the historical feudal middle-class was made up of 170 thousand bread-winners and together with their dependents their number came to 380 thousand persons, i.e. 4.3 per cent of the population of the national territory after the Treaty of Trianon. Of these a mere 4 thousand were medium landowners and/or medium tenants, a negligible fraction of the population; all the rest were officials and/or intellectual employees of public administration and state enterprises as well as of the church and the great manors.

This class position meant the status of an employee, but it was an official's job which radically differed from those of workers. Such employees represented an educated working-class, that is an intelligentsia which, on account of this quality of theirs, in the course of historical development emerged as a better paid, more valued class with a more guaranteed means of living than the working-class. This stratum of employed intelligentsia extended to become a full-fledged middle-class—not only in public administration but in capitalist production as well—formerly being a classless intelligentsia having different social status and linked up with different social factors. Originally the middle-class was made up of the independent bourgeoisie of medium wealth and the landed gentry. As the independent middle-class of the bourgeoisie and the landed gentry declined in the course of capitalist development, the intellectual officials had become a broad stratum both in public administration and capitalist production. It was the middle-class of officialdom which occupied the social status of the independent middle-class. This meant a peculiar transformation since a stratum living under entirely different productive circumstances had grown into the unchanged social condition of the middle-class. This development had been of a peculiar character especially in Hungarian society. It had been basically different within the middle-class of the historical national society and that of the modern bourgeois society.

In the earlier stages of Hungarian history, the stratum of the intelligentsia was similar to that of the Western societies. In addition to the clergy of church, the intelligentsia comprised the teachers of the church schools as well as the literate elements of the clerical and state chancelleries and those employed in county and urban administrations. The intelligentsia was not an integral element of the ruling estate but it also kept aloof from the lower strata of society. It was a classless intelligentsia indispensable for the feudal regime because of its professional competence which was simultaneously also an obstacle to the absolute predominance of the upper-class. At the time of royal absolutism in Western societies a bourgeois-type officialdom had developed out of this literate intellectual stratum becoming an integral part of the bourgeoisie. However, history took another course in Hungary. This was so because in Hungarian feudalism the number of noblemen had

46

been numerous, and because this feudalism had not been a ruling superiority like that of Western societies, and therefore the actual social leadership, the Hungarian nobility itself had developed into an intellectual stratum. Thus it had not only a hold on the upper echelons of leadership and government as a whole but settled the problems of the intellectual roles of its dominance, i.e. administration within its own ranks as well. In addition to the nobility there developed a stratum of professional persons of non-noble origin, the members of which nevertheless were educated in the same cultural atmosphere and lived in the same social situation and therefore they entirely assimilated to the nobility. Intellectual occupations thus had become gentlemen's professions in Hungarian history because these, too, were monopolized by the ruling stratum, i.e. the nobility. In that way all the intellectual professions which took shape at that time almost uniformly became upper middle-class professions and represented more or less the social status of the gentry.

This however, was not the only direction the development of the Hungarian stratum of intellectuals took. Like everywhere else in Europe, a stratum of intellectual officialdom was called into being by the Austrian imperial government for administrating its empire by royal absolutism. This was a class of typically bureaucratic civil servants which did not fit closely into the societies of any nations of the empire but by way of its administrative erudition served the interests of the empire. In the course of history, however, this stratum integrated into the societies of different ethnic groups and/or nations of the empire: it became assimilated to the prevailing social structure thus becoming similar to the middle stratum of the given society. In Bohemia for instance it fitted into the characteristically philistine middle-class. In Hungary, however, it could orientate itself only to the gentry, the more so as this, too, was at the same time a stratum of intellectual administrators.

It was these two lines of development which merged following 1867, at a time when the modern organization of public administration and the activities linked with it were called into being. The positions of developed state life were occupied by Hungarian intellectuals of noble origin and by the stratum of imperial Austrian-German officialdom, thus shaping together the social status and style of activity of the Hungarian civil servant stratum. The gentleman's prestige and trappings of the profession were supplied by the intelligentsia of noble birth, and could be easily adopted by the stratum of civil servants transferred from the imperial public administration. The civil servants supplied the more sophisticated bureaucratic professional competence which was adopted—though with somewhat more difficulty—by intellectuals of noble origin. The two kinds of intellectual attitudes could easily merge the more so as they were identical as regards the fact that both of them were abstract formations superimposed on the people and subservient to the dominant power, thus being part of and dependent on the ruling classes both as regards their high-handed attitudes and their intellectual erudition as well as the nature of their mentality alien to the people. The corps of farm managers, i.e. the intelligentsia of manorial farming consisted of similar elements merged with similar success. And similar was the emergence of the clerical intelligentsia with the sole essential difference that the two lines did not merge in a single organization but lived on separately in the great churches. In the Catholic Church mainly the traditions of the imperial church continued and the influence of the Hungarian gentry intelligentsia made itself felt but only as a secondary factor, whereas in the Calvinist Church the traditions of the intelligentsia of noble birth developed further in a more bourgeois and popular form.

In the course of this development, the civil servant intelligentsia of the Hungarian society evolved into an upper middle-class. Its inheritance from both the paternal and maternal side was of such a nature that it took on a position elevated high above the people, and its activities as intellectuals were rather abstract. Therefore it must be considered unavoidable that this civil servant intelligentsia penetrated the positions and social forms of the old middle-class of noble birth, and this framework was preserved together with the elements of the lesser nobility, irrespective of the fact whether these have become civil servants or have remained landed gentries. Moreover, these elements of the lesser nobility did not preserve the bourgeois ideals of the Reform Era, where the middle nobility became almost a revolutionary force. After the Austro-Hungarian compromise of 1867 the middle nobility supported a liberalism taken over from the nobility of the Reform Era, yet under such social conditions that this liberalism was not democracy but a sort of liberal conservatism.

The social development of the stratum of civil servants continued on the same lines between the two World Wars. It preserved with only slight modifications its upper middle-class character and the typical features of both the paternal and maternal heritage could be clearly identified. This heritage has been considerably revised only by the fact that in the period beginning with 1867 the stratum of foreign origin of the middle-class had strengthened. Society had not even enough time to assimilate the early Austro-Bohemian element when a great number of young people of ethnic—particularly of German—origin succeeded in finishing their formal education and found mainly employment in public administration. All these assimilated people impeccably adapted themselves to the upper-class framework of their career, moreover they deepened the gap between the mentality and proceedings of their jobs and the lower strata of society. Thus, though these were professions demanding considerable erudition or these intellectuals were mere employees, the activity of this stratum—be it in public administration or public education—did not conform to the objective skills of intellectual work but to the upper middle-class nature of its social status. Though in terms of its class position this stratum was composed of employees, it developed as a ruling class which, in addition to the employers' and the leading political class took the position of an associated dominant force. Actually, its position was one of dependence and defencelessness, nevertheless its existence was guaranteed by this very dependence, and therefore it fully identified itself with its employers, that is with that of the conservative national society.

The social position of belonging to the upper middle-class on the one hand and academic qualifications and/or the employee's and civil servant's relationship on the other had naturally created antagonisms in two ways. As dependent white-collar workers, members of that stratum could easily slip into a position when their employers did not guarantee their livelihood at a level they anticipated on the basis of their work and social position. Such was the situation in the post World War I situation. In that period the clerical stratum actually became pauperized: the revision of wages, the so-called B-lists (the investigation into the former political activities and attitudes of public servants accompanied by firing undesirable persons from their jobs), the revision of pensions and the depreciation of the war bonds — all these factors shook the livelihood of these middle-class people to the foundations. All these phenomena were observable to an even higher degree among the war refugees. However, even in that situation, this stratum did not behave as the working-class did, that is it did not turn against its employers but displayed infinite patience, it did not initiate an opposition policy. In fact, it staunchly supported the conservative consolidation. From its own point of view this attitude proved to be correct in the long run since consolidation actually did take place and brought about a livelihood for the white-collar workers by and large equal to the pre-war level. Yet, the contradiction in this situation was evident, and it could threaten stability in the long run. A leading publicist of this very stratum was fully justified therefore to raise the question at the time of consolidation: why did the white-collar middle-class cling to the conservative regime which brought about wealth and possibilities of development mostly for other strata of the society. As a matter of fact, they did not stick to it infinitely even at that time. In the years of prime minister Gömbös' reform experiment as well as during the era of the extreme right policy a part of this middle-class became "revolutionary-minded" and hoped for a radical change in its dependent situation if these movements succeeded. On the other hand, there was an element of tension in the very existence of the middle-class: their qualification as intellectuals clashed with their actual social position. The position of being a member of the feudal middle-class superimposed on the people has been an inherent obstacle to the ambition of the members of this stratum to proceed with their work as intellectuals according to the objective nature of their profession or their own creativity. The feudal middle-class was prevented from doing so not only by the higher levels of the social hierarchy but also by the gentlemen's inhibitions originating from their own feudal middle-class existence. The menacing memories of the revolution have smoothed over that antagonism at the beginning of that era, but later on it asserted itself stronger than ever. This stratum became susceptible to the movement of the populist writers because they had a foreboding of the correct linking up of their intellectual's existence with getting closer to the people. Naturally, the feudal middle-class could not shake off its inherent nature when getting closer to the populist movement, nevertheless the direction of orientation already pointed towards the possibility of solving the contradiction of expertise and social standing.

The evolution of the whole era, however, did not bring about a change in the social profile of the upper middle-class. It became immensely more numerous, the unsolved contradictions of its existence became more evident in the course of the events during these years of change; various commotions were triggered off within the formerly homogeneous stratum, but no decisive change took place in either direction. At the end of that period, this stratum had reached a point where on the one hand the uncertainties following from the dependent employee's position, and on the other hand, their preferences to identify themselves as intellectuals still remained closely linked with the conservative social framework of their upper middle-class existence.

In that era the verdict "guilty middle-class" was often to be heard. Yet, this class was not guilty, it was simply true to itself. Intentions and moral endeavours were all in vain, they could not break through the strongly established social limitations of the existence of this class. It is also true that there were very few who nurtured such intensions and ambitions. Under the conditions of our history—which were unpropitious in many respects—the social position of this intelligentsia took a course which determined its activities. Thus, it emerged as an upper middle-class and as such it developed its relation to the lower strata of society, that is to the peasantry and the working-class accordingly. Nevertheless, it is justified to hold it responsible since there were certain elements of this class which ran counter to a fully developed upper middle-class status, and therefore it would have been the historical responsibility of this stratum to develop these, too, even contrary to its own interests. It was this responsibility which was taken seriously by those who called their own class to account passionately.

Despite the tendencies of internal evolution and external changes, on the whole the upper middle-class of that period still retained its historical nature. It was a sort of intelligentsia whose existence and activities were defined rather by the gentlemanly character of its social framework than either by the demands of being an employee or the quality being an intellectual. Thus this class was not an intelligentsia of the people; neither was it an intelligentsia of the bourgeoisie. By means of its activities, this class as an intellectual stratum did not fit into the world of the lower strata of society but identified itself with the abstract world of an upper society and furthered its preservation. Thus the qualification of this class as intellectuals was subordinated to its own gentleman-like attitudes and to the conservative structure of society, that is it could achieve its goals only within the framework of this social formations. Anyone who wanted to become a priest, a teacher or a mayor without subordinating himself to the consecutive system came up against the upper society as a whole, and either he compromised or had to resign himself to being ostracized.

The two elements of middle-class existence, intellectual competence and a gentleman's attitudes were interlinked in several ways. One of the extremes is represented by leading positions of public administration where expertise was fully subordinated to upper middle-class quality, i.e. political qualifications which were regarded to be the decisive factors. This is the reason why such dignitaries were of highly aristocratic character being almost void of the experts' detached attitude. The other extreme is represented by professionals qualified in engineering. These professions were by their very nature absolutely contradictory to upper middle-class forms. For this reason and because they were fitted in the order of the upper middle-class much later, the engineering professions were the least gentlemanlike ones among all occupations. Here upper middle-class character was subordinated to professional competence, but even here it was mostly exceptional that expertise was entirely more important than social standing. Between the two extremes, we may find all the other occupations representing not only transitions but an order of rank as well. Heading the list were those occupations which reflected most markedly the forms of the gentleman's existence: such were the legal and the general public administration careers, i.e. those whose traditions had been established by the nobility holding clerical posts. Next came agricultural and special public administration careers whose traditions were also rooted in the nobility. Next came other professional jobs but not all of them. Engineers and physicians have more or less adjusted themselves to the upper middle-class environment. The same applies to economists and veterinarians, whereas the more modern professional skills were still regarded as somewhat alien to a true gentleman. There were two exceptional cases: those of the lawyers and professors and/or teachers. The most conservative traditional careers, i.e. that of the priests and officers have to be treated separately.

The most dignified origin could be boasted by the legal professions since these were the occupations of the lesser nobility and the professional persons of non-noble birth associated with them. The legal professions by themselves were a characteristic product of the historical national social development. For a long time they maintained this social nature of theirs, the more so as the legal profession was closely related to political activity. Before World War I, in addition to landowners, lawyers were the most active group in political life. However, in the course of capitalist development this career, too, had become infiltrated by the bourgeoisie as the lawyer's activity became more and more associated with industrial-commercial and financial occupations. At that time the legal professions were already to a great extent associated with the capitalist economy and they had become increasingly colourless bourgeois careers. Among the lawyers those conservative upper middle-class solicitors who had become the legal counsels of one or another latifundium constituted a separate caste and so did all those who were linked in some way or other to activities of the state or the church. Nevertheless the memories of the legal professions being a gentleman's career did not fade away, and the striving of the lawyers to become judges or find jobs in public administration was a characteristic feature all through that period.

The teaching professions, particularly that of teachers had quite another background. Teachers were the direct heirs of the literate stratum which had developed under the wings of the church, and they did not cast off entirely their more objective intellectual character. Though all through the ages the reputation of the profession was enhanced by outstanding authorities, it could not become a truly gentleman's profession in Hungarian development. The famous poet János Arany wrily complained even in the fifties of the past century that a teacher had a difficult position among the gentry of the country town Nagykőrös. As a matter of fact, the gents of Nagykőrös were rather petty gentries, moreover the staff of the Nagykőrös high-school consisted of top-quality teachers at that time. Bit by bit, however, this career, too, acquired as much gentleman's prestige that it came to establish itself as a more or less gentlemanly profession at the edge of the truly gentlemanlike careers. Its full development was hindered not only by the fact that pursuing that profession demanded a highly intensive absorption in its material, but also that from early times on many people of lowly origin had endeavoured to become teachers and therefore the prestige of that profession as a gentleman's career was considerably impaired. As a result of this insufficient upper middle-class training, in the second part of that period when the movement of the populist writers caused considerable commotion also among the middle-class it was primarily the teachers who joined that movement in great numbers and propagated its ideas in debating societies and at people's academies. And quite a few of them represented not only a West European type culture but the Western type of bourgeois intellectuals as well.

The lot of the teachers was particularly hard: this profession was never admitted among the gentlemanly careers. Teachers remained all their lives small school masters (in Hungarian: people's teachers) being the only profession which reflected in its very name that it was rooted in the people. It was not only the objective character of this career which practically prevented it from becoming a gentlemanly profession; it never enjoyed the prestige of other upper middle-class occupations. It had no precedents in the feudal society of the nobility since there were no people's schools in the church schools, only elementary instruction common with secondary schools, and within that structure elementary education, too, was performed by the magisters and professors of the common schools. Moreover, those who taught writing and reading at the early beginnings of primary education were of very low status and their education was correspondingly low. Following the development of the system of state schools and the primary church education, both the training and the existence of the teachers had become more settled, yet this profession never reached the status enjoyed by other gentlemanly professions. Later both teachers' training and the very existence of the teachers had risen in status, however this status always remained at a lower level than that of the high-school and university professors. The prestige of the profession was not enhanced by the fact that later many young middle-class misses had decided to become teachers when forced to choose an independent career because of their impoverishment. However, they did not socialize with the teaching staff but haughtily kept the distance and remained separated from their colleagues. Moreover, whenever they got a chance, they turned their back on the teaching career. As a result of these developments, the teachers' profession, the lowest order of civil servants, continued to have the lowest prestige among the upper middle-class occupations. In spite of this even teachers were affected by gentlemanlike attitudes. Most recently, teachers were very much attracted by the movement of the populist writers; indeed, the populist writers' influence was greater among teachers than among the high-school and university professors.

In the period between the two World Wars the upper middle-class started to pursue new professions and careers and its internal structure underwent a significant change. But none of these developments had essentially transformed the structure of the middle-class.

Because of the historical gentlemanly status of the civil servant career there has been an almost unbridgeable gap between the professions of public administration and the private careers all through Hungarian history. The liberal professions, industrial and commercial venture as well as white-collar professions at private enterprises and firms which required technological and commercial qualifications—all these enjoyed an extremely low status in terms of the historical national society. The feudal upper middle-class had adopted the views held by the historical classes (the landowning and civil servant nobility) according to which careers in industry, commerce and engineering were not worthy of gentlemen. If descendants of the feudal middle-class families had to pursue such a profession, this was regarded to be downward mobility. Following World War I, there was no change in this attitude. However, by that time economic careers had assumed great significance in national life, and, at the same time, all the gentlemanly occupations in public administration had become overcrowded. For this reason, right after World War I, middle-class youth

53

was encouraged by government propaganda to enter economic careers. However, the political leadership initiated no such economic policy as would have made it possible to realize these intentions. Thus, this propaganda had very little effect at that time, and even those who had no other choice but to enter such careers, did not regard this as a life-long decision. Following the Great Depression, however, the situation had changed dramatically. The supersaturation of public administration jobs became more and more oppressive and, at the same time, economic policy started to put a greater emphasis on industry and in increasing number the feudal upper middle-class took up positions in industry.

When the feudal middle-class started to have a greater role in industry, this was similar to the process when certain professional activities came to be controlled by public administration. The professional requirements of various branches were not met by the feudal middle-class intelligentsia. In contrast, this middle-class succeeded in moulding the various jobs in industry according to its own attitudes. Thus the members of the middle-class who had chosen to enter economic careers did not become a bourgeoisie and did not accept the social forms which had developed in these particular bourgeois professions. Instead, they had transformed the given professions into gentlemanly careers according to their own social character. They performed the duties of the business like those of an office. Naturally, it should be taken into account that the process was at its very beginning before World War II. At the same time, a wartime boom gradually gave way to a wartime command economy: consequently, the management of production and commerce became increasingly bureaucratic. It is still to be seen where this trend eventually leads.

Although the feudal middle-class was a well-preserved social entity, the events of the inter-war period started to indicate its decline. The possibility of a radical social transformation started to gain acceptance and the absolute dominance of the conservative national idea was shattered. Radical nationalism on the one hand, and bourgeois democratic aspirations on the other, started to influence the feudal middle-class. As regards political ideas, however, at that time, the middle-class did not reach the point where it could find the radical solution of its ambiguous social position. In the political orientation of the middle-class, the only possible solution, i.e. the fact that as a stratum of intellectuals the middle-class ought to shift its dependence from the conservative social forces to those of the lower strata of society had appeared. However, at that time the masses of the middle-class still regarded this perspective as frightening.

6. THE NATIONAL PETITE BOURGEOISIE

Ticket inspectors, postmen, policemen, gendarmes, officers, office messengers, farm stewards and bailiffs of big estates as well as the non-intellectual employees of the church were all specific but also highly unambiguous formations within Hungarian society. The majority of them were of peasant descent or came from village artisan families, thus being by all means offsprings of the lower strata of the society. Nevertheless, the social situation they represented was inseparable from the historical national society. As a result of this contradiction they were regarded as a stratum of the peasantry which had formed an alliance with the upper classes, and for this reason even at minor squabbles city dwellers easily cursed them as "peasants" in the most derogatory sense of the term. Peasants, however, did no longer regard the petite bourgeoisie as peasants but as a stratum which had turned its back on the class of its origin and had joined the upper strata of society. Peasants harshly criticized this stratum's right for pensions. Their official naming was *altiszt* in Hungarian (meaning attendant, messenger), these words more or less correctly characterizing their social position.

In the same way as the historical national society had transformed its stratum of intellectuals into a peculiar and closed social formation, it also succeeded in forming a closed and typical stratum of its non-intellectual employees. A more open and liberal bourgeois-like stratum could not develop even in the administrative, service and executive situations of the conservative national society. The stratum which occupied these positions had developed according to the historical nature of this social structure. Thus, the national petite bourgeoisie was not a gentlemanly stratum though it represented the lower section of the upper society and, as a result, it was inherently connected with the upper middle-class and constituted a national lower class.

The class position of this stratum was a qualified working-class position. It consisted of workers labouring for wages but both its work and work relations essentially differed from those of the proletariat. Their work was of a confidential nature blending elements of physical work and low-level administration. This class held stable jobs and, similarly to the white-collar workers, became institutionalized. Compared with industrial production, the prestige of these jobs was equal to that of the shop-foremen and other non-intellectual but institutionalized employees. The petite bourgeoisie received monthly wages, pensions, that is their existence was as secure—though at a lower level—as that of the white-collar middle-class. The class position of the petite bourgeoisie is dependent and actually this stratum was a peculiarly developed variety of the petite bourgeoisie in the same way as the feudal middle-class used to be a variety of bourgeois middle-class. This stratum, too, was linked in all aspects of its existence to the very same employers as the feudal middle-class, i.e. in the long run to the conservative

55

national society. With the totality of its activities and consciousness the national petite bourgeoisie was rooted in the given social structure. Consequently this class had developed under much less direct circumstances than the genuine petite bourgeoisie. As a result, this class was not only a dependent petite bourgeoisie but a class whose existence was in all respects limited. In contrast to genuine petite bourgeoisie, Hungary's national petite bourgeoisie readily complied with a conservative social structure; thus it became a "national" petite bourgeoisie.

The members of this stratum led a petit bourgeois life guaranteed by old-age pensions. Their livelihood was often supported by inherited land and therefore their lives were even less subjected to the changes of economic life than those of the petit bourgeois of moderate means. As the majority of them practised peasant thriftiness, some of them even managed to collect small fortunes which were always invested in land at their places of service or in their native villages. The overwhelming majority of them succeeded in buying small one-family houses at the outskirts of major cities or in the central areas of smaller localities. Most of them lived under circumstances of modest wealth, had abundant food and thus were physically fit. Their physique had become strong and resistant owing to the proportionate alternation of physical work and intellectual activity and a well-organized way of life. As pensioners they returned to the peasants worn out by hard field labour with whom they shared a common youth; compared with peasants, by that time there was such a marked difference in their physical condition which in itself made it clear why the peasants harboured an unappeasable hate against these pensioners. It was also characteristic of the members of this stratum that the majority of them sent their children to higher educational institutions and tried to push them into the upper middle-class. They felt themselves entitled to this, since even if on a lower level, they themselves had managed to get close to the feudal middle-class. As a result, they felt justified in trying to encourage their children's upward mobility. Their status as civil servants, too, encouraged them to do so since by means of this they were able to guarantee the same advantages to their children at school which the children of the middle-class were entitled to.

None of these professions had a competence or qualification of a higher level, i.e. a more general and intellectual proficiency in certain fields of administration or production. However, almost all of these careers required high-level practical training. The precondition for most of these jobs was a lengthy, severe period of instruction and training, and before anybody got his final placement he had to go through a series of assignments. Therefore most of the members of that stratum were characterized by impressive and commanding practical common sense demeanour and capability of giving orders, and most of them were outstanding and competent workers. As a consequence of a limited education coupled with a level of self-complacency, a certain degree of priggishness and mannerism of behaviour was almost unavoidable. Moreover, among those of them who worked as civil servants a marked superciliousness and exaggerated self-assurance manifested itself. This, however, was not the reflection of upper-class superiority but a kind of lower-level and more brutal civil-servant haughtiness which turned into absolute subservience and respectfulness when facing their bosses.

The consciousness of the members of this stratum was a closed system in conformity with the constraints of their social views and world outlook and the nature of their education. Their very existence was guaranteed by the conservative national society and therefore they lived within the world of that society without knowing the tensions and problems rendering so uneasy the consciousness of middle-class intellectuals. Putting it in a simple platitude: they were adherents of the conservative national order, and they obediently adapted themselves to all the teachings they got from their superiors in the spirit of that conception. It was for this reason that even in difficult times they persisted in their dependence and discipline and were hardly susceptible to establishing links with any other ideas. All through the critical periods of that era the members of that stratum always staunchly supported the conservative order. Even at the time of the upswing of the extreme right movements which appealed to antisemitism, the extreme right failed to gain mass support among the petite bourgeoisie. Rightism succeeded in attracting masses only among the bus-conductors and drivers. However, these occupations were hardly representative of the petite bourgeoisie, since they belonged rather to the petit bourgeois of the urbane bourgeois society than to the national society.

The stratum developed fully in the period between the two World Wars growing into a genuine class at that time, since its earlier and most recent historical antecedents had been but isolated formations. 100 thousand wage earners and their dependents, altogether 230 thousand persons representing roughly 2.5 per cent of the total population were included in this stratum at the time of the census of 1930. The rate of the numerical increase of this stratum considerably accelerated in the second half of the period.

III. MODERN BOURGEOIS SOCIETY

1. CAPITALIST ENTERPRISE

The higher stage of capitalist enterprise is characterized by unrestrained calculation with capital, material, market, mass labour and production technology. Society does not restrain the development of business ventures anymore, and enterprises do not face a labour force with a secure background who might demand security from the enterprise as well. At this stage only the state intervenes in the operation of enterprises enforcing its priorities both as regards the direction of production and labour relations.

Capitalist development had come a long way until it reached this point and the remnants of this development can be identified even at the higher levels of capitalism. In the original bourgeois societies the artisan skilled labour organized itself into ever higher units, and also the big enterprises developed by means of drawing into their orbit various skills and trained labour. Business venture did not start its operation with hiring mass labour force which it could have made use of unhindered for its own business interests. It could get ahead only by using the labour of specially trained strata of artisans and peasants, and these remained obstacles to the free utilization of labour force even in the large-scale capitalist enterprises. In addition to this kind of skilled labour, it naturally could utilize to a great extent unskilled woman and child labour as well as crude mass men's labour to operate its mechanic equipment. In the long run, however, business was compelled to adapt itself to the resistance of skilled work and skilled workers. For this reason, business venture is hampered in such societies by certain social resistance even at the more advanced phase of development, i.e. by the reliability of the venture and the historically developed self-defence of the workers in the interest of both skilled labour and the very existence of the workers.

In Hungarian society, capitalist business did not develop in the course of such a gradual historical evolution, consequently the kind of social resistance I described in the above could not develop. Hungarian capitalism developed based upon ready-made patterns and complete production technologies relying on the needs of the market, imported capital, mass labour as well as imported skilled labour. Thus it was not organized by utilizing Hungarian artisan work and peasant homecrafts but it operated by unscrupulously making use of the needs of Hungarian society as well as its

58

vast free labour force. Hungarian capitalism did not continue to develop the production skills of the artisans and peasants but, disregarding them, it organized its enterprises by hiring unskilled mass labour and merely the absolutely necessary skilled labour coming from abroad. Under such circumstances it was natural that the working class could not resist exploitation; nor could society as a whole put a stop to the brutal profit-drive of business. Capitalist business progressed within Hungarian society by utilizing the lower society as a pool of unskilled labour in its enterprises, whereas the higher levels of society furthered its political aims. Neither workers nor entrepreneurial competence nor resistance hindered this colonial process. The workers organized only at a later date to defend their interests. The same applies to society; it was only at a later date that the society started to influence business through the state.

This colonial-like development also left its mark on the capitalist business ventures of the period between the two World Wars. But even at that time enterprises were not founded on skilled labour developed at the lower levels of Hungarian society, and they did not adapt themselves to the social needs of that society, they only availed themselves of market opportunities by undisguised business calculations. Of course, this was unavoidable since in that respect there were no countervailing forces in that society which could have checked capitalist ventures adjusting them to more general social interests. Thus, at that time, too, development was controlled by market possibilities and emergencies.

Following World War I, when the country became independent such an emergency situation emerged and domestic market possibilities opened up. Possibilities and demands arose for the development of independent Hungarian industrial as well as commercial and banking ventures. Actually, such a development did take place, however—according to the social conditions—it assured the same forms as in the period preceding World War I. For the modern development of independent Hungarian capitalist venture, the following conditions were given. There existed a stratum of entrepreneurs which had developed under the Monarchy; this stratum had strong ties with European capitalism. Naturally, this entrepreneurial bourgeoisie represented the school of colonial capitalism and was able to conduct business only in this way. A small stratum of skilled workers also developed under the circumstances of previous capitalist production, and a broad stratum of craftsmen and retail dealers also operated but on such a low level that it proved unable to start larger business in great proportions. At the same time, there existed a huge agrarian surplus population supplying business ventures with unskilled mass labour force. Though the dismembered country had access to but very restricted raw material resources, it was able to guarantee—as regards certain raw materials—the conditions necessary for large-scale industrial production. However, domestic capital supply which could have boosted business was negligible or

59

at the most extremely limited. As a consequence of the defeat in the war and the dismemberment of the country, Hungary touched rock-bottom in this respect. Given these production factors, the independent country represented an underdeveloped and unsaturated consumer's market. As a result of Hungary's social conditions, market demand was rather limited; nevertheless even under these conditions, the demand could be met only by a large-scale and developed industrial production and commercial network. Thus, the social factors and the conditions of capitalist production were insufficient, whereas there existed a considerable market demand and also the necessity for the independent development of Hungarian industry. Under such circumstances, business, simultaneously with political consolidation, started to operate under inadequate circumstances and inherited colonial antecedents.

In the twenties a dynamic upswing ensued in large-scale industrial production, in commercial activities and in banking. This, however, later turned out to be but a pseudo boom just because of the insufficiency of its preconditions and the very nature of business venture. A great number of enterprises were founded at that time, the spirit of enterprise was stimulated by the unquestionable market possibilities. However, but a few enterprises proved to be actually viable and trustworthy ventures. All things considered, only a slight increase was reached in production in that period, and even that was achieved under rather colonial-like conditions. At that time, the Hungarian manufacturing industry operated with foreign capital, mainly foreign raw materials and to a considerable extent with imported semi-finished products. As a natural consequence, the capitalism of independent Hungary was not much less dependent on foreign countries than at the time of the Monarchy. Since Hungarian manufacturing industry could achieve even moderate successes only by adopting protective tariffs, domestic consumption was considerably taxed.

In the post-war period banking enterprises organized mainly capital import and they insured domestic capital accumulation to a much lesser extent. But as early as that time they participated intensively in financing industrial production, thus reflecting the strong finance-capitalist character of Hungarian big enterprises. At the same time, trade activities were primarily aimed at agrarian exports and industrial imports. Production and commercial activities resulted in a very moderate upswing, the growth of Hungary's industry and trade was rather slow. This growth rate lagged far behind the demand of Hungary's consumer's market. In these years, the post-war boom was much more restricted than that of Europe. The boom the nation experienced brought profits for business only; the workers did not benefit from it.

This moderate growth came to a halt at the time of the Great Depression. Nevertheless, by relying on a new economic policy, in the years of this new emergency Hungarian capitalism succeeded in reorganizing itself laying the foundations for a more rapid growth. Under the pressure of the economic crisis, an economic policy based on autarky was adopted. As a result, capitalist enterprises, instead of relying on capital import, foreign raw materials and semi-finished products, were forced to make use of domestic capital, domestic raw materials and semi-finished products which at that time were more difficult to purchase. This meant that temporarily profits declined. The pressure of the Great Depression forced business to take a course which it would never had taken owing to its entirely business and colonial type character.

It is on this basis that a new boom started in Hungarian capitalist venture from about 1933 on. At the beginning of the boom, banking and industrial production had to make equally great efforts. The banking system had to supply domestic capital; industry had to exploit domestic raw material sources. Commercial enterprise, too, was compelled to solve more difficult tasks both in the extremely deteriorated foreign agrarian markets and in a rather diminished domestic buyer's market. As a result, Hungarian capitalist venture became better organized and this resulted in a more stable and well-founded development. State economic policy, too, supported business venture more successfully than in the previous period. Within a few years astonishingly fast results were produced: Hungarian large-scale industrial production succeeded in meeting the demands of the domestic consumer's market and its exports even caught up with agrarian exports. These results were achieved mostly with domestic capital and raw materials. In this period also banking had reached a point when it was able to organize considerable domestic capital formation and at the same time industrial enterprises were drawn increasingly into its orbit. In trading, too, certain changes took place: more developed methods had been developed for agrarian exports, while stronger organizations were established in the domestic industrial market.

At the end of the period the direction of this boom was modified by a new emergency situation. However, the boom continued. The demands of war preparations became the dominant requirements in industrial production and this gave further impetus to the boom, whereas adjustment to the changed conditions in Germany rendered industrial growth and trade somewhat more difficult. Taken as a whole, however, these obstacles did not hamper economic growth; they made only partial adjustment necessary.

As a result of the development between the two World Wars, the conditions for the independent existence of the country became more or less guaranteed. Thus a strong and efficient Hungarian manufacturing industry emerged, and an adequately developed bank and credit system evolved which was not entirely dependent on capital import. Last but not least firmly established and strengthened commercial enterprises came into being.

Thus the achievements of capitalist big business were relatively rather significant. This, however, was only one aspect of development. It was also the consequence of this development that, in conformity with European and world capitalism, domestic business life showed the same symptoms. That is, it tumbled into the Great Depression in the same way as other nations, and both prior and following the crisis it also established its higher-level organizations, the cartells and trusts. Finally, Hungarian big business created a situation in which public intervention became necessary. At the same time, business succeeded in benefiting from state intervention. This capitalist development has another aspect, too: under the specific and backward conditions of Hungarian society, business produced a number of disproportionate and abnormal consequences. Generally these consequences manifested themselves in the fact that capitalism did not influence proportionately the whole of society.

The most conspicuous consequence was the further expansion of the capital city to the detriment of the countryside. Similarly to the capitalist development prior to World War I, the new boom advanced in areas which held out the most advantageous opportunities for business, and in this respect the capital city had undoubtedly a dominant position. Though the raw materials consumed by production were extracted somewhere far in the country, all the other conditions of business could be primarily found in Budapest. For this reason, the capital city became even more the hub of the economic life of the country than it used to be. Excessive growth was characterized among other things by the extraordinary high rate of population increase contrary to the more moderate increase of the provincial town. Though in some places in the provinces industrial production and business ventures related to them also developed, the overall weight of these enterprises was smaller than that of the Budapest enterprises. Even at that time the unfavourable consequences of this over-centralization were so obvious that the slogan of decentralizing industrial production and economic life as a whole was unceasingly repeated. In spite of this, no actual initiatives were taken to that effect in that period.

The development of Hungarian capitalist business venture was characterized also by the fact that in addition and beyond world economic booms and slumps it showed uneven upswings and recessions. The obvious reason for this phenomenon was that this development was much less well-founded and reliable than in the traditional capitalist and bourgeois societies. A relatively balanced growth could only be observed in the engineering and food industries, two old and most firmly established industries, whereas in other industries—though the upswing seemed rather significant on the whole—growth was much less balanced. In that period also electrical engineering and the textile industries showed a growth rate which assured further perpectives.

The most crushing consequence of this development was the extremely heavy burden on the agrarian production, particularly peasant farming. The advance of capitalism expanded the buyer's markets of agriculture and supplied agrarian production with more up-to-date machinery and other

62

industrially produced means, at the same time, however, a disproportionate commodity trade relationship became stabilized between the two sections of production which went far beyond the difference stemming from the objective nature of the two production branches. All through that period the gap between the relative prices of agricultural and industrial products more or less prevailed and particularly at the time of the Great Depression it subordinated agriculture to an incredibly high extent to industrial production and banking. In addition, the peasantry was heavily taxed by this capitalist development because peasant farming was in a worse position than big landlord farming both as regards the marketing of agrarian produce and the purchase of industrial consumer's and capital goods. The reason why the complaint against the cartels found such a strong response among the peasantry was that small holdings were much more defenceless against them than the large estates or any other consumer strata.

Also consumption, as a whole was disproportionately burdened by the development of Hungarian manufacturing industry. Obviously it badly needed protective tariffs, these, however, were themselves rather dispro-portionate and in addition, partly by a dumping and partly by the large-scale organization of cartels, this burden was heavier than objectively necessary.

The extension of commercial venture has similar consequences. As regards agrarian export—which was the major single issue of Hungarian foreign trade in the first half of the period—the performance of export companies was of a markedly dubious value. Trade was directed by narrow business considerations and in the organization of production, in the field of stabilizing buyer's markets trading activities were not up to the demands of circumstances. Ideal results of course could not be achieved in this respect in this epoch but even the Bulgarian foreign trade which operated under similar circumstances was more successful. Agrarian production, export activities and consumer's markets were not integrated by business activity, they were connected only by transactions based on the principle of minimal risk and maximum profits. It seemed but natural that, under the cir-cumstances of such business activity, agricultural production did not develop in the direction of a total exploitment of export opportunities nor could the Hungarian export markets be stabilized. Only towards the end of that period did this situation change when agrarian export monopolies were organized and the agrarian market was compulsorily stabilized. These developments, however, were enforced solutions, moreover they were by no means more successful than operations based on the principle of free-trade. In this respect it was the foreign trade activity of the government economic policy which did most serious work; not by introducing monopoly but by promoting exports by means of political and organizational measures.

The extension of commercial business activities resulted in a similar drawback in the domestic market. A colonial-like variant of soliciting trade and instalment business developed in that period which not only went beyond all limits of civil decency but was not consistent with the business standards of a developed bourgeois society either. It was in this field that the colonial character and unscrupulous nature of Hungarian capitalism became most obvious. This phenomenon cannot be simply explained by the Jewishness of Hungarian trade and commerce. It is the outcome of the social structure since it is hardly conceivable that facing the peasantry and an urbane consumers' mass which had but recently entered the road of capitalism, there could have been any decent industrial production, any stratum of traders who would not have been enticed to totally exploit the alluring possibilities. In other countries where such phenomena could not develop the reason for this was not the different character of the entrepreneurs but mainly the fact that the peasantry and the urbane consumers' strata were of entirely different nature.

The root of this phenomenon, and of other aspects of Hungarian capitalism are to be found in the ill-preparedness of the society for business ventures. Because of such ill-preparedness the economy was guided uninhibitedly by profit-greed since society was unable to exert any material resistance. The only defense of society against profit-greed was state intervention, and this was established on a large scale in the second half of the period. But because of the nature of public administration even this was not and could not be a complete and uniform defense organization of consumption, and neither could it be a detailed control of production. It was but an emergency measure which could make up for the most striking insufficiencies and more or less balance the most conspicuous disproportions. Yet, this kind of state intervention was rather comprehensive. The settlement of farmers' debts, generally the fixing of the interest rate, the subsidizing of production branches of vital importance for economic policy, the so-called cartel bill, the regulation of instalment transactions were all measures which more or less succeeded in remedying in certain fields the most striking irregularities resulting from disproportionate development. The legal settlement of labour relations and social insurance for workers were even more extensive. The introduction of the eight-hour day, the fixing of the lowest hourly wages, the compulsory payment of overtime wages, paid holidays, compulsory social insurance were all measures touching on vital interests of the life of the workers. As a matter of fact, things guaranteed by state intervention were more than the minimum that could be legally secured in this respect. These measures actually provided much greater security and protection to industrial workers than had the corresponding regulations to agricultural workers. And this was but natural since state intervention was not a superior power standing above society but a state manifestation of such an actual social balance of power which had developed in society. In this respect the working class was a better organized force than the agricultural workers, and therefore state intervention too, guaranteed it more rights. Industrial and commercial business also played a different role in public life than great estates.

Society itself could directly organize resistance at only a few places against the power of business venture. Both in the fields of production and consumption it was the working class which had the most developed organizations. Within certain limits the workers' trade unions succeeded in defending the interests of the workers in the sphere of labour relations, whereas the same was achieved in the sphere of consumption by the relatively well-established workers' consumers' cooperatives. Cooperative organizations had considerable results among the middle class, too: the consumers' cooperatives of the civil servants achieved a marked success in serving the interests of its members.

The cooperatives of the peasants, however, proved almost entirely inefficient, though the peasantry had a great number of larger or smaller marketing and supply cooperatives which were organized in defense of its production and consumption interests. These cooperatives were of two kinds. Some of them were small local organizations, others were a cooperative network united in a great centre. The small local organizations were more or less the organizations of the peasantry but for this very reason they were extremely weak both in terms of capital and expertise and therefore they could not seriously safeguard their members' interests. The majority of them actually ceased to function after a shorter or longer period of operation, and though similar new organizations followed in their steps their functioning had no well-founded basis. As regards the great central cooperatives, there were two factors which prevented them from serving and safeguarding the interests of the peasants. Firstly, such cooperatives had an enterprise character. They were without exceptions marketing or distributing enterprises functioning as capitalist business ventures and therefore by their very nature they were compelled to operate on the same business-like basis as all the other non-cooperative enterprises. Though their members or customers were peasants, the enterprises themselves had to establish with them connections according to the rules of domestic capitalism, i.e. transactions were actually the same as with joint stock companies or private firms. The second factor was that within these great cooperatives—even if they were of an agrarian nature—peasant representation had almost no influence on business management and thus it was not in the position to shape the activities of the cooperatives according to its own interests. The leaders of these organizations were either great landlords or businessmen who were able to deviate from the general commercialism at the very most according to their own points of view. Commercialism prevailed to the smallest extent in the cooperative credit association network though there, too, it gained some ground.

The social character of Hungarian capitalist business venture was clearly reflected by the fact that it hardly covered agricultural production. This is not at all surprising since in agriculture both the objective nature of production, professional qualifications as well as the labour force were of a totally different social character than in industrial production. In agriculture business had to adapt itself to restrictions and limitations, this, however, generally meant falling rates of profit. Moreover, in agricultural production it was more difficult to make economic calculations and at the same time there was much more objective resistance which could only be overcome or integrated with the enterprise only by means of self-sacrificing work and organization. For this reason, joint stock companies were able to strike roots in agriculture but exceptionally and even in these rare cases they established themselves mostly not in primary production. At that time, there were altogether over 65 of them in the country, and characteristically 43 of them had their headquarters in Budapest, i.e. closer to their business partners than to the objective factors of production. However, a greater number of capitalist enterprises in agriculture functioned in the form of land tenures. A considerable percentage of holdings exceeding 1,000 holds (1 hold equals 0.57 hectares) were farming leases in that period, and though these were not all estates organized on the basis of real capitalist large-scale enterprises, some of them were undoubtedly of such a nature. The percentage of leaseholds in Jewish hands might indicate the true situation since it was first of all the Jews who also in agriculture represented the spirit of genuine business. Somewhat more than one-third of the big leaseholds were owned by Jews. The great estates owned by Jews were less of capitalist nature. A great part of them were not business ventures but reflected the accumulation of wealth earned by other ventures.

In contrast to the traditional farming methods of the manors, in the capitalist great estates production actually had assumed an entirely business-like character. This manifested itself both in production technologies and labour relations as well as in the specialization of production and the marked role of skilled and qualified labour. As a result, the performance of capitalist estates generally exceeded those of the great estates of a more feudal character. At the same time, however, this kind of production used to be more risky. It was a business venture which ran the same sort of risks as industrial enterprises. Moreover, since in addition to market adversities, agricultural production is susceptible to natural calamities, its risks are in general even greater than those of industrial enterprises. And against the latter capitalist agricultural enterprises were less resistant than either the traditional great estates or peasant farms. As a rule, agriculture was not a good business; therefore business was reluctant to invest capital in it.

Capitalism was the production order of Hungarian society as a whole and consequently, capitalist ventures were not confined to great enterprises, factories, big trading houses and banks. At the same time, it was not the universal production form of Hungarian production and commerce and thus, the overt and unrestrained businesslike character of venture did not

66

assert itself in all aspects of economic life. Branches of production which had become organized in historical social frameworks preceding the bourgeois period continued to produce—despite their capitalist foundations—not in the forms of capitalist bourgeois society, i.e. they did not produce as business ventures. Such were the overwhelming majority of agriculture, including both peasant farms and manors, as well as that part of industrial and commercial activities which was more closely connected with demands or with skilled labour and therefore could not become genuine business ventures (the artisans and retailers). Due to the restrictions of their roles, also these latter industrial and commercial occupations had preserved a number of historical traditions, though by far not as many as peasant farming. Within these limits, however, that is in the area bordered by the manor and the peasant farm on the one side and the workshop of the artisan and the shop of the retailer on the other, the social organization of production and trade was everywhere a capitalist business venture.

Factories and commercial enterprises also included the most varied types of smaller and medium-size enterprises which all had a common feature: they were production organizations of the same nature as the great enterprises. No sharp line can be drawn between them. The definition of statistics which regards enterprises employing more than twenty workers as big enterprises is just as correct as if they drew the line between small and medium and big enterprises at hundred workers. They were all formations of the same nature and were not only differentiated and stratified according to their sizes but also overlapped since growth was in the very economic and social nature of business ventures; small business could be regarded prosperous only if they incessantly expanded. Nevertheless in Hungary there were some differences between big enterprises and medium-sized or small businesses; namely the biggest enterprises, factories and firms lost their mobile and venturesome businesslike attitudes to a greater extent. They were old-established firms in business life deeply entrenched in both production and trade, and their business operations were restricted by exactly their own traditions and prestige. Their blue and white-collar staffs, too, had become institutionalized and thus they were in a more restricted position as regards their labour force than the upcoming and smaller enterprises. Moreover, also state control and intervention affected the established major firms to a much greater extent because supervision was easier within the broader frameworks, and also because in their own interest these enterprises more readily adapted themselves to such a control. For this reason, such old-established big firms resembled to a much greater extent the capitalist enterprises of the original bourgeois societies than the smaller and medium-size enterprises. In defense of competent, efficient and reliable work they themselves have built up such a social framework as society generally did not require of business venture.

In Hungarian society capitalist business venture as whole was the product of the development of modern bourgeois society and therefore, its social forms developed together with the advance of capitalism. They had nothing else to do with the historical social structure than to adapt themselves to it. These forms were basically different from both the gentleman's society and the lower strata of the peasantry. These enterprises offered careers for middle-class occupations and as such they were of a novel nature in history. They offered occupational careers which were different from the careers of both the upper or lower societies. Members of the middle-class and the working class entered clearly defined careers and became distinct types even within this shorter historical period. The bourgeois was just as clearly a product of history as the gentleman of historical society. The businessman, the "director", the "boss" represented business mentality relying upon risk-taking and resourcefulness, whereas the gentleman represented the landed estate and office in a more reserved and supercilious way. The different historical backgrounds made themselves felt beyond the nature of different occupational activities. The bourgeois was regarded to be an upstart as compared to the historical classes of grand traditions, and as such he had no historical heritage. The bourgeoisie which developed side by side with the historical professions but sharply separated from them, did not inherit the traditions of the feudal burgherhood since it did not evolve out of these but was constituted of new elements in new situations.

Since Jews had a decisive role in the development of Hungarian capitalism, business venture was regarded as a Jewish career. When someone said: a bourgeois, he meant a Jew in Hungarian society, quite apart from the fact whether the person in question actually was a Jew or not. Business career itself was of such a nature, and the concept had not only a popular but also a professional and social meaning as well. In the same sense of the term, professionals employed by business were regarded as a bourgeois, too. The job of the white-collar worker at an enterprise or that of a clerk at a private firm was looked upon as a bourgeois Jewish career just as that of an entrepreneur. Trade, business administration or engineering qualifications were professions—according to their objective nature—which were attributes of bourgeois society and therefore, they were alien to the gentlemanly upper middle class. As the producing class of business, the working class, too, had developed in this modern and unhistorical bourgeois society. Therefore it was a new formation from the point of view of the historical society, and regarding its objective nature it was also alien to it. The effect of this was enhanced by the fact that also the working class was not a "Hungarian" occupation even in recent times but the rallying and class conscious organizing of new-comers headed mainly by leaders of Jewish origin. Nevertheless, the working class itself was not regarded as a Jewish occupation by the historical society—actually Jews represented only a fraction of the proletariat—but as a mob linked to and led by the Jewish bourgeois society.

68

It was a highly important aspect of the social development in the interwar period that industrial and commercial venture had extended enormously and as compared to the nature of the previous society, new strata, too, were drawn into the orbit of its social functions. In addition to entrepreneurs and employees of private firms, the gentlemanly upper middle class penetrated into these professions, whereas together with the workers great masses of peasants poured into industrial production. However, these new elements did not change as a rule the bourgeois-proletarian careers which emerged in the course of capitalist bourgeois development. The objective, social nature of employees of private firms and entrepreneurs or of the workers remained unchanged. All these careers were formed despite different influences in the course of earlier development and thus, those who entered those careers at this later stage of evolution adapted themselves to its already existing compulsory forms. The only exception was part of the gentlemanly upper middle class which had entered the economy. This class did not get rid of its own social character even when it entered business. It succeeded in moulding business activity according to the social quality regarded as obligatory for itself, and did not adjust to the social forms of business life. But even at the end of this period, this part of the middle class protruded like an island from the sea of business life and its bourgeois society. This is understandable, since it is a law that in the long run one either adapts himself to the objective framework of capitalist business or one has to turn one's back on it. Both the nature of capitalism and the requirements of business careers are in the long run incompatible with non-business attitudes. Those who wanted to be successful in business inevitably adapted themselves to its standards.

2. SMALL-SCALE INDUSTRY AND RETAIL TRADE

The handicraft trade and retail trading of Hungarian feudal society merged with capitalism only to a very small extent. Capitalist trade had been built up somewhere above their sphere, and these underdeveloped crafts and trades were unable to switch over to large-scale activity and more businesslike attitudes. At the first stage of capitalist development both small-scale industry and retail trade passed through a crisis because of capitalist commodity trade; at the later phase however, they succeeded in catching up with their rivals in spite of having to face great enterprises and large-scale entrepreneurial activity. The social course of this development was somewhat different in small-scale industry and retail trade.

The more or less developed guild industry had been totally ruined by capitalist large-scale industry and industrial freedom. In the first decades of this phase handicraftsmen passed through a deep crisis complaining equally of proliferating bunglers, the competition of large-scale industrial production and imported industrial products as well as of the deficiencies of professional training. Later on, however, these complaints were mostly redressed, the level of professional training was raised, and, side by side with capitalist commodity trade and large-scale industrial production, small-scale industry once again managed to find and establish its sphere of activity. New demands and needs were created by urbanization and the development of bourgeois mentality, and small-scale industry grew into these more modern forms. The role of small-scale industry in industrial production was important in the interwar-period. It employed almost twice as many workers (master workmen included) as the big industry, and the value of its production came up to close half of that of the big industry.

The development of the retail trade was less dramatic, since it was not basically affected by either industrial freedom or capitalist trade. Established trade practices were upset by commercial big enterprises and the direct sales effected by domestic and foreign factories. Nevertheless even big commercial enterprises could not circumvent the established commercial practices; consequently, they rather made use of them. The development of large-scale export trade had a most devastating effect on the purchasing and exporting retail trade as well as on the inter-regional trade organization based on the balancing of internal needs. By the centralization of the country and the emerging of export markets, purchasing and exporting retail trade was transformed into a large-scale venture. Similarly to small-scale industry, the extension of capitalist trade had brought about new needs which could be met only by a new-type retail trade.

However, owing to historical factors, the strengthened small enterprises which assumed more modern and urbane forms retained basically their dual social character. One type of small enterprises was linked with modern small-scale industry tied up with capitalism and the urban way of life, whereas the other type was made up of traditional handicraft industries, shop-keepers as well as purchasing retail trade responding to the needs of village life and the peasantry.

Urban small-businesses grew simultaneously with capitalist production, trade and the urban way of life. As regards small-scale industry, this meant rather the personal, servicing activities and the industrial functions of the home and the household than the turning out of artisan wares and quality products of individual nature. The sophisticated crafts of artisanship maintained their capacity for development only in societies where the traditional skills of the handicraft trades of the guilds succeeded as a whole in passing into the large-scale industrial stage of capitalism. In the course of Hungarian development these types of industries were bogged down and perished almost as a whole, and the artisan industries of later times were all entirely new formations which emerged under totally different social and professional circumstances. Yet, guild-like handicraft industries still existed in this period, moreover some of them were considerably successful. These

70

latter, however, were the products of the same modern, rational production as those of the big industry and therefore could not be regarded as truly traditional arts and craft. They rather copied and prudently adapted themselves to the daily necessities, and thus their products were not highly superior in quality to those of manufactured goods. In general there prevailed a rational professionalism in all the branches of urban small-scale industry and at the same time mechanical methods and standardized processes were made use of as well. The raison d'être of these trades—which guaranteed their role even at the time of large-scale extension of the manufacturing industry—was their capacity to satisfy the demands of various individual needs and tastes. And this was exactly how the production of small-scale industries developed. Small business came to a standstill and even declined in all the branches of production which met typical mass demands, whereas it developed further in areas where individual needs predominated even if these were not of vital importance.

Urban retail trading had a similar role in provision with goods and in services. This role expanded simultaneously with urban growth, large-scale industrial production as well as wholesale trade. The place of production of this kind of business was determined by sales and its prompt response to needs, and therefore by its very nature it expanded proportionately with the increase of both production and needs. Later, in the course of the creation of department stores the awareness came that this role could hardly be substituted by large-scale organizations. However, again by the very nature of small business the emergence of specialized shops, i.e. the appearance of larger organizations based on specialization—for instance the factory-owned sales organizations—posed a serious threat to small business.

Village small-scale industry and retail trading differed from its urban counterparts. These activities did not become specialized to the same extent as their urban counterparts. Accordingly, their rational occupational specialization was less developed, and tended to be linked rather with traditional needs and production methods.

At that time, handicraft activities were mainly linked with agrarian production and, for this reason, this craft was strongly connected with the traditional forms of production. Nevertheless, here, too, rational occupational training had its effect which was extended by the higher institutions in the same way to this domain as to urban small-scale industry. However, this process was less complete here since it had to face the traditions of needs. As a result, its work-methods were less stereotyped, and its products less standardized. Two culture complexes mixed in their work the result of which used to be as a rule ill-assorted and tawdry products. The retail trade of this same social domain was also much more traditional than that of the cities and towns. Its specialization remained less developed and its qualifications for fulfilling requirements was of a lower standard. At the same time, its function was to create the demands of the peasantry. For products which were turned out to meet the demands developed in other areas, this retail trade itself created the demands by offering these goods and popularizing them among their consumers.

All things considered, the social position of urban small-scale industry and retail trade was entirely different from that in the villages. The former ones satisfied existing needs, whereas the latter ones occupied a superior, directing position in their social environment, and the needs met by them were partly created by themselves. Village small-scale industry and retail trade were therefore of educational importance and played a particularly significant role at that stage in furthering the progress of the bourgeois development of the peasantry. The level at which these newly created needs were fulfilled is another matter. Due to their specific roles, the rural sector of small-scale industry and retail trade occupied a position on the verge of the modern bourgeois society and peasant society, and was linked rather with the fate of the peasantry than with that of the urban middle-class society.

Handicraft was a trade based on rather professional strict conditions in the inter-war period; in addition to a lengthy practical training, certain theoretical knowledge was also demanded. Though not an absolutely necessary requirement, according to wide-spread practice, graduation from junior high-school was required from apprentices. Thus handicraft required serious professional qualification which was at the same time rather an abstract skill and competence. The traditions of historical handicrafts were further developed but to a very small extent and were mostly a rational adaptation of the more advanced experiences of the individual occupations and abstract technical sciences. As a result, modern handicrafts were not satisfactorily adjusted by the Hungarian society. As a rule, craftsmanship always links up only by some jerks with the materials and needs, and practical activities tend to deviate from studied skills. A typical example of this tension is the peculiarity of technical terms. Tools and technical procedures generally have German terms in the Hungarian language indicating the German past of crafts, while in theoretical professional training these are substituted by such Magyarized terms which are unknown in the everyday vernacular and are used only in the official language.

Small-scale industrial and retail trading careers did not have an unambiguous social quality in that period either. Seen from above, from the position of the gentlemanly upper class—and under its influence also from the point of view of the bourgeois middle class—it was regarded as an inferior career involving manual work and service thus being regarded neither a gentleman's nor a bourgeois occupation. From the lower levels of the social hierarchy, i.e. from the point of view of the peasantry it was regarded to be a superior existence with a stabilized prestige. Handicraftsmen and retail traders were rather despised by the workers regarding them as the scum of the middle-class society. Workers regarded their own organized unions and their social consciousness as superior. Under such circumstances, these careers were not taken up lastingly by several succeeding generations. Peasants continuously strove to rise among handicraftsmen and retail traders, whereas the ambition of the children of this stratum was to become intellectuals and quite a few of them became skilled workers in factories. Thus, small-scale venture and handicrafts could not become established as stable social formations in that period either. They remained the transitionary stratum of modern bourgeois society, but even in this position they represented a much more temporary stratum than the handicraftsmen and retail traders of the historical middle-class societies.

In the original bourgeois societies the transition from the guild industries and shopkeepers to capitalist ventures was continuous, and as a result they had more to do with each other even at the time of modern development. Something was presented even by the factories and trading concerns from the nature of the workshops and stores, and, at the same time, also handicraftsmen and retail traders became more generally entrepreneurs. More generally, these two kinds of activities are interlinked as a common social pattern because they are equally general economic and social enterprises of society as a whole. In Hungarian social development, however, these two courses have parted. Business venture did not develop from the workshop and store but came into being as response to market requirements and business possibilities, whereas small-scale industry and retail trade did not develop further than the workshop and the store. Neither under feudalism nor at the time of bourgeois evolution did these two occupational frameworks grow into a definite, objective social situation in the course of Hungarian history. The working area of the land—both as peasant farms and manorial estates—fully developed and the same applies to the administrative activity in the form of the office, and finally there came into being the lower and higher working places of capitalism represented by the entrepreneur, the privately employed white-collar worker and the industrial proletariat. The workshop and the store, however, were not affected by this social development because they could not strike roots in the feudal economy of the feudal society; neither was the bourgeois society of capitalism of a nature under which they could have further developed. Thus, under the influence of modern capitalist venture, workshops and small shops were built up on their rudimentary foundations, and thus they could neither completely retain the traditional character of the store and the workshop nor could they assume the rational nature of business venture. Both of them were of a mixed character as regards their social structure but neither of these elements gained the upperhand. Persons owning workshops or small shops respresented careers which were not of a middle-class nature (because they remained too close to materials and needs). We must also see that the actual job was done by manual work instead of entrepreneurial management. Thus the members of this stratum were not workers because they were independent and owned capital and their own business.

3. THE LIBERAL PROFESSIONS

In the course of Hungarian history, capitalist business provided the organizational framework for intellectual work. The social forms of intellectual activities were moulded partly by the office and partly by jobs with the enterprises, and both left their marks according to their inherent nature. Office jobs were transformed into gentlemanly upper middle-class careers linked with the historical antecedents of the intelligentsia of noble birth of the feudal society, whereas business jobs underwent a transformation producing the stratum of bourgeois intelligentsia patterned after the capitalist bourgeois society. As a matter of fact, no other social course existed for intellectual activity in Hungarian society. Truly liberal professionals were only those who on the basis of an adequate landed estate or other property were able to be engaged freely and not professionally in intellectual work. However, this was such an exceptional case that it could be neglected as a type. Nevertheless, both statistical investigations and everyday language use the term liberal professions to describe all those occupations whose occupants are not employed either by the state or by enterprises. All these professions like those of the physicians, lawyers, chemists, etc. were truly independent careers within the productive organization of the community, while not being independent formations in the social structure. These careers are so closely connected with the careers of the white-collar workers of the offices and the stratum of employees of private firms that it would have been extremely difficult to separate them from these. Thus, the liberal professions were either office-like or enterprise-like, but could not develop any autonomous structure.

The older intellectual careers with a historical past (the representatives of which were professional persons of non-noble birth) were office-like gentlemen's professions, while those which have emerged in the course of modern capitalist development were business-like bourgeois careers. This division, however, was valid only mostly for the past since the two types have been mixed up by the modern urban way of life, and the two kinds of social qualities became intertwined in each of the separate professions. Partly, individual varieties developed in each profession, and partly the social qualities became mixed up in general within one or another profession. The material basis of interaction was the fact that although the representatives of the liberal professions were not employed by the state or by enterprises, by the very nature of their activity they became dependent on both of them and therefore, their social communication developed in both direction.

In general all those careers which are usually termed liberal professions were linked up with the conservative national society, due to their past as professional careers (their representatives were of non-noble birth) and due to their educational background at that period. The everyday practice of

74

these professions, however, was generally linked up with the business-like middle-class way of life. Thus they increasingly became bourgeois professions, while not entirely discarding their gentlemanly upper middle class character. In this respect these professions underwent an interesting change. In the past century the old traditions still asserted themselves unambiguously, i.e. these careers were regarded more or less as gentlemen's professions. Such careers as for instance the legal profession which were old-standing occupations of the intelligentsia of noble birth were held in higher esteem than those of the physicians or engineers which were entered by the nobility more recently. In the seventies and eighties of the past century such terms as e.g. "he is but a land-surveyor" or "a mere chirurgeon" could be still used as affront to the dignity of a gentleman though these professions were otherwise regarded as respectable careers. However, beginning with the end of the past century these careers came to be increasingly held by young Jews coming from wealthy business families. As a result, the social character of these careers had considerably changed both in terms of prestige and its internal structure. These careers became more businesslike with a less conservative mentality and a modern orientation to Western bourgeois societies. Thus, these careers more or less assumed a middle-class character. Following the war, however, there ensued a reverse process. As a result of the *numerus clausus,* the number of graduates of Jewish origin decreased and, owing to the supersaturation of public administration, members of the gentlemenly upper middle class began to penetrate the liberal professions. Thus, the representation of the gentry became stronger in these professions and this trend was rather enhanced than weakened by university and college education. The new turn, however, did not blur the middle-class character of these careers, as it did not diminish considerably the percentage of Jewish intellectuals. Moreover also the modern businesslike way of life tended to strengthen that nature of the liberal professions. Under these circumstances, these careers became even more markedly bourgeois professions than occupations of the upper middle class. And those representatives of the liberal professions who were still accepted as gentlemen were regarded as such not because of their having intellectual jobs, but rather because, despite their occupations, they were gentlemen due to birth or successful assimilation.

All intellectual occupations call for a high degree of professionalism and modern technical skill, and this trend strengthened considerably in the inter-war period. It was particularly the medical and engineering professions where training was outstanding and up-to-date, and these professions had active connections with the West. The other element, which contributed to the social prestige of these professions, was the fact that, in addition to their guaranteeing independence, they generally were rather lucrative and as a rule exceeded the income level of salaried intellectuals. For these reasons the liberal professions were regarded as attractive occupations, and though they were not considered truly gentlemen's professions they faced less aversion from the gentlemanly upper middle class than the economic careers. Nevertheless, these professions were unable to absorb permanently upper middle-class intellectuals and there was an incessant outflow from these professions towards administrative jobs in the inter-war period. The more bourgeois like elements seeking financial security tried to get employment with enterprises, whereas the more gentlemanlike elements attracted rather by the dignity of office, tried to get jobs in public administration.

Significantly the liberal professions in this period began to develop their professional organizations. It was only the Bar which functioned at the end of the first World War as a professional organization with legal status, but even the Bar functioned mainly as a trade union of jurists. Later, however, the socio-political trend gained the upperhand: it was demanded that the liberal professions should form professional associations, which in addition to being an autonomous federation were at the same time directing and controlling organs as well. The main intention was to grant a certain amount of offical status also to the liberal professions—accordingly the office-like character was emphasized also in these professions—and so to say to integrate them with the upper national society. The goal was to direct the activities of the liberal professions according to this conception, and to oust the so-called unreliable elements, first of all the Jews from these careers. One after the other, the associations of engineers, physicians, actors and journalists were created, and attempts were also being made to establish an association for the fine arts which, however, could not be realized at that time. But the organization of associations met with several difficulties; after their establishment their activity was hampered by continuous political and professional strife. This was but natural since all these professions were of rather a bourgeois character and resisted strongly the idea of being controlled officially. They much more easily fitted into the earlier unions of interest assertion which used to be autonomous middle-class organizations. Only those associations could function without considerable difficulties which confined themselves to purely safeguarding professional interests.

The liberal professions represented an abstract high culture both in terms of theoretical training and their practical experience. The liberal professions relied heavily both on abstract theoretical expertise and the urban way of life of the upper middle-class. These professions were closely related to the ideas of more advanced bourgeois society and Hungarian urban way of life patterned after European examples. This meant that none of the liberal professions was able to process and understand anything of the living conditions of the lower levels of the social hierarchy. This applies especially to the peasantry. The whole professional training and social existence of the members of the liberal professions were so much separated from the lower strata of society that the intellectuals of the liberal profession had merely stereotypical attitudes to the lower strata. All intellectual occupations waged a hopeless fight against the conventions and traditions of the lower society; the intellectuals rejected from the start to learn from the concrete social life circumstances of the lower classes. Instead, they tried to respond to these conditions by composing their prefabricated formulas. Thus the lawyer had first to persuade his client that his notions of justice were false, the physician had to explain to his patient how to change his diet, and the architect had to fight the taste of the builder and to press upon him his own concept of good taste.

In this respect the gentlemen's and the bourgeois intelligentsia were not different. The first represented the culture of the historical upper strata alien to the people, whereas the second was the representative of the modern bourgeois way of life developed in other countries but equally alien to the people. This alien high culture was not only the characteristics of liberal professions which were linked to the lower society by their practical activities but also of the intellectuals who were active in the field of intellectual culture, i.e. in science, literature and the arts. They also worked with abstract materials from the world of fellow intellectuals, while the lower society as a whole appeared in their work only in the forms of ideas and concepts. An almost identical situation existed in the so-called "urban" literature, science and art of the bourgeois world and in the national literature, science and art of the conservative gentlemen's society. Both cultures were equally drifting high above the people, and intellectual activity in both of them was similarly abstracted from the real life of the lower society.

A significant change took place also in this respect in the second half of the period under survey. The populist movement penetrated this abstract world with the concrete image of the lower society and indicated an alternative to traditionally accepted attitudes by conjuring up an image of reality. However, this influence originated from two sources. The more active members of the middle-class intellectuals went back to history and they identified the peasantry as the successor of the deep-rooted Hungarian character of the old Hungarian society. The character of the intellectuals became alienated because both in their social position and their culture they became estranged from the Hungarian people, and therefore they felt they ought to draw lessons from history and immerse in the peasantry and thereby regenerate. As a result, the science of Hungarianism came into being; the collection of folk music and ethnographic research started and attempts were made to identify and save the patterns of Hungarian ways of thinking and popular talents. Later, the influence of the populist movement reached film-making literature, the arts and attire as well; populism became a fashion. At the same time, from among the people there actually arose intellectuals who did not turn their backs to the real world of the peasantry despite of their higher educational standards. This was first reflected in a type of literature which started to depict an entirely different world from that described by both "urban" or conservative literature. The effects of this type of literature naturally intermingled with the populist trend but never fully merged with it. Some members of this group of popular origin had close contacts with both middle-class, bourgeois and working-class intellectuals but they did not merge with any of them. In their education, they benefited a lot from connections with these three intellectual strata, yet, even under the influence of so varied effects they did not lose sight of the concrete material of the lower society. Least of all did the members of the populist group become assimilated to the conservative intelligentsia; better connections were established with the intellectuals advocating working-class interests and even more so with the working class itself.

This effect, however, triggered off a countereffect as well. As a reaction to the influence of populism which was felt to be boorish, the conservative intellectuals—both the gentlemanly upper middle class and the bourgeois middle class—increasingly withdrew into their abstract world of high culture, partly to the realm of the mind, and partly behind the walls of the intellectual constitution of the conservative national society.

4. BOURGEOIS ARISTOCRACY

At the highest level of Hungarian bourgeois society there were to be found no patrician notabilities but "a bourgeoisie given to playing the gentleman". Refinement and nobility were achieved by this bourgeois aristocracy not by way of its own bourgeois development: it had acquired only its wealth in the course of capitalist development, and with this wealth it purchased nobility from wherever it could be purchased. This was possible from two sources: first, from the historical Hungarian aristocracy and second, from the haute bourgeoisie of the Western societies. The social character of this stratum evolved under the influence of these two patterns, and because in Hungarian society it was the historical aristocracy which represented the highest prestige and also because it was nearer to this stratum, it finally assumed the social traits of the aristocracy.

Families which made their fortunes in the first stage of capitalism linked up with the historical aristocracy in three ways: by marriage, by purchasing landed estates and by acquiring family coat-of-arms. Most of these families succeeded in joining the aristocracy in all the three respects: they became related with them, purchased landed properties and were made barons. Nevertheless they did not merge completely with the historic aristocracy and neither did they develop independently in the same way as the latter. The difference between them was something like that between the lawns of the British and American tennis courts: they both have been mowed, watered, attended to for quite a long time, yet, British lawns have been more compact and confined since they have been clipped and attended to in the same way for about for or five hundred years. We may say that the Hungarian aristocracy of bourgeois origins lacked the historical background and thus in vain did it acquire all the prerequisites of nobility; these could be supported only by constant and up-to-date achievements and not by mere traditions. Therefore wealth, education and an upper-class life style were not only concomitants but also preconditions of this way of life. Any of these preconditions were indispensable prerequisites and all of them had to be cultivated concurrently because time alone did not enhance but erode them.

The first prerequisite was wealth. This was mainly capitalist wealth even when it consisted for the most part of landed property. For these landowners it was not enough just to own the land but they organized it as a productive enterprise and made it profitable by means of entrepreneurial activity. This was not a rule—since many of them were so much occupied with their other enterprises that they found no time to look after their landed properties—yet, for a significant part of such cases it held true. By its very nature entrepreneurial wealth demanded top managerial activity and therefore it would have been rather difficult to get rid of it. At least they had to "govern" their enterprises, but there were quite a few among these aristocrats who actually controlled their enterprises. Some of them reminded one rather of American managers than of noble patricians or traditional Hungarian aristocrats.

Education and learning were not traditionally established components of the big-bourgeois way of life either. Unlike in the case of the historical aristocracy it was not a broad and superficial erudition acquired by several continuous generations but an incessantly enriched fresh stock of knowledge which had its own dynamic of growth. It was for this reason that literature, the arts and science found more readily patrons, benefactors and active supporters in this stratum than among the members of the traditional aristocracy. There were a number of examples when such an aristocrat himself became actively engaged in some spheres of culture. And since this was not traditional education and culture, many of such aristocrats turned to revolutionary theories.

Neither was life as settled or even rigid, stereotyped and boring for this fraction of the aristocracy as for the other one. It was a life of permanent activity and pursuit of sensations and new pleasures. It was not just living a disciplined life restricted by chilly forms but making most of the possibilities offered by life.

The role of this active aristocracy played within the social structure also differed considerably from that of the historical aristocracy. It had no traditionally established leading role as against society as a whole, only the role of a co-regent wherein—due to its capitalist influence—it was the stronger though by no means the decisive partner. This bourgeois aristocracy has influenced the direction of society always only by real power factors and not by its consolidated political leading role. Therefore its

79

activity was not founded on political professionalism but on entrepreneurial inclination and talent, and its members participated also in political life by using these methods.

This stratum played a rather multiple role in the interwar period. At the time of the counter-revolution its members—as big capitalist Jews—were regarded simultaneously as the representatives of liberal reaction and revolutionary subversion but by all means as the enemies of the Christian-national society. In the period of consolidation, however, this stratum by and large succeeded in reconquering its pre-war influence and as an indispensable factor of the consolidation of economic life it was granted representation in all the important positions of the regime. But at the time of the Great Depression there appeared an intense hostility against this stratum; though Jewish capitalists had a significant political role in the years following the Depression, they increasingly became the targets of attacks in public opinion. Later on, also the political influence of this stratum declined, moreover its role in economic life, was considerably curtailed. Thus, this stratum slowly began to approximate the social position of the bourgeoisie and the conservative middle class and brought its influence to bear on the defence of the constitution.

Apart from the ups and downs of its political position, this stratum lost some of its prestige and influence as a social factor in the second half of the period under survey. All the affairs of this stratum were exposed in such detail by the antisemite and anti-capitalist right-wing parties pointing out exaggeratedly both the wealth and political influence as well as the international connections of this aristocracy that its prestige was marred considerably even in those circles which were unaffected by right-wing radicalism.

5. THE BOURGEOIS MIDDLE CLASS

The middle stratum of modern bourgeois society comprises three kinds of class positions within the framework of similar social forms: the medium-sized entrepreneurs, the white-collar employees of enterprises and free professionals. The middle stratum of entrepreneurs was the bourgeoisie which used to be the middle class in the more advanced bourgeois societies. This class position assures to its occupants moderate wealth, the ownership of an industrial or commercial enterprise employing a great number of employees, managerial activity rising high above the level of manual and administrative work, a broad though superficial education and a decent middle-class existence. The white-collar employees of enterprises are as much salaried intellectuals as the public servants, and their work relations, too, were mostly similar to the conditions of those working in public administration. However, there were some differences: their salary in similar jobs was generally higher, whereas their pensions were lower, and old-age insurance was less common among them. The way of life of the two strata of officials was also similar: the members of both of these groups received salaries agreed upon in contracts which were sufficient for a modest middle-class way of life, but apart from that they were considerably differing social formations. The middle-class members of the liberal professions led an independent way of life in a similar way as the stratum of the entrepreneur bourgeoisie, however, its independent existence was guaranteed not by ownership of enterprises but by its intellectual occupation. Thus, the elements of the intellectual official and entrepreneurial bourgeois way of life were mixed in the class relations of this stratum.

Within the limits of their material living conditions this middle class could have completely united with the upper middle-class since they were of the same social standing and held the same class positions in the productive organization of society. This, however, did not happen at all, and this, too, can be explained only by historical development. The bourgeois middle class was the product of modern capitalist development; its social patterns and culture were moulded by capitalism and by urban life which evolved together with capitalism. Moreover, its development took place in fields not entered by the historical middle class. Entrepreneurial activity as well as the intellectual pursuits characteristic of urban life, industry and commerce were yielded by the historical society to people who had no social inhibitions to exploit new opportunities. Under such circumstances, these occupations attracted people who were not bound by the traditions of feudal society, i.e. mainly Jews and to a lesser extent immigrants coming from the West. Out of these heterogeneous elements, however, no separate bourgeois social evolution began in the first stage of capitalist development and modern urbanization. The overwhelming majority of these people busily assimilated to the historical society and strove to be absorbed both as regards apparel, habits and political sentiments. They identified themselves with the same national liberal idea as professed by the gentlemanly upper middle class, and in general they adapted themselves to the historical classes in all walks of national life, yet, by the turn of the century, this loyal cooperation came to a stop on both sides. Jealousy and a sense of danger threatening from the new bourgeoisie quickly growing rich and acquiring positions took hold of the historical classes, whereas the former—in the possession of bourgeois wealth, intellectual education and industrial and commercial enterprises—began to develop a sense of middle-class consciousness and no longer held in respect unconditionally the requirements of loyal adjustment. A wide gap opened between the two kinds of middle classes which—though from time to time it decreased in intensity—could never again be bridged completely. The gap between the two strata of the middle class became ever greater through the influence of modern Western ideas and bourgeois radicalism which influenced also political life. The new middle class became strongly susceptible to these ideas. The bourgeois consciousness of the bourgeois middle class became stronger owing to these movements which were highly critical of conservative national society. However, not the whole of the new bourgeois middle class was affected by these radical tendencies. A considerable part of its established close ties with the historical classes and united with them on the basis of a genuine community of interests. But both genuine bourgeois transformation and new attempts of assimilation on the part of the bourgeois middle class were frustrated by the lost war, the disintegration of the Monarchy as well as the bourgeois and communist revolutions; thus the two strata of the middle class became estranged.

Beginning with the counter-revolution of 1919 the antagonism between the Christian middle class and the Jewish middle class became chronic but this, too, was not an even development. At the time of the consolidation a reconciliation took place on the surface but beneath its contradictions and tensions became more embittered than ever. Though the bourgeoisie compromised itself with the revolution, it succeeded in maintaining most of its positions partly due to its indispensable role in economic reconstruction and partly because the influence of liberal democracy predominated all over Europe at that time. Thus, as regards all its roles, it again took possession of its former positions and continued to flourish in the economic life, literature, the press, the theatrical world as much as prior to World War I. With the onslaught of the Great Depression, however, the relations between the two kinds of middle classes deteriorated manifestly and, at the time of the so-called new regime, the Christian middle-class made undisguised attemps at driving back the Jewish bourgeoisie. Actually the anti-Jewish laws and the large-scale state intervention in economic life achieved their aims: the Christian middle class succeeded in ousting the other middle class from part of its positions. At the same time, anti-bourgeois political endeavours asserted themselves, and the Hungarian representatives of this policy very efficiently attacked this bourgeois middle class together with the upper stratum of the middle class even as regards their social mode of existence.

Another consequence of these times was the fact that as a result of partly the Great Depression and partly state intervention the members of the independent bourgeoisie were pushed to the background and the bourgeois middle class itself was increasingly transformed into a dependent stratum. In 1930 when this stratum consisted of 190 thousand bread-winners and together with dependents of about 400 thousand people, i.e. 4.7 or 4.6 per cent of the total population, the minority of it was still independent. By the end of that period, however, the percentage of independent careers dropped by 50 per cent.

Just as in the earlier stages of its evolution the bourgeois middle class developed between the bounds of contradictory influences. It opposed the conservative national society and tried to emulate the European patterns of bourgeois societies continuing to represent middle-class progress and liberal democracy in Hungarian society as well. From this aspect its relation

82

to the West was snobbish, feeling its social environment backward and feudal and regarding the capital and the major provincial towns as islands of civilization. At the same time, it was not a real Western-type bourgeoisie because its whole development took place too abruptly and in rather a colonial way, and therefore no harmonious bourgeois culture could emerge. Literature, the press, film, theatre, the arts and science as well as fashion and ideas were characterized by the fact that they did not reflect the actual life of the middle class according to the standards of a high culture while they also failed in fully absorbing Western effects. Compared to the bourgeoisie prior to World War I, in this respect the bourgeois middle class of the inter-war period represented a regression. At that time the bourgeoisie was capable of being beneficial to the whole of Hungarian society; it succeeded in drawing into its orbit the talents of the conservative society and also those of the lower strata contributing to their development by newspapers, journals and the founding of societies. This impetus petered out after the war; the intellectual life of the bourgeoisie became introverted and dried up. This can be explained by the after-effects of the revolution and by the pressure exerted by the conservative regime which efficiently defended itself. Nevertheless the symptoms were significant. The bourgeois middle class proved unable to transmit its own social ideas and culture to the other strata of society, yet part of its own youth, drew closer to the conservatives joining their intellectual circles. This throws a light on the other aspect of the social character of the bourgeois middle class. In the same way as it was snobbish as regards the West and the examples of the true bourgeois societies, it felt attracted also by conservative historical classes which it regarded as being deeply different from itself. Therefore, this stratum, too, was prone to playing the role of the gentry. Between the two World Wars this trend proved to be stronger than before World War I. All the characteristics of the Hungarian upper (gentlemanly) middle class were with some modifications transferred to the bourgeois middle class as well: conservatism, i.e. conscious and unconscious loyalty to the gentlemanly middle class world, arrogant, haughty attitudes towards the lower strata of society, repulsion of manual work, employment of domestic servants to a much greater extent than demanded by a civilized urban way of life—these were all features clearly similar in the character of both the gentlemanly and bourgeois middle classes. The bourgeois middle class, despite its bourgeois consciousness and modern attitudes, proved to be unable to shake off the spell of the conservative gentlemanly manners.

As regards its political consciousness, liberal democracy was the guiding star of the bourgeois middle class. In festive mood its speakers recalled the ideas of the 1848 revolution, whereas in its everyday activities the liberalism of the era of the 1867 compromise was thought desirable. Thus, in its lofty ideas the members of this bourgeoisie formulated the demand for the assertion of a total democracy, while their actual wish was to guarantee the removal of restrictions imposed on careers based on purchased land estates and on a higher-level social background. And since in this period such restrictions were created and even acquired estates were not respected unreservedly, the bourgeoisie increasingly advocated the ideas of liberalism. Abstract humanistic ideas and the lofty ideal of freedom had no truer believers in that period than the bourgeois middle class. At the same time, in its actual political attitudes it approached only with great caution and a lot of reservations those real political forces i.e. the peasantry and the working class which progressed under extreme hadrships towards humanity and freedom. It managed to establish closest contacts with the working class, more precisely with its middle-class type upper stratum. With the populist movement, started from amidst the peasantry, it sympathized only as long as it revealed the serious situation of the peasantry. The moment that populism voiced more radical views, the bourgeoisie as the advocate of bourgeois outlook turned against it considering the aims of populism a reaction against the ideas of bourgeois liberalism.

The history of the period provides ample evidence in the same way as did the collapse of the bourgeois revolution. The bourgeoisie did not develop into a strong formation capable of emerging as a large-scale and broad foundation; it was far from being like the middle class which created the bourgeois society of the West. The Hungarian bourgeois middle class did not grow strong and vigorous in the course of bourgeois revolution but took shape in a process of assimilation to the higher levels of society: as a result it could never become a bourgeois middle class in the proper sense of the word.

6. THE PETITE BOURGEOISIE

Society is not a mass, not an incoherent community but a permanent organizing substance in history giving rise to a definite stratification. According to living conditions, the formation of society is a long historical process of building up or disintegration. This means that society is not always in a state of progress. If the life of a community is restricted by a hereditary structure, which does not permit the development and growth of either material or intellectual life, then society ceases to develop. At such times the material and intellectual forces do not build but rather destroy the social edifice. However, simultaneously new social forces may start to unfold.

Modern bourgeois society is not a mass society either. It emerged as the result of a long development and its foundations had been laid by pre-capitalist Europe through the work of the bourgeoisie and peasantry of the feudal society. In the course of capitalist development, however, these frameworks immensely expanded, and bourgeois society became a structure comprising the whole community. Expansion released forces, too, which

84

threaten to burst the very structure of bourgeois society. This could be termed "massification", but it is more than that. Despite considerable expansion, the developed formations, i.e. the bourgeoisie and the petite bourgeoisie did not disintegrate for a long time but proved to be stable components of the social structure. Recently, these two strata have actually begun to disintegrate and are practically threatened with destruction; this would already mean "massification". At the same time, however, at the foundations of this social structure a new evolution is also commencing through the existence and activity of the working class. And though the working class shows the same symptoms of "massification" as the bourgeoisie, a contrary social process is taking place behind the screen of these symptoms. In the first case we face the disintegration of the historical social formations, in the second, a new society is in the making.

Social structure developed in another and in many a respect different way in Hungarian society since a new mode of production which was brought into this society from the outside started to affect the historical evolution of the society. The historical social structure, which had evolved under different conditions, had ready organizations, institutions and forms which just because they were stably developed survived the changes in the relations of production and adapted themselves to the changed conditions. Also at the time of capitalist development, owing to the historically developed social structure, almost the whole of agrarian production as well the life of the agrarian population remained within the old forms. Thus the manor, the peasant farm, the landed gentry and the peasantry basically carried on its historically preserved forms. The same applies to the life of the churches and the whole of the state organization. Simultaneously, another social structure emerged owing to capitalist production and urban life; this was a different social structure, yet was also made up of stable formations. This new structure was the result of capitalism and it penetrated the old social structure from outside and above. Business venture gave birth to the bourgeois entrepreneur, to the stratum of intellectuals employed by business and to the working-class. And since the process of expansion of capitalism progressed from above towards the basis of society, small industry, retail trading and the lower spheres of middle-class life in general were not affected by this process. The workshop, the store and the petite bourgeoisie were the very spheres from which capitalism and generally bourgeois society had developed in the original capitalist societies. Hungarian petite bourgeoisie had not inherited any resistant historical forms; as a result, these social groups did not continue to grow but rather perished in the course of capitalist development. Thus the Hungarian petite bourgeoisie remained socially undeveloped. This, however, did not result from bourgeois society, nor did it result from the specifics of Hungarian history. The weakness of petite bourgeoisie resulted from the fact that Hungary's capitalism started to develop as a consequence of external forces.

Thus in Hungarian history the petite bourgeoisie was not a formation of society in the same way as the landlords or the peasants, the bourgeoisie or the workers. It was not an independent social formation, not a finished structure in itself but the result of various intermediary social forces. In terms of the social structure, it remained a blunt mass in the same way as its work remained an underdeveloped activity.

The genuine productive forms of the petite bourgeoisie had developed in the feudal society. These were the peasant farm, the store and the workshop. In the course of time, capitalism and bourgeois society grew out of these and though they remained the lower levels of production and bourgeois society above which higher-level organizations were built, they retained their developed institutionalism. However, since in Hungarian history the farm, the store and the workshop did not develop to such an extent, also their further development took a different course. The peasant farms did not develop to such a point that they could be transformed into bourgeois enterprises, and thus they remained the conservative loci of production of the lower society. But neither did the stores and the workshop develop to such an extent that they could join the capitalist economy. Under the pressure of capitalism, they more or less collapsed and adapted themselves to the order of capitalism. Thus, the peasants did not maintain their social structure, and neither did the handicraftsmen and the shop-keepers preserve their middle-class way of life after becoming a petit bourgeois stratum. At the same time, capitalism did not start new organizing activities in the petit bourgeois productive situations, i.e. in the small capitalist enterprises and in the intermediary stage between the productive situations of the middle-class and the workers of the big enterprises. More exactly, something came into being which comprised somewhat of all structural elements. The petit bourgeois production united the elements of the workshop and shop-keeping; in addition certain rudiments of business venture and those of being a worker or clerical worker were also made use of. Nevertheless, being petit bourgeois meant rather a social position in a state of flux and not a fully developed social form. Thus, to put it quite precisely, in Hungarian society, the petite bourgeoisie was such a social stratum which was made up of neither gentlemen nor peasants, or bourgeois or workers.

This stratum comprised rather a great number of people: in 1930 there were 430 thousand such bread-winners (1,100 thousand together with dependents), that is 11 per cent (altogether almost 13 per cent) of the total population of the country. This group of the population was in fact a mass since in terms of social structure it was a shapeless, not fully developed formation held together not by its own structure but by external forces. The productive situation under whose conditions this petite bourgeois mass lived was of a dual nature. Partly it was a petty capitalist business venture, or more precisely, an independent form of small-scale industry and retail trade, and partly a job between the productive situation of white- and blue-collar workers within the capitalist enterprise—an institutionalized and therefore secure worker's position. These class relations could no longer develop into an independent structural form in the productive system of capitalism; they could only adapt themselves to other, more developed forms since they had not shaped into a resistant formation in the course of history. Thus small-scale industry and retail trade became business ventures which, however, were subordinated to capitalist ventures while the intermediate productive situation came to resemble the white-collar jobs to be held at enterprises.

The petite bourgeoisie played a considerable role in the emergence of the counter-revolutionary regime after World War I, but due to its very nature it proved unable to make the best of this role. Of all the revitalized counter-revolutionary social forces the petite bourgeoisie, more precisely, the smallholders and the Christian petite bourgeoisie was the first to turn against the revolution. It was a peculiar feature of the historical situation that these two petite bourgeois strata joined forces. The small holders became active in defending their existence as small landowners, the Christian petit bourgeois mobilized itself because of its anti-Semitic and anti-capitalistic sentiments. But these two strata of the petite bourgeoisie differed to such an extent that any efficient actions were doomed to failure by their differences. Though they succeeded in gaining political power at the time of the first counter-revolutionary wave, they were unable to make use of it. And this was but natural, since the smallholders were a part of the peasantry which raised entirely different demands from those of non-agrarian petit bourgeois. They could not even elaborate a common political theory. The smallholders represented the concept of petit bourgeois agrarian democracy, whereas the petite bourgeoisie was the representative of a rudimentary sort of fascism. It was for this reason that the historical classes succeeded in reducing their influence. Following their defeat, the smallholders became parts of the lower sections of the peasantry, whereas the petite bourgeoisie entered the stage of consolidation as a mass linked to the lowest level of the conservative national and the modern bourgeois societies. That fraction of the petite bourgeoisie became mobilized in the second half of the inter-war period at the time of the upswing of the extreme right movements. But even then it was not an independent social force, only the mass basis of the rightist movements headed by the middle class.

Just as in previous years, the petite bourgeoisie failed to develop into a compact social structure in that period. Under the same conditions and subjected to the same forces it once again remained an inarticulated mass. It gave free vent to any external forces without any resistance whatsoever and joined the leading social strata according to its direct interests. Therefore, it did not follow a consistent line even in its political theories. The petite bourgeoisie advocated the popular-racist radicalism of fascism in the same

87

way as it supported the conservative nationalist idea or the programme of democracy. It was only as consistent in its political ideas as in its social status. And since the consolidation reconstructed the old social order burdening the lower strata of society both politically and as regards their economic situation, the petite bourgeoisie was inclined to political radicalism throughout the whole period. It always embraced those ideas which seemed to be on the upswing but most sincerely those of fascism which was regarded as the most characteristically petit bourgeois aspiration.

The petite bourgeoisie showed also a high degree of susceptibility to the technology of civilization. It is conservative only in societies where petit bourgeois existence has socio-historical forms. There it is bound by its traditions. However, in Hungarian society the petit bourgeois way of life had not been developed to such an extent and therefore it was exposed like a raw material to all kind of influence. And since it had no development of its own, it gave way to these influences without resistance. All the trends and schools of thought left their mark on the way of life of the petite bourgeoisie replacing each other almost as quickly as ephemeral hit-tunes.

As regards intellectual culture, the petite bourgeoisie served again as raw material because it had no cultural traditions of its own, which could have provided the background for absorbing new influences. As a result, the petite bourgeoisie could absorb only superficial effects, i.e. exciting, thrilling ones because for profound sensations it lacked both education and experience. Irredentist nationalism, bourgeois idealism, populism—all the intellectual fashions of this era had a superficial influence on this stratum.

Even less so than in the more advanced bourgeois societies, the petite bourgeoisie had no traditions in productive work either. It was not bound by either professional traditions or by material determinations of its position in production. The intelligentsia and the working class are not bound by established traditions either, but the work itself they perform is a kind of expertise which demands training and skill from anybody who is engaged in it. For those who are active in these occupations and professions labour is the means of living, i.e. they can make a living only by work and this implies that they are bound to continuously develop their occupational skill. On the other hand, petit bourgeois existence, be it independent small-scale venture or an employment status which is neither blue-collar nor white-collar, is but to a small extent an objective scope of activity. Most often it is a kind of service work which does not demand vocational training. Though it demands adaptation and the continuous acquisition of new skills, it does not call for serious training. Any kind of job attracts the petite bourgeoisie in an abstract form since this involves much more risk-taking than the tasks to be solved by intellectuals or workers. That is the reason why this stratum more easily changes jobs than the intellectuals or workers. For a worker the employer may also frequently change but the trade, the craft itself as an objective work task seldom changes.

88

Nevertheless the petit bourgeois became the hero of the age. All over the world, it had a powerful influence on the intellectual and political trends of the age. This is easily explained by the fact that it is this very stratum which reacts the most sensitively to any change because it is the least skilled and puts up the least resistance to any change in life. Thus, it is this stratum which is affected mostly by any crisis or prosperity. At the same time, however, it does not represent any constructive moment in these processes; it is only the assertion of its force as a mass which it displays without being capable of furthering the development of society and culture. In Hungarian society even that role of the petite bourgeoisie was less significant. In Hungary the petite bourgeoisie was bound by a large number of restrictions and therefore the above-mentioned characteristics of the petite bourgeoisie proved to be unable to influence decisively the course of events.

7. THE WORKING CLASS

The Hungarian working class, too, had grown together with capitalism but its antecedents differed markedly from those of the original capitalist societies. Workers did not come to the factories of capitalist business from the schools of the guild industries and the specialized peasant crafts but they were recruited by business from places where a considerably mobile labour force could be found. Thus skilled labour was brought mostly from foreign factories and unskilled, mass labour from the less restricted spheres of Hungarian society.

The skilled workers of the first business ventures were for the most part foreigners, mostly Germans, and for this reason the first newspapers of the workers were published in German. Even the majority of workers born in Hungary were not Hungarian because they came mainly from towns where the handicraft industry was overwhelmingly a German trade. From the point of view of further development this meant that the organizing work and the whole social formation of the Hungarian working class was launched by a foreign generation which established connections first of all with the German working class.

As regards the social development of the Hungarian working class, it was a significant circumstance that the Hungarian big industrial working class had been recruited in an abrupt way. Even if workers came to the factories from industrial trades this did not happen by way of a continuous transformation; therefore the workers could not bring with them their professional or social traditions. As a matter of fact, the overwhelming majority of these workers had arrived at the factories as unskilled mass workforce. Under such circumstances, the social development of the Hungarian working class started almost from scratch, and all kinds of previous training or organization were eliminated in the new situation.

Thus, this working class was an abstract labour force at the beginning of its history; it put up no resistance against the management. Neither vocational self-defence nor the social defense of the workers' life and existence had any traditional foundations, and therefore such organizing work had to begin without antecedents.

Under such conditions, the Hungarian working class launched its organizational work following the ready-made Western, mainly German examples and ideas, and this applies also to the development of its class consciousness. Thus, similarly to capitalist business itself, the organizing work of the working class was begun from above through already available methods. This meant that the Hungarian labour movement relied on purely theoretical-ideological considerations, more precisely, it was rooted in the ideas and principles of the German working-class movement and not in actual situations. Only a single fact stood out: an unskilled and defenceless mass of workers was employed by business which had developed on the basis of uninhibited commercialism. Under such conditions it was but natural that the working class became aware of this situation and tried to defend itself against exploitation by means of ideals and principles adopted from more advanced movements. For this reason, the leadership of the working class continued to be in the hands of skilled workers of German origin and to develop strong ties with the German movements. In the course of the process when modern urban life as a whole as well as the middle class which was forming mainly out of foreigners became Magyarized, the working class, too, underwent the same development. The trend was given further impetus by the fact that the new working class was increasingly recruited from Hungarians. Nevertheless, a change in language could not alter the fact that the working class continued to develop on the lines adopted at the start of its course.

After such preliminaries, at the beginning of the century the social evolution of the working class as well as its organized character and the power of its movements had reached the point of becoming a political force. At the time of the revolution, the working class was already as influential as the bourgeois radical movement. In addition to this, the working class showed its strength by means of both repeated strikes and its cultural strivings.

In the years following the revolutions of 1918 and 1919 the momentum of the labour movement came to a standstill and its social development ceased for a time as well. As regards both its political role and trade union activity, the labour movement was seriously restricted and isolated by the consolidation. The regime hampered not only its extension towards the agrarian workers but serously limited its industrial-urban activities as well. As a result, the working class so to say shut itself up and this had consequences also for its internal social development.

The working class had a very narrow scope for action in defending its economic position and social security, but even within these narrow bounds it succeeded in achieving considerable results. In fact, the working class was a factor to be reckoned with even under conditions which became more difficult, and this was true as regards social policy as well as parliamentary life. Under such circumstances, its internal development did not come to a standstill either, though no considerable progress was made in the sphere of ideology and as regards the expansion of the movement.

The social development of the working class takes place owing to factory work and the political movement, i.e. in the trade unions and in its political party. For this reason, it is almost all through its life a class characterized by politically conscious social movements and this class cannot stop short at the potentialities of its existence but advances to the stages of development with incessant endeavour to shape its fate. Owing to the conditions of its historical development, the Hungarian working class had always been shaped to a growing extent by the movement. Both within its trade unions and its political party the working class movement was much less concerned with shaping the workers' life than in the more advanced bourgeois societies. At the time of the involuntary introversion in the era of consolidation under Prime Minister Bethlen this had a twofold result. First of all the development of the ideology of the labour movement came to a halt since it had no other way but to descend to the level of a given political situation whose prospects were not at all predictable at that time. The Hungarian labour movement was shaken to its very foundations, and the working class was forced to display a kind of activity with which it had been quite unfamiliar. Thus, there ensued the other result: a process of adopting middle-class standards commenced within the ranks of the better paid skilled workers' stratum. The Hungarian working class had nothing like an extensive social and cultural organizational network which could have absorbed and engaged its attention at a time when the political activity in the movement came to a deadlock. The stagnation in the movement and the process of developing middle-class standards resulted in the increase of factionalism within the labour movement which, under the given cir-cumstances, proved to be an obstacle to mobilizing the working class and to achieving success.

Under the conditions of its involuntary introversion, the working class could have had only the possibility to develop its ideology. However, this did not take place either in that period. Though the working class had its own daily newspaper, periodical and publishing possibilities, i.e. such a development would have been possible technically, these chances were not used for two reasons. First, the labour movement lacked the social basis for such an activity, i.e. a sort of worker's life gaining experiences from diversified activity and concerned with all the problems of life. Second, the German labour movement continued to be the source of ideas for the Hungarian working class, and this proved to be the most disadvantageous source at that time. Thus, there happened nothing else but the discussion and general adoption of the general tenets of socialism without any attempts to further develop and adopt them in a more detailed form. As a result, in the long run the working class was unable to influence either the peasantry or the intellectual strata of society by means of the ideals of socialism.

The Great Depression, however, gave a new impetus to the working class. In addition to the general effects of the crisis, which exerted a fruitful influence on the ideology of the working class, changes ensued which had a direct impact on the way of life of the workers. At that time, the state's more active economic and social policy intervened so directly in settling labour disputes that the role of trade unions was seriously curtailed. The reduction of worktime, the fixing of wages, the general settlement of workers' social insurance, etc. had solved almost all the problems of the social policy of the working class, and whatever these solutions were like, wage disputes and social welfare demands had become impossible from that time on. Thus, the activity of the trade unions came to be confined almost entirely to vocational affairs. The strengthening and increased influence of the extreme right movements within the ranks of the working class was another change with serious implications. As a result of rightist activity the membership of socialist organizations was significantly reduced. In addition, rightist forces launched a vigorous fight against the socialist movement. The third considerable factor was the extremely dynamic development of industry which increased largely the numbers of the working class. And finally, the impact made upon the working class by the movement of rural sociologists, who raised the peasant problem, was not insignificant either.

As the joint effect of these various factors, a more developed class-consciousness arose within the working class and consequently the working class moved from its deadlock. As a final result of this process, the working class which used to be primarily concerned with wages, advanced to become a universal social factor. The theoretical insights of the working class into its own specific problems were replaced by a more comprehensive concept of the whole of society, and its ideology materialized as practical policy. Thus, the working class took the step of fitting into the society of the whole nation and sought to solve the problem of its proletarian way of life through the development of the whole society.

Also the internal structure of the working class changed considerably in the inter-war period. Compared with the old, educated stratum of skilled workers, the mass of unskilled workers who migrated to the capital city increased enormously and this became a factor of both workers' participation in the extreme right movements and later on of the internal ripening of the labour movement. A stratum of intellectuals had been trained and/or attracted by the working class already previously, and this stratum neither increased nor changed in the first half of this period. Thus, in these years, the intellectual elements of the working class still originated from the pre-war generation and also in this respect the change took place only after the Great Depression. At that time, younger intellectuals emerged from the ranks of the working class itself and other intellectuals, too, joined forces with the working class. The characteristic feature of this transformation was that while earlier it was bourgeois intellectuals, mainly of Jewish origin, who were attracted by the working class, after the crisis, in addition to these elements, other members of the intelligentsia, too, found their way to the workers.

Owing to its specific and separate social development as well as its cultural activity and the above-mentioned stratum of intellectuals, the working class represented a specific line in cultural life, being opposed to both conservative national and to modern bourgeois culture. In the second half of the period the activity of its cultural institutions was confined to a narrower scope, yet it never stopped; on the contrary, it became even more intense. Moreover, in addition to the activities of its own institutions, the working class—to a much greater extent than the petite bourgeoisie or the peasantry—was a consumer of the products of the entire Hungarian culture as well.

Naturally the works produced within the social framework of the working class were—just as the whole existence of the working class—primarily shaped by the labour movement. Both in its literature and art as well as in its science the dominant viewpoints were of an ideological character marked by the movement. Nevertheless, the whole intellectual production of the working class cannot be described as a closed and tendentious proletarian culture. The achievements of some of its representatives reached the highest levels of Hungarian intellectual culture. Furthermore even when the quality of this culture was of a lower level, the tendency of the labour movement was not absolutely dominant in these works. On the whole, however, the works which can be termed workers' literature, workers' art and socialist science were mainly of an ideological and labour movement character: they were produced less by creative force than by the interests of the labour movement. However, in that period, the works of quite a few individuals active among workers displayed genuine literary and scientific value and they were also rather important politically.

II

THE HUNGARIAN VILLAGE*

* The Hungarian original is to be found in Ferenc Erdei's *Összegyűjtött Művei* (Collected Works), *Magyar falu* (The Hungarian Village), Akadémiai Kiadó, Budapest, 1974, pp. 130—200. This work was first published in 1940.

VILLAGE FOLK

When we see the infinite variety of the Hungarian villages and consider all the time the problem of diversity, the question should be raised: what is the social structure of the Hungarian village in general, which are its component parts, and which are its constant and characteristic structural elements. If the diversity and the perpetual changes of the village are not lost sight of, then it is not the question "What is the Hungarian village like?" which should be answered, but the problem should be put more plainly and correctly saying: what is the Hungarian village like just now and beyond all the varieties what kind of social group is it in general?

The very importance of the problem is reflected by the ratio of people living in villages as compared to the total population of the country, and to the changes this ratio underwent in comparison to the past.*

According to the census of 1930 the population of all the villages amounted to 5,807,068 and this population defined by public administration as villagers made up 66.8 per cent of the total population of the country.

* The subject of this paper is the Hungarian village of today. The examples enumerated as well as the village phenomena analyzed are all phenomena of the present or of recent years and are related to the whole area populated by Hungarians. The numerical and detailed characterizations, however, are referring to a smaller area and earlier date, i.e. to the post-Trianon territory of the country and to the census of 1930. This inexactitude and/or restriction is the result of a necessity easy to understand. It is only the census of 1930 which demonstrates all the data to be considered of the village population as well as their aggregate correlations and referring to the same period. Thus we were compelled to stop at that date acknowledging this statistical basis. The census after the re-annexation of Upper Northern Hungary has rendered a multitude of highly useful data about the villages of that region, however, these have been relating to a situation of almost a decade later than the census of 1930, and therefore their collation and comparison would have been absolutely mistaken and doomed to failure. The statistical data available on the villages of the mother-country from that time were much more deficient and therefore if we had attempted to collect the data on villages of the present territory of the country relating to the time of the annexation we ought to have restricted our analysis to a highly disparate statistical characteriza-tion. Apart from this, the present territory of the country does not represent the totality of the Hungarian village that is the data on the present territory of the country are not identical either with the data of the sum total of Hungarian villages. Thus, a method was chosen according to which village statistics on a certain part of the country well-known in all details and identical for twenty years were used. Naturally we were fully aware of the fact that we were dealing not with the statistics of all the Hungarian villages and therefore, villages outside both the post-Trianon and the present frontiers were taken into account without, however, numerical descriptions.

97

However, of the 3,372 communities rather a great number, a full 50 could not be regarded socially as villages because either they have been towns in themselves or have organized as a district of a major town. Thus, the actual village population is less numerous. The 50 towns or town districts represent a population of half a million, and if this is subtracted from the sum total we receive 3,322 villages with a total population of 5,300,000. This represents 60.9 per cent of the total population of the country. Thus, the majority of the Hungarian population is village dweller but the ratio of rural population continually diminishes. In 1869 the percentage of villagers had been 76.2 per cent, whereas the census of 1940 will certainly show the ratio of village population much below 60 per cent. By 1940 therefore just a little more than half of the population of the country will live in villages. Yet, this still represents the majority of the population and therefore the problem of village society will be at least of as great importance as those of urban population.

Before examining the population composition and grouping of rural society it would seem of interest to sum up and compare the various social types of Hungarian villages and also the significance of these types as compared to the other ones. The factual figures of the survey do not mark off the unincorporated villages since their exact registering would require special surveys. Therefore it should be taken into consideration that about 20 per cent of the rural population is living in unincorporated villages or in village peripheries. The peripherical districts of villages are partly farmsteads and partly unincorporated villages pertaining socially to the villages, and partly independent villages of an identical character with the parent-village or of an entirely different character.

Type of the village	Number of villages	Population	Ratio of the total population
Regular peasant village	1,225	2,750,000	31.6
Small peasant village	1,705	950,000	10.9
Village with farmsteads	280	1,100,000	12.7
Huge village	11	150,000	1.7
Industrial village	30	100,000	1.1
Mining village	43	135,000	1.5
Resort village	6	30,000	0.3
Residential village	22	100,000	1.1
Total	3,322	5,315,000	60.9 per cent

Calculating on the basis of a 20 per cent peripherical ratio, 1,067,000 people of the total rural population are living in peripherical regions. From this, however, there should be deducted the inhabitants of the farmstead communities (about 30 per cent) because these farmstead people are an integral part of the society of their villages, making up a population of 330,000. The remaining population of the peripherical areas actually do modify the ratio of the various types of villages. The number and the population of such kind of villages are increased mainly by the socially independent, rather numerous and densely populated industrial, mining and resort settlements to be found in peripherical areas, whereas the number and the population of the peasant villages are decreased by them. Moreover, a new type of village was inserted: that of the about 2,000 manorial villages with a population of 300,000, by which the number of the peasant villages has not been decreased proportionally, only their population has been rated less.*

The percentage of rural population as related to that of urban dwellers does not reflect the internal structure of rural society; the only value of it is that it indicates the weight of the social problems of villages as opposed to those of towns. Percentages of the rural society become characteristic when they show the stratification of the rural population as opposed to that of the cities. In this respect the statistical frequencies of the rural population are suitable to throw a light on the specific population grouping of the rural society and actually on the social structure of the village.

The age and generation relations are important aspects of the stratification of any society. The age groups of the old and young people are not necessarily active social groups. Most frequently the age groups mean simply a stratification traceable simply by way of similarity and demonstrate—without creating any special social relationships—the fact only whether the social group in question is old or young, i.e. whether taken as a whole it is growing or declining. The generation relationships are, however, quite different. In settled and consolidated societies there are no generation problems. The age-groups are constant, all the members of society pass through all age-groups without becoming the members of any grouping

* Taking into account the breakdown of the various village types by complementing it with the above modifications, we get a roughly true picture of the rich variety of Hungarian villages. However, when taking the sum total of all our villages we speak about the population, social organization of the Hungarian villages, and about their numerically definable differences as compared to urban settlements, it is not these modified data which are taken into consideration since such an elaboration and tabulation are not available. Therefore, we work with the summarized total figures of all the villages, and these data have been processed and published by the census statistics. Ratios are obviously somewhat distorted by this involuntary inexactitude but not to a degree that they could become meaningless or actually incorrect. The only difference is that while the population of the real villages comes to but 5,315,000, that of the villages on the basis of public administration data as published in the statistics is 5,807,068. In terms of percentages this means that the population of the genuine villages makes up but 60.9 per cent of the total population of the country, but all villages contain 66.8 per cent of the population of Hungary. This difference means that the characteristic ratios of the villages are diminished if we deduct the figures of communities regarded de facto as urban, i.e. anything that can be stated on the strength of non corrected data means an overestimation of rural population.

having a specific social role. However, in changing or particularly in rapidly changing societies the age-groups tend to become active, groups which oppose each other, i.e. generations, and here in the wake of generation relations peculiar social relationships appear. This is the case in Hungarian rural society, the generational relations thus meaning characteristic social groupings as well.

In contrast to the cities, the age distribution of the rural population shows the preponderance of the youngest and oldest age-groups. While the age-group below 12 years of the Hungarian villages makes up 27.2 per cent of the total rural population, this ratio is 18.9 per cent in cities. This is a marked difference finding its explanation in the fact that the population growth of villages by far surpasses that of cities. This was the situation at the time of the 1930 census. As compared to previous censuses the difference shows a definitely decreasing tendency and therefore this trend demonstrates that the high rate of fertility of the villages has begun to slow down and has even come to a standstill. In all probability a further highly significant decrease of difference will be demonstrated by the census of 1940 stressing emphatically the alarming decline in the fertility of the villages. On the other hand, the present ratio illustrates the average of all villages. However, highly differing phenomena are behind such averages. The difference in the averages are explained by the great number of villages where the natural population increase is extremely high and thus the age-group of the young people considerably exceeds the average. At the same time, there are also many Hungarian villages where the age distribution is either similar to that of the cities or the number of youth is even lagging behind that of the towns. Villages characterized by the system of having only one child in the family belong to this type. In villages where the drop in the birth rate is extraordinarily high, moreover where a natural population decline takes place an abundant demographic survey material is available. All these data prove that instead of the normal, broadly based Christmas-tree-like age pyramid the graph of such villages has become a narrow, shapeless spot, moreover in villages which have been for a long time one-child villages it has taken a mushroom-like shape which clearly indicates that rural life is in a deep crisis in these villages. There is a marked trend towards the considerable increase in the number of decaying villages because of the declining birth rate.

An age-group is not yet a generation in the social sense of the term, or if it is called a generation this only means that according to the difference in age it represents a different view of life and activity but not as an explicitly acting group opposed to all others. And even this role of it has manifested itself but in a restricted way in rural society. In rural societies the leading role of the elderly has been absolute and well-founded and thus the youth could live only under their guidance.

An age-group becomes a real generation only if it had been exposed to an historical experience as a result of which its whole view of life changed in a way

100

that it came into conflict with other generations attempting to transform the life of society even in the face of their opposition. The Hungarian village has undergone such an historical experience, as a matter of fact a whole series of them. One had been the emancipation of the serfs, the second the pre-war "happy, peaceful world", the third the time of World War I and the crises following it. These three events or rather periods left their imprint on this generation which had been at the beginning and/or on the zenith of its life, and therefore it had immediately to face the preceding generation.

The generation whose early youth fell on the period of serfdom and/or the abolition of it or shortly after that event still represented unambiguously the village peasant of the feudal era, or if they were not peasants the feudal peasant mentality. The generation following in their wake already saw possibilities going beyond the restrictions of peasant life, thus finding itself opposed to the older generation still bound to the attitudes of serfdom. Until the world war these two generations waged a silent struggle: the old ones wanted to live as if they were still serf-peasants, whereas the younger ones wished to make the best of the new opportunities. The impact of the war and the post-war period was even greater and more decisive. The generation which has lived through the war and the post-war years of crisis inherited the great experience of the war, the knowledge of foreign countries as well as the perception of the inherent contradictions of a social order, and first and foremost the shocks of a revolution and a counter-revolution. These impacts were too much for this generation which was therefore unable to adapt itself meekly to the rural world. Its horizon widened and as a result of the dissatisfaction with its fate, its peasant loyalty was shaken. It became touchy and sensitive because of its position of outcasts and the backwardness. Therefore it came into conflict not only with the acquiescent generation of its grandfathers still remembering serfdom, but also with the generation of its fathers rising quietly without major shocks. The members of this generation had become opposed to anything old and traditional. Today they either make life in the villages troubled and unrestful or recoiling from the impenetrable resistance of the village they leave the villages or, if they are individually bound with too many threads to the village and village life, they send their children off, far away from the village or even prevent their birth.

This fight between the generations is waged in all villages, the front lines, however, are highly different. Yet, there is a common feature: the fight has been decided everywhere, and though there are still minor skirmishes the result would not change. In the majority of the villages it was the young ones and the strivings represented by them which gained the upperhand, i.e. the transformation of the village and the nervous hurry to get away as far as possible from its loathed past. However, there is a great number of villages where the older generations came out on top, and the young ones yielded to their laws hopefully that after the dying out of the elder generation they will carry on the inherited traditions. There are but a few places where the representatives of fruitful and creative peasant traditions have been victorious. In most places the victory of the old has not guaranteed the survival of this kind of past but has meant the final domination of reversed peasant laws. This happened in all the one-child villages where there is very little hope that the next generation living under the pampering tyranny of the elder ones would ever be able to achieve a turn in the life of the village. The literature of rural research mentions but a single case where the young generation has reversed the fate of a decaying village and has found new opportunities of development: *Vereb* community in the county of *Fejér*. Ferenc Földes, the very optimistic sociographer could not make it absolutely convincing whether this change would be final.

The unqualified and obligatory unit of the rural society is the family. And this is true not only for the peasantry but for anyone living in a village. One can simply not live in a village outside the family pattern. This is made necessary among others by economic and socio-organizational reasons to such a degree that there is hardly anybody living in villages who is not a member of some sort of family unit. This situation is tangibly characterized by data relating to family status. While the ratio of singles is 49.4 per cent in villages, it is 49.2 in towns. However, this 0.2 per cent difference does not characterize the actual difference because at the same time 39.9 per cent of the village population is under the age of twenty, whereas in towns this age-group amounts only to 31.8 per cent. This means that the number of the age-group of those immature for marriage in the village society exceeds that in towns by 8 per cent, yet the ratio of married couples does not lag behind that of couples in towns; it actually somewhat surpasses it.

The family is not only the obligatory unit of the village but also divorce is more difficult in villages than in towns. The percentage of divorced people is 1.2 per cent in towns and 0.4 per cent in villages. This difference is explained mainly by three factors. First, by the social laws of the peasantry: it is not for personal reasons that marriages are contracted between peasants and neither can it be dissolved for such reasons. Couples are interconnected once and for all by the farm and the children whatever the personal differences. And the peasantry which sustains these traditions still makes up a majority of rural population. The second factor is agriculture. In the case of agrarian populations, be they still peasants or not, both marriage and family constitute an economic unit and therefore they break up less easily for personal reasons than in the case of town-dwellers who are not connected by such ties. It is only the third factor which is a reason rooted specifically in village life. Even couples who otherwise have serious marital conflict are kept together by the close and direct relations of rural society, as well as by the pressure of strong control. In villages divorce is always regarded as a scandal partly because it is an unusual step contrary to all traditions, and partly because the conjugal state is accepted as an obligatory norm of rural society. This applies not only to peasants but to all other strata of rural population as well. Single new-comers, both male and female, are nowhere more liable to such concentrated offers of marriage than in rural societies, this being equally true for peasants and intellectuals in the countryside.

The ethnic relations of Hungarian villages are interesting not only because we have a number of ethnic villages where, despite a lot of similarities, the style of social life is entirely different from that of Hungarian villages, but also because we have multi-ethnic villages as well where the different nationalities constitute strictly marked off groups which in quite a few communities are bitterly opposed.

At any rate, the majority of our villages have purely Hungarian populations but in a number of villages—even if only the present territory of the country is considered—some other nationality constitutes the over-whelming majority. We have 100 fully or predominantly German villages, 16 Slovakian, 1 Serbian, 8 Catholic Serbian, 4 Romanian and 28 Croatian villages. Thus, there are remarkably few purely Slovakian villages, whereas the great number of Croatian villages is quite conspicuous. This may be explained by the fact that a great part of Slovakians in Hungary live in market-towns and even those dwelling in villages are mostly to be found in the big villages of the Great Plain as a rule in mixed communities with Hungarians. The great number of Croatian villages is explained by the fact that all these communities are tiny hamlets in Transdanubia mostly with a population not exceeding thousand inhabitants. The number of such villages inhabited purely or overwhelmingly by a single nationality comes to 354, but there are more of them where different nationalities live together with or even without Hungarians. The most characteristic variants are the following: Hungarian-German as well as Hungarian-Croatian villages in Transdanubia, Hungarian-German-Catholic-Serbian villages in the Bácska region and some on the island of Csepel, Hungarian-Slovakian villages on the Great Plain and in Upper Northern Hungary, Hungarian-German-Slovakian and Hungarian-German-Serbian villages in the vicinity of the capital, and finally, Hungarian-Serbian-Romanian villages in the area of the Tisza and Maros rivers and some Hungarian-German-Romanian villages in the eastern border region.

In single-nationality villages no internal nationality problems exist, but such problems are still acute in inter-village relations. As a matter of fact, there is but one real problem: that of the German villages. According to the unanimous conclusion reached by rural researchers and rural sociologists, German villages are everywhere developing and thriving. The most characteristic case is that of the inhabitants of Harta and Dunapataj. If there are any lands for sale in Dunapataj—and this is an increasingly frequent

103

case—this is made publicly known not in Pataj but in Harta since it is quite certain that such land will not be bought by Hungarians of Pataj but by Germans of Harta. This reverse development trend and disproportionate relationship is primarily explained by ethnic differences. However, this is certainly not the only reason, and the thesis according to which the Hungarian villages are decaying while the German ones are thriving is certainly mistaken. There are characteristic social and historical differences as well. German villages are without exception settlements endowed with privileges: the foreign settlers had started on their life in Hungary with the zeal of colonialists and mostly in the beginning had been granted all kinds of prerogatives to further the success of their activities. At the same time, all the decaying Hungarian villages have been ancient settlements, the majority of them overburdened serf-villages; no wonder if they are rather tired and show little energy and vitality today. In addition, German villages are located mostly near some water, in the vicinity of a town, whereas the ancient Hungarian settlements are as a rule isolated to this very date. All these social reasons, however, do not invalidate entirely the ethnic differences but nevertheless point out clearly one moment: the decaying Hungarian villages are settlements weary of their hopeless situation and their unpropitious past while the German villages are of more recent origins, colonist settlements with a privileged past.

Wherever different nationalities live together within the same rural society, the society of the village disintegrates almost into as many villages as the number of nationalities, and these grapple with each other within the bounds of a greater village. More recent rural sociologies have come to the almost unanimous conclusion that the Germans proved to be the strongest in such internal struggles. Partly because it was the Germans who have retained to the highest degree everywhere their homogeneity and isolation, and partly because it was they who made the greatest headway in production, wealth and village-leadership alike. The Hungarians as well as the southern Slavs (Serbians and Catholic Serbians) have fallen behind in the contest and were compelled to leave the ground everywhere to the Germans who have recently become extraordinarily vigorous. In Hungarian-Slovakian villages the ethnic groups opposed to each other have by and large equal chances: whereas the Slovakians have the benefit of higher fertility, and this is balanced by the Hungarians' greater readiness for work, their more energetic attitudes as well as the help of being able to use the official language of the state.

Rural societies have yet another peculiar and noteworthy ethnic aspect which is discussed much more seldom than the other problems of ethnicity. And this is the ratio of the various nationalities in villages and towns. In this respect the ratio of Hungarians is of fundamental importance being 88.2 per cent in villages and 92.3 per cent in towns. This ratio does not mean at all that in Hungary towns are mainly inhabited by Hungarians, whereas the nationalities were driven out to the villages which are less advantageous areas. On the contrary, this means just the opposite in all respects. It does not mean that the Germans are unable to penetrate the towns, it reflects only that there they have become Hungarians, thus adding to the number of urban Hungarians—a population which has become rather diluted—who identify themselves with the countryside and especially with the Hungarian villages only to a very small extent. No data are available to characterize this ratio, it is only on the basis of foreign names in both the economic life and public administration of our towns that we can form an idea of the dimensions of the nationalities' influx to the towns. And we have to make another modification which can be expressed in actual numbers, too. The ratio of urban population of Jewish religion was 13 per cent in 1930, and they naturally declared themselves Hungarians. Since then, however, Hungarian legislation, though not declaring the Jews an ethnic group, has at any rate distinguished them beyond their religion. Irrespective of legislation, it has to be pointed out that Hungarians of Jewish religion, though not being an alien element, are by no means identical with Hungarians whose ancestors had been born in the country. Or at least they are not identical to an extent that the difference between Jews and Hungarians should be dismissed as negligible. If the Jewish population is deducted from the total population of the towns then the ratio of urban Hungarians drops from 92.3 per cent to 79.3 per cent, i.e. being of a lower percentage than its share in the rural population because there—even if the percentage of Jews were deducted from the ratio of Hungarians—the ratio of the Hungarian population remains 85.8 per cent. If the losing of ground within the rural population of Hungarians as against Germans and those of German origins could be expressed in numbers, the ratio by which Hungarians have lost ground in Hungarian towns would come very close to 20 per cent. This figure reflects an enormous disproportion, and considering the fact that this is by all means the lowest percentage which can be mentioned in this respect, we must see in this phenomenon an appalling upset of the social equilibrium. Considering the disproportionate role towns and villages play in all fields of social leadership, this ratio might be regarded as a specific anti-Hungarian factor of the urban-rural conflict.

VILLAGE ECONOMY

Economic stratification is the key factor in the social organization of both village and town, and in the relation of villages to towns the economic subordination of the former ones is the decisive factor of the disadvantageous position of the village. Not only is the town the settlement of the industrial and intellectual population, whereas the village of the agricultural one (and agriculture is the loser as opposed to all other productive sectors), but the village is weaker and less powerful than the town as regards it entire economic pattern, and first and foremost the village lags far behind the town as regards the class stratification based on production relations.

105

The different ratios of the individual occupational groups in rural and urban societies in themselves do not explain much (Table 1). There are considerable differences but from this it does not necessarily follow that there should be similarly great class differences even if significant social differences originate from this very fact.

TABLE 1

Occupational distribution (per cent)
by place of residence

	Rural	Urban
Primary production	67.7	19.7
Industry, transport and communication, mining	23.0	51.0
Public administration and liberal professions	2.8	9.5
Capitalists, pensioners	1.5	4.5
Domestic help, servants	1.4	3.8

Conspicuous features are the rather high percentage of the urban population engaged in primary production and the ratio of industrial occupations in the villages. The explanation for the first is the relatively great number of the market towns, a specific Hungarian type of town, whereas for the latter the fact that not all of our villages are engaged in primary production. Thus, the ratios of these two lines of occupation reveal but little of the difference between towns and villages and of the nature of this difference. The only conclusion to be drawn from these figures is that while rural populations are engaged mostly in primary production, town-dwellers are employed first and foremost in industry as well as in transport and communication. The considerable difference reflected by the statistics in the ratios of public servants and the representatives of the liberal professions shows a more significant fact which is of vital importance in the development of the economic role of the village. These data show that the village is but a marginal area of society engaged only in part-functions of the social life as a whole, whereas central guidance and control are the privilege of cities. This is manifested by the occupational distribution of the population: the population holding significantly higher occupational positions in the villages is but a third of that ratio in towns. Further, the percentage of capitalists and pensioners is also much higher in the urban society than in the countryside and this indicates that all those who are not gainfully employed go to live in towns rather than in villages for the simple reason that the town offers full comforts while the village offers none. The similar ratio of domestic servants reveals the fact that there are three times as many people in towns than in villages who can afford to keep domestic servants.

The distribution between villages and towns of those occupied in different branches of production casts light on another aspect of the relation between town and village (Table 2).

TABLE 2

The distribution of rural and urban population by various occupations
(per cent)

	Rural	Urban
Primary production	87.3	12.7
Industry, transport and communication, mining	47.6	52.4
Public administration and liberal professions	36.8	63.2
Capitalists, pensioners	41.4	48.6
Domestic help, servants	40.6	59.4
Total	60.9	39.1

In this respect the distribution of those engaged in primary production and those employed in industry and transport is also characteristic. Despite the great number of market-towns, the overwhelming majority of primary producers are living in villages, whereas but a minority of the industrial population lives in the countryside. Naturally if the number of settlements of urban character were deducted from the sum total of the communities the ratio of primary producers in villages would decrease but slightly while that of the industrial population and those engaged in transport and communication would drop considerably. The overlapping would still exist though to a lesser extent, proving that towns could not be described as being inhabited by industrial population and villages as being inhabited only by primary producers.

Similarly, in villages the smaller economic units are concentrated, while the bigger ones are in towns. This, however, is not a decisive criterion of the economic pattern of the village, although such differences are quite extensive. The ratio of owner-producers is 33.5 per cent in villages while a mere 25.6 per cent in towns. However, if the various types of villages were separately reviewed we would find significant differences. It would turn out that the number of owner-producers is actually very high in peasant villages indicating that such villages are made up of small farms and enterprises, whereas in industrial, mining and manorial villages the ratio of owner-producers would drop even below that of the towns because in these villages the majority of bread-winners are employees.

The major industrial, commercial and credit companies do not settle in villages, whereas the majority of mines are to be found in rural districts. Figures from 1930 indicate that there are 1,560 mining enterprises in the country and 1,314 of them are in villages and only 241 in towns. At the same time, of 2,383 big commercial and credit companies 2,363 have their seats in towns and only 14 in villages. The situation is almost identical in the case of industrial enterprises: there are 1,554 of them altogether and 242 of them are operating in villages, whereas 1,312 in towns.

107

The distribution according to size of agricultural enterprises does not reveal anything characteristic as regards the economic organization of town and village as the greatest part of the farms are outside the villages themselves and therefore the farms of the villages are by and large of the same sort as the economy of the country as a whole: small holdings make up the majority both as regards the number of farms (in this respect the majority is overwhelming) and the area covered by them (in this respect the difference is rather small). The ratio, however, is shifting from village to village. In villages where there are manorial villages in the surroundings the small farms in many places are of a smaller area than that of the big estates which, of course, presents an obstacle to the development of the peasant village at such places.

All things considered, the economic pattern of the village reflects the predominance of the smaller economic units. In this respect it is most characteristic that the overwhelming majority of all small farms is to be found in the villages, moreover, even of the industrial enterprises working without any or only with one journeyman the majority (106,000 to 73,000) is operating in villages. These structural differences do not require it, but under the impact of the corresponding, characteristically Hungarian stratification system the village is not simply a settlement consisting of smaller economic units but it is also the home of people who are more insecure and actually weaker in terms of economic power. In this respect the difference is even greater than reflected in the ratio of sizes of the economic units. It is just this point where the subordinate and disadvantageous position of the village is most conspicuous.

Comparing the number of all the people living securely (in the material sense of the term) in towns and villages—irrespective of the fact whether they have achieved a middle-class or a petite bourgeois standard of living—the overwhelming superiority of the city becomes absolutely clear.

The sum total of all farmers with holdings exceeding ten acres as well as their working members of the family and dependants, all agricultural white-collar workers and their dependants, all the self-supporting elements and white-collar workers in industry, commerce and banking as well as their dependants, all the intellectuals, further on the capitalists and pensioners and the dependants come to 1,419,000 persons in the villages, while in the towns they add up to 1,211,888. This represents 24.5 per cent of the total population of the villages and 42.1 per cent of that of the towns. The extremely great difference means that 75.5 per cent of village inhabitants is made up of some kind of proletarian-like elements whereas in towns this percentage is but 57.9 per cent. If the law of population-flow between the various levels of living standard and wages is valid, then the influx directed towards cities is also rooted in such differences. Quite obviously no policy aiming at the saving of villages could be able to counterbalance the temptation of such a difference. And considering the fact that the conditions

108

of villagers are worse than those of town-dwellers even under similar circumstances, the difference in economic levels is so stupendous between Hungarian villages and towns that not only a rather slow migration to towns but a veritable influx ought to be regarded as justified.

The distribution of middle-class and petit bourgeois elements between village and town is almost of an equal ratio: 1,419,000 persons in towns and 1,211,888 in villages, whereas the number of proletarian and semi-proletarian population is nearly three times higher in villages than in towns: 4,387,068 persons in villages and 1,669,363 in towns! Expressed in percentages, 24.5 per cent of the total rural population is middle-class and petit bourgeois, and 75.5 per cent proletarian and semi-proletarian, whereas in towns the ratio is 42.1 per cent and 57.9 per cent, respectively. Thus, the citing of three million beggars in villages is not a fiction but a reality which has to be emphasized when we want to understand population migration to towns and the crisis of village life.

Naturally, the individual villages do not reflect this average distribution. Some are in a better others in an even worse situation. In the notorious villages inhabited by jobbers and navvies the ratio is even more disadvantageous: the percentage of farmers and other strata of secure livelihood is but a tiny island in the sea of landless and unemployed poor peasants. Such proletarianized villages are to be particularly found on the northern fringe and in the northeastern corner of the Great Plain, while the situation tends to be better in Transdanubia; there the ratio of farmers is more advantageous than in the East even where there are huge latifundia but at the same time, it is there that the greatest number of manorial villages, where the percentage of the poor peasants is higher than in any other type of villages, can be found. There is but one difference: while they are of working-age the livelihood of the farmhands on the large estates is guaranteed, though on a starvation level, and thus, as long as they are working on the big estates they do not add to the number of paupers in the peasant villages.

Such is the economic pattern of the Hungarian village. The general social structure, based on such economic foundations could be capable of alleviating the lot of the poor; however, the social structure of rural society in itself cannot do the same. In fact, under the generally adverse conditions of rural life and the pressures of an extremely slow social mobility, the village renders life almost or entirely unbearable for the majority of its inhabitants.

VILLAGE SOCIETY

As a rule, village society is a very simple social organization. It is by and large a homogeneous group supplemented by a small number of people of different social status; mutual social contacts within that group are also

109

rather simple. This is the case in villages which live in the atmosphere of a settled social system and the organization of their society is traditionally crystallized. Even villages of the feudal and the bourgeois order do not differ substantially in terms of the simplicity of their social stratification.

In villages of a feudal nature the great mass of society are serf-like peasants. A rather small stratum of middlemen is followed by the top of the hierarchy made up of a single or a few landlord families. In feudal manorial villages the peasantry is divided into two groups: peasant landowners and landless cotters, whereas in the so-called curial villages even this distinction is missing since there we find only serfs bound to the soil as farm-hands.

In the totally transformed bourgeois villages social stratification is also very simple. At the bottom of the social hierarchy we find the workers (and there is no substantial difference between agricultural and industrial workers), then there follows a less populous stratum of petite bourgeoisie made up of both farmers and the representatives of other occupations. Finally, on top of the social ladder we find a small bourgeois stratum of the richest land-owning farmers, intellectuals and respected tradesmen and merchants. This social stratification is very similar to that of the towns. Indeed, it is somewhat simpler since it is absolutely clear-cut, everybody exactly knowing his place in the social hierarchy.

In the present-day Hungarian village, however, the situation is different. Since bourgeois transformation has not taken place yet, feudal and the bourgeois stratifications continue to exist side by side. The farmer is by no means simply a petit bourgeois and neither is the richer farmer simply a bourgeois. However, there are genuine middle-class elements in the village, moreover also the peasantry itself has assumed somewhat a middle-class character. Thus, village society is structured by two kinds of social orders simultaneously. As a result, social stratification in the Hungarian village has become rather complicated. Feudal stratification is fundamental though it is modified by bourgeois class stratification and as a result rural society is structured by both systems of stratifications. In addition to these two aspects of stratification the rich variety of our village types should also be considered leading us to the conclusion that rural stratification in Hungary is far from being simple. Some of our villages are still entirely stratified in terms of a feudal structure, others have already been transformed alongside bourgeois stratification and between these two extremes we may find an infinite variety of village types. Despite the variety and complexity of Hungarian rural society, there still exists a characteristic rural social order.

The broad fundamental stratum of rural society is made up of the *village paupers*. This lowest stratum of the villages comprises the peasant cotters, farm hands of proletarian nature as well as workers and labourers not working in agriculture but in a number of other fields. Though there are certain differences, their identical economic conditions bring about a unity among these groups: all of them are proletarians owning a small house and

110

a tiny strip of land at the most, but the majority do not own even such a dwarf holding, their only possession being just a cottage. Their social position is also equal: all of these groups are at the bottom of rural society. Peasant cotters are still in the same position as in the time of feudalism: they are workers and proletarians but they have developed peasant attitudes. The majority of farm hands, however, though occupying the same social position, have already got rid of peasant traditions; they have become simply farm hands which has the same meaning in villages as the term "proletarians" in towns. The non-farm hand or not primarily farm hand proletarians also differ from peasant workers in so far as they have become estranged from the peasantry also owing to the character of their activity. As a result the ties binding them to the village are much weaker than those of other village paupers. In different types of villages, the composition of this basic rural stratum is also different: in more intact peasant villages the majority of the population is made up of peasant cotters, whereas in villages (irrespective whether these are agricultural or industrial communities) which have assumed a more or less middle-class character, the majority of inhabitants consists of proletarian-like farm hand and industrial workers.

Above this lower stratum which for all its diversity is uniformly proletarian and plebeian there is the peasant elite of the village—the group of the *well-to-do farmers*. In peasant villages this group is by all means of a class character, however, it does not belong to the middle-class but to the upper stratum of the peasantry. The members of this stratum are peasants exactly like the landless peasants or dwarf holders also working for other farmers. Therefore they regard the same social restrictions and regulations of attitudes as compulsory for themselves just as the members of the above-mentioned strata of peasants, nevertheless they are privileged as compared to those ones because of their own farms. Their relationship is very much like that of the bourgeois with the proletarian. Well-to-do farmers enjoy the more advantageous aspects of peasant existence. In contrast to the gentry and bourgeois elements of the village, these well-to-do farmers constitute a stratum of the peasantry. This means that they are members of a lower estate bound by traditions and external as well as internal conventions. As a consequence, together with the landless peasants, the social status of this stratum is lower than that of the non-peasant strata of the village. According to middle-class standards, well-to-do farmers are on the same level as the artisan petit bourgeois, yet they are considered inferior because they belong to the peasantry. Moreover, even industrial skilled workers regard this stratum as inferior because workers, while being proletarians, are nevertheless defined in terms of the bourgeois world. The well-to-do farmers are everywhere assigned to this social status provided they have remained peasants in an intact form or without radical changes.

The middle-class elite of the rural society is the genuine *petite bourgeoisie*, the group which, owing to its holdings, enterprises or positions rises without

111

any peasant-like restriction above the village paupers. Members of this stratum are the village artisans, merchants and lower-level officials. As a class, these elements are definitely superior to all kinds of proletarian elements, whereas as a genuine middle-class stratum they regard themselves as superior to the well-to-do peasantry. As long as well-to-do farmers are peasants in the genuine sense of the word, the social status of the petit bourgeois is actually higher. However, the stratum of well-to-do peasants is a major, independent and influential factor of rural society, whereas the non-peasant petite bourgeoisie is generally a tiny group as regards its numbers, and therefore its role in the rural society is much less significant than that of well-to-do peasants.

The *rural middle class* is the truly gentlemanly elite of the rural society. Because of its upper-class consciousness and pretensions, it is superior to the peasantry being its very opposite in terms of social stratification. Yet this stratum is also superior to all types of the rural middle class since gentlemanly mentality enjoys a higher social status than being a member of the rural middle-class. This stratum is an upper-class elite the more so since in terms of bourgeois stratification it is not above the level of the village; as a consequence of its restrictions, its social situation is not more advantageous than that of the land-owning peasants or the independent artisans and merchants. In addition to that, all this also follows from the rather feudal social system of the village. Hungarian society, as a whole, has been unable to develop purely bourgeois social forms and the village was even less in the position to do so. He who is on top of the rural stratification system is not a bourgeois, he can be solely an upper-middle-class gentleman. In Hungarian society one may enjoy a really high social status only when one joins the stratum of gentlemen; this is true in general, but it is especially true of rural society.

Above all these middle-strata rising above the lower stratum of village paupers, at the top of the social stratification we may find the *village squire*. The most characteristic representative of this stratum is the village landlord regarded even by the rural middle class as the true gentleman and therefore the members of the middle class wish to adapt themselves to him thus substantiating their claim of their own gentleman status. If, however, there are no such landlords in the village, then it is the chief district administrator who personifies the squire stratum, and he, similarly to the landlord is an absolutely dominating element not only as compared to the village as a whole but also to the village middle class.

Such is the social stratification of village society. The social consciousness of the individual strata is an exact reflection of stratification, though it must be added that the nature of their specific social standing is to a much greater extent reflected by their consciousness than by their place in the social hierarchy.

112

The social consciousness of village paupers is a peculiar mixture of peasant subordination, proletarian class consciousness and the loyal submissiveness so characteristic of poor people; all these are blended into a uniform social attitude in rural societies. This attitude contains certain elements of the peasant outlook according to which there do exist subordinate and privileged people and this subordination has to be accepted. It also contains a certain component of proletarian class consciousness according to which it cannot be an unchangeable law of social life that the minority should subjugate the broad masses; as a result the awareness gradually grows that this order has to change sooner or later. However, we may also discover the submissiveness, so much characteristic of the poor, reflecting the view that the lower strata can expect the improvement of their plight only from the upper strata and thus, such a help has to be deserved by displaying loyalty to those above. All these attitudes can be identified in the consciousness of the village poor. However, among peasant cotters' attitudes resignation is the strongest; among industrial proletarians that of militant class-consciousness, and among the down-trodden poor that of loyal submissiveness. And finally, in the case of farm hands on big estates rebellious resistance is so much rejected that their social consciousness becomes debased and assumes forms of submissiveness and loyalty, that is characteristic only of servants.

The social consciousness of village paupers shows a great diversity also in terms of its forms of manifestations. In all of them there is at least a trace of militant resistance. Since there is no possibility for open rebellion and not even for conscious opposition, rebellion and resistance can manifest themselves only by taking on distorted and muted forms most often one or another form of escapism. The following are the manifestations of such silent rebellion and escapism: the increasing fall in birthrates even among village paupers, emigration, migration to the cities, religious sectarianism and a feeling of constant expectation anticipating that something is bound to happen.

At the same time the majority of poor people in villages have a feeling of certainty that their only chance would be if the privileged and dominant ones would change their attitudes and helped the village paupers. Thus, they patiently and submissively wait for help from above. Though they do not expect much, they are still in need of help because of their plight. With a meek bow and hoping for the next general elections, the village poor look forward to the improvement of their lot.

Peasant farmers are less socially outcast even as regards their consciousness. Being peasants themselves, they are inclined, by force of ancient laws, to accept and endure their lot loyally. At the bottom of this view there is the belief that they have to be peasants, and peasants cannot live in another way since somebody has to do the work. Nevertheless, they are getting restless because they are still peasants and their lot has not been eased for centuries although they know there could be other ways of life as well. Some of them demand another kind of peasant lot from society, i.e. they demand more or less vociferously various forms of easing their conditions, and some of them do not want to remain peasants at all manifesting this demand of theirs by means of various forms of the silent revolution. However, being land-owning farmers, their consciousness has more solid foundations and they are more patient. Peasant lot is also easier to endure for land-owning farmers and for them peasant burdens are also not so heavy. Moreover, owing to their farms, they feel some kind of middle-class solidarity with the upper classes and their absolute discontent is checked this way.

All of their manifestations are characterized by this ambiguity. There are no villages where well-to-do farmers would not resent the subordination of peasants. Some demand economic aid, tax reduction and more respect, others have already turned in mind against their conditions as peasants and entered the way of the liberating silent revolution. They do not want to have children and, if, despite of this, children are born, they do not want to raise them as peasants. If not only the future seems uncertain or intolerably burdensome but their individual life, too, they try to migrate to the city in order to substitute the uncertainty and rigours of peasant life for the pensioners' security and petit bourgeois way of life. However, the land they hold as farmers ties them to the more privileged elements of the village and the solidarity felt with them renders them defensive against all kinds of "subversive efforts". In vain do they feel that they have reasons enough to revolt, when the claim according to which all types of subversive activity are directed against their holdings does not fail to impress them and makes them inclined to take a stand against any radical change.

The consciousness of the rural petite bourgeoisie is of a middle-class nature. The fact that they have already got rid of the peasant restrictions supports their feeling of superiority and therefore strengthens their defensive and submissive attitudes. At the same time, their middle-class status is quite devalued and all things considered they have a hard life. This makes them restless and moderately peremptory. The situation of this group is by no means unbearable since it has certain possibilities to rise socially. The rural petite bourgeoisie makes every effort to achieve a more advantageous position in the social hierarchy.

Both the members of the rural middle class and the village landlords regard themselves as squires, the only difference between them being that the landlord is a squire in the genuine sense of the term and by right of birth, whereas the middle-class official achieves this status only by virtue of his office. There is, however, a common element in their consciousness: they both consider themselves to be integral parts of a social status and power above the village and, while this guarantees their superiority over the village, it also hinders the development of a feeling of total affinity or solidarity with the village. They are standing above the village and even if they spend all their life in the village they regard themselves to be far superior to all the other residents of the village.

The manifestations of such a situation and consciousness necessarily result in the claim for absolute leadership on the one hand and a striving to defend themselves and prevent any substantial changes on the other. The claim to leadership is fully enforced. The members of this stratum not only actually give effective guidance in the fields of all offices and jobs they occupy but they are the dominating elements in all the spheres of social life in the villages. At the same time, their defensive efforts manifest themselves in the fact that—though they may have certain grievances and are moderately dissatisfied—they hold on to their prevailing position and in the last analysis find this situation even proper and just. Thus, either in the name of social order or referring to the unity, peace and development of the village, they react to and resist most vehemently any demand for change, including even the most modest ones which somehow would influence their position.

Political and/or party organizational activity is not a constant element of the social order of villages. The village in itself is living as a specific social unit which cannot be split permanently by party differences and therefore no active party life can develop. Certain party movements may either gain complete control over the whole village or they can influence the village only for a short time since it would be impossible to develop a permanent party life under the strict social constraints of the village. Even as regards direct community-level policy-making like municipal politics, where everybody knows all the participants and strivings, the parties can fight each other only for a short time. The victory of one party over the other instantly liquidates the defeated party because between the narrow bounds of the village a lasting and irreconcilable enmity cannot be accepted. As a rare exception, if some leaders harbour implacable hatred against each other or they have an unappeasable want for reforms, a party may be able to survive under any circumstances. However, without such special conditions enmities are sooner or later eroded by the monotonous social life of the village.

The case is entirely different as regards the denominational structuring of the village. Because of the very traditions and also as a result of the role of denominational differences, rural society is significantly structured this way. Where the whole village is of one religion society naturally is not differentiated according to denominations. In such cases, however, the given village characteristically differs from villages belonging to other denominations. Visiting villages in the course of our sociographical trips we often tried to guess the religion of a certain village without collecting any preliminary information, judging only on the basis of the outward appearance of the village, its houses, the behaviour or its inhabitants. We were never wrong. Denominational affiliation reflects highly significant social differences even

115

between villages inhabited purely by Hungarians, whereas in villages inhabited by nationalities denominations typically coinciding with the nationality bring a strikingly colourful element into the social life of the village.

However, in villages where people of various denominations live side by side—with or without additional ethnic differences—a characteristic conflict is to be found everywhere. Conflict manifests itself not only in larger or smaller denominational feuds; populations with different religions differ in their entire social profile, i.e. there are marked differences in non-denominational and non-religious affairs, too. Calvinist villagers are everywhere more dissident minded, steadfaster and more impatient, whereas the Catholics are meeker, more patient and more loyal. The explanation for this is to be found not so much in the differences of dogmas than in the historical role played by the respective Churches. The Catholic Church has always been the advocate of moderating conflicts and consequently it contributed to peasant resignation, while, by the very virtue of the circumstances of its birth, the Reformation has become the confession of protest. Added the fact that in the age of Hungarian Reformation and counter-reformation the villages kept aloof according to their respective religions, this difference becomes even more comprehensible. The most malcontent and stiff-necked element took on Calvinism since this had been the only form of liberty aspirations at that time, while the weaker and more acquiescent ones persisted in their traditional religion. And when the Calvinists were brought back to the Catholic Church by fair means or foul, it was only the more fortunate or extremely persistent villagers who succeeded in sticking to their faith.

Another rather characteristic difference is that in purely Calvinist villages or among the Calvinists of mixed villages there are at all times more families with one child than among the Catholics. It would be again a serious mistake to explain this phenomenon with the difference of dogmas or with the differing moral views of the two Churches. Here, too, it is the above-mentioned social difference which has revealed itself. Peasants do not come to have only one child in their families because their churches restrict them or give them full freedom but because they have developed the aspiration not to continue to live like peasants and there is no other way to achieve this. Therefore, peasants choose this kind of suicide without taking into account the creed of the church. Among such peasants there are more Calvinists since it is the Calvinists who are freer, less patient and more exacting. But there is a number of Catholic villages as well where the one-child pattern is as widespread as in the Calvinist villages because these, too, are inhabited by similarly restless and exacting peasants. Naturally it should and could not be denied that religious faith plays a role in the inner liberation of the peasantry and in the development of its attitude to life. And this applies not only to the denominational life going on within social bounds but also to the differences of religious life.

It is often claimed by zealous rural researchers that the characteristic

116

social units of the village are the associations, cooperatives. However, they also have to admit that there are many troubles and problems in the life of such unions. This latter aspect of the problem is by all means significant. The more so because the society of the village is in itself such a close-knit unit—even considering its stratification reflecting characteristic and considerable conflicts—that establishing any other unions of lesser importance tends to be rather difficult. Associations and cooperatives which are formed within one or another social stratum to bring about opposition or defence against the other ones are not viable for the same reasons as parties are not fit to exist. It is difficult to maintain such an organization under unceasing control at places where, despite their serious disaccord the individual strata are directly dependent on each other. Unions, however, which are not organized by a single stratum of the village but are called into life by all the inhabitants of a village for some specific reason are not viable either because village people are hard to convince to duplicate the social organization of the village (if it is not for some kind of entertainment). They think it enough to be under the control of their superiors as villagers and deem it unnecessary to have this multiplied in their capacity as members of some association or cooperative.

Nevertheless there are unions in the villages which have been formed within one class and even some which are of an inter-class character. Examples for the first are the various peasant associations and farmers' circles, and for the second one the village choirs and patriotic associations. The difference between the two sorts of unions is quite conspicuous. The first ones are vigorous as a rule but putting some authority beyond their class at the head of the union thus guaranteeing its smooth functioning, whereas unions belonging to the second group just exist after having elected their leadership for the very reason because they are nobody's concern except their president's who administrates himself accordingly.

Rural society is too much of a community to allow its separate units to function lastingly (with the sole exception of the various denominations). Since it is a highly close-knit unit separate class unions are inconceivable, and since it is strictly stratified it cannot tolerate specific common organizations. Those which do exist tend to be exceptions or just vegetate.

THE HUNGARIAN VILLAGE

In general the village is simple not only in its internal organization but in the ways it is integrated into its surroundings as well. It is a rural social unit of simple organization integrated by simple means into the surroundings of a city.

The feudal village has been a social domain of special legal status and special order being simply subordinated to the castle and to the domain of the town having a different legal status and social order. Though the bourgeois village is not a domain of a special legal status and another social order, it is still on a lower level than the towns being but a secondary civic domain. It is not a separate social world but a secondary external component of the very same social domain.

The Hungarian village is not so simply integrated into the external social order either. It is not simple because it is the domain of feudal character of a city which has undergone urbanization separately from and alien to the village.

The usual feudal relationship between town and village reflects the absolute dissimilarity and subordination. This relationship, however, is of the same nature as that of the squire stratum and the peasantry. Despite the antagonisms and subordination they are linked together by an elder and younger brother relationship. The peasant and the village are subordinated to the lord and the castle, nevertheless they are members of a common body or at least of a greater unit which could be compared to a family.

In contrast to this development, the burdens of the Hungarian village were still further aggravated by the fact that it was outside of such a bond. The upper order and the town have outgrown the brotherhood and, instead of being an elder brother, have become an alien body which proved unable to ease the existing differences with the help of being aware of the relatedness of town and village. The village remained in its condition of helpless and pure ethnic character whereas the multiple nationalities reaching back to the times of King Saint Stephen came together in the melting-pot of the towns in a way that taken as a whole the world of towns and cities became totally alien to villages. The Hungarian village is not the younger brother of that Hungarian town but simply its colonial domain. Being alien to the world of towns is by itself enough to severely aggravate the position of the village. In addition to this alien character, the town made great strides on the way of bourgeois development while the village remained stuck almost at the same place where it had been at the time of the feudal world. As a result, the Hungarian village—though at some places it succeeded in developing into a bourgeois society—has become not a secondary but a tertiary civic domain. This is the truth and only so much is true of the truism that the Hungarian village is Asia and in Hungary Europe is represented only by the cities.

To sum it up briefly it can be stated that the Hungarian village is the oriental fringe of the occidental Hungarian town, this being by far a greater and more dangerous difference than any other urban-rural contradiction. In a "healthy" urban-rural relationship, however burdensome, the village is able to live or even if it feels the burden of its lot too heavy, it becomes depopulated at the very most since ex-villagers feel themselves at home in the town, too, leading the very same life as in the village but only on a higher level. The Hungarian village, however, cannot choose either of these paths.

Either it is able to live because it can live under the given circumstances or it gets drifted away or declines.

The case of the German villages is a tragicomic version of our villages. To the inhabitants of these villages the town is not more alien than to Hungarian villagers, and they are able to migrate to the towns perhaps even more easily than the Hungarian villagers. It is true that also German villagers can do this with great difficulties and paying the price for it by radical transformations in their way of life, but Hungarian villagers can go along this way only under much harder conditions and by means of an even greater change in the way of life.

The isolation of the Hungarian villages and their inhabitants' status as third-rate citizens is an excess to the burdens which in themselves represent a frightful pressure upon them both in their capacity as villages and countryside. Even a palm-tree could not straighten out under such a burden; here it is possible to live at the most or to go down in various ways until the total collapse ensues. This is the fate of the Hungarian villages. Only few of them can develop by a stroke of extraordinary luck whereas the overwhelming majority of them live from hand to mouth and a great minority is drifting more or less rapidly towards their doom. Thus, there is a system to be found in Hungarian villages not only as regards their settlement pattern, economic organization but also whether they have strength enough to live or only to decay.

This peculiar list is headed by villages which are still capable of development and flourishing; they are followed by the bulk of villages which are just rubbing on whereas at the bottom of the list are those doomed Hungarian villages which have not strength enough to keep themselves afloat.

The possibility of growth for developing Hungarian villages is provided by either of three lucky factors. If they are highly fortunate they are located in the direct neighbourhood of towns, particularly near the suburbs of the capital city, and this way they share in those things which are otherwise the privileges of the towns. Few villages, however, are so lucky. The majority of the villages situated around the capital city are inhabited by Germans, and the city itself is not too strange for them. If on Sunday afternoons on the boulevard a German servant in Budapest happens to run into a German lad living in nearby Hidegkút or Soroksár who had come to the city to make the most of his Sunday, they do feel very much related and at ease. It is also a lucky case if the village is big enough to start on the way of urbanization. This is, by exception, favourable for Hungarian villages as most of such large villages are inhabited by Hungarians, particularly in the case of communities surrounded by homestead-villages. These are fit for life in themselves; they are not strangled by either their isolation or their narrow bounds and therefore in some cases they even tend to flourish. But a price has to be paid for this: the poorest people are banned for a lifetime to the

119

homestead: either they are farm hands on the great estates or they are toiling on a few acres of their own. The third type among villages capable of growth are the villages of settlers. Having got rid of the burdens of the crippling past, they can make use with fresh energy of the available resources even under village conditions. Moreover, in the course of their shorter history they have not yet filled in entirely the living-space of the village. However, the old settlement policy has not favoured the Hungarians, since hundred times as many foreign settlements have enjoyed such advantages than Hungarian ones.

The majority of our villages live from hand to mouth. Peasants in such communities have just as much land as not to starve and have also some scanty communication lines with the towns as not to be totally isolated. This normal frame of life, however, does not suffice to develop the village in any respect, if the incessant and abundant offspring is not regarded as growth. The village can no longer provide any basis for starting new ways of farming. Neither are there any possibilities for the peasants to develop freer and more human attitudes; the village as a whole does not have the strength to become a part of civilization. These villages are just living along waiting for better days.

Villages which are even less lucky have no other chance than to decline. They are unable to live in a way they would like to, and are unable to live under their given conditions, so they have no other chance than to perish. There are many ways of decline. A village can perish if no more children are born than are absolutely necessary to maintain life without any population increase. A village can perish if people flee from it, migrate to the town, go abroad and overseas. And decay can ensue if people disregard all the laws that have been hitherto respected and, like the outlaws of olden times, grab whatever they can from a miserable life with the attitude of "after me the deluge".

This Hungarian village is by no means the eternal village. Not only alarmist novelists and young hot-heads claim that this is the fate of the Hungarian village but also hard facts and figures and other phenomena. One even does not have to visit a village to understand these facts.

THE LIFE OF THE HUNGARIAN VILLAGE

THE LIFE OF THE RURAL SOCIETY

Though the village is a small society of simple organization squeezed within narrow bounds, its social life in general does not proceed according to such simple definitions. Moreover, the social life of the Hungarian village, the structural relations of which are extraordinarily intricate, is particularly not simple and of a single-track nature. No doubt, the territorial unity of the village has brought about a social community of the village within the range of which social life, too, has identical laws, nevertheless the strata which constitute the village are parts of one or another greater unit beyond the bounds of the village as well, and the behavioural laws of these units extend to the village, too.

There are societies which constitute in their entirety a single sphere of action and in these, both as regards inter-class relationships and relations between villages and towns, identical processes are taking place, with the groups participating according to their roles. Hungarian society, however, is different. Here the various classes and territorial groups represent not only different social roles but also independent spheres of action where the leadership, control and in general all underlying elements of social life are made up of separate circles. And not only society as a whole is divided into a separate upper-class, peasant and bourgeois circles but towns and villages, too, represent separate spheres of action.

Thus, the village while being a part of the whole of society is a social sphere in itself having separate and specific active components of its own. Furthermore every village is connected in some way or other with a town constituting a characteristic town and its hinterland sphere of action. In addition to this, the strata which constitute the village society are also strata of the whole of society, i.e. they may belong to the upper-class, the peasantry or bourgeoisie. This is the reason why the social stratification of Hungarian villages shows such an infinite variety. The social "individuality" of each village is determined by the actually prevailing composition derived from larger social classes and the combination of so many factors brings about an immense variety. Therefore we have peasant villages which almost as a whole come under the social laws of the peasantry, and we have manorial villages which can hardly be considered peasant villages because they are subject to the laws of the squire stratum. Further on, we have

121

bourgeois villages which by and large belong to the bourgeois sphere. And within these basic types there are to be found countless variants.

Beyond and above these variants, however, in every village every greater social class has some representation. There is a squire in every village being not only a villager himself but also a member of the whole Hungarian upper-class order. Even if he is not a resident of the village his place is nevertheless there with the same effect as if he were there in person. The bourgeoisie and the working class, which compared to the peasantry are of a bourgeois nature, are also represented in every village, and last but not least there are peasants in every village. Therefore, in every village we have to consider the fact that, in addition to the characteristic social laws of the village, these village strata retain also the characteristics of their peasant, bourgeois or upper middle class existence. As a result the forms of village life are far from being homogeneous.

Another structuring of the villages manifests itself in their relation to the towns, and this again is so varied that the number of the types of villages can once more be multiplied. We have some villages which are so closely interlinked with their respective towns that these villages follow the patterns set by the towns in all fields of their social life. There are some villages which are interlinked with the towns in a much looser way. These are influenced by the towns only in certain fields. Finally, there are villages which, though maintaining some communication with towns are by no means influenced by them and they tend to preserve the village autonomy of their life—this being, naturally, almost without exception a kind of peasant autonomy.

However, the characteristic social autonomy of the village is not destroyed but only modified and diversified by the above-mentioned relationships penetrating the separate existence of the village. Every village has such an autonomous homogeneity and its peculiar laws do have an influence even on those villagers who actually do not belong to any social sphere of village character. The specific social laws of the villages are obviously fully complying with the peculiar features of the social situation of the villages, i.e. with the rural situation, the small distances within the settlements and the proximity to nature. The social relations in the villages, the connection of leadership and those led and controlled as well as political life and all walks of social life are on the one hand deeply influenced by these above-mentioned three features, and on the other hand, rural social life is also the result of these three features.

Naturally all those attitudes which may develop on the basis of social relationships are subject to the law of these three rural features. In practice this means that any attitude of any villager comes under this influence. Thus, in the final analysis the whole of village life is influenced by the rural situation and the rural laws of the village.

Let us examine now only the specifically social relations, i.e. that kind of social life proper which is totally centered around interpersonal relationships.

122

In spite of the existence of strict social division-lines, the prevailing unity of the village would be proved more clearly than any speculation if we had a detailed sociographical survey comparing the communication villagers maintain with non-village residents with communication that takes place within the village itself. Such a survey would definitely show, and this is but natural, that communication within the village is disproportionately more common than the other type. But it would also show that various rural strata communicate with the outside world to a very different degree, and considerable differences exist also in terms of groups and the purpose of communication. With the exception of agricultural labourers and farm hands, all villagers do communicate fairly much with the town or the neighbouring villages or even with the district town going to the markets, looking for work or settling some official affairs. This proves that the village is closely linked to the town or to the district town having a partly urban function, and thus the village as a whole is linked up with it within a close, sometimes loose circle. The same is borne out by the fact that members of all strata—though to a lesser extent and without any social aim—do communicate much more simply for reasons of entertainment. Most frequently the intellectuals of the village communicate, followed by artisans, merchants, minor white-collar workers, all kinds of non-peasant workers, independent farmers and finally agricultural labourers and farm hands. When we consider communication with social aims, i.e. when those who leave for another settlement socialize within their own social stratum, there is a much greater variety according to social strata. In this respect, it is the village squire who most often travels either to the nearby town or to families in the neighbouring communities; he is followed by members of the rural middle-class who go to see acquaintances in the town and in neighbouring places. Members of the rural petite bourgeoisie travel much less often than the above strata. All strata of the peasantry have the fewest number of contacts with non-village residents and when contact is maintained, it is not with town-dwellers but the residents of other villages.

Thus, of this external communication it is only the connection with the town which characterizes the village, whereas its other relations are the separate concerns of the different rural strata. Independent of the actual participants, it is, however, a telling characteristic of the village what contacts are maintained within the village itself. Communication within the village is primarily characterized by being frequent and direct.

Villagers frequently communicate and this is justified by the very fact of neighbourhood and is necessitated also by the social order of the village itself. A villager possibly establishes direct contacts with fewer persons than a townsman but the circle he communicates with is much narrower and therefore he obviously meets the same persons more frequently. This applies both to peasants and non-peasants. As a matter of fact, the calling on one's neighbours and talking in front of the gates which characterize peasants are not peasant traits either since people living on homesteads and herdsmen do not feel this a necessary form of communication as it requires the circumstances created by village life. Reading Reymont's novel there is an unforgettable and recurring scene: people just pop over to the neighbour to exchange a few words under the gateway. They have no special reason for doing so but they find it gratifying to run over and ask whether the neighbour has heard about a certain event or what his opinion is of the weather. The contact among villager burghers is of a similar nature only the forms differ. They always find occasions for a gathering or if there is no such occasion they create one, but they are always pleased to meet each other. What townsmen settle by calling each other by phone, even if it is not more than getting some sort of information, villagers arrange through personal contacts.

The same applies to informal contacts. Frequent contacts in themselves contribute a great deal to informality. In addition to that, contacts are rendered more intimate by rural proximity and interdependence. Every contact is a manysided affair involving the whole person, and even when a non-routine case is discussed there are quite a few other factors influencing the contact. Naturally, the quality of contact heavily depends on the fact whether people belong to the same or to different social strata. The law of rural communication is also valid if its participants belong to differing social strata; however, in that case class differences also have their role. Class differences can never take the form of various individuals not willing to speak to each other. Members of different strata do speak to each other even if this were avoidable. However in such cases, in addition to informality, also the social distance makes itself felt.

A specific feature of the social contacts among villagers is that they take place at special occasions. There are no meetings for the meetings' sake, they always have some specific aim and if by chance there are no such aims, they should be created. Naturally, it is only the pretext of an occasion which is needed and, once this is given, everything proceeds within the framework of village informality and empathy. Since the whole of the village is actually one society, social connections within separate, smaller circles are taking place only on special occasions or when production or the everyday life provide such opportunity. This is particularly the case with the peasantry. Peasants do not meet just for the sake of meeting; occasions of birth, death, wedding, striking a bargain or cessation of work in winter are needed as opportunities for coming together. Though with other rural strata there are no such opportunities provided by peasant work, this has become the rural law of contact to such an extent that the non-peasant strata cannot act otherwise either. This means that they, too, organize meetings primarily on some given occasion but they also multiply and deliberately search for such opportunities. For instance peasants tend to minimize the significance of birthdays, whereas non-peasants gather together at such dates, too. Or let us take the name-day: peasants just say "God bless you" and drink a glass of wine or brandy, while with rural intellectuals and petit bourgeois people it is always an occasion for a great party with a great number of people participating in it.

It is in the case of the laws of leading and being led where rural stratification manifests itself to the greater extent. First of all every villager belongs to the circle of leadership prevailing in his own stratum. This means that the peasant is under the influence of and follows the leading strata of the peasantry in each village. In contrast, the members of the upper middle class primarily follow the upper middle-class guiding principles and leaders. The local burgherhood accepts the bourgeois leadership as their pattern and in every respect finds examples in the city.

Beyond that the village, of course, constitutes a separate circle of leaders and those led by them. And in this respect we can speak of a significant transformation. The law of the village of old had resulted in the fact that the leadership asserting itself above the classes and concerning the village as a whole was by no means of a total nature. Just the contrary is true. Thus, it was not the same leading figures who exerted their overall influence in all spheres of life but every sphere of action had its separate leadership. The administrative leadership of the village covered only public affairs in the strict sense of the word, while in all other walks of life decision-making was in the hands of various groups. Those having a place in the council and the village mayor himself were all chosen from among the older people because it was chiefly the experience and exact knowledge traditions which was needed for the administration of public affairs. In other fields, however, leadership was in the hands of those who had the greatest expertise in a given activity. Thus, in addition to the administrative leader, every village had separate economic leaders as well: the so-called master of the vineyards, the market headman, etc. The youth of the village, too, elected ceremoniously a first lad who had a decisive say in all affairs concerning young people; in questions relating to arts, entertainments the "poetical" men and/or the groomsmen were the competent ones, whereas in matters of healing and superstitious religious life the advice of the midwives and wise men was followed.

In the course of the present transformation of the village, the habit of this divided leadership declined and a kind of total leadership and guidance has taken its place. The process of transformation began when administrative leadership came to control an increasing number of fields. By now this process has reached a point when the administrative leaders have become the overall leaders of the village being competent in all matters. As a result, with more or less success, village administration tries to assert its leading role in all fields. The leading personalities of the administration have become the presidents of the village choirs, the patriotic associations, the firebrigades, the cooperatives and so forth, and in addition, they are the supreme censors of morals. In short, their sphere of authority extends to all domains.

The prestige of leaders has undergone a similar change. In the past general prestige could only be derived from being old, whereas all other venerable qualities had meant particular respect only in the relevant sphere of activity. Thus particular esteem was due to the strong men, the shrewd men, the poetically inclined men or the wealthy ones but this reverence manifested itself only in matters which were somehow connected with the outstanding quality in question. Only the squire had enjoyed a general prestige; he was the one who had been obviously considered the shrewdest, strongest and in all respects the most outstanding man of the village. This, too, has changed. Today all leading personalities attempt to gain the general prestige once due only to the squire, i.e. they try to extend the particular respect gained at a particular sphere to all the domains of life. Such attempts prove to be successful. The top-ranking farmer of a village is not content to be the outstanding authority in the field of production; although everybody buys sowing-seed and pedigree stock from him, he strives to seize a political role as well. He wants to be the first man in dance-parties, too, and finally he yearns for the title of ministerial counsellor, thus to append the seal of squiredom to the general upper-class prestige. In the past, if the son of a rich peasant began to show off in the village inn, the elected first lad personally calmed him down or let it do by his friends. Now all such barriers have been broken down: he who is the first in the principal things (i.e. farming and politics) is likely to be respected as the first one in all other spheres as well.

Thus in the village, too, wealth and social position have gained a general and overriding prestige in comparison with which all minor distinctions seem to be insignificant. And since these authorities have become separated from the upper-class position insofar that anybody else can acquire such positions by that act also gaining a similar position as the squire, it is only this authority which is held in esteem in rural society. In the traditional village, students originating from the village who have learned abroad and returned either as priests or teachers have been held in high esteem and were regarded as bright and learned men. They enjoyed the position of renowned and respected people without any upper-class privilege for the only reason that they were talented and widely-travelled. In vain does a young man today return to his village upon graduation, he will not be respected only for having become an educated person. However, if he succeeded in getting some upper-class job or in attending some upper-class distinction thus gaining in general a superior position, his prestige will become generally acknowledged. If, on the other hand, he gets down to farming he will have to face total lack of comprehension, distrust and even suspicion instead of earning particular respect. He who takes it upon himself to wage an unflinching political fight in the interest of villagers will be respected only by the most conscious and brightest people of the village and he will be considered by all the others a fool who does not seak his own good but struggles for others to no purpose.

Thus, both leadership and prestige in the village have become very much like those in the town with the only difference that, as compared to the town, they have become distorted within the narrow bounds of the village. They also have become distorted because even the leadership of towns asserts itself only at third hand. The general leader of the village is the gentlemanly upper-class having attained the official consent and the corresponding sphere of authority being itself the follower of urban leadership. It is mostly through them that the influence of the town reaches the village, and therefore this influence is rather a filtered and transformed one.

The guiding ideas of villagers are only to a very small degree common ones having a specific rural character. The village squire lives according to the leadership ideas of the upper class, the village peasants take the guiding ideas of the peasantry as their pattern while the rural bourgeoisie keeps the bourgeois ideals in view. The nature of a given rural society heavily depends on the fact whether traditions are still being followed or not. Villages of the old type still living under conditions of absolute traditionalism have not been affected by the process of transformation. Everything is good provided it is as it always had been; things simply cannot be otherwise and therefore everybody has to adapt himself to the traditions. In transformed villages the opposite is true. Nothing which is old is good, everything is in need of renewal and new ideals are to be regarded as guiding principles. This opposition to traditions manifests in two ways. There are some peasant villages where to this very date it is the peasant guiding principles which assert themselves, however, they are just the opposites of the old peasant way of life. In healthy peasant societies the dual guiding principle of life is production and children, in the latter ones, however, it is reverse: everybody tries to escape from work and the main ideal is childlessness. These are the villages with the system of having only one child in the family where peasant life as a whole has become perverted. In contrast, in villages having taken the road of embourgeoisement, the guiding principles of the peasantry have given way to bourgeois ideals, at least to those which can be realized by the village, i.e. the transformation of the outward appearances of life, more comforts, upward mobility and as a rule "better life" judged on strength of its external trappings.

The rural social life is most definitely and strictly regulated as regards controls. Since the village is a small and clear-cut society linked together by direct relationships, the attitudes of all its residents come under the control of the community. And this has not changed in the course of time and transformation. Rural control is still as absolute as possible and the same as it used to be.

It is absolute in the sense that it covers all spheres of life. There is no sphere which could shake of control. There does not exist private life in a sense as it is possible in the jungle of the city. The community is interested in all attitudes and is forming judgement on the behaviour of everyone. The community is absolute since it is infinite. It does not know any limits neither in actual affairs nor in the measure of judgement. All affairs are judged in their fullness and for this reason there is no opportunity for evading censure. And finally, it is also absolute in the sense that everybody is both the means and the object of the control of the public opinion of the village. It is the means of everybody since everybody participates in forming public opinion, and everybody becomes its object in the minute when he does anything. Even the most high-ranking village squire is no exception to this rule although the form of judgement concerning him is of another nature and it asserts itself in a different way.

The validity of control manifests itself in the fact that every attitude is followed by immediate judgement. In this respect the control of the community is general and absolute, whereas, concerning the consequences of the judgement, the village opinions will differ. The reflection of the judgement in public opinion is general as well as the fact that in major affairs it takes always the form of disapproval. Beyond that, however, the consequences of disapproval are realized in the spheres of the various circles of leadership. In olden times here, too, it was divided opinion which was characteristic. Reprisal followed in each case in the relevant sphere and was meted out by those competent in that given sphere. If a husband frequented young brides there followed neither divorce scandal nor public scandal, it was at the worst his family and old women who passed judgement on him. Today, however, because of the general nature of leadership such general consensus asserts itself in judgement as well. According to the judgement of the general leaders of the village, excesses in any field imply general consequences.

The rules of control taken as a starting-point by public judgement have undergone important changes. The influence of radical changes in the life of the village and particularly the transformation of guiding principles have made themselves felt considerably. In the rural society of the past the sphere of laws of the peasants was a strictly separate field and so was that of all other villagers.

In the morals of the peasantry it was rather the value judgements of the peasantry than that of rurality that manifested themselves. This means the acceptance of the roles derived from the peasant status since it is a crime to violate them. A man who does not work is immoral, a woman who does not give birth to and raise children but shows off in gaudy dresses is immoral, too. This spirit made itself felt even in the conventional rules of minor importance. You had to greet everybody: the peasant because you surely had to know him, the non-peasant because he was entitled to it even as a stranger. There were some specific village rules in this respect; you had to greet, for instance, everybody according to his position and not by a general formula: neighbour, chum, brother, churchwarden, judge, etc. Peasant morals were further characterized by not knowing any absolute and abstract value judgements. Everything was judged according to the circumstances of the action. Theft, murder, adultery were no crimes taken in themselves, they were considered crimes only under specific circumstances, whereas on other occasions they may be regarded even as acts of bravado. Those, who according to peasant judgement, had played their role well and without infringing on the rules could reach a respected old age and were regarded an example to be followed. Peasant morals, however, had known another kind of bravery, too. Subconscious resistance to being a peasant manifested itself, for instance, in the fact that he who complied with peasant morals could be a respectable old man, while he who bravely violated conventional rules putting up resistance to the squires could be a veritable hero. To rob another peasant or a poor man is a crime, but to rob a squire or a rich man may be an act of bravado, too. To fight or pick a quarrel all the time is a crime but to teach the squire or the bossy rich man a lesson is considered to be heroism. Sándor Rózsa, Matyi Ludas or Dani Turi are these types of heroes who were respected by all peasants and who had followers on a smaller scale in every village.

Naturally transformation has radically changed things in this respect, too. The autonomy of peasants in evaluating things has disintegrated, peasant morals have been turned inside out or have been substituted by bourgeois values. The most characteristic changes are the following. In villages adopting the system of having one child in the family, mothers with many children are scorned the same way as sluts had been: "she farrows like a sow" and other contemptuous things are said of the woman having many offspring. In olden times a rich farmer had worked the same way as any other peasant because he, too, had been a peasant and not a capitalist, a bourgeois, and if he had not worked he would have been despised as any landless poor man. In contrast, today those rich farmers are scorned who could live idly, yet they toil taking work away from the poor.

Villagers outside the circle of peasants were characterized at all times, in addition to the moral views inherent in their own class situation, by a peculiar formalism and narrow-mindedness. Within the small circle of the village even small things are played up and therefore everything is judged more seriously. An act considered in the city simply a laxity of morals becomes a gravely judged piece of folly, something regarded in the city as improper behaviour is condemned as immorality in the village. Thus, everything is judged more seriously in rural settlements. Not only the form of judgement but also moral evaluation serving as its basis immediately raises the moral standard higher than in any other fields if those who are judged are non-peasant villagers. Though the guiding principle among them is almost generally the desire to get along, to make a career but at least to

129

achieve modest wealth, in their public evaluations—be it a passing moral judgement on their own stratum or on peasants—it is always Christianity and national consciousness which are manifested in the loftiest terms. Nowhere else in the world are trifling things as severely judged as village affairs by the middle-class leaders of Hungarian communities. But since everything is judged by such standards, these insincere and rather empty judgements should nevertheless be regarded as truly valid evaluations.

Evaluations manifested in statutory provisions also divide the village in two, i.e. in the people not versed in law and the leaders versed in law. The people are at a loss as regards statutory law and are rather wary of it. Evaluations manifested in the written law are either beyond them or incomprehensible to them, and only a fraction of evaluations formulated by the law coincide with their own judgements. Thus, ordinary people are facing the law confusedly. While doing their everyday work they do not consider the possible legal sanctions, and when called to account they are astonished at the consequences.

The leaders of villages well-versed in law do accept the evaluation embodied in the law, since their moral conception gets formidable support from it. These leaders consider village folk a herd to be controlled and disciplined. Therefore they are capable of applying legal statutes with hair-raising formality even in the face of serious obstacles. This specific attitude to the law has often resulted in serious conflicts between the village and its leader. Conflicts, however, do not prevent the leadership from enforcing even the most insignificant regulations with absolute bureaucratism. When having got acquainted with local circumstances, it frequently occurs that a superior legal authority immediately finds some possibility of alleviating the legal practice, whereas the lower-level authorities do not find such circumstances because it is not their guiding principle to find them. Instead, they strive at upholding the prestige of the office by all means, although otherwise their prestige could be much more accepted and effective.

On the other hand, there exists a kind of autonomous customary law among ordinary rural people not versed in law, in the form of partly regulations of an independent legal character, partly as statutory interpretations and supplementary regulations, and partly as agreements filling the gap in the law. Naturally, in many places this type of popular customary law is in the process of disintegration, and often it has been actually annihilated. However, its traces can be found everywhere. It is especially in meadow and field problems where such valid popular legal regulations are still to be found. The same applies to problems of inheritance in the form of the priority right of male heirs, etc. The complementing and the application of law are still rather common especially in settling labour disputes. The evaluation embodied in such regulations of customary law reflects the most specific peasant attitudes. At all times and in all places, these attitudes are also well reflected in the peasant customs of non-legal nature.

130

A society living under such conditions cannot be much different in its political manifestations either; rural societies lead a political life that is possible. The political attitudes of the various strata of the village differ radically but they are rendered similar partly by the narrow-mindedness and partly by the exaggerated nature of the political views of the village communities.

For instance in municipal politics, the leading group asserts its absolute leadership; the taxpayer majority can at the most only strive at achieving a situation in which nothing is undertaken without their participation, whereas the others, i.e. the village paupers can only put questions to the community or object to the decisions from outside and without any avail. The subject of local politics where such fronts are facing each other are the most fastidious routine matters where the will of the village leaders predominates absolutely, due to their competence and privileged position. Those objecting to such decisions can enumerate only arguments based on a social and economic policy whose targets go much beyond the narrow limits of the village and therefore these arguments are of no avail.

Similar is the situation as regards national issues of political life. Actual political struggle is waged on village affairs of minor importance while regarding major political issues villagers only give vent to their imagination—except the leaders who pursue a purposeful defensive and shrewd reformist policy. Farmers regard their trifling affairs as major political issues, e.g. local surtaxes or distillation of brandy at home, whereas the paupers follow the vents and turns of political life with expectant illusions. International affairs are discussed by all rural strata. However, this should not be regarded as political life but as dabbling in politics which serves as pastime for farmers and petit bourgeois strata, whereas among the poor it takes the form of impotent and vain expectations. The artisans and shopkeepers are the most fond of discussing international politics. Every village has its own pot-house politicians, generally the bootmaker, the blacksmith or the barber.

However, it does not follow from the above that simple village folk, e.g. the village peasantry and village paupers were politically immature. On the contrary, they are very mature since their social and economic situation have made them ready for any political manifestations but they are unable to formulate their political consciousness and to launch political actions. They are not immature but helpless. Just because of their helplessness the political life of village commoners becomes a narrow-minded bickering or futile day-dreaming. For this reason, despite certain attempts, village people are not socialized for political life. In spite of efforts to change this situation, the helplessness of these strata is only aggravated by lack of learning and sheer ignorance.

THE ECONOMIC LIFE OF THE VILLAGE

In the division of roles between village and town the most significant element is not the fact that the village is agrarian, while urban people are craftsmen, traders and all kinds of intellectuals but that the village is primarily a productive sphere, while the city is eminently a sphere of consumption. Moreover the division of labour is not so developed in the village being first and foremost not a place of dwelling producing finished goods, whereas the town represents an especially differentiated and higher-level economic life both as regards production and consumption.

Having a closer look at this division of social roles between town and village it is a characteristic of the village that its main function is production while consumption is limited to what is absolutely necessary and it will always lag behind production in importance. Production is turning out primarily raw produce and is specialized in none of its branches to such a degree as in the city. Mainly it is raw material production which is turning out goods for urban consumption or further processing, and only to a minor extent production of finished goods with the aim to meet local needs. In none of the production types of the village can we find such a developed division of labour as in the production of the towns. Farmers producing raw produce are able to meet quite a lot of their industrial needs by themselves and are taking a lot of their goods to urban markets while very often village artisans and merchants are also engaged in agricultural production to satisfy their private needs. Village society has but one stratum which lives and works under conditions of a highly developed division of labour: the village intelligentsia, though even among intellectuals there are quite a few who own their gardens. This stratum is also unique since they do not regard consumption as subordinated to production.

Naturally, the social motives of production differ by the various branches of production.

Thus, in the case of the most typical rural products, the village farmers, this specific rural determination prevails absolutely and peasant traditions enhance everything developed under rural conditions. Under the influence of the social laws of the peasantry, both the priority of production and its undivided nature characteristic of village conditions are expanded to the limit. The peasantry is characterized not only by its dependence on its role as a producer but also by its ingrained attitudes and its moral habits which advocate a social order where productive work is acknowledged as a top priority and guiding principle. It is also a feature of peasant life that the peasant's productive work is primary production not only in the sense that it is agricultural but also in terms of comprising some industrial activities most directly related to agriculture and consumption. The expectations of this rural and peasant productive role are fully complied with by the farmer of the village. He works incessantly not only because he has to in order to make both ends meet—under given circumstances the size of his holding makes this unnecessary—or to acquire some further property but also because, according to his knowledge, this is his social duty. He performs all kinds of industrial work around the house not only because this is cheaper than to have it done by a craftsman but also because he regards it as peasant tradition.

Naturally, the transformation of the peasantry has considerably changed the farmers' attitude to production. There are very few places today where the peasant himself builds his home or fabricates his agricultural equipments and his furniture, but the details of the work he still performs by himself. Women of the family no longer weave and spin—this is quite exceptional— but everywhere they bake the bread and whitewashing as well as washing are still done everywhere by the family. Thus, in the course of transformation, peasant laws have mostly lost their validity, however, the compulsions of the rural condition have survived and this means almost the same as the former peasant condition. Despite all the transformation, village farmers still have to subordinate the viewpoints of consumption to those of work—even if their only aim is to keep the pot boiling—and particularly if they want to pay back their debts or acquire some new land. They have to perform this productive work in a way that the possibly least industrial work be performed by craftsmen; therefore anything that could be produced at home is home-made.

The situation of the village traders and craftsmen is very similar. Rural conditions demand from them, too, to give top priority to productive work even if their sole aim is to eke out a livelihood, and if they wanted to save up some money for their old days they have to do their utmost to increase their productive efforts. The same is the situation with the village shopkeepers with the sole exception that they succeed more often in amassing some fortune. But with them, too, it is a precondition that they have to work long hours and with all their energy.

The same applies to rural workers. They have to work incessantly, often even on holidays, not in order to amass a fortune but for their mere livelihood as well. All types of regulated working hours and benefits taken as granted in towns are unthinkable in villages. Rural life is so much shaped by economic necessity that everybody has to work incessantly. Some of the holidays are actually partly used for leisure, the rest of the holidays is used by villagers for performing some activities which fall outside their expertise but cannot be done by anybody else. Only on such occasions can rural labourers work for themselves; farmers perform industrial work and craftsmen busy themselves in their gardens or vineyards.

Owing to these constraints, it is generally characteristic of rural productive work that in villages more work input is necessary to achieve the same result than in towns. Because of the incomplete division of labour and the less favourable conditions of production, the village is forced to accept this

133

even without some specific urban "exploitation". Compared to the cities, rural economy is in an adverse position. Under such circumstances of production, working hours cannot be reduced. Neither the farmer nor the independent craftsman or shopkeeper can have fixed worktime, they have to work round the clock. But it would be rather difficult to fix working hours for agricultural workers, too, because it is their interest to work as much as possible whenever they have a chance to work at all. And even if there are certain restrictions in certain branches the workers still spend very long working hours, because whenever there is a break in worktime they peg away at their houses or gardens.

As regards the professional aspects of production, the village is once again in a much more unfavourable position than the town. In contrast to towns, educational and training facilities, experimental plants and work-shops, farms and enterprises representing higher technological skills are at a great distance and as a result, vocational training is inevitably of a lower quality than in towns. In addition, the binding force of traditions is stronger than in towns and thus even if there is a desire for learning, grave obstacles have to be overcome. In this respect the various branches of production do not differ considerably.

A farmer can acquire vocational knowledge in two ways. On the one hand, he learns the traditional peasant methods of production at the farm of his parents, on the other, he snatches up some skills from the experiences of other farms and on rare occasions from books, newspapers and at vocational courses. Neither of these guarantee his becoming a good farmer. Traditional production skills offer a great amount of useful and valuable knowledge, since age-old experiences and lessons drawn under local conditions are handed down that way. However, these skills do not explain the laws of plant and animal life or mechanisms of farming methods. Thus actually an inadequate and inefficient vocational knowledge develops. At the same time, inadequate knowledge gained from books as a whole contains much knowledge which has to be adapted to local conditions and if this is mastered only insufficiently and erratically, the results will be rather disillusioning. The village farmer thus struggles with his deficient vocational knowledge of doubtful value, and it is a rare exception if he succeeds in acquiring the science of successful farming.

The vocational competence of village tradesmen is not much higher. Their knowledge, too, is derived partly from local traditions and partly from vocational training but the mixture is not a fortunate one in their case either. The traditions of rural tradesmen spring only to a minor degree from the master strokes of local popular handicrafts. Expertise is to a greater part the result of intricate and priggish methods of semi-educated master craftsmen which can be considered neither true popular culture nor a technical science of higher standards. This is the general rule. There are, however, some exceptional villages where this popular tradesman's knowledge is able to turn out highly viable and outstanding products. For instance in certain regions of the Great Hungarian Plain it is carriage-building, in other regions house-building and at many places the various branches of wood-work which can boast of harmonious and outstanding products. The other source of vocational knowledge of rural tradesmen, i.e. the apprentice-school is not more successful either. Here the vocational apprentices learn the elements of a German-oriented technological science on the strength of examples which are in no way relevant to rural conditions, and therefore it is but natural that both their taste and their knowledge become confused. The hair-raising bad taste manifesting itself in rural architecture, interior decoration and clothing is to be attributed to this mixed and altogether deficient vocational knowledge of craftsmen. Where peasant traditions are still alive the village is harmonious and beautiful since peasant culture has set the artistic forms of everything with rigorous and disciplined taste, whereas wherever peasant traditions have lost their vigour the distorted taste of rural tradesmen is matched by the spoiled and confused taste of peasants who became embourgeoised, and this produces all kinds of freak forms.

The village as a whole and also in its smaller economic units is a subsistence economy. What can trade turnover be here like? Such as is possible in this world forced into subsistence production. There is a small internal circle of trade and there is some trade with villages. Neither of them is similar to commercial activities in towns.

First and foremost the decisive role of trade so characteristic of the market-based urban economic organizations is missing. Naturally, villages, too, live within the bounds of trade-based economy; here, too, commodities are produced after all, but under rural conditions this trade character becomes so much eroded, modified and changed that it ceases to be a genuine market economy. No definite order of either producing for the market or living from the market has emerged. Intellectuals in villages, rural tradesmen and shopkeepers are mostly living under the influence of the market economy. They produce for the market and do business in commodities, moreover they meet the greater part of their essential needs from the market. But being influenced by the market is by no means so complete as in the towns. The lives of the members of these strata are influenced to such a degree by the garden and the allowances in kind that they do not have to rely totally on the market. More exactly: by means of the production they work for the market but their consumption does not entirely depend on the market.

In the case of rural primary producers even producing for the market prevails only partly. Though they bring various goods to the market, they do not produce for the market. They produce according to traditions or to the vogue carrying along one or another village, but they do not adjust their production to the market and therefore they are unable to follow the change in market demand. If there is market demand for what they have produced they are overjoyed, but if their produces are not sold, they tend to complain and wait for better times. Both the law of observing rural traditions and the vague nature of productive vocational skills contribute to shaping the attitudes to the market. If, motivated by market demand, a farmer nevertheless tries to introduce some innovation, his initiative usually fails, thus strengthening the views of those who from the very beginning refrain from such experiments.

Obviously, such a reduction in the role of the market is in general unfavourable, further worsening the economic situation of the village compared with that of the town. In times of crises, however, it is just the reduced role of the market which guarantees the security of village life. When dependence on the market is not substantial, it is easier to shoulder the burdens of the crisis.

Trade with towns, whether it is strong or weak, is always disproportionately favourable to the towns. This is so not only in the flagrant case of the ratio between the relative prices of agricultural and industrial products but in general the village is in an unfavourable position as regards commodity exchange as a whole; whether it buys or sells there is no difference in this respect. The defencelessness of the village has two causes. First, in the case of commodities, both coming from or flowing to the town, transport costs are paid by the village. Second, the town being the centre of trade turnover, all the elements of economic life develop according to the viewpoints of the town. The village, a periphery in the economic sense of the term, is forced to accept everything in the form as it comes from the town.

The proportions of rural consumption are determined by the overstressed viewpoints of production. Consumption in the village is not a particular concern—except for the paupers living off the market and the middle-class—but a subsidiary function of production. The greater part of the consumption of farmers is covered by their household plot and even traders and shopkeepers produce much in their gardens. The ratio of consumption is characterized by this factor.

However, the technique and economy of consumption are much more significant factors. Consumption had been rigorously and strictly restricted by peasant laws in the village of old guaranteeing at the same time an absolutely careful management of money and resources. No independent viewpoint of consumption had existed: this could be taken into consideration only as the shadow of production and to a certain extent life itself demanded it. Nutrition, homes, clothing—all these had no separate occasions or means. Everything fell into the line primarily with production and only secondarily served the ends of consumption. This law is most strikingly characterized by the fact that the attire of the peasants worn on festive occasions is not a separate holiday attire but a more ornate form of the peasant working dress.

136

As this strict peasant law lost its forces the careful management of resources characterizing consumption came to an end. Exception from the rule are the middle-class and the truly bourgeois elements who live according to the principles of bourgeois thrift. The peasantry, however, having undergone radical changes, has got confused because of the disproportions. The importance of consumption has increased as a whole and particularly in the spheres which are regarded as the easiest ways to achieve bourgeois standards. Thus clothes have become important out of all proportions in some villages. People spend everything on clothing, and even if they live in dilapidated houses and are fed very poorly they want to show off with their clothes. In some villages it is still the rustic attire which fills this function while in other places it is already the bourgeois forms which have come into fashion. While girls proudly display their rich peasant attires in the Sárköz region, they show off fur-coats and silk evening dresses in villages near to the capital city. At other places it is food which has gained importance out of all proportions. People consider food as the only important moment of life and such needs are met even to the detriment of clothing and housing. There are very few places where good housing has gained top priority. There are plenty of examples where big, many-room houses outstripping peasant claims are built in villages but there are much fewer cases where attempts are made to match the enlarged interior of the house with higher quality demands. Most of such cases can be found in German villages. The legend about some peasants having a piano in the house is an extreme case and a very rare one at that.

No matter how the economic roles of the village have changed, the transformation has not been so momentous that the significance of consumption as a whole would have surpassed that of production. It was only in the totally bourgeois villages and in the "degenerate" peasant villages that the reverse is to be seen. At these places, production proved to be unable to cope with that high level of consumption and it got into a crisis. High and wasteful consumption levels resulted either in the neglect of the fields or in running into debts of considerable proportions. Both phenomena are serious difficulties in rural economic life; they are rather deep-rooted and cannot be cured without a radical transformation of the whole of village economy. There exist decaying villages where part of the plots are left fallow, another part of them are leased out and only a small portion of the land is cultivated but even this only poorly; at the same time, however, people dress expensively and eat abundantly (in the village of Dunapataj, for instance, there are two pastry-shops!) in spite of a serious indebtedness. The situation of these peasants cannot be helped by granting credits or protectionist measures. These people can improve their lot only by radically changing their attitude to life. In other words, village life has to be radically changed.

Sociological studies of village-life frequently make the mistake of identifying the rural way of life with the peasants' way of life enumerating specific peasant characteristics as typical rural regularities. It is true that the village is primarily the home of the peasantry and it is also true that rural characteristics are similar in many respects to specific peasant features, but their absolute identification is by all means an error which hampers the adequate evaluation of the village. This is true since the specific rurality of the village determines the social life of villagers from all walks of life though not to the same extent but in an equally typical way. Thus, there does exist a peculiar rural way of life necessarily manifesting itself at all the levels of social stratification. As regards rural realities and village politics, in the final analysis this is the decisive factor and not the entirely different problem of the peasantry.

This distinction is important so much the more as it is exactly the biologically influenced phenomena of man's life—such as sexual life, mate selection, marriage, birth, education, life style, hygiene, healing, as well as playing, sports, leisure, celebrations—where the effect of one's social position is the most conspicuous. Both these life-manifestations and their influence on human attitudes are equally specific indications of the social conditions under which people live. Obviously, this applies to the village, too.

It might be assumed that in the interdependent world of the village so near to nature such biologically shaped attitudes as marriage, sexual life and birth are taking a much more direct, simple and natural form than in the sophisticated and more civilized world of the town. However, reality is quite different. Rural society has also another law of life consisting in the typical and formal determinateness, and it is just on the above occasions that such laws primarily assert themselves.

Let us consider, for instance, mate selection. Obviously the natural state of affairs would be that this should be decided by biological factors. However, in rural society, even more than in urban society, this happens differently. Mate selection is typically predetermined. In the world of the village everybody has his place according to social stratification and mate selection can take place only within one's social stratum. Though literature cites quite a few examples of romantic marriage, in actual life we find very few such instances. Social stratification is so rigid in rural society that in most cases the idea of choosing one's mate from a different stratum is not even considered. Very seldom it may happen that the marriage partners come from different social strata: however, this romance, which is usually much talked about, has a detrimental effect throughout the spouses' whole life.

The wedding itself in a village is by no means a simple affair and is a much more complicated matter than in urban society. It is just inconceivable in a village to have a simple, formal wedding before starting married life. Even in the lives of the poorest cotters or farm labourers the wedding is much more important. Marriage has its ceremonial rules and these, though they may differ, are equally binding for peasants, rural gents or the village bourgeoisie. Naturally, wedding ceremonies are the most formal and ceremonious among peasants; potters or farm hands do not differ from well-to-do farmers. Gyula Illyés, the famous Hungarian writer recorded that in the lives of manorial farm hands the wedding is the only occasion, where the poor can eat and drink to their hearts' content: such a feast may cost as much as a year's income of the newly-wed couple. It is much of a mystery why just this occasion is selected by peasant law for such extravagance since cohabitation does not begin with the wedding in the case of farm hands, and no new life begins with marriage for the young couple. Most of their married life is spent in the house of their parents and therefore the big wedding party cannot be regarded as the celebration of having become independent.

Not even married life develops as a free and natural cohabitation but it takes the form of living according to predetermined roles. Among peasants it is the economic roles which are important. If the newly-wed couple is independent their life assumes the form of a common economic venture strictly defining the roles of both husband and wife. If they live at one of the parents' house, the young couple has rather a subordinated role in the household of the elder generation. The husband has to satisfy himself with playing the second fiddle at the side of his father or father-in-law, i.e. he ranks only second as regards the management of the farm, while the greater share of work is performed by him. At the side of her mother and particularly of her mother-in-law the young wife is assigned the role of a much respected domestic servant. Within the family she is considered to be equal but it is her share to perform the inferior household chores. A similarly subordinate role awaits the young wife at the house of the rural craftsman, shopkeeper or junior clerk. Even under conditions of scarcity, she has to perform manifold household chores, and if she sometimes tries to escape from these tasks she is seriously condemned by the public opinion of the community. In the families of the middle-class leaders of the village, in addition to her household role, the young wife has to meet the requirements of a similarly strictly defined role of rural representation; on Sundays she has to go to church; she is obliged to participate in charity work; she has to assume a leading role in the local women's association, etc. The law of the village makes all these activities obligatory and whoever dares to live differently has to reckon with serious sanctions.

In the peasant villages of old the only natural aspect of married life had been childbirth. Peasant morals had forbidden all forms of birth control and thus as many children were born as nature willed it. However, the natural way of life has been terminated in this respect, too, by the transformation of the peasantry. All kinds of forms of birth control have been accepted among the rural peasantry, too. Indeed, it is the most brutal methods which have been adopted. Since peasants have generally no opportunity, and nor are they civilized enough to adopt the less dangerous but more expensive methods of birth control they resort to the simplest but most risky methods. The most frequently adopted method is that of *coitus interruptus,* the physical and mental consequences of which are regarded as highly perilous by doctors. In regions where the system of having one child in the family has emerged, men are characterized by peculiarly nervous, confused and uncertain attitudes. When examining the roots of this behaviour, it always turns out that its cause is the *coitus interruptus* adopted continuously for a long time. It is unanimously stated by doctors practising in regions characterized by the system of having only one child in the family that initially they had had difficulties in identifying the cause of the mass phenomenon of nervous disorders, because among peasants its incidence is very low. In all communities this explanation has been given. The other most common method of birth control seriously endangers the health of women. The most brutal intervention is to hurt the womb to start bleeding. Since superstitious beliefs determine what objects can be used for this purpose, the danger of infection is quite considerable. It has become an everyday event that as a result of such intervention, young women often die or they become disabled at an early age.

Among non-peasants birth control is practised at least with the same incidence but its methods are more civilized and therefore the consequences are less perilous. Naturally, birth control itself is not a village law, but that people living in villages are compelled to resort to the more primitive and dangerous methods and often medical help is to be found only at a great distance, this is a characteristic of the plight of the village.

Another characteristically rural phenomenon is also connected with this sphere of life. In the villages of past ages love-life had taken place before and outside marriage. Folksongs, love superstitions and magics are rooted in and are still connected with times preceding marriage because marriage is such a strictly determined and disciplined way of life that it leaves no room for love. At that time, partly as an exception and partly more generally pre-marital sex life did occur among young people who then resorted to the various peasant methods of birth control. However, the very same peasant mores, which permitted birth control in extra-marital connections, prohibited it in the case of married couples. As a matter of fact, peasant mores presumably forbade romantic love, since they did not provide any place or opportunity for the love-life of the young. No matter what change the mores of the villages underwent (embourgeoisement) or becoming more conservative, the restraints imposed upon love-life have changed. Today it is possible to marry for love and together with love also the various peasant methods of birth control have appeared in married life. Naturally there have remained quite a few restraints, moreover, a new one has appeared: the number of children is limited to one. This rural one-child system is not similar to urban childlessness. In urban families there are no children because the parents do not take upon themselves the sacrifices involved or they are unable to raise children according to their wishes and ideas. This, however, is always explained by unfavourable circumstances and those who have several children are not despised but especially respected. However, with rural one-child families it is not harsh circumstances which limit the number of children but an unwritten law. Those who violate this law of community have to reckon with disapproval. This is the most brutal restraint in this sphere but there are many other constraints as well in such "degenerate" villages: "emancipated" love-life is often poisoned by ever new restrictions such as the incessant intrusion and control by the elder generation, the restriction of sexual intercourse and other monstrosities.

With rural people who are not peasants there are no such awkward regulations; there, in addition to the general constraints, love-life is as free as permitted by the village mores. Actually such rural mores are stricter than the urban ones. Rural mores are stricter because love-life takes place within the same social stratum. Occasionally, persons from different social strata establish contacts but these are always exceptions even in such flagrant cases as that of the manorial hired maids or jobber-girls establishing sexual contacts with men of higher social standing. Men belonging to the privileged classes, might force women to have sex with them, and this may even become general practice; however, this is not approved even by the public opinion of the manorial village; it is only tolerated out of shere necessity. The case of the village Dejtár is quite an exceptional one since free lovemaking for money is accepted there by village mores—but Dejtár is a "corrupt" village in other respects as well.

To sum it up: though the sanctimonious sermons on the clean life, the fertility and mores of simple village folk are not true, it is a fact that, partly despite the constraints and partly because of them, their sexual relationships are more balanced than those of urban residents. The so-called "corrupt" villages are exceptions because there mores are more scandalous than those of the towns. And when all is said and done, in rural communities—again with the exception of "corrupt" villages—more children are born than in urban societies. This being an undeniable fact it would be a premature conclusion that according to a social law more children are born in rural districts simply because the parents are rural people. Let us recall that in certain cases rural society is capable of limiting births to a much greater extent than the urban communities. We also have to see that villages experience a much greater decline in fertility than the towns. It would be more exact to state that the birth rate is higher in Hungarian villages than in towns despite the fact that they are villages. Actually, we could face a situation in which rural birth rates will be lower than those of the towns just because of their rurality.

Another caharacteristic sphere of the rural way of life is education.

First of all there is a crucial difference between the educational background of the village and the town. István Dékány, a well-known Hungarian sociologist repeatedly pointed out that the rural educational milieu is totally different from that of the urban educational environment. The educational milieu of the villages is clear-cut: it is a world in itself in which the child is able to find his way and to learn not only words but relationships and meanings as well. The child understands everything which surrounds him since no relationships are beyond his grasp. Since the pace of life in the village is slower than that of the city, everything a child experiences leaves an imprint on his whole frame of mind. The child participates in work at a very early date of life; he gets tasks and thus his sense of responsibility and his social consciousness increases. And finally, he is surrounded by the phenomena of nature and therefore he learns to identify them and understands even the most delicate facts of biological life at an early age. All this means that the world of the rural child is simpler, more clear-cut, and more comprehensible than that of the urban child. However, it is naturally smaller as well, and therefore, in contrast to urban children, the child's scope of interest remains limited.

Regarding the deliberate educational influences, here again we find some specific rural relationships. Rural children—even the children of non-peasant families—are subject to fewer educational influences than urban children. They are given more freedom than children of the same age group in towns. This is explained by the fact that they are not exposed to so many dangers as the children in the streets of the cities. Thus, children grow up in the company of their peers, that is to say in a society of children and develop in many respects without the intervention of adults.

Similarly, rural education is characterized by the fact that even if the effects of conscious and deliberate educational influencing can be felt this concerns less general human affairs but rather the future social role of children. Peasant children are tought by the adults what a peasant has to know and how he has to behave, whereas middle-class children are tought what is done and what is not done by a future gentleman. It is a more recent phenomenon when peasant children are reared to be "gentlemen" and are painstakingly separated from the other "peasant children", moreover are spared any physical work. It may well be imagined what an influence such a peculiarly distorted and inadequate education exerts on children.

Peasant, bourgeois and gentlemanly upper middle-class lads jointly roaming the countryside have the time of their life exploring all kinds of secrets of the world without having the remotest idea about how they fit into social structure; they only fear the society of the adults. And all of a sudden they begin to experience disappointedly that the upper middle class bourgeois lads are ordered off their gang by their parents because they learn "bad things" from peasant children and it is considered indecent to socialize with them. This discrimination is upheld even at school where they sit in the very same class room, and the gap becomes unbridgeable when upper-middle class and bourgeois lads attend higher educational institutions. Naturally, children learn early about class distinctions in towns, too, but there children never live in close togetherness. The significant feature of villages is that children living in a children's society ignorant of social stratification are exposed to such a forceful and severe social lesson which makes up for everything omitted in that respect up to that time. This is guaranteed by the whole rural social order.

As regards the everyday life of the village it falls into two radically different life styles. When speaking of everyday life it is absolutely true that we may speak of a peasant and a non-peasant village. However, in everyday life, too there are some common particularities stemming from rurality. We should think of those features that we have discussed when describing the attitudes of villagers to civilization.

Our civilization being a characteristically urban civilization (as reflected by the etymology of the word itself), the attitude of the city-dweller to the comforts of city life tend to be natural and simple. The bourgeois makes use of these comforts, and the proletarian would like to do so. As regards, however, the villager, to whatever stratum of the rural society he happens to belong, this relationship is not as simple as that. It is a rather ambivalent attitude. The peasant, as a matter of course, faces civilization as a strange phenomenon and even if he comes under its influence he makes use of it in an inadequate way. On the other hand, the rural bourgeoisie and gentlemen demand the comforts of civilized life and even under unfavourable rural conditions they make considerable efforts to get these facilities. As a result, peasants live either without the comforts of civilization or they use these facilities inadequately, whereas the rural bourgeois and gentlemen live under conditions similar to a colonial civilization.

Thus, even the common features of the way of life of villagers show considerable variation. The only thing which remains common is the fact that both peasant and non-peasant strata equally differ from the urban way of life; however, the degree of difference differs.

According to the rules of the peasant way of life, meals are not the basic concern of life. For cooking peasants do not need any sophisticated tools or special place or time. Preparing meals is not regarded as a specific scope of activity but it is done by any person at a time when be/she finds it suitable since it does not require much time anyway. As a natural consequence of this philosophy peasants never cooked complicated meals and neither did they eat particularly well. However, as all aspects of peasant life, this, too, has two sides. The above rule applies to workdays only, on holidays this order is reversed: then the most delicious food is abundantly served that

143

peasant ingenuity can invent. We can say, therefore, that generally peasant women cannot cook well, yet there exist excellent folk and peasant dishes.

The role of meals has been radically changed by the transformation of the peasantry. This was perhaps the first field in which the peasantry has broken with the rigid peasant laws. Nowadays meals have become much more significant, almost the entire activity of women is absorbed by preparing food. And this is but natural, since now they cook such bourgeois dishes which have developed under entirely different circumstances, and if somebody wanted to prepare them in a village house it involves twice as much trouble, leg-work and hot haste. Nevertheless, this new way of cooking is accepted and, as a result, women have left hardly any time to engage in productive work. Naturally, this applies only to farmers since peasant well-being is only possible in this stratum.

Whether they live according to peasant laws or not, village paupers live in such abject poverty that they eat what they have, and since they have scarce food, they hardly eat anything. For them meals do not represent a social problem; the problem of eating and meals is economic: it is a question whether there is anything to eat or not. Through the research work of Zoltán Szabó and others the diet of the village paupers is a widely known problem, and this gave rise to the idea that the women of the villages should be taught cooking. However, such efforts are doomed to failure since farmers' wives who have the ingredients of cooking can learn it from various cooking books, whereas poor women are bad cooks just because they have nothing to cook with.

The system of meals seems to be most harmonious in the case of the village petite bourgeoisie. Their life is adjusted to rural circumstances but they are by no means bound by peasant traditions. The same applies to farmers if they have liberated themselves from the restrictions imposed by peasant conditions.

The problem is more difficult in the case of the rural bourgeoisie and gentlemany upper middle class. They lay claim to more than is simply possible in village and therefore they have some trouble in procuring everything they require. This means they lead a colonial type of life. Housewives have often serious difficulties in buying fish, coffee, spices and drink but whatever the hardships they procure these goods exactly like the white men in the colonies. In addition, they have to consume all this in a colonial atmosphere watched by astonished and hostile eyes, moreover, they have to fend off even the hostile intervention of the air, the dust, the flies and the wind. Nevertheless they are able to procure everything and live accordingly and even more lavishly than in the towns.

Rural life is characterized by the house and its furnishing and installations better than by anything else. In this respect the peasant way of life is most harmonious. This is the field in which the village farmer, who started on the way of embourgeoisement, has rejected traditions to the greatest extent. As

144

regards their housing, village paupers are most miserable, and the village bourgeois and upper middle class elements are the most colonial.

According to peasant laws of long standing the house was built strictly of local materials and its internal division was rigorously determined by needs. The typical village house plan consisted of an entrance-hall-like porch from where there opened in front of the entrance the kitchen; on one side there was the so-called "clean" room, on the other the living-room with the stove. This lay-out of the house was absolutely adequate to the requirements of the peasant way of life. Heating meant no problem because it was solved by the stove which was suitable for burning any kinds of local materials, and since the furniture, too, was made according to needs, all the functions of a dwelling could be located in a single room. A table with a right-angled bench under the window served for meals as well as for just sitting around and any kind of room activity. Around the stove there was the chimney corner seat for sitting around in winter time; in the corner opposite the table there was a bed for the old couple, and a so-called "lower" bed behind the door for the young ones whereas all the children had their place on the den or a mean bed near the stove. The middle of the room was left free to facilitate leaving the house for the yard or under the eaves. The clean room served the purpose of keeping the better, newer, more richly decorated furniture (similarly to the order of the living-room), and it was also used as the scene of entertaining guests on various festive occasions.

This strict order has been totally upset by the transformation. In most places the first change took place when there was put an end to the separation of the porch and the kitchen as a result of which one had to enter the room through the kitchen. Naturally, this did not suit the more exacting people who therefore built a so-called lower kitchen behind the rooms with a door opening on under the eaves. Thus the upper kitchen lost its significance as "cold kitchen". It became a clean kitchen, like the clean room. When the closed peasant order has thus been broken down there followed an infinite variety of other changes as well. As a consequence, a farmer's house today is about twice as big than it used to be, yet, not a single part of it meets the requirements of its original functions. When people lost the soundness of their peasant taste they began to build according to bourgeois patterns and standards, and since these patterns themselves were bad, and in particular did not suit the way of life of farmers, various torsos were built all over the country. A huge collection of examples of the pathology of architecture could be compiled on the basis of the plans of rural Hungarian farmers' houses. A veritable orgy of bad taste and derangement has spread over the countryside as regards building and decorations, the reason being that peasants have lost the soundness of peasant taste required by local materials. Their houses were built following the "decorations" of the worst secessionist bourgeois buildings. In addition to the confused mind of the builder and the unsuitability of the examples, this was made even

145

worse by the ill-matched taste and innovative efforts of the foreman-builders. If the disintegration and confusion of the way of life of the peasantry which has entered the way of embourgeoisement were to be judged according to these houses only hopeless confusion and desperate disintegration could be pointed out.

Rural bourgeois and petit-bourgeois houses are similar which is but natural since it was these houses which were imitated by peasants well on the way of embourgeoisement. The most degenerate substandard examples of the styles of recent decades have appeared in the villages. Unheard-of mongrels of secession, neo-baroque and neo-classic styles were built along the broad, beautiful streets of the villages compared to which any peasant house or upper middle class mansion with all their social drawbacks seemed masterpieces of architecture. By good fortune these houses are more hygienic than the old ones, further on there have remained some villages which have not yet been inundated by this terrible flood of architectural innovation. A particular kind of luck, nevertheless some sort of consolation.

The form of the gentlemanly upper-middle-class mansion is different. Though they are fortresses of a colonial style of life, they are still respectable buildings. They, too, are characterized by provincial taste but are constructed with taste aiming at harmony and thus, despite their colonial seclusion, they tend to be pleasant to the eye. They are homes based on a life of exclusive comfort and are protected from the colonial surroundings by intricate barriers: fences, dogs, gardens, shutters, nets and curtains. Despite all their seclusion, they are an integral part of the scenery of the Hungarian village and as regards their form, they are undeniably the most pleasing views of that scenery. And one more point: they have not changed through the times.

The homes of village paupers have not changed much either. Such houses are built according to peasant standards of local materials and to a strict pattern based on needs but without any hygiene and comforts. These are missing from such houses to an extent that most of them tend to be wretched, overcrowded, damp and stuffy homes which are cold in winter and stifling cool in summer, where to live amounts to getting ill. Once again the social problem is not why they do not build better houses but poverty which means the total lack of better building materials. It is not the architecture of the house and the taste of its inhabitants which cause the problem (most often a very healthy taste has been retained). The homes of village paupers are inadequate because of abject poverty.

In spite of its variety, rural homes have a common feature which has developed owing to the proximity of nature. Every rural home is surrounded by nature. This means both the benefits of nature (sunshine, fresh air, a garden around the house) and the adversities caused by nature (mud, wind, cold and rain) which are further aggravated for lack of a protective shield offered by civilization. Villagers are directly affected by both the beneficial and harmful effects of nature. Moreover, the influence of nature varies as a function of social stratification. Clothing, too, in rural society reveals a lot of the actual social processes.

According to the peasant order of old the basic form of attire had been determined by peasant work, and it was on this basic form of boots and wide skirts that trimmings and ornaments were put according to popular traditions. A great variety of national costumes has developed in the various regions of the country, yet the basic form has remained the same everywhere. And it is a general custom, too, that village peasants did not wear many kinds of dresses—they usually wore only holiday attire and working-clothes. Holiday clothing could have been rather ornamental but working-clothes, "fatigues" were always simple. Moreover it used to be a binding rule that as soon as the holiday attire became worn-out it was used as working-clothes.

The transformation of rural society has considerably changed this strict and practical custom. At most places working-clothes have by and large retained their traditional peasant character, the holiday attire, however has been adjusted to bourgeois patterns: it consists of suits with neckties, boots are abandoned, whereas the attire of women is a one-piece dress with a tighter skirt. In many villages transformation has reached a point when ex-peasants actually wear bourgeois dresses, though not always with the best taste.

A peculiar rural phenomenon is insistence on the return to the national costume. Though villagers sincerely would like to get rid of national costume, considering it a public stigma of their peasant condition, official propaganda—intending to strengthen Hungarian character by re-establishing the national costume—proved to be so strong that at some places national dress is worn again. The case of the people of Mezőkövesd has become the most famous. But even here it happened that for persons turning up in national costume free entry was granted to dance parties; as a result, young men carried their ornamented aprons under their arms and put them on only in the doorway. And when the national costume came into vogue again, a group of young Mezőkövesd men suddenly declared "No fuss!" and have been wearing pullovers and cloth caps ever since.

It is exactly these two pieces of clothing which are characteristic of the progress of embourgeoisement in villages: the pullover and the cloth cap and in addition to these, the yellow shoes. Such attire is worn even by the more proletarian strata of the village paupers and it has gradually become a uniform with villagers aspiring to embourgeoisement but still remaining proletarians. This attire is a city form disguising rural misery.

Rural upper middle class and bourgeois attire is not without significance either. The forms are the same as in the towns but the clothing itself is much more ostentatious and well-pressed than in towns. Rejecting the idea that a less elegant attire "is good enough for the village" such villagers painstakingly concentrate on their outward appearance and want to be by all means distinguishable from other rural social strata. Too much attention paid to outward appearance is characteristic of the whole of Hungarian society, and this is obviously a manifestation of internal insecurity. The above statement is particularly true of rural society. It is only the truly grand seigneurs who occasionally dare to show up in well-worn or disorderly clothes, whereas anybody whose privileged social status could be challenged takes much care to look like a gentleman. And as everybody is afraid of being spoken about, everybody takes pains over his proper clothing.

Under such conditions, rural life is not unambiguously favourable for health. On the one hand, we find the beneficial effects of being close to nature (sunshine, fresh air and the strict rules of rural life demanded by hard work) on the other, however, the adverse effects of nature make themselves felt as well (dust, mud, flies, etc. and also the harsh and even cruel ways of society). As a result, health conditions in villages are at least as bad as in towns. The incidence of illness is higher in villages and an emphasis on remaining healthy is less pronounced than in towns. Medical care is much less available in villages.

The traditional way of life of the peasantry to be found at many places is rather indurative and does not pay much attention to illnesses. According to the ancient law, the ingenious ones stay alive while for poor wretches there is no place in this world anyway. Illness was regarded therefore definitely as a burden by healthy peasants who did not make great efforts at healing the sick. Naturally transformation has brought about momentous changes in this respect, too. Life has become more hygienic, illness has become a greater concern. Both in villages where people became embourgeoised and in settlements which are branded "corrupt" because of their one-child family habits illness has become a serious matter and the healthy ones do their utmost to cure the sick ones, particularly if these are children. (As a matter of fact, it was in particular children who were neglected by the old peasant order because of a high fertility.) Public health policy—which was initially looked upon with distrust but has recently been increasingly accepted—contributed a lot to rendering life more hygienic and to the medical care of the sick.

In the case of village paupers, in addition to peasant traditions, the hazards of life are increased and the efficiency of medication is decreased by incompetence. Though rural health care is mainly concentrating on them, no radical improvement can be achieved with the sole exception of reducing infant mortality. Actually the main reason of their illnesses is not the lack of medicine and the insufficiency of health care but their destructive way of life. For village paupers health policy is identical with social policy and economic policy, i.e. the health of this stratum can only be improved by a positive change in social policy and the economy. Otherwise, only their most recognizable suffering can be alleviated.

148

Rural life is extremely favourable for health just because of the proximity to nature. This is indicated by the fact that village squires, bourgeois and well-to-do farmers are much healthier; among them the incidence of disease is much lower than among any social strata of the villages or towns. The reason is obvious. Well-to-do rural strata may enjoy the benefits of both nature and society without being exposed to harms. Those benefits prove to be advantageous to health.

Rural way of life as depicted above is the everyday and shady aspect of life in the villages. Villages, however, have also a more serene and sunny aspect reflected by the feasts and holidays. Holidays are much greater events here than in cities. On holidays the whole village gets transformed and heaves a sigh of relief. For a single day it becomes what it would like to be. Thus, if the calendar is the law of life of the village in the sense that it is the seasons which determine the pace of life, it is also a law in the sense that it is controlled by the red-letter days of the calendar.

In the traditional peasant village festive rural life did not transgress the limits of the peasant way of life either, it only took on a more cheerful appearance. It was on holidays that peasant art manifested itself in its most manifold forms. That was the only leisure time, the only occasion when tasty dishes were served, and the rural youth got an opportunity to amuse themselves, to play; young and old alike had a good time within the bounds of the strict peasant laws.

In the village of today, however, Sundays are no longer such peasant holidays. The longings and ideals of the village have gone beyond the bounds of the village, and on Sundays villagers try to move in the world as if that other world were already a reality. On Sundays the village takes on a rather bourgeois character the only exceptions being the villages of peasant regions which have remained more or less intact in their peasant nature. But these are a minority of all villages. On holidays everybody dons his most urban clothes and participates in entertainments of urban character, does various sports and, last but not least, everybody who has an opportunity goes to town. This is just the reverse of the city week-end which is a different phenomenon; it is an escape from the town in an urban style. In contrast, what villagers do is an escape from the village (which has retained its rural character) with urban illusions and urban desires.

THE INTELLECTUAL LIFE OF THE VILLAGE

The intellectual life of the feudal village had been divided between two spheres of culture. The owerwhelming part of intellectual life was a manifestation of the colourful and rich world of peasant culture representing manifestation of the colourful and rich world of peasant culture representing a closed circle in every village, whereas the rest of it belonged to the culture of the nobility extending over the whole country. There had been a sharp division-line between these two spheres of culture, nevertheless there also had been some sort of communication between them, though in a filtered and elaborate way. Both types of culture had organically, extensively and harmoniously developed, i.e. all members of the village had been integral parts of a fully developed intellectual life.

The culture of the nobility was not entirely rural but it enriched feudal tradition with the experiences and colours of rural life. In contrast, peasant culture was typically of a rural nature. Though from times immemorial peasants lived also beyond the bounds of villages, the true creative communities of peasant culture have always been the villages. Thus, in addition to the integrating community of the village and the peasantry, every village had its own specific cultural profile.

This was undoubtedly a deep culture but not a primitive rather a concentrated and mediocre one. It had yet another particular feature, too: not being independently the culture of intellectual life, it was the elaboration, including the most mature artificial forms, of spiritual manifestations associated with the various events of life and production. However, it was a full and complete culture. It was full and complete because it covered all the ranges of intellectual life and particularly because everybody was an equally creative contributor to this culture. The peasant culture of the village prolifically created mediocre works expressing, however, deeply felt collective experiences both in the spheres of learning and erudition as well as in the fields of the arts and religious life. Though this culture certainly had some known or unknown initiators and promoters, actually all the members of the community contributed to this culture. In comparison with contemporary villages, where even the traces of such an influential culture have vanished, this general cultural life was remarkable.

With the transformation of the peasantry peasant culture has begun to disintegrate. A few of its works are still to be found in most of the villages but living together with this culture has ceased to be of the same nature as it used to be. Peasant works of art are considered today only more or less dull objects of tradition and not elements of a buoyant cultural life. The transformation of the peasantry was not directed against this colourful and rich culture, it was rather the consequence of the patient rejection of the prevailing social conditions. In vain were the creations of this culture beautiful if the social conditions which gave birth to them have become intolerable and, consequently, the rejection of the peasant circumstances of life was bound to result in destroying the works of art of the peasantry.

The creations of this folk culture have perished and no new works of art have been created instead of them; rural society has become the follower and consumer of urban culture. And since embourgeoisement has to a great extent demolished the structure of the culture of the nobility as well, the creativity of the cultural life of the villages has ceased to exist. Villages have come under the influence of urban culture. No single stratum of the village population is an exception to this. However, there is still a difference: various social strata have been influenced by urban culture to differing degrees. Inhibited by the memories of the traditional peasant culture, the peasantry has accepted the most easily accessible lowest level of urban culture, while the members of the village upper middle class have adopted the higher level of urban culture with qualifications and contradictions. The rural bourgeoisie has unconditionally accepted urban culture.

The transformation of rural intellectual life has not been fully completed yet. However, its debasement and disintegration are complete. In addition to the historic cause, i.e. that two organically developed cultures creating harmonious works have perished in the villages, disintegration and debasement were increased by the fact that the Hungarian village had come under the influence of an urban culture which is alien to the village not only in its urban qualities, but in its popular character as well. A culture removed from its historical traditions and of a diluted Hungarian character has developed in our towns. This culture has entirely lost not only its rural but its historical and Hungarian roots as well. This is true as regards at least the majority of the towns and the flourishing cities. This culture is the product of the town and for this very reason is very much alien to the rural world. In addition, this culture has become considerably estranged from the Hungarians living in villages; it represents an entirely alien culture within rural society. Thus, even if the best of its works were to reach the village it would create only confusion and a cultural life full of contradictions. However, it is not these works but the most trashy mass products of urban culture which reach the village representing Hungarian and urban culture in the eyes of the villagers.

Under such circumstances, intellectual life in the villages presents a dismal picture of disintegration and confusion; it is unable to create harmonious forms of culture, moreover it does not receive such even second-hand versions. The intellectual life of the village cannot be regarded as a cultural life; the culture of the village drifts between absolute illiteracy and the wishy-washy creations of an alien culture. All efforts at education prove to be futile, since there is no ideal cultural level to be attained. It is possible to fully switch-over to the available sphere of urban culture but this means the repudiation of all rural, peasant and Hungarian folk experience. The other possibility is to break away entirely from the village or by relying on examples of the historical past of far-away regions to make efforts at creating a Hungarian culture going beyond the intellectual limits of both town and village. He who is unable to realize any of these two possibilities has no other chance but to live a life-style of barbarism and lost perspectives.

Considering the outstanding spheres of culture, one becomes fully aware of this desolate and distressing state of culture.

Intellectual confusion has the most dangerous, though not the most far-reaching, consequences in the field of learning and science. In this respect the only educated and informed stratum of the village is that of the

151

intellectuals. With but a very few exceptions all intellectuals living in villages are qualified and well-versed as regards expertise. The villages would never need better educated village doctors, priests, notaries and young teachers than the present ones. Yet, they do not find their place in the rural world, and villagers are also at a loss and uneasy with them. The reason for this is that the spirit of their knowledge is absolutely alien to villagers and they are unable to share the experience of the village or to transmit their knowledge to their fellow-villagers.

As regards the other strata of the villages, the knowledge of craftsmen is not adequate. The skill of the craftsmen consists in a mixture of local traditions and the results of an unsuccessful technical schooling furnishing them with the most elementary scientific knowledge but proving insufficient for using such knowledge independently and with good taste. Thus every rural tradesman knows something but only exceptionally is he capable of performing his work with good taste and well. The expert knowledge of farmers is even more inadequate. Farmers still remember the production traditions of peasant culture, but as a result of incessant instruction, they are so confused, that they do not rely even on what they have learned and try to learn from whatever source they can. And since they have no schools for elementary training in the natural sciences, they try hopelessly to acquire the elements of agricultural sciences which are very much different from an agricultural knowledge that should be applied under Hungarian circumstances. Thus, only those villages can boast of a higher agricultural expertise, where peasant knowledge has been successfully developed to a higher level, or a good teacher, sometimes a model farmer was able to influence his fellow-villagers by his example, or such development was furthered by adequate training. However, these are rare exceptions.

Concerning more general knowledge and learning, there is absolutely no difference between rural tradesmen and farmers and rural paupers. Their education is inadequate making it impossible to understand the world. These strata helplessly face the worlds of nature, society and intellectual knowledge feeling totally helpless. In vain have they learned at school, and in vain have they acquired some knowledge ever since. These strata are unable to relate their poor knowledge to their own lives, and finally they realize that all such efforts are hopeless. No matter how often popular lectures are given, there is no use in attending them. For villagers to know about Árpád, the leader of the ancient Hungarians or maritime navigation or perhaps the structure of atoms is of no use—these strata do not see what they could do with this kind of knowledge. Considering the traditions of the village, adult education does not make much sense, since any kind of learning is strictly connected with a given life cycle.

Partly because the inhibitions of villagers and partly because the nature of the body of knowledge, books, periodicals and newspapers are of not much help either. Rural people do not understand most of the books and periodicals, and even if they do understand them they cannot adopt knowledge thus obtained as they do not understand its relevance to their lives. In addition, the majority of newspapers is written in such a popularizing style that they prove to be too didactic even for villagers. So villagers are content to satisfy their curiosity by reading just the news. Every village has the library of its own: some people attend lectures, and in most settlements there are some "educated" peasants who know things like when Queen Maria Theresia had been born and how long the Persian emperors had reigned. However, village folk, as a whole, generally knows but little about the outside world.

In the realm of art and culture the situation in rural regions is absolutely hopeless. The majority of villagers have no such needs. Since they have got rid of the creations of peasant art, they feel neither need of nor the longing for such works of art. Life either means shapeless poverty or shapeless "affluence"—both of them representing a barbarous condition.

However, art does exist in the villages, as a matter of fact there exist too many kinds of it. The official leaders of the village feel themselves committed to a kind of Hungarian pseudo-folk and pseudo-national art and propagating and fostering such art they do everything in their power to spread the products of such art in the village. The village, of course, repudiates that sort of art feeling nothing in common with it. The mentality expressed by these works of art is alien both as regards its Hungarian origin and its social outlook. Thus we find statues in villages which villages do not regard as their own. There is a great number of folkish books in the village libraries which are read perhaps for their romanticism but are felt alien both in content and style; therefore villagers do not identify themselves with such books. Readers in villages unanimously seek books for a single reason: romance, since this offers some entertainment. Nevertheless they are uneasy about the message and the style of these books. The whole range of that intellectual realm remains incomprehensible to them, and as for their form of expression, they are felt to be perfectly strange even if official village education policy regards them to be genuinely Hungarian.

In the villages another trend of art is represented by debased urban works be they in the forms of chromotypes, books or plays. The only aspect from which they are able to shape the kinds of the villagers is their being interesting and romantic. Villagers need these "works of art" just for these reasons and for being entertained. They have no sense anymore to look for a feeling of solidarity and a possibility of identification in a work of art; they do not want to enjoy style. They desperately want to get excitement and entertainment from reading. Reading, amateur performances mean entertainment for them, and they display the cheap-quality prints hung on the wall with pride. All forms of music or singing are also fun. They are not "delights in art" as demanded by aesthetics but opportunities for escaping the harsh realities of life. The only quality that is expected from a work of art is that it be fun and a means of escape from reality. For this reason, films and the Hungarian popular tunes are the most favourite forms of entertainment. The fact that none of these forms of art are produced by peasants and peasants have nothing to do with the mentality or style of these genres does not matter since only excitement and means of escape are sought for.

The time has come when villagers simply cannot suffer the old peasant works. These works of art have reflected the peasants' own genuine experience and a real solidarity of the community, whereas in terms of language they have been genuine reflections of the Hungarian peasantry. All this has become insufferable because all what is needed is escape from the realities of life. For this reason, it is a vain effort to try to bring back the old peasant works of art. Villagers do not want them, and if ever they would want anything, that could be only a higher-quality art with which the collectivity would be able to identify itself. Such works are very rare and do not reach the villages, though if occasionally such a book finds its way to the villages it becomes extremely popular and people begin to look for others of its kind as well. Outstanding examples are Áron Tamási's hero *Ábel,* József Nyírő's protagonist *Bence Uz. Ábel* has become a beloved figure; wherever the book was read people identified the hero as a member of their families and he was spoken of as a relative. *Bence Uz,* however, has met with cold reception though Nyírő, too, is a good writer. However, he writes for the middle class, whereas Tamási is a writer of the people.

In spite of all what has been said in the above, the movement aimed at reviving peasant folk art seems to be indefatigable. The ensemble *Gyöngyösbokréta* tries to revive truly beautiful folk songs, dances, tunes, and it seems as if villagers were willing to accept them. Young people like to "perform" and make a show of themselves. This, however, is not a genuine revival but a kind of role-playing for the sake of entertainment and profits. Some young people do participate in folk art programmes but there are others who feel it degrading to take part in them. Thus, in vain is the art beautiful which this movement would like to revive. Such efforts are doomed to failure because they do not really revive peasant art, they are only a new form of role-playing.

Similarly, assistance given to especially talented rural persons is bound to fail. These peasant geniuses would have been outstanding naive poets or playwrights in the period of peasant art and could have initiated the creation of peasant works of art in their own communities. If they could get proper education, they could become renowned artists outside the rural world. Under present conditions, however, as natural peasant talents they are no longer the initiating artists of rural life and neither are they artists of a higher community because for lack of proper education they are unable to create art according to higher standards. These peasant geniuses are but pathetic figures of the disintegrating village and also deplorable victims of the pseudo-Hungarian cities.

III

THE HUNGARIAN PEASANTRY*

* The original is to be found in Ferenc Erdei's *Összegyűjtött Művei* (Collected Works), *A magyar társadalomról* (Studies on Hungarian Society), Akadémiai Kiadó, Budapest, 1980, pp. 113—121. The text presented here is part of a greater study entitled *Magyar paraszttársadalom* (The Society of Hungarian Peasants) which was first published in 1942.

THE SPECIFIC FACTORS OF THE DEVELOPMENT
OF HUNGARIAN PEASANTRY

All things considered, the emergence and social formation of the peasantry has taken place in Hungarian society in the same way as anywhere else in Europe. However, in all the phases of Hungarian social development there have been some specific elements. First of all it is significant that the formation of the peasantry began much later in Hungarian society than in the West. The nomadic society of aristocratic class structure had been still at its height even after the conquest and settlement in the 9th century, at a time when Western social development was well-advanced on the way of feudalism. As a consequence of this time-lag, the period of formation was shorter and as a result, the evolution of the peasant formation was more superficial, moreover the elements of the previous social structure did not dissolve totally.

A more significant specific Hungarian evolutionary factor of the development of the peasantry was the fact that Hungarian social development was in many respects a mere copying of Western evolution. Whereas in the Western societies social development began following the disintegration of the ancient forms with a totally new start and by taking autonomous forms, the Hungarians integrated themselves with a fully developed social order and shaped similar forms by means of adoption. As a result of this initiative social development, the feudal forms evolved less profusely and with less variety. At the same time, also some elements of the nomadic society, survived and/or remained in a somewhat transformed way. This doubly specific social development was reflected most clearly by the country-building activity of King St. Stephen. This outstanding king strove to build up a European social order for the Hungarians with the conviction and ideological determination of a Christian prince realizing his goal, however, in the style of a leader of nomadic horsemen. Copying foreign institutions, he built up a society based on the principle of centralization; the development of Hungarian society was just the opposite of that of the West. As a result of this society-building policy, the popular forces did not participate in the formation of the institutions of society and for the time being they were forced to retreat. For this reason, the Hungarians did not experience the formation of feudalism as deeply as the Western societies. And when following the weakening of royal power the self-formative forces of society, too, got a chance to assert themselves, the traditions of the clans which survived from the nomadic era, immediately gained ground.

As regards the formation of the peasantry, this specific development of society had the peculiar consequence that the estate of the peasantry was shaped not within the body of the Hungarian society but outside, so to speak under it. In a nomadic society the servants and the conquered people had not been members of the society; they were just subjugated elements of a society structured within itself; similarly in the society of noblemen the peasantry, developed like a sub-social world preserving the clan units and traditions. This peculiar relationship survived even at the time of the full development of feudalism and the organization of the counties of the nobility. The Hungarian nobility became not such a small leadership group as in the West but a broad, full-fledged society comprising all free people. As the heir to the free Hungarians of the time of the conquest who had lived in clans, the Hungarian nobility regarded itself as "the nation" and regarded the state and the whole of society as its own possession. In contrast, the peasantry as the social descendant of the captives of the period of conquest and of the subjugated people of this region maintained its peculiar sub-social status even when it merged with impoverished freemen to become the stratum of serfs.

Within feudal society the interrelationship of the nobility and the peasantry was somewhat like that of an elder and younger brother. Despite conflicting economic interests and different and mutually complementary economic roles, the noblemen of the feudal society have maintained a mutual and intimate, close relationship with their serfs; notwithstanding the system of subordination and superordination, their relationship had a lively human-popular touch, moreover cultural connections between the two strata were significant, too. As opposed to this trend, the relationship of the Hungarian peasantry to the Hungarian nobility could be characterized all through its history by a far more distant relationship than that of the elder and younger brother. Right at the stage of formation a considerable distance developed and in later periods this took the form of institutions which made their effect felt up to this time. The sub-society status of Hungarian serfs was institutionalized by two factors: the county of the nobility and the code of laws elaborated by Werbőczy. The first established—by means of the self-government of the nobility— an autonomous and absolutely powerful organization of the nobility which in all respects tied down the serfs below its own society, whereas the second succeeded in raising the legal status of the nation of the nobility as a whole above that of the serfs.

Another specific feature of Hungarian history was the fact that a relatively broad stratum of the agricultural population escaped the fate of full serfs though these people were not town-dwellers in the Western sense of the term. Those privileged regions which succeeded in upholding their clan freedom originating from the time of the Hungarian conquest, though individually they did not become members of the nobility, remained outside

158

the domination of the counties and thus also escaped the fate of the serfs. Such regions were the districts of the Jászkunság region and the area of the Székelys in Transylvania. Though in both of these privileged regions time and again the nobility succeeded in asserting its power, the Jászkuns and the Székely people never degenerated fully to the status of serfs. As a consequence of this privileged position, the Székelys and the Jászkuns have differed from the peasants of all other regions to this very date.

The peculiarities of the development process and the specific pattern of subordination and superordination of the centuries of serfdom could in themselves suffice to explain why the Hungarian peasantry became so to say petrified. Later, however, also other factors contributed to the survival of the social forms of the peasantry at a time when society was already structured in general according to other principles. It had been the result of backward industrialization, urbanization and in general the retarded bourgeois development in Hungary that the peasantry still existed in Hungarian society at a time when the Western societies as a whole assumed a bourgeois character. The backwardness in industrialization and urbanization, towns and industry could absorb only a fraction of the agricultural surplus population, while as a consequence of the underdevelopment of the bourgeois society the feudal social forms survived in a number of areas. As a matter of fact up to this very date the bourgeois elements of Hungarian society have proved unable to completely liquidate the feudal forms replacing them by overwhelmingly bourgeois structures.

In the history of the Hungarian peasantry the period of serfdom was longer than in the Western societies, and even in the period of free peasanthood we can speak of a feudal peasantry. This was caused by the Turkish wars, since after these wars the life of the whole Hungarian society had to be redeveloped belatedly. Following the era of Turkish occupation there began a new process of social development, and consequently the subsequent stages of development followed only later.

THE PLACE OF
PEASANTRY IN HUNGARIAN SOCIETY

The specific nature of the development of Hungarian society had two consequences. The nobility became over-developed and the peasantry became a too closed stratum.

The over-development of the nobility meant that as regards its number it became too numerous and on the other hand, internally it became over-organized. Similarly to Poland, Hungary, too, became the country of the nobility strong in numbers, and this resulted in the fact that in both of these societies this nobility incorporated all those elements which otherwise could have become a middle-class, that is, the nobility eliminated an

159

important condition of bourgeois development. At the same time, the nobility comprising broad strata and occupying several class positions has gained a much broader social basis than the social order of the narrowly defined upper-class nobility. This has been the other reason for its persistent survival. The over-development, i.e. the excessive growth of counties' power and as a result, the strengthening of the power of the nobility as well as the fact that Werbőczy's code of laws has become ingrained in society further enhanced the process of preservation. Where nobility is such an entrenched legal status and social form as in the counties and such a legal attitude as the nobility was imbued with by jurisprudence, the feudal forms of the nobility were bound to survive for a long time despite the various changes in the economy and constitutional regulations.

The fossilization of the peasantry was partly the consequence of the above position of the nobility, and partly of the specific inferior social position of the Hungarian peasantry. Since the nobility succeeded in establishing the social forms of feudalism broadly and securely, the peasantry necessarily had to sink down deeply within the structure of society and had to develop the social forms of this inferior position. At such depth and under such pressure it would be rather difficult to dissolve the fossilized forms even if they were exposed to a full liberating effect. And as it is well known, they were not exposed to such an effect in Hungarian society.

In general the bourgeois economic organization of Hungarian society has emerged. The technological framework of everyday life has been transformed and the intellectual atmosphere has changed, nevertheless, feudal forms have not been entirely eliminated. The peasantry still lives under feudal social conditions and the heir of the nobility, i.e. the gentlemanly upper middle class and landowning gentry have also preserved a lot of feudal traits. All this means that Hungarian society is not a homogeneous social unit which is homogeneously exposed to social forces but a bourgeois structure whose functioning is hampered by feudal forms first of all within the peasantry, but also within the ruling strata.

This specifically Hungarian pattern is rather an unusual formation since no similar structures can be found either to the East or to the West of the country. Polish society is the most similar to ours, particularly as regards the position of the peasantry; the Croatian situation is similar to ours in many respects but as regards other countries of Europe both near and far, the peasantry–if there still exists any peasantry–is integrated in the society as a whole in a different way.

In the West, both the development of feudalism and the bourgeois transformation had been complete: by now feudal forms have withered away or have entirely perished. Society as a whole, farmers included, has assumed a homogeneous bourgeois character and structure. In the West the former serfs have ceased to be peasants and have become agrarian bourgeois, petit bourgeois and workers occupying their social positions

160

according to the bourgeois class structure. There are still to be found some memories of their peasant past, e.g. apparel, etc., however these are no longer rigid forms of everyday life but mere symbols. If those employed in agriculture in such societies still experience certain backwardness and restrictions, these are not the consequences of the survival of the feudal forms but the results of the disadvantageous position of the village and agriculture within bourgeois society. This disadvantageous position has resulted in a certain inferiority and economic disadvantage for those active in agriculture. This, however, no longer reflects the crisis of the peasantry but is an inherent structural problem of bourgeois society.

The situation in the North differs somewhat from that in the West as there the elimination of the peasantry has not stopped at the liquidation of the feudal peasant forms but society as a whole has to a certain extent assumed an agrarian character. Thus, the peasantry has not only gained a bourgeois position but has become a significant factor and has succeeded in considerably shaping society to its own image. As a result, no disproportions between town and countryside, industry and agriculture have developed. This more balanced development has been furthered by two social and technological factors: co-operatives and farm settlements.

In the East, more precisely in the South-East, i.e. first and foremost on the Balkans yet another situation has developed. Here neither feudal development nor subsequent bourgeois evolution has been complete, in fact it has not reached even the level achieved by Hungarian society. Neither the upper middle class nor the peasantry has developed such manifold forms as West of the Balkans and thus in Hungary, too. As a result of the permanent instability of state power and Turkish dominance, the feudal formation of the leading strata could not be supported by state power, and therefore the backwardness of these societies must be regarded as natural. A significant factor of this development has been the differing role of the Eastern church from that of the Western church. Under such circumstances, in that part of Europe both the leading-ruling stratum and the working-subjugated population have got stuck at a more rudimentary stage of social formation and therefore, their social forms have not become as traditional as those in the Western world. For this reason, bourgeois evolution did not replace a fully developed feudal society, but a rather undeveloped structure was built on the foundation of economic and political factors. Thus the Balkan peasants, who had not been totally peasants in the cultural sense but had remained rather primitive and servant-like or free farmers, living in the mountains, had the following development prospects: they could easily become members of the bourgeois class; they could go on belonging to the stratum of primitive farmers (either living in the freedom of mountainous regions or in rural servitude) or they are just becoming peasants in the genuine sense of the word. Apart from the latter development prospect which is of minor importance, the life of these peasants is less

161

likely to be troubled by a specific peasant crisis. Among the peasants of the Balkans peasant fertility rates are still very high.

In the societies of the West and South-East having a calmer life, yet not exempt from agrarian and peasant crises, the life of the peasantry did not experience open stagnation. Indeed, these societies do not know the special problems posed by the serious crisis of the peasantry. Neither in the West nor on the Balkans have the state and social position of being a peasant become so pronounced. This has been the specific experience of doubtful value of primarily Hungarian and perhaps also of Polish societies.

IV

PEASANTS IN PRESENT-DAY
HUNGARIAN SOCIETY*

* The original is to be found in Ferenc Erdei's *Összegyűjtött művei* (Collected Works), *A magyar társadalomról* (Writings on Hungarian Society), Akadémiai Kiadó, Budapest, 1980, pp. 169—237. The text presented here is part of a greater study entitled *Magyar paraszttársadalom* (The Society of Hungarian Peasants) which was first published in 1942.

PEASANT HOLDERS

1. THE FEUDAL PEASANT AND THE MODERN FARMER

Hungarian society is in fact a bourgeois society in spite of the fact that its basic stratum is formed by a massive feudal block, the peasantry, and that very many feudal forms of the upper classes remained valid even in its upper stratum. As a consequence the structural principle of Hungarian society is fundamentally stratification by economic power and interests, and all of the other vestiges of the feudal system are but modifiers of this bourgeois structure. And since the peasantry itself is also deeply immersed in the crisis of transformation and its feudal forms have disintegrated in most of its strata, we can examine also the peasantry in terms of the stratification of the bourgeois society as the most massive component of present-day Hungarian society.

At the present phase of the transformation the situation of the peasantry in Hungarian society shows that its position and role already conform to the bourgeois criteria, yet it still fills this position partly under peasant forms. For this very reason, we can no longer speak of a homogeneous peasant mass, but must find the class stratification of the peasantry in the bourgeois sense adding that a part, indeed, in a sense the whole of the peasantry still retains feudal-peasant forms in its bourgeois, petit bourgeois or working-class class positions. The peasantry is therefore neither an order of society, nor a class, but a conglomerate of regular bourgeois class stratification coupled with common feudal-peasant social forms.

Even when the peasantry was synonymous with the order of serfs only its feudal social forms were common, while it was rather broadly stratified in terms of its concrete economic situation. Nevertheless, the difference between the past and the present state is essential. In the past the peasantry occupied an unambiguously feudal position in the great structure of society; therefore the members of this feudal order, no matter under what economic conditions they lived, were held together not only by the common social form, but by a genuine village community and a jointly shared social structure. Today, however, only the traditional feudal background of the peasant holder and the peasant worker is common; otherwise the peasant holder and the worker belong to social strata of differing interests and in reality their relation is no longer an intimate community, but it is characterized by conflict.

Thus the feudal peasant and the modern holder completely differ in terms of their social position; they also have completely different attitudes to the lower strata of the peasantry independent of the fact how much they still retain peasant forms. The feudal peasant is also a farmer, who is in command of a farm and of those, who work there, but his social position and attitude do not embody a self-validated power and supremacy based on an objective economic position, but a role living on in the traditions of a small community and defined in interpersonal relations. Just because he was a farmer, the feudal peasant was not an independent and self-supporting member of bourgeois society but a person who in the social intercourse with the landlord, the members of his family and his workers had to act and behave according to traditional forms. In contrast, the village farmer is not just acting according to a role, but he is the master of an estate, which objectively ensures a free position to him, which he fills as he pleases freely choosing the examples to be followed. In present-day society each peasant farmer has this objectively guaranteed position of a free farmer. However, not all peasant farmers are the same; some still follow traditional peasant forms, while the village farmer of bourgeois mentality follows the dictate of his interests without scruples.

The change in the role of farmers also transformed the relationship between the farmer and the working peasant. The feudal peasant was bound in the feudal age not only by the rules of the village community, for his role as smallholder also meant his automatic selection for institutional leadership. Thus in certain fields an unqualified leadership role was accorded to the smallholders within the autonomy of the peasant society, and generally they controlled the development of the village communities and every member of the community followed them. The modern farmer no longer enjoys such an institutionally guaranteed role as a leader. The owner of the land enjoys the prestige due to him according to the bourgeois set of values, but this prestige does not necessarily give rise to leadership. The modern farmer can be unconditional leader in his own farm due to his rights as an employer, yet he can set an example for society only if he gains the respect of others by his special achievements.

The situation has also changed in other respects. In feudalism the whole village was a uniform field of social action in each part being exposed to outside influence to the same extent; for this reason the village had a homogeneous culture. And the feudal peasant was just as much part of this homogeneous social circle as the last cotter living on the fringe of the village, save that he enjoyed certain primacy or a leading role. Today even the smallest villages are not uniform fields of social action; this applies even less to agricultural towns surrounded by homesteads. Village society is now divided into special sections even within the peasantry; consequently in the various sections different effects assert themselves and differing cultures take shape. Thus the culture of the well-to-do farmer and the peasant labourer is no longer identical today even if both of these strata still live

166

amongst the old peasant forms. These two strata have completely different social worlds affected by completely different influences.

However, the transformation left one aspect intact: just as in the old society, the independent farmer is a leading and character-lending member of also the new society. This is the very reason why the disintegration of the peasantry's social forms is indicated to the greatest degree by the independent farmers; this is also the stratum which shows the most clearly the extent to which the feudal peasant forms have come into irreconcilable contradiction with real life. Therefore our inquiry will classify those who owing to their bourgeois position must be regarded as independent peasants necessarily relying on hired labour because of the size of their land by the extent of their peasant or bourgeois ways, while the other strata of the peasantry will be examined according to their position in bourgeois society and in terms of their currently valid social forms.

2. FEUDAL PEASANTS

In regions of the country, where the transformation lagged we could summarily characterize the peasantry by saying that they are still peasants. This means that in spite of their changed social environment and changed mode of life they still did not break loose from the peasant forms of the feudal age; thus even if they are strata of bourgeois society they continue living as if they were serfs.

Such feudal peasant societies exist today only in the Land of the Palóc, on either sides of the Upper Tisza, in some isolated districts of Transdanubia and in Transylvania, and even there only in small and medium-sized villages. In many respects the societies in these villages are even today village communities similar to those prevailing in the feudalism although their external and internal life circumstances have radically changed. No matter how weak the transport links of such villages are, the influence of a changed world still reaches them and if nothing else but their economic relations have completely changed. If, in spite of that, the traditional peasant forms survived this must be a manifestation of obvious contradictions. For this very reason, this peasantry is no longer the balanced peasantry of the feudal age living a secure though hard life; the external life circumstances should not lead us astray. Some of these communities show signs of some peculiar decadence: they turned to a system of having only one child in a family and are tired, while others incessantly try to turn against the obligatory force of their traditions and to break loose from it. The way they look today, these villages do not at all represent a stable and an established structure but rather a phase of an increasingly accelerating process of transformation. Each of these villages is on the way of either perverting their peasant traditions (as in the villages where a system of having only one

167

child in the family prevails) or starting to develop alongside bourgeois lines in the same way as the more developed villages did. Both the above-described types of villages will soon catch up with those which outpaced them.

The development problems and the sharp contradictions of these conservative peasant societies are to the greatest degree manifested by the representative leading stratum, the independent farmers. The feudal-peasant farmer is the most obviously anachronistic figure of Hungarian society.

His economic situation is unquestionably bourgeois. He is the master of a big, sometimes vast capital, controlling an inherited farm and the labour of two or three families. No matter how backward the village is or how far it lies from the transport network, it still has some access to the market, and the life circumstances of the farmer force him to produce as much as possible for the market. In spite of this situation the economic activity of this type of peasant still retains its purely feudal-peasant character. What production he does is no planned production, but a many-sided one partly determined by the needs of the household and partly by traditions. Thus the farm of that peasant cannot become specialized in any direction. The farmer has a vineyard, some grazing land, produces wheat, maize and fodder, even some vegetables; he keeps all sorts of animals, sometimes a lot of each kind, but the production of none of them becomes his speciality; the farmer manages this complex production unit with the traditional peasant method instinctively doing in each branch what is usual at the appropriate time. With such agricultural methods there is not much to be taken to the market; it may easily happen that the peasant runs into debts and the land has to be mortgaged. In any case, the farmer often faces difficulties. The extremely high proportion of indebtedness is to a great extent to be attributed to the traditional farming methods of these peasant estates. Indebtedness is a necessary consequence of the contradiction of this form of farm management. Such a livelihood is of bourgeois character, that is taxes have to be paid and expenses (such as the cost of hired labour and fixed assets) have to be covered just as in any company. In contrast, the production of the farm is of a feudal-peasant character; thus it is natural that the holding cannot always produce sufficient money income. The disproportion is even more conspicuous, because these peasant farmers work just as much with the whole of their family as if they were not owners; even the family's consumption is entirely on the same level as that of other peasants, thus it hardly exceeds the workers' consumption level. In spite of all of the paralyzing contradictions, some of these feudal-peasant farms prosper. However, that prosperity is never the result of production, but it always has some other cause. Such a cause may be that the otherwise pitifully small quantities that are being produced enjoy a boom on the market—like the wheat boom of the post-war years—or the family of the peasant works inordinately much in order to save the cost of labour, or they cut back on consumption as much as possible. In this case the family of the farmer

168

suffers just as much as the hired hands. This is why agricultural workers say in many districts that they "would rather serve the Jew for his renown than the peasant for his wages". This saying is true; the consumption of the landholder peasants is often of a pitifully low standard.

There is one point, where the feudal peasant adjusted to his bourgeois position; he possesses his land with immeasurably strong conscience. The myth of the land, sticking to the land is the feature of this peasant type. He became the exclusive owner of land only three or four generations before, but that time was sufficient for developing a profound consciousness of being the owner of land. Yet this consciousness of ownership is not the same as the pride of the feudal lord or the capitalist bourgeois in the possession of land. This manifests itself in a completely irrational peasant attitude. It is not expressed in the realization that he can use his freehold land now as his pleasures and interests dictate; he can produce the way he wishes or he can exploit the possibility of letting the land and living on its rent. This attitude does not even urge him to build something, some outstanding culture or a homestead, or a forest, a fruit plantation on the land; this consciousness of ownership exhausts itself simply in making the farmer move in the world with the haughty, lordly attitude of the landed farmer. In reality the estate yields no positive advantages to him. He does not live better and does not work less than he would if he had less land, or if he were only a tenant; he does not undertake creative tasks with his land or some individual performances that would satisfy his ambitions; he does not avail himself of the bourgeois advantage of the possession of land that he could live on its rent, he simply enjoys the fact that the land is his possession. A worker may live much better, a tenant may produce far more efficiently, yet the landed farmer considers himself superior to them just because he has land. It seems as if the possession of land were the only thing the farmer needed as the consummation of his peasant desires; this is a possession without interference and supervision implying a complete control over crops.

This entirely peasant attitude to the land made the peasant way of life of the feudal peasants even fuller in fact, instead of destroying it. This is just the same life bound by its own forms as it was in the feudal age. Every movement is determined by the same traditional forms, and the reason for these forms is now also that this is an independent, land-bound world, but now the absolute and exclusive possession gives these traditional forms and objective basis. Thus it is no longer the villainage relation that preserves the common validity of the laws of peasant life, but the freehold land. The absolute contradiction of the situation is obvious. Feudal-peasant social forms are being supported by a bourgeois estate. It is invariably just a question of time when the farmer realizes that his land enables him not only to live on it in the security of his peasant life—indeed, it is often not suitable for that—but also to pursue some ambitious and profit-aimed bourgeois production there, or to let it and live on rent not on the peasant standard but in bourgeois comfort. The younger generation is already making progress in this way. Part of them, who have bourgeois ambitions want to produce more, better and newer products on the family estate, while others, who simply want to live better and more easily, would gladly let the land and escape the peasant labour and peasant life. Their elders, sincere guardians of traditions, are still preventing this process, but there will be nothing to check it once they die.

3. PEASANTS OF NOBLE DESCENT

In the feudal age a lot of members of the lesser nobility also lived on land held in villeinage farming as the villeins did. The noble standing of these "single-block", "armaliste" (patent-holder) "squireens" was unquestioned under the principle of *"una eademque nobilitas"* (one and the same nobility), but their actual social situation was still not identical with that enjoyed by the feudal landlords. It differed partly because most of them farmed their small holding just like the peasants did, or even lived as cotters, partly because even though their political privileges were valid, their political role has always been inferior. In spite of all that they still were not common peasants.

The essence of the peasant existence is the very fact that it fills the lower regions of a social structure, and separated from the upper layers it filled that with forms developed by itself. Thus the peasant has no right as owner of the land in feudal society, neither has he any right of assembly and voting in the bodies of the nobles; in other words, he is separated from the nobles by sharp and decisive forms. People of noble descent are always independent members of society, while the peasants are always inferior. And this difference asserts itself in definitely differing forms even in the less significant aspects of everyday life. Thus when a member of the lower nobility farmed an ordinary peasant estate, or even if he worked for a peasant holder, he was still always distinguished from the peasants by his social rank. The man of noble descent was always an honourable gentleman even when he was herding the swines of peasants or dug the soil; he always expected to be greeted first by the peasants and regarded his descent as some magic attribute that ensured him privileges. The peasant work he pursued was but a class situation for him, that is a consequence of concrete situation, which, however, was always believed to be provisional. In contrast, his nobility was a more general and abstract social status that, in principle could be restored to its old glory at any time. Thus if he could afford to educate his children or if he could get a scholarship for them in some college his sons could become the district administrators or even sub-prefects of their county, which was an almost impossible career for the peasants. Thus even though the actual life of these farmers of noble descent conformed with that of the peasants, that fact did not do away with their descent; therefore in terms of social forms the peasants of noble descent were by no means equal to peasants.

In spite all of the similarities of their lives, the feudal, thus the objective social differences of the peasant farmers and the peasants of noble descent are therefore not only a distinction in principle but an actual social reality asserted all the time and under all circumstances with sharp divisions. Where farming nobles lived in the village community of serfs the different feudal status meant personal privilege for the farmer of noble descent. Thus if his land was the remnant of a noble estate, then he was his own landlord, and owed no villein socage to anyone, and even if he farmed a villein's land or had no land at all, he was not a subject of the manorial court; his affairs did not belong to the authority of the village mayor, he could attend the county assembly and enjoyed privileges in his dealings with peasants. Therefore he was always exempt from subjection to an alien power, while the situation of the peasants was precisely determined by such subjection. And where a whole village was such a settlement of lesser nobles—like Bori in the Garam Valley district, Nemeskide in Transylvania, or Aporka in County Pest by the river Danube—the farming lesser nobles did not live by personal privileges but in an independent noble social world. Having the same technical conditions as the peasant villages, these villages of the nobles developed completely different communities and social systems. Seemingly these nobles worked and communicated amongst each other as peasants, yet the rules of social intercourse completely differed from those of the peasants. This community did not exist below society but lived in it, and the individuals, who formed the community were not people of inferior rank but free and independent persons. For this reason this society did not develop the forms of some inferior social role characterized by being at the service of others, but the general framework of a free life valid in itself. First of all the attitude to work was entirely different in the noble villages. These people worked too, but not under the compulsion of an incessantly pressing moral obligation to work, but as they needed to; if it was necessary they worked harder than the peasants; when it was possible much less, or nothing at all. But they differed from the peasants mainly in that their whole life was not under the pressure of labour and production all the time. Their home was a mansion even when it was the same thatched and mud-walled house that the peasants had, because they had separately functioning rooms. Their meals were not just snacks eaten during the breaks of work but separate and separately lived acts of life. The peasants did not understand the way of life the peasants of noble descent lived; they regarded these nobles as showing off, even if they only lived under different forms and more freely and not better than the peasants.

The differences between farmers of noble descent and of peasant origin have faded a lot by the present phase of development. Those two strata became free people of identical rights and live in the same transformed society, yet very many of the vestiges of their differing past survived. The people of Kide, for instance, wear long boots, riding-breeches, and hats decorated with wild boar bristles, the customary outfit of the gentry, while the progressive or quasi progressive peasants of the district wear ordinary suits, and while the entertainment of the one-time serf villages is the cinema and the billiards, the inhabitants of Kide go hunting and race horses. The difference is even more conspicuous in the case of Bori. The villages of the Garam Valley are populated by one-child, tired peasants with a disintegrating way of life amongst increasingly bourgeois forms and turning against their peasant past with some irrational frippery and high living. Bori, right next to them is a viable and developing village, with a population of noble descent, which works hard even today, lives a disciplined and moderate life. Birth rates have not declined. The sons of the village go to occupations but they also become farmers all over the whole district. It seems therefore that traditions enabled the free and independent inhabitants of Bori to develop and increase in numbers, while the peasantry of the environs tried to discard its magnificent peasant traditions thereby starting on the way of slow destruction.

The case of the *Székelys* is different again. During the Middle Ages the *Székelys* managed to preserve their freedom as nobles relatively intact. Accordingly, their settlements were village communities of nobles with complete independence and noble forms appropriate to that. Later, however, the *Székelys*' privileges were increasingly eroded; by the dawn of the era of bourgeois development the *Székelys* became hardly distinguishable from the peasants. They never became completely and unreservedly peasants, and the traces of their more-or-less noble past are still evident in their present life circumstances. The *Székely* farmer never became a peasant in the sense of getting stuck to his land and developing a strict, closed and shackling system of forms to fill that destitute role. The *Székelys* have always preserved the freedom of movement, enterprise and social mobility; in their village communities they lived a life of coexistence in the noble style instead of following the life-style of oppressed village folk. The consequence of this half-peasant past is that the *Székely* people are even today much more freely moving and enterprising; in spite of that, they still preserve their traditions far more than the peasants. They can do that because their traditions are not so much peasant traditions not capable of following the developing life circumstances and the changing requirements.

The people of the *Jászkun* district and the *Hajdús* were also distinguished by privileges, but since they mostly lived in large town communities, they deviated from the common peasant forms not like the nobles but in a way the bourgeoisie was different from the peasants.

172

4. MIDDLE-CLASS PEASANTS

Where the bourgeois transformation penetrated society most deeply, thus in the North-Western and the Central Plains, the holders were the first to break the validity of the peasant forms and to try to fill their bourgeois status with bourgeois forms. For this very reason, by now the peasant holders of these regions have hardly anything in common with the feudal peasants. They are much more agrarian citizens than the peasants tied to their peasant holding.

Their farming is no longer the traditional peasant farming; it is rather an agricultural enterprise specialized as much as possible to suit market demand. These farms represent every variety of specialized agricultural production. Fodder and animal production as well as the production of sugar-beet and barley are highly developed in the North-Western plain. The middle-class peasant farms pursue these lines of production there with particular zeal and with continuously developing expertise, which enables them to market yields far exceeding in value the peasant production. There from among the small holdings dairy farming is also the most advanced owing to the expertise in the selection of breeds, registration of the herds, the proper stabling of the stock and a highly developed fodder production. Between the Danube and the Tisza vegetable and fruit production became similarly specialized. The standard of expertise, the botanical and general farming knowledge of these holders far exceeds that evidenced by the peasants, thus each fruit and vegetable garden and vineyard is rather a specialized agrarian enterprise than a peasant farm. There are wheat, poultry and horse breeding farms in the region east of the River Tisza producing similarly developed mass-products.

The production of middle-class peasant holders specialized not only by the district, but by special enterprises sprung up also individually completely in the spirit of bourgeois economic life. Farmers are getting into mechanization everywhere. They operate threshers, clover-shelling machines, grist-mills, and hire these out to farmers, who do not yet have such machines. There are also pig-raising farms. They produce pigs either parallel with general open-field farming or without that, and often couple their activity with dealing. Elsewhere specialized animal breeders spring up. They breed animals with particular expertise and care and let the best of their own breed serve the animals of other farmers. Besides or instead of working their own land, many farmers lease major holdings and follow completely capitalistic production there. Yet another variety is the capitalist farmer, who lends money or produce to those needing it and charges interest, thus engaging in banking activities.

Thus the varieties in which these farmers utilize their land once they break loose from the traditions of peasant farming are almost endless. Land is no longer the basis that provides these peasants' security, but capital, which they use according to the principles of capitalist management. And these farmers do that not only by developing special branches of production thereby trying to increase their profits, but by also converting the land, or the profits of the land into some other kind of capital. There are many wheeler-dealers amongst them. They buy cattle, horses and pigs on the markets of the neighbourhood and keep them for a while to get them into better shape; somewhat later they try to sell these animals with some profit.

The letting of land assumed huge proportions in the past decade. The major part of the larger peasant holdings are let in the towns of the Plains with extensive farming districts, which means that the owner broke loose from the troubles of production and now he enjoys only the rent of his land. Such owners then prefer living in the town; some work a little in their garden, in the vineyard, others deal in animals or produce, and quite a few take a job in the office of some association, church, cooperative or interest-representation body. Still others do not engage in anything, but live an idle life from the profits of their capital. In villages close to the capital city a new custom spread a few years ago; the farmers sell their land and buy apartment houses in the vicinity of the capital and live like landlords since the apartments are rented to others. It is rather characteristic of social change that these people are not condemned; instead they are looked upon with respect and envy because these landlords are capable of understanding the new trends of the age.

In terms of economic behaviour these farmers have completely turned bourgeois. They no longer respect the old peasant tradition that one should farm the land according to customary forms. They use the land as capital and they utilize it in a way to get the maximum of profits. Even if they keep the agrarian enterprise, they no longer work as a peasant should according to peasant rules. They have all works done by labourers and manage the farms as the overseers and stewards used to do. Owing to the fact that the owner does not have to live on the farmstead, the system of homestead farming is particularly suitable for this sort of bourgeois farm management. The middle-class farmer may run a respectable house in the town and he may go out to the homestead to see how things are getting on once a week or, if necessary, more often.

Their consumption is no longer limited by peasant customs either. They are trying to live well in the bourgeois sense, sometimes at a too high standard. They often keep a virtually open house, where they offer such an abundance of food and drinks that exceeds the ordinary bourgeois standards. Their whole way of life lost the limitations of peasant traditions also. Their home, their attire follow the bourgeois style completely; there are only a few traces around them telling that they are still rather beginners of this life style.

Their social life and their external circumstances have lost not only their peasant character, but they themselves also try to avoid the peasant forms consciously. Thus they socialize only amongst each other and with bourgeois and gentry strata; they treat workers in a gentlemanly way and insist upon all possible titles; they christen their children to nice, noble-sounding names instead of the old peasant names; they avoid every turn in their speech that might have a peasant "smell", indeed, they even make a special effort to get rid of their provincial dialect. Finally, they encourage their children to choose other than agricultural occupations having a higher prestige in society.

The middle-class farmers of the North-West (the transformation in that region is more balanced) differ from those of the Great Plains mainly in that they show the liberation from the peasant forms rather in the capitalist development of agricultural production, than in a bourgeois way of life. One of the reasons for this difference is that the smaller size and closer society of the North-Western villages do not provide as much opportunity for a bourgeois life-style as the urban societies and the homestead system of the towns of the Great Plains. In addition to that, the difference in their historic past also has a decisive influence. In the privileged towns of the Great Plains the development of bourgeois mentality has been going on since the end of Turkish rule and the forms of the old burgher-peasant society had already laid the foundation of the development trend that occurred later.

SMALLHOLDERS

1. THE SMALL PEASANT AND THE PETIT BOURGEOIS

The medium-stratum of the bourgeois society, the petit bourgeois making a living from small-scale enterprise or from some qualified employment is the medium stratum of a social structure only owing to the actual power relations of society. As far as its aspirations are concerned, it lives in the same world where the upper stratum lives, and as soon as its economic power changes it immediately rises or sinks to the appropriate level in respect of its actual living standard. Contrary to this, the small peasants of the feudal society, those who lived on a small plot of land or were cotters tending the vegetable garden did not form the middle of society as a whole, only the middle of the sub-society of peasants. Thus the movement of their course could not go beyond the limits of the peasant world; this stratum's ideals and ambitions go only as far as the upper stratum of the peasants, the peasant holders. The small peasant wants to become a peasant holder, and even if his desire is unfulfilled he lives in the same world as the peasant holder, the only difference being that he lacks the security and prestige of the larger holding. The difference in the living standards of the small peasant and the middle-class peasant is not even as great as that between the petit bourgeois and the middle classes. Every peasant is bound by the same system of forms and peasant morals force each peasant stratum equally to constant work, frugal consumption and to the subordination of the entire life to production.

In present-day Hungarian society the situation of the small peasant became complicated. His economic position conforms with that of the petite bourgeoisie: the economic foundations of his life may be the following: his small or dwarf holding, where he farms independently, a vegetable garden on his own or on a leased land, some petty leashold or small enterprise outside agriculture or a job as some minor executive for a large estate. In contrast, the social world in which he lives, that is the village, the agricultural town, or the large estate do not present a uniform environment. A structure based on bourgeois principles dominates the agrarian towns and the villages of middle class peasantry; backward villages are dominated by a peasant community, whereas the large estates are subject to the rule of their own world.

The petit bourgeois economic position of the small peasants is not in as

176

sharp a contradiction with the peasant social forms as the bourgeois position of the middle-class peasant holder. Capital itself cannot ensure such a degree of bourgeois affluence on a small holding, some leasehold land or a few acres of vegetable garden that the small peasant would consider the peasant laws, that bind him to the land and force him to work as a distressing burden. Indeed, the only way the small peasant may get along in life and make both ends meet is the type of work ethic that is demanded by peasant rules. On the other hand, precisely because of the smallness of his land, the peasant production traditions can no longer ensure progress to such producers in the system of market competition. Thus he has to learn more advanced production technologies, and no matter how alien such activities are to peasant traditions, he has to experiment with new production methods. Owing to the contradictions of being a small peasant, part of this stratum — most of all peasants having a few acres in the feudal-peasant type villages — are more conservative socially sticking much more to peasant forms, than the middle-class farmers, while other small peasants — the leaseholders, share farmers and gardeners — for example town-dwellers, or those who have assumed middle-class characteristics break the validity of peasant traditions at least in their productive work.

This contradictory economic situation determines the life of small peasants in accordance with the social environment. In an environment that has increasingly assumed bourgeois traits, thus in the towns and the more advanced villages of the Plains, this stratum of the peasantry became bourgeois to a great extent discarding peasant forms in the same way as the peasant holders, the leading peasant stratum of this process did. Thus, similar to middle-class peasants, these small peasants no longer live in a peasant autonomy, but have become participants of the bourgeois structure of the whole of society. These bourgeois small peasants and middle-class farmers embrace the same bourgeois values. In the backward peasant communities, however, the binding tendency of the economic position of small holders asserts itself more strongly resulting in a strong adherence to peasant forms. Since this stratum is poorer, it can much more easily conform to peasant laws resulting in a life with less tension. In their ideals the middle-class holders already pass the limits of feudal peasantry even if they actually still live as peasants. They are not yet followed on this course by smallholders who still adhere to peasant rules. The situation is different again at the big manors. The medium-ranking employees of big manors, the head-men of the manor, the overseers, machinists stand in the middle of a strictly feudal hierarchy separated by feudal restrictions downwards as well as upwards. They cannot possibly follow the upper-class ways of the owner and his executives; and in turn they cannot be examples for the labourers to be followed since — from the perspective of the lowest levels of the social hierarchy — their life style is rather gentlemanly. Under such circumstances the small peasants of big manors form an isolated and petrified intermediary stratum having semi-peasant forms; as a result, this stratum is unable to mediate interests between the upper-class world of the executives and the feudal peasant existence of the labourers.

Thus in their petit-bourgeois position small peasants live in a confused social role very much like the middle-class peasants who also experience confusion as regards their class positions. Small peasants are influenced by various factors owing to their economic situation, while their social environment also induces them to act in different ways. As a result, they also experience the crisis of peasantry; this is so even when the binding-force of tradition is still strong; small peasants try to escape their peasant lot to a degree which is allowed by circumstances.

2. SMALLHOLDERS

After World War I a new figure, the smallholder emerged on the social scene of Hungarian society. The concept suggested that smallholders were the modern successors of the villeins of yore, thus the long-awaited true representatives of the Hungarian people. As a social group, smallholders were capable of becoming a considerable political factor for a few years; this stratum still attracts the attention of economic policy. In social life smallholders often become the target of ridicule or they often figure as the embodiments of the romantic expectations and dreams of the people. This smallholder—with István Szabó Nagyatádi and Ferenc B. Tóth as proto-types with many minor figures around them—is different from the small peasants. The sole reason for being named smallholders is that—compared with the estates of others—the size of their holdings is really small. In reality smallholders were the uppermost stratum of the peasantry; they belonged to those holders, whose middle-class situation brought them into conflict with peasant forms; as a result, even in its name, this stratum rejects anything to do with the peasantry calling itself smallholder. And this leading stratum of smallholders forms a homogeneous social group only in terms of its economic and bourgeois character; otherwise, it represents the most heterogeneous strata of peasantry ranging from feudal and middle-class peasants to peasants with a feudal background.

Up till now, smallholders have never played such a historic role. They are an anonymous mass of landed peasantry, the most populous of the independent farmers; even compared with the whole of the peasantry, their numbers are very high. All the independent holders who have enough land for independent farming without ever working for others belong to this stratum. Smallholders rely on the work of their own farming and they use hired labour only occasionally. Leaseholders farming a piece of land larger than the size of a small holding, or just a plot to supplement their own dwarf holding also fall in this category.

The farms of this stratum follow peasant traditions to the greatest extent. The size of the holding is not large enough to move production out of its traditional organization; however, the land possessed by the smallholders is not so small either that it would encourage the profit motive. Most land possessed by smallholders has been inherited; the holdings' origins can be traced back to feudal times; thus the circumstances of ownership are always complicated. The separate possessions of the family members and the rights of usufruct, which are of the greatest importance in this stratum of the peasantry, have always rendered the farm's management uncertain; this is one of the reasons why the traditional peasant technologies of production have been preserved. Smallholders produce according to the traditions of the district; this means that part of the produce is taken to the market; production, however, is not rationally organized it rather needs a great effort. Most of what is produced is consumed by the family; this renders a specialized agricultural production based on market demand rather difficult.

The majority of these farms are operated from the villages, that is several parcels of land scattered around the village are managed from the farmyards of the village. This involves a waste of time and the transportation of crops and the fertilizers; thus the productivity of labour is necessarily low. The homestead farms of the Plains represent a higher standard. This is where one of the most advantageous forms of the system of homestead farms has developed; the homestead of the smallholder, where almost no hired labour is needed. All the able-bodied members of the family live on these homestead farms permanently, while the old generation lives in the township or the village. Thus farming is carried on on the homesteads and the family's labour force is at hand, while the home of the family is in the village or the agricultural town, and this ensures a direct contact with the urban life of the community as well as closer ties with the market. This is one of the reasons why agricultural specialization developed in many regions of the Plains. Poultry production, for instance, is mostly based on these homestead farms.

Together with his whole family the smallholder works long hours. He is forced to do this partly by his petit-bourgeois economic situation, partly by his peasant traditions. The smallholder must work hard to make both ends meet, but the peasant work ethic also plays its role. As a result, productive activity is carried on also beyond the subsistence level. And since every smallholder has some bourgeois ambitions either to amass more land or to build an easier, more civilized life for his family, he must work more than what his traditional livelihood would demand. The only instance, where this attitude to work ceases to dominate is where a strongly civilized environment began to dominate the life of the smallholders in spite of the economic situation. It is increasingly common in the townships of the Plains, and evident also in the more civilized villages that the woman, particularly the

179

younger women, who worked very hard, if possible even harder than the man now often avoid field work. Thus in the villages they do not go out to work in the fields which used to be a natural obligation; similarly they avoid work and spend as little time on the homestead farms as possible.

Within more or less similar economic circumstances the smallholder peasantry represents as great a variety of the peasant existence as the whole of the peasantry. Not only the attitude to work, but the entire life is manifested in the traditional peasant forms in the still peasant-dominated districts. Thus the whole way of life, the education of children, family life, leisure and the whole culture are determined by peasant conventions. Therefore, in these peasant communities, life develops not according to individual interests and ambitions but is structured by typical peasant forms. Any violation of peasant mores results in the condemnation and disagreement of the village community. No wonder that in these communities only the strongest personalities endeavour to violate peasant mores and to shape their lives according to their own ambitions. In the social world of smallholders big-holders were the ideal and the example to be followed. The smallholders themselves also wanted to be big holders, thus their ambitions were confined to the culture of the peasantry and they seldom attempted to copy the bourgeois examples disregarding the life style of big-holders.

The other stratum of smallholders lives in strongly middle-class villages and particularly in agricultural towns. In this environment the big-holders also adopted the bourgeois ways; thus the smallholders also try to discard peasant mores either because they want to follow the big-holders, or because their own ambitions induces them to develop a more highly civilized life in their own way. Even the labour ethics of these smallholders is in a process of a change; thus as soon as there is an opportunity to work less or to free the family members from the necessity of work they immediately reduce work hours and the community no longer condemns them for doing so. The smallholders' life style and culture also undergo a radical change. Their home and their clothing no longer conform to peasant traditions. They bring up their children not in the peasant ways, but insist on attaining higher schooling levels, often spoiling children. They often hope that their children will leave the land and seek jobs somewhere else. Amongst the daughters of these smallholders there is a general reluctance to marry smallholders, "peasants"; a tradesman, or persons with a steady job eligible to pensions are the desirable marriage partners. Often these girls succeed in getting such partners.

Even if they are not exceptional in their clear form these two extreme poles are not the characteristic. Peasant smallholders in such clear form exist only in some very isolated and backward villages, and petit bourgeois smallholders only in some leading towns in the Plains. The majority of smallholders are somewhere between these two types: they are still bound by peasant traditions, but at the same time life is already freed from many of the peasant ways gradually assuming a bourgeois pattern following the forces and interests of the community. For these reasons, the smallholder stratum is rather mixed made up of the most different social types; this is why for the objective observer the smallholder is not an attractive figure.

The smallholders' life is exposed to two cultures, thus the rational of neither culture is realized. The smallholder makes concessions to one culture because of necessity and to the other because of his ambitions. There is not a single aspect of this life-style he could completely identify with. They feel the peasant mores and social forms pressing and uncomfortable, unfriendly and backward, thus they accept them only with aversion and compelled by necessity. At the same time, smallholders get the patterns of bourgeois life in a distorted form; they have no experience with this life style, thus they rely on it only clumsily and foolishly. Peasant and bourgeois elements are mixed in the behaviour of smallholders in such an unbalanced way that the resulting life-style is completely barbaric and shapeless; this life is not civilized either in terms of peasant or bourgeois culture. The smallholders have no homes where they could live decently, peacefully or enjoyably. The interior of peasant homes was suited for work. They also had a corner where the family and its guests could sit down and have their meals on festive occasions or during the period of winter rest; they also had a large oven where people could warm themselves in their winter-time isolation and rest on the ledge to their pleasure. The bourgeois home can also meet these needs in its own world, indeed, it offers better facilities. However, a house which is both rural and bourgeois at the same time is absolutely dysfunctional. These houses have not got a table, where people could have a quiet meal. Neither do they have a corner where the family could quietly sit around. There is no really good heating. Instead, there is a kitchen in the house which absorbs the work of women without any visible result and where the life of the family is lived in an awkward transitoriness.

The same applies not only to the home, but also to clothing, the education of the children, family life not even mentioning intellectual life. Yet all of this is understandable. The socio-economic situation in which the smallholder lives is in a state of transition between bourgeois and peasant forms. There is no sufficient conserving force to keep the peasant forms intact, that is to preserve a rather primitive, yet ordered and cultured life. Neither are the bourgeois forces decisive enough to liberate life completely from the burden of traditions. Thus both possible ideals of this life, the bourgeois one as well as the peasant ideal are in an irreconcilable conflict not only with each other but also with real life. The peasant ideal of life, the orderly and secure life of the smallholder is impossible, because he must produce for the market and to a great degree live from the market; however, smallholders expect something different from life than what is possible under the given circumstances. The bourgeois ideal is impossible to realize in this life because the smallholders are unable to experience middle-class life in its

181

genuine forms and because neither their economic power, nor their occupation make them suitable for this life style. We may say, therefore that peasant forms have become obsolete and the bourgeois life-style does not yet suit the situation. Smallholders can no longer live according to the peasant traditions, for that contradicts the social environment, yet they cannot follow the bourgeois pattern either, for that disagrees with their social position and occupation.

They live as determined by the opposing forces, thus lacking the balance of culture, and when all is said in drudgery. This is one of the reasons why the number of those, who want to flee this fate is increasing. Giving up their lives as a smallholder more and more of them flee to the towns to fill jobs in industry and commerce with the promise of old-age pensions. Smallholders send many of their children to other careers, while their daughters try to marry others than smallholders. The prestige of being a smallholder is indicated by outflow mobility. Any clerical position even with low prestige or even the job of an office-attendant is not only equivalent to being a smallholder but very often even more prestigious. While the feudal peasant would not have liked to become a soldier, a tradesman or low-ranking clerk; present-day smallholders see all of these occupations as superior to theirs and more befitting a man. To be a member of the gendarmerie or a police officer, a post-man or a railway employee is considered a desirable career for nearly all smallholders.

A more characteristic course of escape from being a smallholder is the restriction of births. The birth-control of this stratum generally does not differ from that of the bourgeoisie: they limit the number of children enabling the parents to build the foundations of a better life for them. This symptom is a consequence of the given situation; therefore, as soon as people become richer they also are prepared to have more children. The general experience is that smallholders, who rose on the social ladder bring up large families. In the districts, known to practise the principle of one family-one child, the declining birth rates are not the direct results of the environment; birth control has become an institutional defence against the spread or continuation of the smallholders' life-style.

3. TENANT FARMERS AND DWARF-HOLDERS

These two strata of the peasantry represent an unambiguous economic existence. They are both peasants independent but working for others. The tenant is a completely independent farmer, who not only utilizes all of his own labour on his leased farm, but occasionally even hires labour. However, he produces about half of the yield for the owner of the land. The dwarf-holder on the other hand, cannot make both ends meet on his own land; thus he is forced to work for another farmer, too.

182

Economically both strata conform almost exactly to the feudal economic positions of the peasants. The tenant is like the feudal serf, an independent producer obliged to pass part of his product to the owner of the land, and the dwarf-holder is like the peasant farming only on a fraction of an ordinary villeinage holding: besides cultivating his small holding he must find work as an agricultural labourer often also with his wagon and draught animals. Such situations are obviously material supports of the peasant social forms, thus there are objective reasons for sticking to traditions. Peasant rules provide the best conditions for living in such situation, since they have precisely emerged in feudalism to render these life circumstances bearable and socially approved. It follows that the only way to make a living under these conditions requires people to work in the peasant manner, so that labour and service fill all of their time. At the same time, this existence is now in the world of capitalism, thus it has to function under market conditions. The peasant production is no longer sufficient, the tenant must produce considerable quantities of produce in order to pay the lease, and the cotter must work for the wages developed on the labour market in order to supplement his own production. And this contradiction produces a mess and a crisis just like the ambiguous situation of middle-class peasantry does. The tenants' and dwarf-holders' lives are a mixture of peasant work ethic, rural poverty and a bourgeois-style wage labour and individualism. The actual life-styles are determined by joint effect of these factors.

The enterprising cotter, the conservative cotter, the small peasant owning a homestead farm, the independent tenant and the share-cropper are but a few varieties of this social existence.

The enterprising dwarf-holder's is the small peasant of regions more affected by bourgeois development. In the atmosphere of some livelier and more progressive village or agricultural town, where people broke free of the peasant forms the dwarf-holder builds an independent agricultural enterprise on his own land or one, perhaps a few "holds" (1 hold = 1,42 English acres), even though this is considered entirely insufficient for independent farming by the standards of peasant farming. So he starts intensive production there and does his best to use his labour entirely according to the principles of enterprise and market production. Thus he keeps cows, produces poultry, accepts transport for hire; he cultivates the garden so he can sell some of the products at the market; in other words, he uses all the possible intensive production methods to make sure that he does not have to sell his own labour. This kind of existence springs from a more progressive environment and bourgeois ambitions from the start, and it would be absurd to pursue it throughout one's life with bourgeois work ethic. The only way such an enterprise can exist is that the dwarf-holder lives and works according to peasant laws. Therefore, the dwarf-holder works all the time with inexhaustible diligence; he consumes not more than allowed by peasant circumstances; even when there is no work to be done, his work and the problems of production do not let him relax completely. Since this life is bourgeois in respect of all of its external conditions, but peasant in all of its psychic factors and social forms, the dwarf-holder looks equally towards the peasant and the bourgeois opportunities. Thus the enterprising dwarf-holder would like to own more land and a bigger and more independent farm, and if he is lucky enough to get it he turns into a viable unit. Others would prefer some steady employment as skilled workers, in other words, a career in bourgeois society, and are glad to leave their former lives if an opportunity presents itself.

The small peasant owner of a homestead farm is another variety of the independent dwarf-holder. Existence of this kind develops in two ways in districts, where the homestead system is alive, that is mainly in the Plains. They are either results of the repeated division of the family farm, so that only a few holds were left to each of the present owners, or they owe their existence to the fact that a labourer or a descendant of a feudal farmer, who inherited nothing of the feudal unit of land was lucky enough to save up enough money to buy a plot of land.

With the practice and the ambitions he acquired on the independent farm, the owner of the divided and inherited plot built a farm house there; he gave up his home in the township and went to the homestead to live his own life there. Everyone of these dwarf-holders tries to have the greatest possible poultry-farm and a cow is also kept. The dwarf-holder takes his products to the market each week; in other words, he uses all of the advantages of living out on the farmstead trying to maintain an independent existence. Even there, naturally, he can preserve his independence only as long as he works as hard as the peasants, but since the hard circumstances of homestead life also force him to do so, the dwarf-holder of the homestead is more likely to make both ends meet than those who live in a village or township. The culmination of all the dwarf-holder's desires is to acquire a house in the village or the agricultural town to which he could retire in old age. This is the ultimate pay for his labours that keeps his spirit of work and energy alive from day to day: if he succeeds, he spends his old days with the comforting knowledge that he achieved what he wanted: he can live like a middle-class farmer in a more developed environment.

The career of the other type of dwarf-holder having a farmstead is harder and it often has a tragic end. Most people, who bought such a plot usually with rather poor soil far away from the villages, either sold their village house or their little gardens, or they sacrificed the "capital" they saved as workers hoping that they could live as independent farmers in the new environment. The situation which they thus created really offers many advantages in farming. By living on the farmstead, the owners save the time devoted to travel; thereby the efficiency of their labour increases and they can devote more attention to agricultural production. They all work steadily and with a peasant devotion rare even amongst other peasants; they cut

184

back on their own consumption to the greatest extent and they can be regarded as genuine peasants. Still only a few of them succeed in growing rich achieving a somewhat easier life or buying a house in the township. The major reason of this stagnation is mostly the isolation of their land; these plots are far from the markets and they are to be found on sandy or saline soil which hardly yields more than the sowing seed in adverse years. Even though they own the land they farm, these peasants just do not have the external preconditions of production. The population of the homestead villages between the Danube and the Tisza is primarily made up of this stratum, whose life is a perpetual drudgery. Other groups of small peasants living in centres East of the River Tisza have a better life. The soil is better there, the markets are also closer, and with just as much hard peasant work, that is already a sufficient advantage to ensure a more independent and easier life.

Tenancy is one of the newer forms of peasant existence. Letting the land is an entirely capitalist phenomenon and by now not only the non-agricultural owners let their land, like some decades ago, but also an ever increasing number of the farmers. Most of the acreage owned by farmers in the towns of the Plains is already let, while the proportion of leasing is much smaller in the villages even in the more advanced regions of the country. It is the system of homestead farms that facilitates leasing in the Plains partly because these farms are usually established on a single parcel of land, partly because normally there is a house on the plot, so the tenant can live there and this ensures better conditions for production. Due to these circumstances, this mode of farm management is a purely capitalist enterprise. In essence it is a capitalist enterprise only from the aspect of the owner. Leasing for him is but a bourgeois way of utilizing capital, therefore this form spreads parallel with the advance of the bourgeois mentality, and provides an opportunity for the middle-class life of land-holders. The tenant's position would be also capitalistic only if he could reliably calculate the rent which would have to be paid in cash. However, that is not the case. Even a few decades ago it was customary to set the rent in wheat and to set it rather reasonably, at an average of two quintals per acre or even less for poorer land. The pressure of the constant competition of would-be tenants, however, gradually pushed the basic rent in wheat higher and higher, and the bidders also offered various extras, such as milk, eggs, pig, fire-wood, labour etc. By now in the agricultural towns of the Plains tenants pay as much as 3-4 quintals wheat per acre for the poorest land, the sandy and saline soils, and as much as 5 quintals for the better, wheat-producing land. In addition to that, tenants also pay a whole lot of extras. The situation almost reverted to feudal tenancy, because the tenant has to render services of a feudal character to the owner of the land, who also exercises as much supervision over the production of the tenant as the feudal lord used to have.

In order to meet the extremely heavy rental conditions, the tenant must

185

farm with maximal efficiency, and therefore ultimately in the most capitalistic way; the tenant must be very sensitive to the needs of the market; if he hires labour he must exploit it as much as possible; in other words, the tenant must produce for profits. Under these circumstances, the tenant and his family must live like peasants, since only a ceaseless peasant devotion to work and frugal peasant consumption can make the tenancy successful. Since all tenants would like to be prosperous buying a few acres of land or at least a house in the village, they all live according to peasant rules. In other words, they must live like peasants even in their strongly bourgeois environment, under the capitalistic production forms forced onto them. Undoubtedly, this kind of peasant life is not a form with which they made peace and to which they acquiesced, but it is enforced by necessity just as strongly and firmly as if it were kept in existence by an unchanged feudal world. The confusion and contradictions of this tenant life are further exacerbated by the completely class-war character of the opposition of lessors and lessees. The tenants as the weaker party and also as working peasants dislike the idle landlord. No matter if the tenant is a farmer who has grown poor or a small peasant rising from the ranks of labourers, this hatred still remains.

In the villages the lot of the tenants is not that hard even where leasing is relatively common and the community reached a higher standard of bourgeois conditions. Tenancies in the villages are always infrequent, and usually do not involve independent farms. These tenants do not constitute a populous class anywhere, but are exceptions in the village society both as regards their economic and their social position.

In spite of all of his economic difficulties and social contradictions the independent tenant is an independent peasant; he is master of his own lot in his economic existence and thus a separate factor of the life of his society. There is, however, a lower category of the tenancy, which gives rise to a stratum of semi-independent working peasants; this stratum represents a transition between the lives of the peasant labourer and the farmer. In fact the share-croppers, whether they pay half or third or some other part of the yield for rent are in a lease relationship with the owner of the land where the rent is not a fixed sum but a given part of the yield. This arrangement establishes an even more strongly feudal relationship between the tenant and the owner than the lease for a predetermined rent. Accordingly it gives less independence to the tenant and more intervention to the owner right to the point where the tenant ceases to be an independent farmer and changes into some special employed labourer. Most of the tenants of this kind are upwardly mobile workers or agricultural labourers; therefore this social position implies an even stronger assertion of peasant laws. The share-cropper is always subject to an alien will, just as the villein was, thus he gets stuck in the peasant forms not only in respect of his labour morale, but also in his whole existence. He works incredibly much, lives frugally and his whole world is the same as that of the villeins was in the feudal age. It is not his objective lot, but only the changed atmosphere that caused his life ceviate from the course of undisturbed peasant existence. His aspirations are gradually increasing and diverting him from peasant standards, and he does not only bear his lot impatiently and with incessant lament, but he also turns more and more against the peasant forms of his life. Therefore he escapes, if he can, to some other career, or he moves to another town and if he has not enough luck or courage to do so, then he breaks the peasant laws in his own circle. The only reason why birth-control and sending the children to other careers are not more wide-spread in these peasant strata is that in these families the labour of each child is absolutely necessary.

4. PEASANT GARDENERS

The peasant farmer is not inclined to gardening. There is no garden culture anywhere developed by peasant farmers. Wherever gardening is done on a property of a peasant it is either the work of share-cropping gardeners, or is a tried and common branch of the peasant production.

While peasant farmers themselves developed no vegetable production, their womenfolk did so in some districts, that is the vegetable-producing region alongside the Danube and in some Transylvanian villages. These vegetable cultures evolved from the home-garden work of women, and when they were extended to the open fields they were also controlled by women, who knew every trick of growing them; they grew the seeds and did the lion's share of the labour themselves. On the other hand, this kind of gardening never grew into a large production branch that would create its own market.

The large-scale garden cultures were everywhere developed either by cotters, or by bourgeois gardeners, or by gentleman farmers. The only exception was wine and fruit production which developed before the age of capitalism, because every social stratum (agriculturists of every possible rank and social status just as tradesmen and professionals) had been engaged in such production there for centuries. Peasant farmers joined the production of garden products only when they had already become common, and particular products started to enjoy good markets. But even then they did not always rely on their own labour.

The paprika production around Szeged, the fruit and vegetable culture at Gyöngyös, the flower gardening of Szőreg, and the fruit-growing of Jánoshalma were all developed by dwarf-holders. They were popularized by peasants holding tiny parcels of land, who were already deeply immersed in the diligent peasant labour and the small size of whose land forced them to take on branches of production promising better market results. The onion culture of Makó, and melon culture of Csány were developed by cotters, who had only tiny plots and later acquired some more either by ploughing up some grazing land or through subdivision. Keeping in with this origin, most of the garden production is done even today in dwarf-holdings or leases, while only a part of the larger peasant estates engaged in this production on their own land.

Tobacco differs from the other branches of garden production insofar as it became widespread on all types of farms, but it also conforms to the other branches of garden production in the fact that the actual work of production is done here also by gardeners of small, or no property on their own either as tenants or on the basis of share-cropping.

Each of these garden cultures, thus the overwhelming part of the Hungarian gardening production represents special production skills. All of them were generated by capitalism, yet they are still peasant cultures without exception. In other words, peasants developed the mastery of production entirely according to the laws of peasant culture in appropriate market and economic situations. The mechanism and the technology of production were not created overnight by some rational calculation, but they took shape gradually, every intermediary result being inherited from generation to generation. These garden cultures differed from the common achievements of peasant culture in the circumstance that owing to market demand and economic factors there has always been an economic incentive to increase yields and crops; thus these gardens could develop more vigorously than other spheres of peasants life which served only the comfort of the peasant life itself. The melon-growing at Csány, the Makó onion production, and the paprika culture of Szeged were all results of entirely peasant development, and yet all of these products are not only noted but the most respected of their kind at even the greatest markets. Vini-culture and horticulture, on the other hand, were not such independent peasant achievements. The cultivation of these noble cultures had long been the pursuit of a section of society much broader than the peasantry itself, therefore highly developed special knowledge and the art of the improvement of the varieties also played parts in their production. For instance, the fruit culture of Kecskemét was initiated by feudal landlords, who initially began fruit production motivated by an interest in botanics as a sheer hobby as well as by the possibility of attaining higher expertise and profits. The peasants joined them later, when the success of the venture was obvious.

Although the vegetable cultures developed by peasants got hardly any impetus from the science of botanics, they still represent a standard of expertise, a profound trade knowledge and fail-proof calculation which do not exist in any other fields of agriculture. This production culture reached a stage in the hands of peasants, at which it can hardly be distinguished from the production science of non-peasant origin. Although it lacks the fullest degree of rationality, a close and intimate contact with plants, soil and the tools gave rise to skills which cannot be found in horticulture just because of its rationality and abstract nature.

Thus the expertise of the peasant gardeners is of peasant character, but not much else of the peasant ways can be detected in them by now. Even the gardeners' attitude to work is no longer that of the peasants. They can work incredibly hard, harder than any peasant, but they can also relax and break free from drudgery, when there is no need for it. They regard their economic position, which is bourgeois and not feudal, with bourgeois consciousness and pursue an efficient market production and bourgeois principles also in their consumption. They readily adopt any innovation demanded by the market; thus they experiment with the latest production methods, even if they do this somewhat hampered by peasant culture. Gardeners who really grow rich are ready to undertake production on the largest possible scale; they are no longer peasants in their consumption either. Peasant gardeners live according to their financial position; sometimes they spend lavishly, sometimes they live frugally. When production is successful and after having satisfied their needs, instead of buying land they accumulate capital and even if they buy land, they do not hesitate to live up their capital when production is not profitable, in the hope of saving up again. And if some of them go broke they do not feel finished as a peasant holder would, who would feel absolutely lost without the security of his land.

Very many of the small peasant gardeners attain bourgeois positions as owners thanks to such production based on the spirit of enterprise and hard peasant work. This rise, however, does not mean that they become peasant holders; this implies an advance to the status of middle-class farmers. Thus they become entrepreneurs or they use their land in some other form as capital, and live like the middle-class. The result of this visible capitalist progress is that even those, who are less fortunate in production adopt bourgeois attitudes. For this reason they often look down on peasant holders, who continue living as peasants in spite of their bourgeois position; they do not want to socialize with them or to win their particular respect. The fact that these enterprising gardeners spend much more time on the market and generally in the world than the peasant holders also gives them a more bourgeois polish. They are glad to undertake production at far-away districts; if necessary, they take their product to the farthest market, and while moving about in the world they accept its influences and develop accordingly instead of keeping aloof as peasants normally do.

This stratum's fertility has also changed; they no longer conform to peasant fertility. However, the birth-control they practice is far from being the quite common peasant system of having only one child in the family. They have only one or two children because they want to live life at a higher standard, but this birth-control is not to be followed strictly; those who can afford it or have more courage often have more than two children. The prestige of this social form is well demonstrated by the fact that very few

189

people flee from it in a panic. Members of this stratum may switch to some other course or train their children for some other occupation for some plain and purely bourgeois reason. Since peasant gardeners are equal in social ranking with the more respected tradesmen they do not think of changing their status to something inferior; also the same consideration leads them when they marry outside their own stratum. Peasant gardeners became a genuinely petit bourgeois group. In other words, it has completely liberated itself from the bonds of the peasant traditions, and it is hardly affected by the crisis of the peasantry. They did not become completely free, neither is their life smoothly ordered, but their way of life is much less ambiguous, than that of smallholders.

5. PEASANT TRADESMEN

Peasants are not only the people, who cultivate the land in a peasant way, and live according to peasant forms, but also others, who practice a trade, yet live in a world shaped by the peasant laws. If someone acknowledges as binding the same system of conventions, which the peasants tilling the land do, that is he occupies the same position in the social structure, he is a peasant no matter what his occupation is. In fact, there are everywhere members of peasant society, who are organic parts of the machinery of the peasant society even though they are not farmers, but practice some supplementary trade. The peasant tradesmen may be cited as examples.

Tradesmen living in the midst of the peasantry, not only in everyday contact with them but also subject to their conventions are in fact peasants, and they constitute one of the strata of peasantry. They do not only live like peasants, but in their own field they also know the best what the peasant needs and they produce their industrial products accordingly. It often happens that a peasant would like to follow his own individual need or taste when he has a house built or a wagon made, but the peasant tradesman persuades him to stick to conventional forms by pointing out the unusual and novel features of his special expectations.

Tradesmen pursuing various simple peasant-industries, such as walling, thatching, bush-carpentery, plastering, brick-making and adobe-making are peasants without any perceptible difference. They are not even regarded as tradesmen, but seen just the same peasants as the others. Although their occupations are regular industrial ventures, they follow them in an absolutely peasant way. They do not learn their trade first as apprentices; neither do they sit for any examinations. They learn their trade from practice and traditions just as the peasant learns agriculture. They do not even learn their trade as a separate occupation, but as part of the occupation of being a peasant. Thus they also learn agriculture in the traditional way, and can switch to tilling the land any time, when there is not enough work in their trade or the jobs available are not satisfactory. Usually these traders are landless labourers, who learn a trade to suit their talent, inclination or some opportunity, and then practice it as a job that gives them a better livelihood. By doing so every one of these peasant entrepreneurs rises above the ranks of labourers and reaches a status equal with that of the small peasants. But this applies only to the entrepreneur himself, for his workers, who usually know their trade as well as their boss remain peasant labourers and work in the field or in their industry as needed.

The various tradesmen of peasant standing, who properly learnt their trade, do not easily mix with the farming peasants. From an abstract point of view they are the same tradesmen as their counterparts in the towns; they learn their trade in the same way; they also pass the same examinations and set up separate workshops to practise their trade. Yet in rural social life they organically belong to the farming peasantry. On the one hand, they have a little land, if nothing more than a big garden or a vegetable garden where they work themselves, so they have a direct tie with agriculture. Even more important than this is that they work almost exclusively to meet peasant needs; as a result they are also bound by peasant laws. The peasant tradesman's position in the village hierarchy also agrees with that: the leading big holders enjoy a higher status, while the various groups of landless peasants are lower on the social level. Thus the peasant tradesman has a small peasant status in the village community, and he achieves the social status of the leading farmers only if he acquires exceptional respect and grows rich. In other words, these trained tradesmen, the joiner, the bricklayer, the smith, the tailor, the furrier, the barber are all considered peasants in spite of all of their marks of distinction and other circumstances; this is beyond doubt for the urban masters of the same trades.

It is also the consequence of this peasant status that from the totality of expertise these tradesmen use merely the tricks of their trade no matter how thoroughly they studied their trades. Their taste and sense of form are completely peasant and they do their work accordingly. This is why masters, who learnt their trade in the town rarely succeed in village societies, while village-trained ones do not find their place in the towns. Besides knowing the trade, rural demands must also be met. This proves to be quite easy because these tradesmen have grown up in the village world, knowing the peasant laws. The accepted village tradesman, the peasant master does not only understand and identify with the peasant forms, but he also shapes them. Needs and tastes originate from the rural world, but the things are actually produced in the workshop of the tradesman.

In any case, the tradesman moves on a different course than the farmer. He has more frequent contact with the town, and generally with the world, he adopts more influences and is more inclined to follow the bourgeois examples if for nothing, but for the reasons of his trade. Thus, the tradesmen are representatives of progress even in the most backward of villages. Naturally, this is also felt in work. The tradesman always tries to modify the taste, the customary forms of the village bringing them closer to bourgeois forms. The town tradesman, who supplies goods to the peasants simply because that is his business, does not shape the village so directly, because he is willing to meet the demand as it is, without trying to add to it. Towards the end of the last century town traders used to copy the peasant patterns in various villages, and had cloth and kerchieves made in Bohemian factories based on these patterns. Even today there are many stores in the towns, where various peasant-style goods are kept separated.

By virtue of living where the demand arises the peasant tradesmen in the villages can also shape the appearance of their products. They add their own more highly developed bourgeois taste to them with the outcome that the taste of the whole village changes through their influence from year to year. Thus these tradesmen are the trend-setters in terms of rural environment; tradesmen bear the heaviest responsibility for the emergence of ill-shaped forms in clothing, buildings and tools. Were the village tradesmen not peasants but people with bourgeois background pursuing their trades according to the taste of their class, the village would obviously cast off its peasant forms more easily.

6. PEASANT TRADERS

Similarly to tradesmen, traders can also be peasants. Traders whose lives are completely embedded into rural society acknowledge the peasant laws as valid to themselves and they are just as much peasants as tradesmen. In other words, their occupation distinguishes them from farming peasants, but their social status binds them to them. Traders are similar to tradesmen insofar as they are also the trend-setters and the examples to be followed in rural society. And since traders do not have to have special qualification, numerous people began trading while they were peasant tilling the land; these traders are even more intertwined with the rural world than the tradesmen of similar situation.

All in all, similarly to peasant tradesmen, peasant traders also have two characteristic strata. Those belonging to the first stratum are members of peasant society without any distinction, while the others are somewhat distinguished from the farmers by the more highly developed general conditions of their occupation.

The marketers, the middlemen and gatherers are the equivalent in social ranking to the thatchers and peasant masons. Although their occupations make them small-scale entrepreneurs, they need no special training or equipment, but follow their chosen occupation without breaking away from their peasant-farming background even when business becomes quite regular. What they need they usually learn in practice; they calculate

192

instinctively, as peasants do and they really do not aspire to be traders. They only intend to earn some money by filling the role of the trader. The market-woman is usually a distributor selling goods brought from other districts, while the gatherer is a small-scale procurer, who buys up small quantities of products for the bigger traders. The middlemen engage both in buying and selling and generally act as agents in most deals. The market-women and the gatherers are usually small peasants transacting small-scale business using a tiny capital; often they are rather poor, without any real means. Amongst the middlemen, however, there are some who act as brokers in sizeable deals; therefore even the wealthier farmers may become middlemen but then they have a higher social prestige.

Big or small, the peasant traders travel much; they are familiar with the urban markets and they mediate much influence from town to village. These peasant traders are not really leaders, for they are not highly respected members of the village society. Usually they display facile mores and are treated with contempt by peasants having a more settled life.

The other stratum of the peasant traders is made up of professional traders, i.e. the shop-keepers and the inn-keepers who, whether they have special qualifications or not, work full-time. Just as the qualified tradesmen, they transmit influences coming from the outside and are leaders of the village in this respect because of their higher-prestige occupations. The shop-keeper offers the latest in consumer goods and household items, the women get the latest recipes in his shop, while the inn-keeper provides news and music to the village besides drinks.

Tradesmen and traders fill such roles only in the village communities, thus in places where the peasant members of a closed social world descended mostly from farming peasants. In the larger and more advanced villages and the agricultural towns where trade and commerce are special occupations employing many people, the followers of these two occupations do not follow so closely the peasants. In these communities tradesmen and traders form a separate bourgeois stratum and as such they become leaders of the peasantry on the path leading to bourgeois civilization. In other words, in the same social world tradesmen and traders represent a different way of life and influence the peasantry by their example. In the villages the peasant tradesmen and traders only transmit influences and they themselves develop also only by the influences adopted, while in the town and in the larger villages their direct example shapes the peasant forms. This transmission and example are equally important in both rural and more urbanized environments and the actual situation of Hungarian peasantry is to a great extent explained by the nature of the influence of tradesmen and traders. Putting it another way, the life of small peasantry assumed ambiguous and awkward forms and this is to a great extent explained by the fact that the bourgeois stratum which is part of the peasantry or is closest to it has not advanced very far on the way of bourgeois civilization.

PEASANT WORKERS

1. THE LANDLESS PEASANT AND THE WORKER

The ultimate difference between the feudal and the bourgeois class situation becomes clear in the class situation of the worker. The worker lives in an undisguised worker class situation, thus his economic and social status are identical, since he lives in his class situation directly, without social forms of an objective validity. In contrast, the peasant worker, the landless peasant, the descendant of the cotters is not a worker, but a peasant even if the class situation in which he lives is abstractly similar to that of a worker for his social status is given a concrete form by the traditional social form quite independently of his direct economic position.

The worker lives in bourgeois society; he is influenced by this society and his efforts are aimed at achieving a better position. In contrast, the landless peasant, even if he is similar to the worker in terms of his economic and social status is made independent of society at large; he is member of the lowest stratum of the peasantry which in itself is also in a subordinated position within the society. Owing to this, the ambitions of the landless peasants also remain within the limits of the peasant society and do not run on the bourgeois course of the greater society.

Summing up: the difference between the worker and the landless peasant is that the social status of the workers is a social fact, it is always capable of change, while the status of the landless peasant is a norm that exists with the abstract validity of a social form, therefore it encompasses the requirement of permanence instead of that of change. The peasant worker is not resigned to his status either, but his ambition to get out of it is not directed at rising out from the status of worker; becoming an independent farmer he intends to remain within the peasantry.

In the abstract the peasant's social status does not contradict the class situation of the worker. In essence the peasant social form is a conservation of the worker class situation and its ossification under detailed social forms. In fact, however, the peasant form attached to the worker role clashes with the class situation not only when the peasant is owner of the land, therefore a bourgeois according to his class situation, but even when he is a landless cotter. Social forms prescribing and binding every step not only forced the peasant of the feudal society to lead a working life, but also gave him protection and security. The social mechanism of village society obliged not only the cotter to spend his life working, but other stipulations obliged also his employer, the farmer and the landlord to take care of the life conditions of the cotter, that is to guarantee him an interest in the grazing land and the forest of the village, and some sort of social security, when he becomes too old or sick to work. Undoubtedly, helping the invalid cotter was but an act of charity, but since that did not depend just on pity but the power of a social convention it was in fact obligatory. In complete contrast, the bourgeois society is ready to acknowledge the fact that the landless peasant lives under social forms, which force him to work more readily, in a more servile way and more cheaply than others, who are not bound by such traditions. On the other hand, this society knows of no obligation to give any protection to these peasants above and beyond their wages. There are still some patriarchal farmers who, motivated by compassion or by a respect for traditions, feel some obligation about their peasant labourers and take care of them in one way or another, when necessary, but now this is charity only and not a duty made obligatory by the existing laws of society. At present, even in the agriculture, the worker and his employer agree on the labour market and the employer is not obliged to pay anything but the wages, while the worker is also bound by the peasant form, in which he is expected to live and work devotedly and completely in his worker role. In the most recent years, only the obligatory wages set by the government and the introduction of the old age insurance changed this position; however, these new measures are far from being actually realized. Even if the new laws are strictly observed it is only an actual situation which does not get support from bourgeois society or from ingrained peasant attitudes.

Thus the situation of the peasant worker has its social tension just as well as that of the smallholders, only in a different direction. The peasant farmer came into conflict with the peasant forms because they bind him to the role of a worker in spite of his owner status, and the peasant worker experiences the conflict because his peasant status forces him to hard work and a servile attitude, while his employer, except the payment of wages, has freed himself from every obligation. Because of this contradiction, and the nature of social development, the landless peasantry has not yet discarded its peasant culture; however this contradiction is likely to result in abandoning peasant attitudes. Where the landless peasant is strongly bound by the rural world, the disintegration of peasant attitudes has just started, but where he is subject to the strong influences of a changed world with a society increasingly becoming bourgeois, a fast disintegration of peasant forms may be observed transforming the landless peasant into a worker in the genuine sense of the word.

2. AGRICULTURAL WORKERS OF LARGE ESTATES

The people of the large estates form the worker-peasant stratum bound most thoroughly to its peasant forms by their environment. The manor on the large estate is a technically isolated territory of society at least for the workers living there; it is a place hardly influenced by the outside world, and the workers have not much opportunity to leave it. Besides that, agricultural workers form little groups living under the direct and close control of their masters. As a result, change, innovation or individual ambition is less easily asserted in this social world. Thus technical isolation prevents the external influences from actively shaping the life of the agricultural workers, while the feudal mechanism of society makes sure that in spite of internal development peasant forms are strictly preserved.

Tension is, however, present in the social situation of the agricultural workers of large estates even if it did not yet produce striking change. The peasant forms have not yet disintegrated because the agricultural workers still live in the mechanism of a feudalistic society. Peasant laws have become distorted here too, however, just as with land-owning peasants exercising strict birth control, their meaning has become perverted also under the effect of an unsolved contradiction. The peasant law demands hard work; it makes sure that everybody works all the time. This is being supervised by the whole of the community, which condemns not only those, who do not work at all, but even those who do not work hard enough, like peasants should. But the social form, that crystallized around him in the course of historic development did not only force the peasant to perform such work, but it also developed the kind of work morale in him, which developed his voluntary diligence at work. That was how contemporary observations described the good old agricultural labourers of the large estates, partly because they were still bound by the "healthy" peasant conventions, partly because work on the large estates was less exhausting and strenuous. Later, however, labour became more burdensome, and the world changed. One of the changes required the agricultural worker to work harder, while the other wanted him to work as a proletarian, and not as a peasant, therefore at a more measured pace. Since a solution did not come in either direction, the result was that the peasant work ethic underwent a change. Instead of hard and devoted work, a slow and self-sparing pace of work evolved. The peasant duty to work incessantly was not discarded. However, a more lenient attitude to work was adopted. Labour discipline asserted directly from above also forces the labourers to constant work, which they themselves feel obliged to do anyhow, but they slow down every movement and stretch the time of everything a little in a conscious effort at giving enough work but not to get crippled in doing so. The body instinctively slows down the work-process as if it were defending itself against reckless exploitation, and the soul rebels against the never-ceasing servitude.

196

Yet this "peasant strike" of the labourers of the large estates does not go beyond sparing themselves at work. Besides that all of their life activities proceed in the regular peasant order which could hardly happen otherwise under the given technical conditions and at the given standard of life. In fact, the peasant form is even favourable in this respect, for it makes life at least bearable with its little tricks and constant self-discipline. The peasant law of fertility is still retained, thus from among the various strata of the peasantry it is the agricultural labourers of big estates who practice birth-control to the smallest extent. But just as they did realize a peculiar form of instinctive strike they may also start a life-denying strike; then the critical state of the labourers of the large estates will not differ from the peasants practising a strict birth-control with the result of having only one child in the family. There are already signs that such a trend got started. With or without change in the life-style of agricultural labourers, fertility is likely to change. The isolation of agricultural labourers or measures for their protection could only delay but not prevent a drop in fertility.

3. PEASANT SERVANTS OUTSIDE THE BIG MANORS

Peasants in servant relationship invariably live in the tension of opposite forces, but these forces do not assert themselves in a concrete form in every situation. The effect of both of these opposite forces is the weakest in the case of agricultural labourers of the big manors; as a result they live the most balanced life among all farm servants. They are bound by a feudal community, and the big manor gives the best protection against outside influences. However, in any other kind of service, peasant servants outside the big manors are exposed to stronger influences; as a result their peasant status becomes uncertain and unsettled to the extreme. Whether the servant lives at a farmer or in a bourgeois household, he is no longer in a feudalistic position bound by many ties. Instead, he is constantly exposed to the influence of bourgeois life.

There are two distinctly different versions of the lives of servants; one in the service of a farmer, the other in that of a bourgeois household.

Provided he is not yet a landowner affected by bourgeois influences, the farmer himself lives in the same peasant world as his servant does, therefore in a formally common world. This is the reason why their relation becomes patriarchal in such a situation. However, this patriarchalism is different from that which characterizes the landlord-peasant relationship. The farmer's attitude to the servant is of intimate nature, yet it does not assume an air of superiority; the farmer's and the servant's position are not different in terms of social standing; the farmer has a vast influence on the servant's life because he is in a leadership position. Thus the standing of the servant is similar to that of the members of the family. It is similarly directly and minutely subordinated. Thus, going beyond the farmer-servant relationship, the farmer feels entitled to interfere with even the most intimate aspects of the servants' private lives and discipline. In other words, the farmer treats his servants just as they were members of his own family, i.e. with the same harshness and roughness. The feudal peasant farmer thinks just as little about his minor children—often even when they have come of age—as about his servants and he treats them equally strictly. Thus he knows no tolerance in working, he is ready to use any humiliating method of punishment, ready to hit even besides the commonly used abuses. Since he keeps down his own demands too and dares to eat no more than his peasant forebears, he keeps back as much as possible from his servants and children, too. The servant does not have to be given a decent bed, the male servants should sleep in the stable and the servant girl in the corner of the kitchen. Only adult servants can sit at the table. The younger ones must eat on the threshold or in the door-way of the kitchen, eating there what is meted out to them; thus they are always hungry and unsatisfied. Although the peasant treats also the members of his own family rather harshly, the family ties naturally soften the fatherly strictness, while there is nothing that would soften the head of the household towards the servants. As the change progresses the members of the family become progressively free from the fatherly terror, but the same change does not bring similar benefits to the servants. They are gradually becoming workers employed for wages, whose labour must be exploited to the limit, and whose payment in kind must be postponed as much as possible. Although, at a more primitive level, the farmer treats his servant strictly, he feels himself responsible for his servant's whole future. Though the farmer sometimes treats his servant with cruelty, he also gives him an appropriate gift when the servant gets married. Similarly, he gives assistance to the old servant should he be in need. However, in more advanced regions, the servant is increasingly regarded like a worker. Though the servant is expected to do his work with peasant zeal, the employer thinks his only duty is to pay the servant's wages.

In recent years peasant farmers keeping servants complain more and more about the poor quality of the servants. They consider them demanding, disrespectful and careless. According to them, servants demand high wages, object to the meals given to them; they want to have free time of their own and immediately leave their job if the farmer punishes them. This complaint characterizes reality from the aspect of the farmer. The present-day farmer really could be of the opinion that the servants became completely spoiled and it is impossible to deal with them. (In many instances, the land is a consequence of problems with the servants.) But the same situation seen from the side of the servant means that the farmer is unbearable, for he wants the servant to work like a member of his family, with the same responsibility and diligence, that is from dawn to dusk without holidays. At the same time the servant should be satisfied with wages that are due to an ordinary worker.

The deterioration of the situation is entirely understandable. The conflict of the master-servant relation is so sharp that a peaceful relationship cannot be possible for a longer period, and influences coming from the environment also jeopardize the earlier balance.

In spite of all of their peasant fellowship the peasant servant is in an unbalanced relationship with the peasant farmer ever since their peasant status came into conflict with their bourgeois status. In practice the farmer treats the servant as a peasant and expects work attitude from him, but in principle he relates to him as a farmer holder, that is in the bourgeois sense, therefore he no longer feels any responsibility for him but only the obligation of paying his wages. Thus the farmer preserves only those peasant attitudes which render his position more favourable, while he expects his servant to respect the less favourable peasant attitudes, too. It is obvious that this practice cannot be maintained for long, sooner or later it must be eliminated. This inequality of rights and duties could only be remedied if in the relationship of the farmer and the servant the peasant forms of mutuality would be restored again. That would force the servant to devoted and responsible work performance, while it would also oblige the farmer to a responsible attitude, giving security against sickness and old age. The only other alternative would be the development of a plain and honest bourgeois relationship, in which the farmer, as the employer could not demand more than a definite amount of labour, and the worker, once he performed the labour he contracted for would be his own master disposing of his time and himself as he wishes.

The direct cause of the change in the servants' behaviour was the external influence on the lives of servants living in villages or in agricultural towns. The social environment has changed and that gave rise to the revolution of rising expectations and to a social character expecting more humane treatment. In spite of his servitude and hard work, the servant does not live in isolation in the world. He receives influences day after day when working and when resting. He socializes with people working in other occupations, he sees examples; therefore it is natural for him to demand a more humane life. The fact that the servants keep in touch with one-another, thus they exchange their experiences, convictions, and immediately transmit their personal impressions is of tremendous importance. The farmers have good reason to complain about the influence of the *"levente"* training (a para-military youth organization in Hungary between 1928 and 1944). They believe that the situation began to deteriorate since the start of this training, since the servants gathering there have the opportunity of adversely influencing one another. This is true; servants meet there without the supervision of their masters, therefore they can freely exchange their opinion, which is definitely unfavourable from the point of the farmer.

Obviously the *levente* training itself is not responsible for this, since other servants and servant women above the *levente* age changed just as much as the younger lads receiving *levente* training. And even if there were no compulsion to attend *levente* training, young servants would still meet on Sundays, only perhaps not that frequently.

The situation that shapes the position of the bourgeois servant is entirely different. Servants in bourgeois households, even in those found in the villages live in an alien world. Torn out of the society of their village they become participants of a bourgeois world only technically. They learn mechanically what falls into the area of their service, and they fulfill their duties in the peasant way. In other words, all the time they find it natural that they can eat only at the kitchen table, which conforms to the nature of the peasant laws. It is also accepted that they sleep in the servant's room, and that the only time they can have a day off is Sunday afternoon, since they lived at home under the same rules. Apart from the service itself, they have nothing to do with those living in the household. The servant acquires her duties in detail. She might even sympathize with her masters, but that does not alter the fact that she does not live together with the family employing her. Her separate life exhausts itself in doing the service in the peasant way, and in meeting the other servants on the promenade on Sunday afternoon. For the same reason, when such a servant returns to her village she can step back into the farmwork she left as if nothing had happened, that is she completely forgets the life-style she learned for herself in the town. What she learnt in the town was not a life-style, but service. That she ate spinach and cooked bourgeois dishes was just part of her service. Apart from this, her own life remained intact within the peasant forms, thus when she left service and went back to her village she did not adopt a different life-style; she only finished with service.

This is the good servant. Bourgeois households esteem her not only for her diligence in and devotion to work, but also her modesty and loyalty. She is a peasant, who can work only in that fashion. But for the servant herself there is even more contradiction in this situation, than there is in the case of those serving farmer families. Besides being exposed to bourgeois demands, or more correctly demands less formal than those of the peasant life, she also lives directly in a bourgeois mechanism and enjoys its comforts and advantages as long as she is in service. It is absolutely impossible to stay unchangeably peasant in such an environment and work according to peasant rules. Only those servants who came from very traditional villages remained unaffected, the others discard peasant conventions in work and in aspirations and begin to live a bourgeois life. And that also means a change for the worse. The servant is no longer really committed to the service. She starts to demand higher wages, more free time. She will have her own leisure time, she will no longer be modest and obedient. In other words, she

200

gradually reaches a stage when her employer finds her spoilt, immoral, impudent and unbearable, and she is dismissed from job.

Servants working in bourgeois homes have also another variety. In peasant societies that developed a bourgeois mentality, which also means a change in aspirations and ambitions the peasant farmers have almost completely disintegrated. Those, who go to the cities, mostly to the capital city, to become servants are fleeing from the dirty, uncomfortable and hard agricultural work and are seeking easier work and a more bourgeois form of life for themselves. Such a servant is no longer a peasant in such bourgeois service either. She may already be a worker, who performs her work with expertise. However, she also wants to enjoy life in the town; her aim is to have as much free time as possible which is already spent in an urban way. And this change of life is complete and real. From the agricultural life in the village, the servant switched to the urban way of life of a worker. She might have left behind a smallholder life, but she considers even the service more bearable than the discomforts of rural life, thus she is glad to go to and stay in the town. The life she lives is not really good, for she believes she lives in a bourgeois way, although in fact she is a proletarian. However, it was this illusion that enticed her from the agricultural life in the village, and this illusion makes the change worthwhile in her eyes. Naturally, she would be even happier if she could live a real urbane-bourgeois life, therefore she attains the height of her happiness when she marries a petit-bourgeois man on whose side she can participate in bourgeois life by her own right.

4. CONTRACT WORKERS

Contract workers are partly labourers of the large estates, partly poor village peasants. They live half of their life—from spring to autumn—at the large estates, and the other half in their home village.

These two places of stay differ in many respects. The large estate is unquestionably a feudal world, where the contract worker lives in isolation from the world in ceaseless work, while his village is a disintegrating rural community which still preserves part of the peasant forms, but is already being influenced by a changed world and is on the way of disintegration and transformation. The most essential difference between the village and the large estate is that hardly any outside influences penetrate the latter, which is constantly under the supervision of overseers and stewards, while the contract workers are in constant touch with similar people in the village in a society exposed to uniform influences. The consequence is that the life of the contract worker alternates between the poles of two opposite worlds.

In essence contract workers are hired hands although the forms of this employment are traditionally set. In other words, his wages are not simply paid in money, but partly in kind, which may be either a pre-set amount of produce or a proportion of the yield, and the rest in cash. The work to be done is not determined either simply by the number of hours or shifts, but in a composite way as the conditions of the farm require. The principal difference between this contract work and more formal wage work is that it is not confined to the completion of one particular job. The completion of the principal job involves also the performance of various supplementary tasks. Thus a group of contract workers can contract to do hoeing, but it is also obliged to reap and to work at the threshing etc. The contract work is partly specialized, and it is partly made up of various agricultural works. In fact the special assignment of the contract workers is hoeing, particularly the hoeing of sugar-beet, but they also reap, thresh, collect hay etc. during the same summer season. Thus the working situation itself is of a set and feudal nature even though it is a wage worker situation on the basis of employment conditions.

The actual performance of the jobs undertaken by the contract workers takes place under purely peasant forms. Thely live completely a life determined by their work. They spend unspecified length of time in shift work, but their day work is also extremely long, and they have practically no life beyond working. They cook for themselves hastily and frugally, and besides eating they have no time for anything but to sleep a little at their lodgings, which are suitable only for a temporary stay. The overseers and foremen of the large estates treat them in the same way as the full-time workers, that is with the same feudal attitude.

Contract workers earn, more precisely save up the winter provisions of their family with their hard work. They usually spend the winter with their family in their village constantly looking for work, yet mostly finding none. Therefore, they spend their day in a state of hibernation, coming together from time to time to discuss current news and to exchange a few words. Naturally, they are completely exposed to the influences of the village, therefore they usually feel rebellious and think that their lot is unjust and intolerable and all the time they try to devise ways of escaping it. They all come to the conviction that life at the large estates is unbearably servile, thus they hope to find some freer way of making a living instead of going back there. But since no such opportunity arises, they are forced again to go back to do contract work in the spring and to continue where they finished last year. Thus, each spring the contract worker becomes proletarian again. No matter what he wants, he must live that life from each spring to each autumn. Yet he changes slowly from year to year under the impact of his increasingly rebellious attitudes. Although he goes back to the large estate each spring, he gradually loses the characteristics of agricultural workers. Simultaneously, he becomes more proletarian, thus trying to break free, indeed protesting against the peasant forms which bind him to this role so strongly. As contract labourers change, they become less and less valuable for the large estates, giving more and more cause to complaints. Unlike the agricultural workers of the estates, contract labourers are becoming increasingly demanding, disrespectful and worse workers. Their situation gives a rather plain explanation of this deterioration.

When the contract workers decide in winter-time that they would not return again to work at the large estate they give equal consideration to agricultural job possibilities in the villages and to industrial ones in the towns. The far-away possibility of becoming an independent farmer is a glimmer of hope to him just as much as the more respected and better paid career of industrial workers. His yearnings could take him either way, the only difference being that in the more backward and traditional villages the life of the independent smallholder seems to be more realistic, whereas in the more advanced and urbanized villages, particularly in the vicinity of industrial or mining settlements, the prospect of becoming an industrial worker is more attractive.

5. PEASANT WORKERS

The numerically largest part of the poor peasants live under the conditions of being free workers; that is they do not enter into service but contract to work from time to time. The two most common forms of contracting to work are day-labour and work for a share of the yield. Day-labourers work everywhere in the production of vegetables, in the mowing and gathering of hay, generally in the more specialized branches of agricultural production, while working for a share is the rule in the production of the two most traditional and popular cereals, wheat and maize. The result is that throughout agriculture the jobs involving animal husbandry, thus also carting, are done by permanent agricultural labourers, others related to wheat and maize by share workers, and the specialized jobs by day labourers. This also means a certain order of rank. The labourers tending to the animals and driving the carts are the most tightly bound; they live on the estates and they are not independent. Therefore their life is still determined by peasant forms to the greatest extent. The share workers are working for wages, but their work has some traditional forms and their wages are not cash payments either, therefore they are closer to the more or less independent life of smallholders than to that of the workers. The day-labour is the least bound due also to the specific nature of production. Thus it is least influenced by the power of peasant traditions. These various forms of employment do not constitute separate peasant strata, for most of the poor peasants engage in one or the other form of employment alternately. The agricultural labourers of the large estates form the most closed group, while mostly the same people work sometimes as share croppers, other times as day-labourers. Only the skilled workers of some of the branches of production specialize completely in day-labour. They normally do not take share cropping, for that traditional form of employment limits the worker in many respects. Often it involves additional labour obligations. Generally, share cropping is still a traditional form implying a personal relationship and servitude, while the free day-worker no longer wants that, since general experience proves that such a relationship ultimately does not favour the worker.

Generally the supply of labour determines the situation of the free peasant workers. Besides the influx of peasants to the towns and their endeavour to find other occupations there is also an agricultural labour supply even if it is not as competitive as it used to be. The latter circumstance is the reason why wages are getting lower. Although the nominal cash value of the wages is increasing particularly since the law set the limit of the minimal wage, the earnings measured in purchasing power generally deteriorate. This is reflected by the constantly diminishing size of the share received by the share cropper. A few years ago share workers used to receive one-fifth of the maize yield for hoeing and snapping, today only one-sixth, or even one-seventh. And reapers used to earn one-eleventh or even one-tenth of the crop for reaping, but today only one-thirteenth or one-fourteenth. Thus the worker is in supply situation, therefore he is more and more likely to agree to the harder conditions of labour, and these conditions are in fact getting harder. On the other hand, the peasant worker is still more or less motivated in his work by rural attitude. The inevitable result of this contradiction is the constant deterioration of the labour morale; from the former agricultural labourer who was committed to his work the peasant worker is becoming a calculating proletarian trying to adjust his performance to the wages received; the rural peasant commitment to work has disappeared. This is the reason why farmers think that even peasant workers are no longer what they used to be. They have become demanding, they do not have a positive attitude to work and they abandon the work they have undertaken rather frequently.

All this becomes even more understandable, when we realize that this stratum of working peasants lives in the most changed environment. In other words, this stratum lives in the field of the greater society. With changed attitude to life, it can no longer work in the old fashion as peasants, but it increasingly feels his position to be a proletarian one, and regards his work accordingly, free of a peasant work ethic.

However, the working peasants discarded the traditional restrictions not only in their work, but also in their whole way of life. These peasants are already trying to live better. Their consumption is often more demanding than that of the smallholders, and they no longer regard the latter as their leaders and examples. Instead of this, bourgeois examples are being followed. The fertility rates of this stratum are also declining. Birth-control asserts itself amongst them not in the peasant form of having only one child in the family but as the necessary adjustment of the proletarian to the hardships and needs of life. Fewer children are born because it is difficult to bring them up even though their children would reach the wage-earning age early. Thus fewer children are born, and in many marriages not even one. We can no longer speak of a moral obligation to have children. Indeed, the conviction has become accepted that birth-control is the justified and necessary method of defence of the worker against social exploitation.

The more backward villages have not yet reached that stage. Even if the employment conditions have become increasingly capitalist, peasant workers work under these conditions preserving their rural attitude to work. Thus they recognize the binding force of the peasant rules of life, and regard the independent farmers as examples in this respect, too. In such places, social attitudes do not reduce fertility; these poor peasants provide the greatest part of Hungary's population increase. For this very reason, the supply of labour keeps increasing in their villages, which is the most common reason why they must take on contract work.

In the more closed order of the peasant society and under its more monotonous production conditions the poor peasant has no opportunity to advance, therefore an independent life remains only a desire. Poor peasants either take on contract work, or they try to get out of their village in some other way, often by going to the town. Those who move to the towns are more strongly motivated by the impossibility of rural life than by the attractions of city life. In contrast to that, on the great Hungarian Plain there is a refined form of rising social mobility in agricultural towns surrounded by homesteads, particularly where vegetable is being grown. Quite a few poor peasants base their lives on this rise on the social ladder. First of all, wages are generally higher in these places, thus there is a better opportunity to save up a starting capital. And as soon as one has enough "capital" to live for a few months, one is not forced to constantly work for somebody else, but one can try to enterprise himself. Leasing a small plot for vegetable growing, or growing vegetables freely at the homestead farm are possibilities of enterprise. In the former instance the peasant worker leases a small plot on which he grows vegetables according to market demand. If his crop is good and the market is favourable, he may make enough money to lease a larger piece of land next year. And if the crop is particularly successful, or if it happens to have an especially favourable price on the market, the peasant may even be able to buy a house or to lease an ever larger piece of land. Lessees on homestead farms live on the farm for which they are obliged to do some work, but they are also free to use a piece of land, where they can grow vegetables. This may prove to be so much profitable that they may lease a homestead farm for ordinary farming, or a larger vegetable plot on which he could produce while living in the village. Possibilities for upward social mobility are more limited in regions which do not produce vegetables, since the garden where production can be successful even on the small-scale is not feasible there. Getting into the business of leasing a homestead farm

205

may give the opportunity of rising in such places too, since the lessee can also produce poultry, which may be just as profitable as vegetable production.

All the above avenues of social mobility are not wide or straight enough for the rise of broad strata. They are, however, good for keeping alive the possibilities of rise with their realistic examples, thus giving a glimmer of hope to the peasant workers of getting out of a hopeless proletarian existence.

6. AGRICULTURAL SKILLED WORKERS

The peasant worker is a Jack of all trades, thus he is conversant in every branch of agriculture, but he undertakes also various types of industrial work. All that means that he has no trade qualifications at all. There is only one thing he can do as well as anybody: to work with complete devotion, and to subject his whole being to work. That is to consume little, to live extremely disciplined, to bear every hardship, fatigue and trial. All that is the consequence of the peasant state. The lack of special training and of any specialization and the peasant social forms are mutually interdependent. Even when peasant workers become proletarians for other reasons they also try to become skilled workers, and where they develop into skilled workers through some local production culture, there they soon become workers.

There are two massive groups of skilled agricultural workers in Hungarian society: the pick and shovel men and the gardeners. Even together these two groups do not represent really great numbers, but that is not surprising at the present development level of Hungarian peasantry. The stratum of landless peasants becomes overwhelmingly a mass of skilled labourers only in a completely bourgeois society, but in Hungary, where the agricultural workers are still partly bound by peasant traditions, this process did not yet take place. This process is being delayed also by the fact that the production of the farmers has not yet become specialized enough to demand skilled workers.

The pick and shovel men are the typical products of the large agrarian townships of the Great Plains. They are descendants of feudal peasants picked out from the peasant-worker life by the capitalist upsurge of demand for labour, the great earth-work projects of harnessing rivers and building roads and railways. Relying on their boundless capacity of work and their low aspirations, which almost became their blood in their peasant situation, and also on the culture they developed through the economy of physical work, masses of them undertook the construction works offered and worked in that occupation as long as there were opportunities. Their work produced a separate trade complete with its own culture. It is similar to the horticulture of peasant gardeners. It emerged from peasant traditions and developed in a peasant way, but this skill became also competitive under constant and hard tests. The pick and shovel work, that eventually became a skilled work, then shaped the workers engaged in it also in their social forms. The worker situation made them workers, and elevated them out of their peasant traditions. Also their constant travels and their free and independent lives might have played a role in that. As a result, this stratum could be shaped by the influence of their economic situation and without the presence of a rural society. Once their attitudes have changed, the pick and shovel men are no longer like their companions who still work on the land. In spite of their almost incredibly hard work they live more easily. Their work became skilled, thus an objective task, not the purpose of life. This is a good example of the fact that rural attitudes are also capable of developing a skilled culture, when forced to do so by some non-peasant need. But when that culture developed as a skilfully pursued occupation, it had already liberated this stratum from peasant forms. Therefore the pick and shovel man works with a skill, that represents peasant culture, but he is no longer a peasant. When there is a demand and an opportunity for it, he works as much as a man possibly can, but when there is no work, he dares also to accept an existence freed from work. When their chosen occupation could no longer be pursued, the pick and shovel men, who could not save up some capital found it difficult to return to the peasant world to pursue a simple peasant life. As unemployed pick and shovel men they either just manage to subsist waiting for some job, or they take some other skilled, or unskilled industrial job.

The skilled gardeners are the agricultural workers of the districts where a gardening culture developed. The separate district culture of their region developed the specialist, the skilled worker also in work, and at the same time transformed peasant workers completely into a bourgeois-capitalist pattern. These are all day-labourers, with the exception of the vine hoers. Their lives are thus determined by the labour market, and they may work for any number of employers in a season, for the personal restrictions are no longer valid in their respect. But even when they work a whole season through for the same gardener, they still strictly remain workers, who do their work for wages without any additional informal obligations.

And their own ways are no longer the peasant ways. They live in a bourgeois world and even if they are on its lowest level they are in fact completely immersed in that world accepting its influence. Many of them consciously recognize the nature of their social position and establish a community of interest with the industrial workers. This is made easy since many of them work in industry and commerce at plants packaging, transporting and processing agricultural products.

The ideals of the skilled gardeners are also borrowed from the bourgeois world. They would like to become enterprising gardeners themselves, or they would like to be in industry, even if only as industrial workers. Getting rid of every tradition, the skilled gardener sends his children to careers which suit his son's or daughter's interests. This often means that children choose an occupation differing from that of their parent's. Since these agricultural workers get about the same in their environment as they could in a town—in any case, they live in an agricultural town—,they do not flee to the town. Their wages are anyhow the highest in agriculture; their standard of living is also as high as that of an urban worker. Indeed, the skilled gardener's own little garden ensures him more and better food than an industrial worker can get. The gardener is not attracted by other life-styles. In terms of social prestige, his standing is rather high, because he is already part of the bourgeois society. Within this world he would not like to be something different having the same class position. If he is truly aware of the nature of his position and has a sufficiently strong personality he would only want to be at the higher levels of bourgeois society (becoming a bourgeois or middle-class farmer) or in another society.

V

THE STUDY OF URBAN LIFE
IN AGRICULTURAL TOWNS*

* The original is to be found in Ferenc Erdei's *Összegyűjtött művei* (Collected Works) *Magyar város* (The Hungarian City), Akadémiai Kiadó, Budapest, 1973, pp. 98—188. The monograph was first published in Budapest in 1939.

1. AS IF IT WERE A CITY…

As if it were a city—this is the picture some of our agricultural towns show from a bird's-eye view. The aerial photographs of Hajdúböszörmény, Hajdúszoboszló, Kecskemét and Hódmezővásárhely present magnificent and startling pictures. If our knowledge were based only on these photographs these towns could be ranked among the big cities of the West. Viewing the dimensions, the regional divisions and the road network, an exciting and thrilling question presents itself. What kind of society is to be found in these towns and what is the role of such a settlement in the life of the wheat-producing and fruit-growing Great Plain?

However, if an unsuspecting traveller happens to get to these towns he is bound to gain impressions contradicting the above statement and he will escape hurriedly from these rather provincial regions. Such a traveller will find a tiny urban core but even this is lacking the ceaselessly pulsating activity, and the town atmosphere is upset even in such urban cores by dust, mud and various rustic phenomena of agricultural character. And if he ventures farther out from this urban core he will surmise to see a bleak and insufferable mixture of village and Asia. Dust or mud everywhere, gaping huge houses and rows of houses interrupted by vacant lots—the illusion of a town is irreparably shattered by such phenomena.

In the above, I have described two impressions. If a casual or passing observer were asked about the society of such towns he certainly would answer that each of these towns are huge rural societies though all of them have urban cores of strikingly high standards. Anybody who has visited such towns will surely remember market places and streets crowded with people of rural appearance; however, he will not forget that while attending to his business or official matters or doing some research he unexpectedly ran across people of true urban and European stature. Probably he will admit that it was hard for him to understand that these two types live in the very same town side by side.

The outward appearance indicates a great variety of contradictions and, if these are surveyed one by one, the scientifically accepted forms of views about agricultural towns can be discovered in each of them. Urban studies passing judgement perfunctorily declare without doubts or misgivings that such agricultural towns are essentially nothing else but huge villages and only in their middle are to be found some tiny urban cores; these, however, cannot be regarded as true towns until such cores do not displace the rural districts and take possession of the whole area of the towns.

It was enough to reflect in general on the town and track the course of urban development to prove that agricultural towns are not incidental mixtures of town and village but they represent the emergence of a town specializing in primary production; however, further details are still to be clarified. Who are the inhabitants of these towns? How do the inhabitants live in this type of settlement which is primarily engaged in agricultural production yet is still to be regarded a town. What are the institutions serving this strange urban life and finally, why should a settlement be considered a town though on account of all general rules and regularities it is not a town?

On the basis of detailed research exploring concrete interrelations I intend to answer the following questions. It will be attempted to throw light on the social factors of the life of agricultural town by means of urban studies founded on sociographical aspects. At each step we shall consider the question whether the phenomena under survey are of an urban nature and if so, what do they mean in the life of an agricultural town.

Before discussing the details, we should consider the problem in general as well. As it was pointed out, rather contradictory judgements can be formed on the basis of superficial observations both as regards the outward appearance of a town and the society living in it. Let us now examine this strange urban phenomenon less superficially and find out whether the picture of the agricultural town and its society actually presents such an un-urban picture even at first sight.

Since the Great Plain is the "home" of the agricultural towns, this fact in itself may lead us to misleading judgements. Relying on ancient traditions we associate towns with some, if not the seven hills or a valley. We are fully aware of the fact that a considerable number of towns are situated on plains but since the classical urban pattern is associated in our minds with hills and valleys, settlements on the plains are believed to be towns only if they are able to prove on the strength of many decisive criteria that they are towns despite their geographical location. None of the agricultural cities, however, can boast of hills or valleys. Just like the Eternal City, Szeged was thought to have been built on seven hills, but what were these hills like? They represented just a few meters of difference in level as compared to the surrounding countryside. However, any agricultural town on the Great Plain can boast of such hills, though perhaps not seven of them, since all of them had been originally built on some protuberant point because of the frequent danger of floods and have expanded to low-level areas but later.

As a rule towns are thought of as traversed by some river or as having a river under the town walls. Although many settlements justifiably regarded as towns do lack natural waters just as some of the agricultural towns, on the strength of comprehensible traditions, it is felt a shortcoming if a town has not been built along a river and only other urban characteristics can move us to disregard this. Of the thirty agricultural cities it is only the four towns situated on the banks of the Tisza river which can boast of a river: Szeged, Szentes, Csongrád and Szolnok as well as the two ones on the River Körös: Gyula and Békés. In addition, there are some towns which had once been situated on river-banks and the whole structure of the settlements had been adjusted to the water. However, either the water has dried up or the town itself has resettled farther away from the river-bed. Szarvas represents a transition between these two types of towns since it is still situated along a river but this is already a back-water and it might easily dry up in the future. Makó and Hódmezővásárhely, however, which were built along rivers have removed themselves entirely from the water.

Thus it is true that our agricultural towns are situated on the plain which is but seldom mitigated by water or protrusions, but only by viewing them emotionally can this be considered an insufficiency of their urban character. Though losing their specific scenic attraction because of that circumstance, their urban character can be absolutely intact in spite of this. It is also true that the environs themselves have a contrary effect, they do not enhance but reduce the urban character of such towns since it is difficult for a settlement to assume an urban character on the boundless, parched and dusty plain or along reed banks crowded with frogs and water-fowl. Nevertheless this can happen despite all difficulties.

Still strictly in terms of the adaptation to the environment let us see where our agricultural towns are geographically situated and what the position of these places is as compared with other regions of the plain. Of the riverside towns Szeged, Makó, Hódmezővásárhely, Szentes, Csongrád, Szolnok, Gyula and Békés are crossing places which guarantees them advantages though only Szeged and Szolnok benefit from them considerably. Lacking waterways and crossing-places other agricultural towns have developed at the junctions of traffic routes; thus the place where the town is situated is important in terms of transport. Such towns are Debrecen, Nyíregyháza, Békéscsaba, Cegléd and to a certain extent Kecskemét. However, it is a peculiar and significant symptom that none of these agricultural towns developed at market-places or road-crossings are to be found at the meeting points of two different natural regions; they are rather located at the internal intersection of the traffic routes within one region having a uniform character and production structure. Even so, only a minority of these towns can boast of geographical endowments. Where have the other agricultural towns been built and what is their function? In the case of most of them their place of settlement has not been justified by geographical factors whatsoever since they have been built mostly at arbitrarily chosen places within a region of absolutely homogeneous character. These places have later become regional centres. However, this function did not result from geographical endownments, but the towns themselves have become centres. Any of these towns could have settled at another place as well and developed into a centre in the same way. Thus, the majority of our agricultural towns have not drawn their urban energies from geographical endowments but they themselves have created urban energies. In the course of time, however, the agricultural town influenced its environs: today every agricultural town is the centre of a given region and we can no longer say that there are no differences between the various environs of towns in terms of production and social life.

In short, despite the monotonous surroundings lacking energy our agricultural towns have developed into towns and today also their environment has adapted itself to the urban function.

A central location meaning urban energies and functions is the common characteristic of our agricultural towns such as Szeged, Szolnok, Debrecen, Nyíregyháza and Békéscsaba. Towns which originally were not so much at a location with geographical endowments are today agricultural cities as traffic centres though they have not lost part of their agricultural character which has been a crucial factor of their urban character at a certain stage of their development. Agricultural towns which have developed their geographical endowments themselves are simply country towns without any specific traffic functions, i.e. they are the centres of restricted areas from where every road leads to the urban centre. These are places therefore, where, owing to geographical factors, no towns were likely to develop but since people have clustered around those places and founded towns the whole environment has gradually organized itself around these centres which took on an urban character. This is an absolutely common feature of all our agricultural towns: a rather big area has been organized around them with all of its life functions and this social unity is geographically reflected by the fact that the whole road system has a radial structure around the town. Without having any geographical justification the area covered by the environs of a town amounts from 25 thousand to 166 thousand holds (1 hold equals 1.42 English acres) and this means an area extending radially from 15 to 50 kilometres around an urban centre. Homesteads and villages included the population of this town environs may range from 20 to 200 thousand people. If only the persons strictly belonging to an urban organization are taken into account, we can speak of a population of at least 20 and at the most 140 thousand which has been organized in an urban pattern.

Such a central location means that the settlement in question is a town by all standards of judgement and this urban character becomes immediately clear whether one looks at the map or observes the whole landscape. The urban character becomes increasingly unambiguous if the central districts of the towns are examined. The basic area of such a town is thousand holds at least but sometimes it amounts even to four thousand holds, and though the picture of this urban area resembles that of the villages in certain respects, it radically differs from them when viewed as a whole. In the centre of the radially converging roads there rise towers and spires and around them there are spacious squares which have the functions of both market-places and public meeting places. Around the squares there are public buildings and institutions of traffic and communication, and these are surrounded by a belt of residential streets. Along the periphery of the town there are districts of a village-type. Being in the vicinity of the town, these are not real villages but rather suburbs. Such landscapes are no longer of a rural but rather of an urban nature; as regards the structure of these urban territories we are reminded of big cities.

If our agricultural towns and their environs are examined one by one, we get acquainted with the individual character of the surroundings. As it will be seen, the various towns with their environs represent an individual urban character and an individual colour lending variety and beauty to the countryside.

The countryside around Szeged and Debrecen is of truly urban proportions and style. Their public squares and streets in no way differ from those of big Western cities and their functions, too, are the same as those of Western cities. Their residential quarters, both the housing developments in unbroken lines and the villa-like ones are fully similar to the residential quarters of other European towns. The same applies to the inhabitants' way of life. The residential areas on the outskirts are regular suburbs whose life blends in perfectly with that of the town. This is true also of the more remote settlements of these towns: both in Debrecen the villas and cottages of Nagyerdő and in Szeged the country houses of Újszeged and Fölsőtanya are buildings meeting the very same needs as those in the suburbs of Western cities. The villages and farther-off homesteads of the precincts are settlements of agricultural production in the same way as the villages to be found near the Western cities with the sole difference that in Hungary they are more integrated into the structure of the town, i.e. they are of a more urban nature than their Western counterparts. The paprika fields and orchards of Szeged have something of an urban character in the same way as the kitchen-gardens and corn-fields of Debrecen.

In terms of the urban character of the downtowns the three agricultural towns with busy traffic (Szolnok, Békéscsaba and Nyíregyháza) follow right after the two great towns mentioned above. If they were not located on the Great Plain and were not surrounded by rural suburbs and homesteads, these three towns could be listed in good faith among smaller Western towns. And only a biased observer could say that the village-like districts and homesteads of these three towns are not of an urban character. In each of these three towns traffic is so busy that their whole area would assume the appearance of an urban centre even if they were not country towns on the strength of their homesteads. Though the agricultural settlements of these towns are different in these three towns, all of them markedly show the characteristics of belonging to an urban centre. The so-called cluster homesteads of Nyíregyháza—though they gradually grow into villages—are different from Western villages: they are linked up much more strongly and decisively with the town. Being villagers to all appearances, the Nyíregyháza homestead-dwellers lead an urban way of life, too, since all of them have a dwelling in the town as well and spend a considerable time there. People living on homesteads in Békéscsaba are not villagers even on the face of it. Here the homesteads are isolated from each other and each of them is linked to the town individually. In Szolnok the homesteads are linked to the town by direct traffic channels. It is in this not primarily agricultural town that the fitting of homesteads into the urban pattern is most conspicuous.

The two classical agricultural towns, Kecskemét and Hódmezővásárhely represent the outstanding example of organizing a huge agricultural area into a homogeneous urban structure. Kecskemét is a major fruit-growing town the market and processing organizations as well as the orchards of which are integral parts of the town endowing it with a characteristic local colour which fully compensates the lack of some urban institutions. Hódmezővásárhely is the centre of animal husbandry and corn-growing. There are hundreds or rather thousands of poultry on the spacious courtyards of its homesteads, and the yield of grain-crops of its black earth are higher than anywhere in the country. In the centre of the town, in addition to the comfortable houses of the farmers, it is the markets and shops selling local produce which represent the urban way of life. The passing observer might be inclined to regard Hódmezővásárhely a sleepy and sluggish town. Actually, however, even this slowly moving energy has proved sufficient to raise Hódmezővásárhely to the status of a town. It is yet to be seen whether this town would be able to develop further without some new kind of dynamism.

By means of their urban organization, Makó, Nagykőrös and Cegléd, the three horticultural towns have raised islands from the level of extensive farming of the Great Plain and have developed a horticulture of urban standards. Each of these three towns has developed different lands in a different way and style their only common feature being that each of them is a town and each has succeeded in developing both its agricultural production and the character of its environment so that they meet urban standards. Cegléd and Nagykőrös have turned the sandy soils into gardens or open woodland. Nagykőrös has developed the black earth area and the town had been transformed into a veritable vegetable-garden. The huge desiccated grasslands and corn-growing areas around Makó have been turned into a countryside almost resembling the fields of the Netherlands. In contrast to the towns enumerated thus far, in these three towns the central areas are smaller, but the houses of the owners of gardens and farmsteads as well as the processing and the sale of highly valuable agricultural produce have created an urban life.

216

Halas and Félegyháza, the towns of Little Cumania in South-Central Hungary are following in the footsteps of Kecskemét and Cegléd introducing a similar type of garden production and are developing along the same urban lines. The towns of the regions of Jászság, Nagykunság and Hajdúság on the other hand are towns of the *"puszta"*. In the surroundings of these towns large-scale livestock-breeding and corn-growing are still carried on and therefore the towns themselves and their suburbs resemble to a greater extent the picture of the old *"puszta"* than those towns which have switched over to more intensive farming. These are towns of the *"puszta"* but of a *"puszta"* which has come under the influence of culture. The only reason why they were able to raise the surrounding region to an urban level while retaining their original characteristics is their specific urban organization which they have preserved and improved from time immemorial.

There are some towns in Békés and Csongrád counties which represent individual local colours in the group of the urban regions of the Great Plain. Thus Szentes and Orosháza are similar in character to Hódmezővásárhely but both of them are more vigorous and capable of further development. In addition to retaining the agricultural character of its production, Orosháza has attempted with increasing success to introduce more intensive methods of production and may follow the lead of Makó or Cegléd. Szentes is very similar to Hódmezővásárhely but its inhabitants are livelier and its production is more diversified. It is a town just like Hódmezővásárhely, however its way of life is more brisk and thus it does not only preserve its present standards but it develops even further. Orosháza is one of our most typical market-towns displaying without any special character the features of an agricultural town.

There are a number of smaller country-towns as Békés, Szarvas or Gyoma which were raised to urban status but recently; the quality of their surrounding areas reflects the recently acquired urban character without any specific features. The trend of their development points towards the example of some other country-towns but owing to specific local energies, they might be able to establish individual agricultural town profiles.

This is the spectrum of our agricultural towns from the point of view of an outsider. However, even a brief account suffices to show what kinds of landscapes have been formed from the monotonous *"puszta"* by the urban structure of one or another town. Thus, as we have seen, the landscape itself is of an urban character and as regards the society embedded in this surroundings, we shall discover even more unquestionably urban phenomena.

*

Agricultural towns have not become towns overnight and particularly the development from village to town has not been an abrupt transformation.

217

Their present form and structure have been shaped by many subsequent generations and these generations have been townsmen ever since the resettlement following the devastations of the Turks. Thus, today all the generations of the agricultural towns consider themselves town-dwellers meaning that the society of agricultural towns has urban traditions. Both old and young regard their communities as town and are equally aware of the circumstances making their urban organization possible.

The society of the agricultural towns has been influenced by the idea of local self-government and social autonomy and both in mind and feelings also the homestead-dwellers have been definitely aware that they belong to the town; living at the far-away homesteads has been a temporary way of life forced upon them by the need for production. This urban consciousness is a living tradition of the society of agricultural towns regarded by all generations as their own. An agricultural town could also become a town if it burst open suddenly its rural limits, aspiring to urban qualities with the younger generation advocating this new aspiration. In the present situation, however, when urban way of life and urban qualities are the only traditions common to all the generations of the townspeople, the urban character of a given settlement cannot even be doubted. At present, these towns are regarded not more urban than they used to be a hundred years ago. The fact that these towns were regarded towns even then is vividly shown by an urban tradition which has been passed from one generation to the other in the society of our agricultural towns up to this very date.

Let us now examine this urban society in terms of its class stratification and let us try to establish whether this stratification is really urban.

The greater part of the society of our agricultural towns still belongs to the peasantry. There follows the basic question whether an urban society can be made up of the peasantry or not? It is well known that primary producers—even if they are not of peasant character—can form an urban society only on rare occasions, whereas peasants are able to do it only quite exceptionally. The earth-bound, static peasantry is necessarily living in villages and therefore such a society can by no means be a city constituting factor. The methods by which primary producers can become townsmen, i.e. homestead settlement and garden production are also beyond the reach of this kind of peasantry. Actually it is only a peasantry which has put an end to its static position and managed to rise to a higher level that is able to bring about homestead settlements, develop garden production and, as a result, it is only this kind of peasantry that can become town-dwellers. Or to put it in another form: a town can be created only by a free society, whereas the peasantry—if it is truly and totally of a peasant character—is not a free society and consequently, it can never become a city constituting factor.

The peasantry of our agricultural towns, however, is a free peasantry. It had entered on the road to an urban way of life when it had been able to substantially alleviate its social conditions by gaining more freedom. It

218

developed the homestead system when it got rid of its landlords, and it succeeded in maintaining its communities greater than the village communities because it managed to develop a free and autonomous society. However, these town-dwellers remained peasants, even at the time of developing the urban structure despite the fact that they succeeded in attaining freedom; but the more they were able to defend their urban organization and to develop further their society into an increasingly urban and free community, the fewer peasant features they retained. Even if we accept the validity of the fundamental thesis according to which the peasantry and urban way of life are incompatible, it is also true that the reduction of peasant traits improves the capacity for an urban way of life.

On the basis of this connection the peasantry of the agricultural towns could become an urban population and its social development reflects the validity of this connection up to this date. At the time when the pattern of the agricultural town had taken shape the town-founding peasantry had already moved out of its earth-bound immobility and in the course of its subsequent history it lost its peasant character simultaneously with urban growth. By now our agricultural settlements have assumed an almost totally urban character while the primary producers in these towns have almost totally lost their peasant character.

The peasantry of the agricultural towns can be regarded as peasantry in the genuine sense of the word only in the times before urbanization and the gaining of urban rights. In the free districts of the Jászkunság and Hajdúság the peasantry had got rid of its dependence even before the rise of agricultural towns. In these regions peasant subordination and dependence have been continually diminishing from that time on; by now the agricultural population in these regions can be regarded as true agriculturists. If the members of this agriculturist stratum nevertheless prefer to call themselves peasants this does not mean the acceptance of peasant status but it rather reflects a protest against the rule of the surviving peasant laws. They call themselves peasants partly because they are actually still peasants experiencing everywhere contempt owing to this origin. However, this stratum is no longer willing to be looked upon as peasants.

When pursuing sociological studies, it must be realized that the peasantry of the agricultural towns has already been integrated into the bourgeois pattern of society. If these people are nevertheless called peasants this term can be used only in order to indicate the surviving vestiges of the past or to define a political aspiration.

Thus, the society of the country-towns represents by and large a homogeneous bourgeois society; the peasantry has already fitted into this pattern, and even the peasant past filling in the earlier periods of the history of such towns had not been a genuinely peasant life because of its urban environment.

Concerns about the peasantry are therefore needless: the society of the

219

agricultural towns has become a truly bourgeois society and for this reason it can certainly be a truly urban society.

Naturally the differences of occupation have not been eliminated by the transformation of the peasantry, i.e. by the class stratification having assumed a unified character. Thus we have not to reckon with peasants in urban societies though agriculturalists are still present there. The question arises whether devoid of its peasant character this occupation is not an obstacle to regarding these societies as urban ones? As it has been pointed out, primary producers' towns are a feasible alternative, and Hungarian agricultural towns pursuing garden farming and assuming a homestead pattern are perfect examples of such towns.

If the criteria of town were linked with large-scale technological equipment it would certainly be a necessary criterion that urban society be bourgeois without any remnants of feudal stratification and with an economically strong bourgeoisie also capable of developing urban technology. Since we regard the social function and not the technological equipment and institutions as the essential factors of the town, this consequence can be easily ignored and the society of our agricultural towns can be examined without this bias.

The society of the agricultural towns is thus a bourgeois society the average proportions of its class stratification being equal to those of Hungarian society as a whole. About ten per cent of the population of the agricultural town can be regarded as belonging to the bourgeoisie, about forty per cent to the petite bourgeoisie and the remaining fifty per cent to the working class. Such class relationships in themselves do not reveal anything about urban character, but if we take into account that the settlement having such social stratification is a town, then it can be pointed out unequivocally that it is a poor town. This explains the fact that despite their excellent urban nature our agricultural towns proved to be unable to develop the technological facilities which, even with a superficial approach, are regarded as indispensable accessories of urban life. This poverty is somewhat alleviated in some of the agricultural towns by the fact that the town as a legal body is rather wealthy thus being able to develop from its revenues those public facilities which could not be subsidized by its own citizens. Taken as a whole, however, the society of our agricultural towns is nevertheless poor and this will not change until this society prevails hindering the building and development of technological facilities needed by such towns.

The bourgeoisie of the country-town is every bit an urban factor; indeed it is the leading stratum of the society of the agricultural town. Both as regards leadership and the way of life there are but very slight differences between the various groups of the bourgeoisie. In most of the towns the gentlemanly upper-middle class elements of the bourgeoisie have retained their leading role while at county seats, and in addition in Nagykőrös and

220

Kiskunhalas, they are absolute masters of urban society. The descendants of the old urban bourgeoisie with the new arrivals partly of Jewish, partly of German origins also lay claim everywhere to the leading role by right of old traditions. This stratum tries to justify its claim by adapting itself as far as possible to the upper middle-class way of life and by absolute identification with the upper middle-class. There are but few agricultural towns where there has emerged an independent bourgeois consciousness which, as opposed also to the upper middle-class influence, developed a true urban-bourgeois (industrial-commercial) way of life. The bourgeoisie of German origin has faded everywhere into the bureaucratic order which has become the follower of the upper middle-class way of life. It was only the bourgeoisie formed of tradesmen and merchants of Hungarian or Jewish origin which managed to develop in some places an independent way of life and social function. For instance the industrial-commercial bourgeoisie of Szolnok, though of absolutely mixed origin and not devoid of a strong German strain, was able to emerge as a peculiar Hungarian urban burgherhood. Similarly in Debrecen the descendants of the well-to-do town-dweller peasants and Jews both pursuing industrial and commercial activities succeeded in forming an independent bourgeoisie. In Szeged the bourgeoisie has been of a somewhat similar origin, however, there the influence of the Roman Catholic clergy is strong representing an upper middle-class and feudal impact as opposed to the burgher character of the Debrecen Calvinist clergy. In the other towns — if there is any independent bourgeoisie to be found there — the bourgeoisie consists mainly of Jews, and this group everywhere only embarrasses the gentlemanly nature of local leadership. Though most European and most bourgeois in its way of life, in some places it identified itself rather with the peasantry and the working class.

The well-to-do elements of the former peasantry have become totally integrated with the leading group of the bourgeoisie participating in leadership according to local traditions. This peasant burgherhood has preserved its independence in all privileged fields, and though it tends to be conservative or loyal in its relationship with the upper middle-class leadership, it has not acquired the upper middle-class way of life. These privileged towns have developed a peasant democracy where the most wealthy farmers who became embourgeoised retained their independence both downwards and upwards and especially in the face of the elite of the merchant bourgeoisie. Their class consciousness is of totally bourgeois nature but since they go on living imbued with agricultural town traditions they managed to retain solidarity with the lower strata of the population. In all the other agricultural towns these peasant-burghers have become the supporters of the gentlemanly upper middle-class and, owing to class solidarity linking them to this class, they have tried to adopt their way of life as well. Leading farmers strive everywhere to become aldermen or get titles

221

like honorary counsellor, and if they have succeeded in obtaining such status, they tend to consider themselves as members of the upper middle-class with genuinely upper middle-class rights. It is an absolutely exceptional case when ambitious and rising farmers ally themselves with other groups of the bourgeoisie. Makó may be the only settlement where this phenomenon can partly be traced. As a rule, however, this is not the case and therefore the urbanization and embourgeoisement of the peasantry follows a totally unbeaten path. With the exception of the privileged towns nothing indicates the possibility that this stratum would ever be able to reconcile its urban and embourgeoised way of life with its existence as agriculturalist and working-class.

This bourgeoisie consisting of three elements is the leading stratum of the society of agricultural towns but its leading role means only on rare occasions a leadership of country-town traditions. The gentlemanly upper middle-class and the bourgeoisie of German-Jewish origin do not feel any affinity for the traditions of the agricultural towns. On the contrary, both these strata would like to maintain an isolated and separated urban way of life. As a result of such a leadership, our agricultural towns are urbanized, even as regards their outward appearance only in a tiny downtown core, whereas the remaining zones despite their perfect urban patterns, are increasingly forced to live on a village level. A broadly founded urbanization can be observed only in towns where the traditions of a free peasant democracy are still alive and the leadership socialized along these lines associates itself with the whole society of the town. However, even at those settlements leadership has undergone a certain change, and if the present trend continues here too, an isolated urbanism is going to prevail.

In all the agricultural towns the broad stratum of the petite bourgeoisie is a stratum of followers and if occasionally it displays any independent attitudes, they are not aimed at a homogeneous urbanization but at preserving popular traditions. For this reason, the petite bourgeoisie of the agricultural towns is to a certain degree less of an urban character than the bourgeoisie though none of its groups are alien to urban traditions.

The greatest stratum of the population consists of petit bourgeois small-holders. This stratum leads a life of even more peasant character than the large farmers and this conservatism respresents both a smaller and greater extent of urbanism from the point of view of urban development. This group is less urbanized because its living standards are lower, its way of life is simpler and its attitudes are more hesitant, whereas its urban character is more developed insofar that it is this very stratum which actually upholds the homestead pattern and, as a result, is the vanguard of a broadly founded urbanism. This strange duality could be best defined by pointing out that agricultural town traditions are preserved mostly by this semi-peasant stratum of small-holders; just because of this and as a result of its peasant character it is least willing to accept a rapid and isolated urbanization. In the

222

municipalities it is the representatives of this stratum who oppose the building of theatres, yet simultaneously it is these persons who most vociferously protest against proposals to disannex the surroundings of their homesteads from the town or against relinquishing a homestead road project.

The petite bourgeoisie of traders and shopkeepers with an urban past is the least Hungarian stratum of agricultural towns. In addition to Jews who are to be found in all towns, German, Serbian, Romanian and Slovakian nationalities are also to be found. The number of Germans is negligible in agricultural towns and they mainly belong to the overwhelmingly assimilated white-collar bureaucracy, while the Slovakians, Serbs and Romanians are represented as indifferent groups in some of the agricultural towns. The urban petite bourgeoisie of Hungarian origin is to be found only in places where urban development did not begin with the evolution of agricultural towns, for instance in Szeged or Debrecen. However, in those towns, too, the Hungarian element has fully merged in the colourless mass of the petite bourgeoisie. Thus, the masses of this petite bourgeoisie have urban aspirations and though they are not susceptible to the traditions of the agricultural towns, they definitely want their communities to grow into genuine towns. Within the limits of its economic strength this stratum realizes as much as possible of this way of life.

The Jewish petite bourgeoisie is of a definite and peculiar character. While the majority of the Jewish bourgeoisie has unconditionally assimilated and developed an urban way of life patterned on Western Europe and as regards its denomination it belongs to reformed synagogues, the Jewish petite bourgeoisie being isolated and belonging mainly to orthodox communities continues to preserve the way of life of the ghettos. Nevertheless this Jewish population represents an urban group but only insofar as its members tend to live in the centre of the town engaging in industry and trade. Jews belonging to the petite bourgeoisie maintain continuous contacts within their own group but have no affinity whatsoever to either the urban traditions of the agricultural towns or the European patterns of development. For them urban way of life is a simple fact and no traditions or requirements are deduced from this fact. In the long run they are not a dynamic force of the society of agricultural towns.

The working class, too, is split into two parts. The majority of them works in agricultural, the minority in industrial and commercial enterprises but apart from an exceptional stratum they are almost equally urban factors of the society of agricultural towns. The exceptional stratum is that of the homestead labourers. These workers have been excluded from the town by the homestead system, they have been sacrificed as the only ones to the life of the *puszta* by urban development. In most places these homestead farm hands are destitute and helpless cotters who are not allowed to participate in the life of either the city or society. Neither can they communicate with each other because of incessant hard toil and great distances, whereas communication with the farmers is taking place under the conditions of strict subordination; this cannot be regarded as social communication but only as a status of being employed. However, in a few towns where local working-class organizations succeeded in influencing this stratum there has been a lively response to the ideas of the working class. Under the influence of socialist theory calling for urbanization, homestead labourers became factors of urbanization, though this stratum was expelled from the towns. Thus, in Hódmezővásárhely the most enthusiastic adherents of the working-class party are to be found on the homesteads, and the fact that the town has a socialist representative is mainly to be attributed to homestead labourers.

The great masses of agricultural workers, too, are to be considered urban factors insofar as they participate in the labour movement. Those who do not are town-dwellers only to such an extent as they live at a separate housing estate of the town but this zone is an integral part of the urban pattern. Workers participating in the labour movement are most energetically demanding the urban development of the town, the liquidation of the penury of their housing estates and the fastest possible transformation of the town.

By virtue of their occupations industrial workers are town-dwellers and thus, whether they are participants of some movements or not, they are by all means genuine urban factors of the life of the agricultural towns. Just like the petite bourgeoisie these workers naturally have no feeling for agricultural town traditions but their call for urbanization is so strong and sincere that they have become the most active elements of all efforts aimed at urban development. It is of no importance that they were not educated by the traditions of the agricultural cities because they represent the longing for a kind of overall urbanization most fiercely rejecting an urbanization limited to certain town zones. Thus, their energy points in the same direction as if it helped consciously the further development of agricultural towns. Even without class-consciousness agricultural workers are the most energetic town developing stratum and since they live in agricultural cities they promote the development of these settlements.

After having outlined the social stratification of agricultural cities, there can be little doubt about the urban character of their society. Examining the functioning of this society it can be pointed out even without a detailed analysis of the individual attitudes that some of its social phenomena are inherently and specifically of urban character necessarily linking up with the urban idea.

The towns of the German regions have probably developed only to fulfil the functions of a role demanding an urban framework; this is known of all such towns whether their original function was that of a fortress, traffic centre, trade settlement, church centre or royal court. The Mediterranean towns, however, particularly the towns of the ancient world have not come into being with such specific purposes. Athens and Rome had been founded by shepherds and ploughmen not as industrial or traffic centres but as residential settlements around the forums. It was not the market-place which had been the core of the ancient town but the forum, i.e. the place where people gathered without any definite aim just to communicate with each other and to live public life. This shapeless gathering-place established without any formal purpose had been such an undoubted and ancient phenomenon of urban life that wherever such a forum is to be found the settlement around it is a real city even if the population which came to live there does not fulfil urban functions or does not live in the direct neighbourhood of the forum.

The community of our agricultural cities is well acquainted with such forum-like gathering-places; town life is regarded first and foremost as this kind of informal and aimless gathering by all the members of the community.

Homestead farmers drive home to the town every Sunday morning, and also on the occasion of the weekly market, and having groomed their horses and taken a rest they set out for "the inside". The same is done by those who live all the time in the town, and if they meet an acquaintance in the street they answer his question by "goin' inside". And the place where people tend to meet is none other than the market-place. For a certain time it is actually a market but after having closed down the "forum life" there begins the shapeless and "aimless" public life with the sole purpose that people should be able to meet and talk over problems of common interest. They hear about news, give their opinions and go home assured that they have been part of the course of the world. It happens that a farmer drives home from his homestead twenty kilometres from the town only to be able to turn up on the forum, and it also has happened that when following some decree Sunday markets were closed down the crowd gathered on the place just as if there were a market-day.

However, since there is no special term in Hungarian for "forum" such gatherings are simply called "markets" by the people. But since either nothing is marketed at these places or commodity trade has only an inferior role at such gatherings, they are also called "men market" and "women market" depending on whether men or women participate in the gathering. It is a tempting possibility to search for the original core of agricultural towns in these "market" gatherings and not in some kind of Germanic urban function. It seems quite probable that it was this forum which prevented the inhabitants of the villages clustered into town from returning to their original settlements because they have become so much obsessed with that form of public life that even the harsh realities of production could not tear them apart. No matter how obvious such an explanation would seem, it does not make any sense to set out for such distant and uncertain explanations,

225

when it is an indisputable fact that such forum-like gatherings are today the most central aspects of both the life and the urban character of the towns.

Naturally, owing partly to technological development and partly to the fact that the population has been increasingly divided into clearly defined classes, these forum-like gatherings have assumed several forms today. With the more well-to-do farmers the function of the "men-market" is slowly shifting to the farmers' club, but no matter how bourgeois in terms of their consciousness the members of this club are, all the farmers turn up at the market because it is here where they most readily find those with whom they have to settle some deal. In many a town it is not only the well-to-do farmers of bourgeois consciousness who have their own club but the tenants, the gardeners and the workers, too, have the clubs of their own. None of these, however, can fully replace the common "market" because all are meeting-places based on class position, whereas the "market" on the main square is common to all the classes, this explaining its exceptional significance. The "woman-market" is disappearing in most towns since bourgeois women do not frequent such places and in towns where the club life of women is not taken for granted to the same degree as with men, women rather stay at home. Though the "market-place" tends to lose its old function as a women's forum and is degraded to be a sort of servant exchange and gossip corner, in many towns it still functions up to this very date.

In the agricultural towns, too, there came into being the promenade for the youth, being a gathering-place without class distinctions just as the forum with the only difference that here there is an age limit. But even this is not always absolutely observed. Sunday morning and late in the evening on workdays the promenade is the gathering-place of the bourgeoisie and the petite bourgeoisie and the members of this stratum make the best of this social opportunity disregarding any age limits; only the most illustrious families do not mix with the people. On the other hand, Sunday afternoon and early in the evening the promenade is crowded with common folk, but it is only the younger generations which go there clearly with the aim to meet the other sex. This "peasant promenade" is still very much of an urban nature because it is rather different from the Sunday gatherings in the villages where the members of small communities knowing each other very well gather together. In contrast, on the promenades of the agricultural towns there assembles a greater crowd with the only aim of enjoying the exciting presence of the members of the other sex. For young people this promenade plays the same role as the "market" for the older generations. Young people come home from the farmsteads only to show up on the crowded promenade just as the older ones for the sake of "market" gatherings. And when old and young return late at night to the homesteads, both of them are satisfied to have participated in urban life and are longing to repeat the experience next time.

226

The heart of the matter of such shapeless gatherings—lending it the significance of a real urban way of life—is the fact that they embody an occasion for gathering together which is open to all and true enough, everybody does avail himself of the opportunity. The forum of the agricultural town is not identical with the market-place, i.e. not only those are interested in it who want to buy or sell something but everybody is attracted by it—young and old, paupers and the upper middle-class alike, i.e. all the inhabitants of the town. The fact that anybody residing in the town or working in the surroundings is by its very organization a member of the town represents only an abstract relationship, an abstract urban way of life. But when on the occasions of such a gathering anybody can meet any other citizen of the town, the unity of the town becomes a tangible fact thus laying the foundation for genuine community ties.

Naturally other gatherings and meetings according to various social functions also strengthen urban relationships. However, these get-togethers are all of a specific and partial importance. Only the gatherings at the forum are occasions for general and universal relationships and therefore this forum can be regarded as an unquestionable evidence of the universal validity of the urban character of the agricultural town.

2. HOUSES

The agricultural town has developed in the same way as the residential town and has preserved this character up to this date. Naturally every town is a residential town since all those who make their livelihood in a town usually live there, too. The agricultural town, however, is a town not only in this sense but also because those engaged in a distant productive labour live in the town as well. For this very reason these towns were not called into being by the necessities of production. On the contrary, they were developed by the social energies of living together as opposed to the requirements of porduction. Even today it is only a part of the population which finds work in the central zone of the town; the majority have jobs outside the town, whereas their homes, their actual and constant places of residence are to be found in the town.

In the course of time when the pastures along the precincts of the town were brought under cultivation just like in the villages, the number of farmers who regarded the town both as their workplace and home increased. Yet, these primary producers never became decisive factors of urban life, and if they had determined the decisive character of our agricultural towns, these towns would certainly have declined into the state of being a village.

Simultaneously with the increase of the number of houses with a rural character, also the houses of persons employed in industry, commerce and

227

the homes of intellectuals became more numerous. Naturally, for these persons the town has become not simply a place of residence but also a place of production; in the same way as in the houses of primary producers in the villages, home and productive work found their place on a single plot or under a common roof.

Thus the originally purely residential town character has partly been transformed by agricultural production and partly by commercial, industrial and intellectual work, i.e. the town experienced two simultaneous trends: on the one hand, because of the spread and expansion of urban occupations the town slowly grew into an industrial and administrative settlement, on the other, it slipped back into the state of a village. Though all the three types of homes mentioned have definitely developed in the agricultural town, the town as a whole did not lose its original character. It continued to be a town whose most characteristic house is the residential town house of a primary producer working on his homestead.

Taken the national average of all agricultural towns, the three types of houses are equally common in the areas of such towns.

The urban dwelling-house of the homestead farmer used to be the original type of house of the agricultural town. This kind of house is not of agricultural town origin as regards its outside form since it could already be found in olden times in rural settlements. However, since the emergence of agricultural towns, the development of the traditional Hungarian house has taken another course, and having rid itself of its production function, it developed into a peculiar dwelling house.

The prototype of this type of house, as of all Hungarian houses, was a unicellular crude shelter, a roof for both man and beast, the still existing form of which can be found in some places of Cumania in Central Hungary in the form of heatable stables. While peasant cottages have preserved the common roof for beast and man, in agricultural towns the dwelling has been separated from the sties and stables, and has started to develop independently. The heatable stable has been banished to the homestead; here it became primarily a shelter for the beast and only a tiny corner of it has been retained for human habitation.

Thus the house most typical of agricultural towns has developed from the dwelling section of the ancient Hungarian house. In its form and structure, however, even this separated dwelling-house has retained the character of its forerunner, the house uniting dwelling-place and stable.

While the house became a place of residence only, it remained a free-standing building and it was but much later that it took the form of undetached house in a row. Though it had distinct front and rear parts and upper and lower ends all of its sides were of the same shape and the smooth gable roof had no projecture to either side. For this reason, such a house could be placed absolutely free-standing at any place on the plot and could be oriented at will. Old maps actually verify the assumption that both in

228

garden-towns and in agricultural towns which had developed out of a number of smaller settlements the dwelling-house was situated on the ground-plot most whimsically all through the eighteenth century. Some houses were built deep on the site parallel with the street, some took the same position only near to the street, and quite a few faced the street with their rear part. All of such towns houses had, however, a common feature: they were never built at the end of the ground-plot. The ground-plot was surrounded by a fence, the house itself being situated in a way that man and dog could walk around it unhindered.

Regarding its inner structure this house differed from the house of olden times which had served as a stable and sty as well, insofar that opposite the living-room, the door of the porch did not open into the stable but into a cubby-hole or later more often than not into another room on the other end of which a pantry was built with a separate door.

Thus, the Hungarian house was not a row house either in its homogeneous form at the farmsteads and villages or in its internally separated form in the agricultural towns. But neither was it of a pattern which could not have developed into an undetached row house for reasons of its structure. The block house of the German regions for instance is absolutely unfit for ever becoming any kind of a terrace house. This type of house was formed and shaped at all sides separately; each side had its own function, and therefore it could by no means link up with the line of a downtown building-plot. As a matter of fact in regions where this type of house is dominant the villages are not settlements consisting of undetached row houses but houses are situated freely and haphazardly next to each other.

The Hungarian house, however, could and actually did develop into an undetached row house both in village and agricultural city settlements. As a first step a pent-roof was built as a projection of the roof above the entrance and by this very fact the differing roles of the sides of the house were determined. The front of the house became elongated towards the ground-plot and therefore this side had necessarily to face the rear end of the plot. And when they began to put on board, painting or plaster decorations at the upper part of the house where the bigger room was to be found, this end of the dwelling assumed a separate function; now it was this end of the house which necessarily had to face the street. As the next step of development the house was built in one of the corners of the plot with its lower part towards the neighbouring house and its front facing the rear of the plot whereas the decorated end overlooked the street. With this the building has become a row house and from this time on its further development could take place only along this path.

Even after the emergence of homesteads in the fieldlands, the detached dwelling-house was the most common type of house in our agricultural towns. It was quite common that the dwelling-house was situated in the back of the plot crosswise to the street; the outhouses and stables—which were necessary despite the farmsteads—were facing the street and, as it is pointed out in the history of the town of Szentes, manure was thrown out onto the street. In towns consisting of houses with gardens outbuildings did not belong to the dwellings but the living-house itself was situated as freely and waywardly as in places where houses were not surrounded by gardens.

From the beginning of the 19th century, however, i.e. when the urban organization of agricultural towns assumed its final form, houses began to line up in rows and the innermost parts of the towns increasingly assumed the character of an organized residential town. Decoration on walls facing the street became more and more common, the eaves extended all along the front forming a porch in front of which a tiny flower-garden was to be found at pretentious houses. The outbuildings, necessary even in the case of homestead farming were inevitably located under separate roofs in the back of the yard and, compared to the dwelling-house, had an inferior part. For this reason the well-known Hungarian researcher, Zolnai has taken notice of the fact that in the past when heirs divided the ground-plots there were rarely any references to stables, barns or sheds. And this is but natural since these were buildings of only secondary importance and often but rough-and-ready makeshift sheds serving to shelter cattle when they were driven home from the farmsteads.

This type of dwelling-houses underwent changes and further developed only from the middle of the 19th century when demands on homes increased and people needed more and more rooms. The inner structure of the house did not permit to build more than two rooms within the house since the unicellular system continued to be effective. A house could be built only with two roms: one to the right, the other to the left of the porch. If more rooms were needed there seemed to be only a single solution: to make the house crooked in the line of the street next to the room overlooking the street, and there to build one or if necessary even more rooms. Indeed, the ensuing type of country-town dwelling-houses was the crooked house meeting fully the requirements of the homestead-farmer living in the village. The arrangement of the ground-plot remained unchanged but the part of the house overlooking the street was increased, and here there were plenty of opportunities for decoration and vain display. This kind of elongating the house had yet another effect. It became possible to bring the entrance gate, too, under the roof and thus to build, on the whole street-line, if needed, right to the end of the plot. This possibility has been fully made use of by agricultural town farmers since the end of the past century; as a result streets with closed rows of houses were built by now presenting even in their outward appearance a definitely residential and urban style. Even today these closely built crooked houses are the most characteristic types of buildings in the residential streets of our agricultural towns. However, inside the house the arrangement follows the very same pattern as it used to when only a single room had opened on the street. The combined porch and kitchen are still at the same place and rooms open from it both to the right and the left. However, where there have been built more rooms these tend to have functions of their own, due to the arrangement of the bourgeois home, since the inhabitant of such a house is, in addition to his agricultural occupation, a burgher as well.

The agricultural town house of rural character and function has developed out of the same ancient form, as the dwelling-house but it has retained its unity with the stable and the other farm-buildings. It has become a terrace-house just like the dwelling-house, however, it has been elongated so much along one side of the ground-plot that the stable and the shed, too, could be accommodated under its roof, and thus the courtyard has been divided also in two parts according to the dwelling and farm sections of the house. These two parts are the upper and the lower courtyard, and of these the lower one has become the farm-yard. Such houses with rural functions are up to this date turned only with their rear ends towards the street and as a consequence, streets consisting of such houses are full of vacant lots since houses and their fenced plots of unbuilt grounds are alternating.

In some streets of the agricultural towns these two types of houses of different functions and patterns are alternating, thus producing streets of mixed character. As a rule, however, the dwellings of homestead-farmers are to be found in separate streets and so are the houses of rural character.

In the agricultural towns the dwelling-houses of inhabitants pursuing occupations follow to a certain extent the pattern of house types rooted in past times; however, they embody house forms of alien origin developed independently of the ancient Hungarian types. A frequent bourgeois pattern is the house built all along the ground-plot facing the street; this is similar to the most developed form of dwelling possessed by homestead farmers. In these houses, however, there is no broad gateway instead of which a narrow doorway is leading to the street serving only as an entrance for the inhabitants of the house. In addition to this type of house, however, a great variety of other types of provincial houses are also to be found ranging from two-storey houses with their rear overlooking the street to villa-like blockhouses. The common feature of all these houses is that they have been unequivocally built for the purpose of dwellings; occasionally offices, surgeries or shops occupy at the most a room or two but these do not disturb the structure of the house adapted to the needs of the dwelling.

A separate form of house has developed in the outlying settlements for the only reason that, considering building materials available, the village-type house proved the most economical form. Houses of these workers' colonies have been built without exception patterned after village houses even if their inhabitants tend to be industrial workers. Such workers' houses are similar to village houses only in their external forms, i.e. they are facing the street with their rear end and therefore the streets are discontinuous. However, in their internal order, this differs considerably from the village

231

pattern since only very occasionally are stables in them. As a consequence, the courtyard does not fall into two parts either since there is no need for a farm-yard; instead of it a part of the ground-plot—usually that facing the street—has been transformed into a garden and only the rear end of the ground-plot remains an uncultivated yard. The village-type house farm is quite often further developed at such outlying colonies: the eaves are built in and a kitchen or pantry is formed. Frequently the whole front part of the house under the eaves is built in, and in such cases a kind of hall; the kitchen and the pantry are located here. Whatever the forms and patterns of the houses of such outlying colonies, they are all primarily and in the overwhelming majority of cases dwelling-houses, and despite their rural forms it is a rare exception that they should serve as farm-buildings as well. A small garden in a fenced in corner of the courtyard and a tiny poultry-run in the rear—this is all what is allocated for farming purposes, and such can be found even in bourgeois houses in downtown districts of the town.

In its present form the country-town is only two hundred years old, thus its characteristic houses are at the most two hundred years old. However, houses which could be regarded as historic monuments have not survived in great numbers even this relatively short period of time. The most outstanding dwellings are everywhere mansions built at the end of the 18th and the early 19th centuries as the residence of either the local landlord or of some other official of the county administration, and they have remained exclusive upper middle-class homes up to this date. It is rather interesting that in terms of town-planning these mansions are of the same urban dwelling-house character as the homes of the homestead-farmers since landlords had their homesteads, just like the peasant farmers, far away in the fields; yet because their estates used to be larger they were termed manors. The most beautiful and numerous such mansions are to be found in Nagykőrös which is a veritable museum of the upper middle-class classicist building style of the Hungarian countryside.

The atmosphere of the old town-houses has been preserved only by some short rows of houses in Debrecen and Szeged. In other towns there are only occasionally a couple of such dilapidated houses reflecting a way of life which could not become a dominant form in Hungarian agricultural towns.

The building material of peasant houses had been mud and earth for a long time and therefore rarely can we find houses older than a hundred years. From the beginning of the middle of the last century, however, in all of our towns there can be found historic buildings and some of them are quite valuable. These are outstanding examples of economically and well-built peasant houses; they are not yet terrace-like buildings and have been built of earth and reed, nevertheless they still seem fascinating, owing to the beauty of their form and economic pattern. Most of the monuments and the most beautiful ones of the peasant houses date back to a stage of development when the house itself has been squeezed out into a corner of

232

the ground-plot but has not yet taken on a crooked form. These houses going on the street with their rear end were built by the well-to-do farmers altogether of brick or at least the rear ends and the columns of the portico were made of brick. Owing to their structure and beautiful ornaments, they are the outstanding achievements of peasant architecture in agricultural towns. The Baroque-like decoration of the end of the houses is in itself a captivating sight, and the massive proportions, the rhythm of the rear end of the house as well as of the columns underlined by white or light yellow colours render these peasant houses the most lasting works of architecture in the agricultural towns.

In our time there is a new construction fever in agricultural cities but the present-day houses are rather a cheerless sight. The residential buildings of the burghers continue the secessionist plaster-trifling widely popular in the pre-war years, and only in the case of a minority of recently built houses has at least as much of the modern building style been recognized that the walls of the traditionally designed houses have been left "unadorned". Numerous dwelling-houses with modern structures are to be found only in two medium-size towns though almost every town can boast of a couple of solitary representatives of the new style. In recent years in most of the county-towns some municipal or cooperative blocks of flats have been built which are pointed out as sights of the towns by the official prospectuses. By meeting the requirements of residential buildings of an urban character, in downtown districts these buildings are certainly welcome phenomena. However, with rare exceptions, their form and style are warning examples of the most horrible architectural aberration. All kinds of "neo" trends are to be found among them, the dominant style being the neo-baroque. Such hotchpotch is deplorable not only as regards the aesthetic aspect but it is also an exasperating historical phenomenon; if such a style has become the dominant feature in the present-day life of our agricultural towns it is easy to see that this type of urbanization is entirely alien to the traditions of these towns and nothing positive can be expected from such a town-planning.

Thus, the streets of the agricultural towns do not breathe the air of a historic town and though the style of their buildings are mostly lacking grace they still have some beauty of their own. The old streets of the downtown which have been united and transformed into residential districts are narrow and tortuous, and some road-junctions or streets running into squares provide the visitor with unexpected sights. Here the rows of houses are not similar to the well-known streets of Western Europe either, nevertheless the peasant-style and burgher-style houses lined up side by side and the varied location of both of these types on the ground-plot are certainly interesting and can by no means be termed a rural sight. The boulevards cutting through the town and the rows of houses of streets sometimes widening suddenly and forming squares do not form a homogeneously closed row of houses but their beauty is fascinating. The wide open

233

spaces and the immense dome of the sky above them lend air and light to the townscape unfolding before our eyes. Despite their rustic houses, the residential settlements in the outskirts are not of a rural character because they are lacking wide spaces and huge proportions. The narrow streets, houses lining up beside each other leaving but tiny gaps would seem toy-villages if viewed superficially. A keener eye, however, is reminded of urban proletarian colonies; this desolate picture is slightly improved by the tiny gardens, some poultry in the yards and occasionally a huge acacia tree at the rear end of the houses. Workers' colonies built as a joint building venture are as much of a rural character in their outward appearance as those which have been built one by one; however, the straight line of the rear end of the houses resembling a military formation, the weird repetition of red roof-tiles and the uniformly dim window panes have turned these districts into a phalanster-like settlement, whereas the absolute lack of individual diversity throws a sharp light on the proletarian pauperism of such colonies.

The streets of the truly rural districts are much more harmonious. Broad streets, spacious courtyards and rear ends of houses all overlooking the street are very much like genuine villages; to be more exact, we are reminded of villages situated very close to cities. Such rural streets occupy whole belts around towns and they are both according to their functions and architectural style alien bodies within an urban structure. Their outward appearance will be alien to the general view of the town as long as they remain unchanged. However, the socio-economic role of these rural districts is not absolutely alien to the town. Primary producers cannot be town-dwellers if they pursue their production in the town's central zone; however, if they live in town, their production can become urbanized even without homesteads. First of all they can seriously try their hand in market gardening in the surroundings of the town. The onion-growers of Makó, the paprika-growers of Szeged, the market-gardeners of Nagykőrös all live in the urban village and it is rather questionable whether such a garden culture would have developed if this village were a solitary, isolated settlement far away from the town. In addition to that, the originally village-type house system is capable of urbanization. The first task of the urban renewal in agricultural towns will be to rid the rural houses of economic buildings and to furnish these homes with urban facilities. These primary producers are willing to accept such change; actually they live in villages wedged in towns in spite of their urban aspirations.

Besides their existing structural urban character the residential districts of agricultural towns can assume an astonishingly urban character by the adequate use of vegetation. Though the forms of the houses do not present the usual urban image, afforestation and the deliberate use of other kinds of vegetation can shape the picture of streets lending them a fully urban character. These efforts are still in the initial stages but they promise

234

excellent results. The afforestation of Szentes, Makó and Kiskunhalas has already improved immensely the streets of these towns and at the same time all the three towns set an example to other settlements of how to develop their townscapes. The wall-like lines of poplars, the leafy trees of the residential districts, the covering up of open channels with shrubs, the planting of the spaces between the houses and the roads with flower beds and shrubs are admirable methods of enhancing the beauty and the agricultural character of residential districts.

This function of the vegetation is particularly important if it is taken into account that, despite all efforts, the supply of public utilities serving private dwellings is extremely scarce in all our agricultural towns. It should be emphasized that such technological equipment is not a precondition for urban character. Nevertheless it is undeniable that it is favourable if such utilities exist, moreover they are preconditions of higher-standard housing. With the exceptions of Szeged, Debrecen and Szolnok, in our agricultural towns canalization, watermains, pavement and footwalks are of a sub-standard quality. Though they have been developed over considerable parts of the towns, public utilities are not complete, even in the above-mentioned three towns, whereas in all other agricultural towns they exist only in the small central areas. It is only electricity which can be found in adequate quantity in all agricultural towns; all other public utilities are to be developed in the future. It is also an undeniable fact that if public utilities should be developed as integrated systems a certain increase in population density has to be attained.

Thus, with a few exceptions, our agricultural towns are not of an urban character as regards the availability of public utilities for housing purposes but since the structure and the society of these towns are urbanized, the development and building of public utilities can be achieved much more easily than in villages.

The housing statistics of agricultural towns reflect the astonishing fact that of all settlements in the country it is here that the people/house ratio is the lowest. For this reason it would be easy to draw the conclusion that these towns are absolutely lacking urban conditions. However, this conclusion is possible only for those who are totally ignorant of actual conditions.

First of all it should be stressed that in our view huge structures and many-storey buildings are not preconditions of the urban character of a settlement since also smaller buildings are equally suitable for performing the functions of urban housing or any other urban role. Even so, it is unusual that while in the villages of the nation a house is inhabited on the average by 5.1 persons, in Hódmezővásárhely for instance this ratio is 4.3 persons per house. This is the more baffling as in Hódmezővásárhely there are on an average still more many-storey buildings than in villages. As a matter of fact, if the agricultural towns had not any homesteads the number of persons per room and/or the number of persons per house would be somewhere between Western-type towns and that of villages. The only reason why these figures are much lower than those of the villages is the existence of the homestead system. It is because of this system that while the number of inhabitants per house in Fejér County (the town of Székesfehérvár excluded) is 5.4, in Győr County (the town of Győr excluded) 5.6, in Somogy 5.3, in Vas 6.2, in Veszprém 5.5 and Zala 5.4; it is 4.6 in Békés, 4.4 in Csanád, 4.5 in Csongrád, 4.3 in the town of Hódmezővásárhely, 4.4 in Hajdú and 4.5 in the County of Jász-Nagykun-Szolnok.

A reasoning based on statistics would be tempted to explain this with the fact that the population is much more scattered in homestead regions and very few people are living on the single farmsteads. It should be stressed, however, that there are a great number of homesteads inhabited by less than five people. At the same time we also know that young people living on farmsteads have the highest fertility rates and, in addition to the members of the family, even hired farm hands are often needed. Actually the cause of the above phenomenon is the homestead, however, not because few people are living there but because the farmstead means a kind of dual housing—if staying at the homestead is also conceived as a housing. The homestead farmers have their housing at the homesteads regarded statistically as dwellings and, besides, most of them have their own house or at least a section of a house in the town as well. Therefore there are much more dwellings in the agricultural towns than in the smallest villages if homesteads are considered also dwellings. The case of Hódmezővásárhely is particularly characteristic, where of all the administrative units of the country the number of persons per house is the lowest, though it is a fairly well-known fact that this town has a great number of many-storey buildings of urban character. At the same time it should be noted that it is Hódmezővásárhely where the homestead system has been preserved in its purest form the farmers having two homes one in the town and one on the farmstead.

3. TOWN HALL AND COUNTY HALL

Though our country towns are primarily residential settlements, the places where the population gathered as early as the Turkish conquest were towns already meeting urban requirements to a certain degree. Among these centres, towns with administrative functions were top-ranking. Primarily two towns (Szeged and Debrecen) should be mentioned, which had been seats of public administration before they became junctions. From among the agricultural towns Szentes, Gyula and Makó were also simultaneously county seats.

These towns have preserved their roles as administrative centres up to this date despite the fact that they have gained importance due to their development as agricultural cities. All through their history their function as administrative centres has been growing to such an extent that this provides an essential feature of their urban character; indeed these settlements became more important as administrative centres than as agricultural towns.

But even at the time when the agricultural town had fully developed it used to be a common practice to settle institutions of public administration at locations which had thus grown into towns. The settlement in question had become a town anyway, and therefore it was able to meet urban requirements more efficiently. Thus, Nyíregyháza succeeded in snatching the position of a county seat from Kálló after having developed into a significant agricultural town by means of its homesteads. Similarly, Kecskemét became the seat of a law-court of public administration and of other institutions after it had grown into one of our most important agricultural towns due to organizing vast territories into a single unit. It would have certainly become the seat of the county's administration, too, if it had not been located in a county the seat of which was the capital city.

Under such circumstances the agricultural towns enriched themselves with a varying number of administrative institutions and, accordingly, their urban character broadened partly because they had been administrative centres even prior to their becoming agricultural towns, and partly because they succeeded in gaining new administrative functions following their development into agricultural towns.

The minimum of this administrative function is the town's capability to perform its own administration, thereby avoiding a subordination to the lower-level organs of the county administrations, the so-called district offices of the administrations. Particularly the agricultural towns located in areas that had been granted privileges and an independence of county administration succeeded in preserving their autonomy, and though they did not come to control other areas they did not surrender their own administration to others either. Today, these settlements have the legal status of county towns which guarantees them exemption from the jurisdiction of the district administrator in the same way as it had been by the letters of privileges. Such simple agricultural towns are Kiskunhalas, Cegléd, the four *Hajdú* towns as well as Karcag, Mezőtúr, Túrkeve, Kisújszállás and Nagykőrös. These towns were not vested with any public administrative power beyond their borders, however, they succeeded in preserving their own local self-government to an extent required by their urban character; it is their town halls which symbolize their self-government.

Another kind of minimum of the administrative function is the case when either similarly to the above towns, the town in question has achieved and preserved its autonomous administration and at the same time it has become the centre of the county administration of a major rural district, or—though it did not succeed in attaining its own autonomy—it has become the administrative centre of a greater area and within that naturally of itself, too. Such towns are Csongrád, Jászberény, Kalocsa which, in addition to being agricultural towns, are also district seats. Such towns are also Békés, Gyoma, Szarvas, Orosháza and Törökszentmiklós which are not agricultural towns but seats of districts.

A higher stage of urbanism has been reached by agricultural towns which, in addition to having an autonomous urban orgaization, have risen to the position of an administrative centre of a greater region, i.e. of a county. Such towns are Debrecen, Gyula, Makó, Nyíregyháza, Szentes and Szolnok. In these town the administrative function has become so important that if they were not towns because of their agricultural town organization they would become towns because of their central administrative position. Towns which are not county seats but are still autonomous municipal authorities fall under the same category. These, though not administering counties are not administered by counties either. Such towns are Szeged, Kecskemét or Hódmezővásárhely.

This varying degree of authority of county administration is very well reflected by the various levels of the administration of justice. Every district seat but also a simple agricultural town has its district courts and the same applies to larger towns. At the same time, some of the county seats or municipal boroughs such as Szeged, Gyula, Kecskemét, Szolnok and Debrecen have courts of justice.

Within these two common categories of agricultural towns in some major country towns there are higher-level institutions having a district-level authority. Thus Szeged and Debrecen have courts of appeal, and in Szeged, Debrecen, Kecskemét, Nyíregyháza, Békéscsaba and Szolnok there are one or more district-level public administrative authorities as well. Among all agricultural towns Szeged and Debrecen have the greatest administrative powers because as real district towns they have come to control the higher-level organs of the most important administrative branches.

The administrative functions mentioned all represent the urban character of the town in question not only by linking a greater or smaller region with the town but also because they enrich the town itself with some buildings of urban character and a further group of urban population.

It should be emphasized that the buildings of public administration, in particular the town halls and the county halls are the most beautiful and oldest of the agricultural towns. In Szentes and Makó, for instance, the oustanding buildings are the county halls, but in all other towns, too, it is the town hall or the county hall or both which are the most urban architectural features of the town. The buildings of but recently settled various administrative institutions have brought a new colour, that of a more modern architectural style to the agricultural towns, though sometimes not in its most advantageous form. However, the buildings of the *OTI* (National Health Service) have established in many places the most up-to-date architectural style of public buildings.

Among the urban population the civil servants represent the urban

238

element for whom the town does not only mean a place of residence but the place of work as well. Their ratio is not high in any of the agricultural towns, however, together with other strata working in the towns themselves they significantly add to the increase of the ratio of an urban population which is rooted in the town with all its functions. Civil servants amount to about five per cent of the agricultural towns' population; in subordinate administrative centres this figure is much lower, whereas in higher-level administrative centres it is somewhat higher.

Civil servants generally belong to the leading stratum of the town and even junior clerks whose living standards equal those of the petite bourgeoisie are in a more favourable condition in this respect than the burgher elements of other occupations. The gentlemanly upper middle-class status of old times which had been an attribute of office was inherited by the civil servants, and at present public office itself guarantees them a privileged social position. As a consequence of this legal succession, the town of a peasant character is viewed by the civil servants of the agricultural towns in the same way as by their forerunners. With the rare exception of some naive dreamers the town is regarded as a realm of public administration that has to be kept under strict control to maintain order. As a natural consequence, civil servants are isolated in the society of the town. Civil servants consider themselves as if they were living on a marshland. They are just like the colonial sahibs in their European-style villas which are defended by fences, cross-bars and wire-netting against the attacks of beasts and mosquitos. On the other hand the town is a real agricultural society of peasant character and/or to a lesser degree an urban bourgeois world. No wonder that this part of the society reacts with a similar aversion and defense to the attitudes of the civil servants. A peculiar kind of class antagonism has developed manifesting itself in reserve and arbitrary measures from above, and antipathy, aversion as well as desperate impatience from below.

Naturally this antagonism has rather adverse effects on the social life and urban character of the town. The peasant section of the town denies and attacks the isolated public servants since it still nourishes—though not consciously—the broadly founded urbanism of the agricultural towns, while those in office strive at a different type of urban development, partly because of their own interests and partly taking into account Western examples. Every municipal and county committee meeting witnesses the clash of these contradictory views and almost without exception it is the standpoint of officialdom and the social interests of those in office which comes out on top. Thus it happens that a high-pressure mains is built in the town's central zone while in the suburbs there is no possibility to build even the simplest bibbcocks, or that the downtown districts get asphalt pavement while in the outskirts people have to trudge ankle-deep in mud and slush.

However, it is an undeniable fact that everywhere the civil servants try to do their best to develop and build the town. The only problem is that they have rather strange ideas about how to do this. First they want to realize their ideas in contradiction with the previous history and structure of the town. Second, they want to enforce their ideas against the will of the majority of the citizens and as a result, their plans are often doomed to failure. And third, they pursue an urban development policy as an aim in itself, disregarding the social and economic context, and therefore no real urban development can take place.

This is the reason why the agricultural towns have failed to achieve self-government despite the fact that its legal conditions were given. And even this legal framework is not capable of a decision-making process expressing the will of the townspeople; indeed not even the given possibilities are fully made use of. The present leadership is not only alien but contrary to the life and traditions of the town, and even with a mayor in charge who, owing to his descent, ideals and skills, would be able to realize the autochthonous administration of his town, ingrained leadership attitudes and the lack of a reform-minded staff usually thwart his ambitions.

All these social conflicts are reflected in different ways on the levels of state, county and municipal administrations and accordingly, government, county and municipal officials represent different social forces.

Due to its aims and very nature, public administration does not give much heed to local interests; this in itself, would not be harmful. The dim of the individual organs of public administration is to ensure the collection of taxes and to see to it that nobody could evade state control. However, this is the attitude of the urban burgher, too, when acting in his capacity as a government agent, though his profession keeps him in the town for rather a long period of time. Civil servants are distinguished aliens in the agricultural towns who have been transferred from Szombathely or Pécs to the Great Plain which is felt a hopeless desert of mud and slush; here they frequently speak in a mawkish way about Europe, and lead a totally secluded life either in their lofty offices or among the four walls of their homes. They socialize only with their colleagues from the office; at the very most—if this seems absolutely necessary—with the leading potentates of the town. If, owing to their professions, they have to participate in local decision-making, they totally fail to identify with local aspirations, and believe to perform their duties well if they race through ruthlessly all orders from above even if on the higher levels local needs could be taken into account. This kind of civil servant stratum feels alien in the agricultural towns. This is rather a painful fact, the more so as it is exactly the officials of public administration who are the most influential.

County administration is of an entirely different nature. It is aristocratic and reserved. It represents the local traditions of leadership and, by virtue of its social origin, is rooted in its environs. The members of county administration happen to get to other regions only as guests and if they yearn for anything at all it is not Europe but the gentry past of Hungary

240

when upper middle-class leadership enjoyed a much more privileged position than today. This group of high-placed officials regards itself as the only representatives with a vocation of leadership and any intervention in their realm is considered either churlish impertinence or the consequence of the evil influence of alien ideas. It is not aware of the fact that it is a strange body within the town. The policy of leadership this group pursues as well as its aspirations are alien to the town. The same can be said of this group's social attitudes and its gentlemanly upper middle-class way of life. The members of county administration are surrounded by a peasant society yet they have not a word of goodwill for the endeavours, not a word of agreement for the aspirations of this society, and on the whole they are hostile to any efforts of this stratum to improve its lot. The only sincere contacts they maintain are with the landed gentry of the town and the county, and even those whom this class accepts as *homo novus* from the ranks of the bourgeoisie or the peasantry are permitted only at arm's length in a restrained way. This behaviour and style could be even attractive or justifiable if it were an expression of the uprightness, integrity and independence aiming at preserving durable values under circumstances of social change. However, behind the polished upper middle-class style we find a total lack of principles and servility which could serve any type of government.

Regarding the life of the agricultural town, this gentlemanly upper middle-class is of no importance since this type of settlement has developed against the intentions of the middle-class. The plight of the agricultural town is further aggravated by the fact that nothing good can be expected from this gentlemanly middle-class. At the same time, however, the gentlemanly-feudal attitudes of this class are rather an obstacle than a contribution to the socially desirable development of the agricultural town.

In all agricultural cities municipal administration is the most democratic and is very closely related to urban traditions. In the case of privileged towns it even succeeded in preserving its independent character and is the only institution to preserve a style of municipal administration rooted in the needs of society. However, the unity with urban society and the spirit of democracy do not result everywhere in a progressive leadership. If a clique of traditional burghers happens to seize the rule in a town this means an absolute lack of understanding for the agrarian needs of the agricultural town, whereas if the agrarian burgher class becomes dominant they display an umcomprehending attitude to industrialization and hostility to the demands of the farm hands. If, however, a group independent of classes snatches power in a town, then all local interests of the town are overshadowed by political aims serving individual careers. Whichever clique seizes power in one or another town, its members certainly find cushy and leading jobs for their children. But such leadership—even if it is of local descent—results in a leadership unable to introduce creative initiatives and makes no headway.

241

It is obvious that the various administrative institutions contribute to urbanization and to creating ties between the town and its environs. According to the statistics, also the officials employed in these administrations considerably contribute to the urbanization of agricultural towns. In spite of this, these officials are far from having a beneficial influence on the town. Surveys containing facts and figures could shed light on this antagonism which can be removed only by political means.

4. ROADS, SQUARES AND SHOPS

Some of the agricultural towns were built at places which have been traffic centres for ages. At such places the town was created by energies generated by traffic and the agrarian town agglomeration of later times only increased and further shaped the proportions of the town. Such towns are first and foremost Debrecen, Szeged, Kecskemét, and Szolnok, too, followed in their footsteps. In other towns, however, evolution took a different course. Here the town was created by the agricultural town agglomeration of the population engaged in primary production, and this population developed a kind of production demanding market and/or trade needs of urban dimensions; by meeting such demands significant market trade activities developed. Such towns are Nagykőrös, Makó, Orosháza, Szentes, and also Kecskemét, which has opened up new vistas of trade and traffic by becoming an agricultural town. The third variant is when an agricultural town emerged at a place where it became the centre of important transit trade and traffic thus assuming a considerable commercial role. Such are Békéscsaba, Nyíregyháza as well as Szolnok the commercial role of which has been enhanced by transit trade.

Considering the commercial significance of our present-day agricultural towns, their role in trade can also be categorized into three types.

Some of our agricultural towns play their role as trade centres like any other towns, i.e. they are the centres of the local trade activity of a certain region surrounding the town, with the sole extension that buyers tend to come to such markets of local products even from greater distances as well. Such settlements are mainly centres of live-stock trade; most appropriately they could be referred to as market towns with the qualification, however, that at their markets it is not the commodity trade of two or more regions of different character which is transacted but the central live-stock turnover of a single region of homogeneous character. Such towns are Kiskunhalas, Mezőtúr, Hódmezővásárhely and, in addition to their roles as trade centres of other nature, Kecskemét, Debrecen and Orosháza are also such market towns. Here trade activity has assumed greater dimensions than required by the life of an agricultural town and as a result market and trade activity appear as independent urban factors in the life of the town.

242

The other type of trade centres could be termed export markets. At such places the town which had settled completely as an agrarian town succeeded in developing production with the opportunity of export trade. By making the best of this opportunity actually an export market emerged increasing the urban character of the town by trade activities. Such towns are Nagykőrös, Makó, Orosháza, Szentes as well as Kecskemét. The case of Jánoshalma is of considerable interest. At first this village approached the level of an agricultural town by settling homesteads and thus it could grow to bigger dimensions than an ordinary village. Later on, quite recently it started large-scale orcharding at the farmsteads and fields near to the confines of the town by means of which it has presently developed an export market which is beginning to rival that of Nagykőrös. This village is entering the group of towns indirectly because of its farmstead system and directly because of its export market.

Of the towns ranking as export markets Nagykőrös, Kecskemét and Jánoshalma (this latter setting out on the course of urbanization just now) are markets of fruit exports; Makó is the market of onions and vegetables, Szentes, Orosháza and Kiskunhalas that of poultry, and besides, Kiskunhalas is also a fruit market, whereas Orosháza is a well-known grain and flour market as well. These market places become urbanized directly not only because some kind of trade activity has taken root there; they have also gained enormously by achieving a surplus income which is out of reach in other towns. Such an export market yields an income of one to two million *Pengős* for the town; for any other kind of different produce profits would be by 50 per cent less. The income realized through exports contributes to higher living standards and to urbanization.

These two types of trading towns were entirely of agricultural town character and their role in commerce resulted quite naturally from the nature of the agrarian town. The third type of trading towns, however, is not of an agricultural town character but meets the demands of a regular commercial town. Though in such towns trade involves urban character, it does not reflect and represent the growth and enrichment of the agricultural town but that of the commercial town to the detriment of its agricultural town. Settlements belonging to this type are places of transit trade among which the most outstanding are Szolnok, Nyíregyháza and Békéscsaba, and partly Szeged and Debrecen.

It is remarkable that the agricultural town character of settlements belonging to this third type is declining. To a considerable degree, this is to be attributed to a commercial activity which is not based on the needs of the environs of the town but serves the needs of the transit trade of two different regions. Because of its great transit trade Szolnok as well as Nyíregyháza have almost ceased to be country towns. For other reasons also Szeged and Debrecen are no longer primarily agricultural towns. From among the towns in this group it has been Békéscsaba which has preserved its agricultural town character to the greatest degree.

Taking the population employed in trade as well as transport and communication as a single category (though statistically they are broken down into two separate groups) it can be stated that in our agricultural towns the number of persons employed in trade and transport amounts to 10 to 25 per cent of the total population. It has reached highest percentage in Szolnok, whereas it is lowest in the towns of Great-Cumania (Central Hungary) which have no or no noteworthy markets.

In all agricultural towns the population engaged in trade is made up of two groups. The first group is made up of the heirs of the old urban burghers, the present-day petit bourgeois retailers, market-women, marketers, and the second comprises the bourgeoisie of Jewish origin which is as much an urban element as the first one with the exception that the members of this stratum are not natives but have immigrated earlier or in more recent times. For this reason they have greater impetus and a stronger entrepreneurial spirit.

But even the successors of the merchant bourgeoisie of old are only partly Hungarians. A considerable percentage of them are of German, Serbish or Dalmatian descent and only a minority are Hungarians. Thus, in Szolnok the overwhelming majority of the merchant bourgeoisie is of foreign origin, and even in towns like Szeged or Debrecen, where the percentage of Hungarians is the highest among the towns, certain branches of business activities have been entirely managed by foreigners from the very beginning. Tradesmen of Hungarian origin having merchant traditions represent the highest percentage in Nagykőrös and Debrecen, yet even there they could not assume leading positions in the dynamically developing commerce. Similarly to the merchant bourgeoisie of Serbian, Dalmatian, Slav as well as German origin, Hungarian tradesmen, too, have confined their activities to retail trading and middleman's business. At a time when the proportions of commercial activity have increased, and particularly when local trade has extended to foreign countries, this merchant stratum has fallen behind and is able to undertake only inferior commercial transactions.

Where the Hungarian-German-Slav merchant stratum failed there appeared the Jewish merchants and with matchless entrepreneurial skill and ruthless efforts developed the export trade of the agricultural towns and seized the leadership in trading. The Jews have kept a firm hand on export trade up to this very date, and while they have not fully assimilated culturally and socially in business life they have totally adapted themselves to the conditions of agricultural towns and have developed an enormous trading activity suited to local needs.

As regards the social position of these two merchant strata, in the agricultural towns, we may say that the Jewish merchants integrated with the bourgeoisie, while lesser traders of various national origins chiefly belong to the petite bourgeoisie. However, apart from their influence on

244

economic life, neither of these strata occupied leading positions in the society of agricultural towns.

Together with the bourgeois Jews in other walks of life the Jewish merchant bourgeoisie is of the most clearly bourgeois and European character in agricultural towns. It has remained essentially alien to the other parts of society but by no means more so than the gentlemanly upper middle-class and bourgeois officials. It would be misleading to declare that the new merchant stratum — which by means of the more and more powerful monopoly organizations attempts to assume the role of the Jews — could integrate better with the society of the agricultural town. These people of various social background who have been hastily trained as merchants do not interpret the role of the merchant like the Jews who have adapted themselves to the atmosphere of free enterprise. It is not bourgeois values which are pursued by these new traders but they try to adapt the life-style of civil servants and of the gentlemanly upper middle-class. They do not wish to take the risks of a business venture but aspire to play a secure, stable socio-economic role. This is the reason why they keep on proclaiming collective, production-supporting and popular slogans. They pretend not to represent separate merchant interests but to go into business in the interest of the producers. However, there is no truth behind the slogans, their actual trade policies are not changed by the fact that they are Jews. What has been said in the above is by all means characteristic of the older generation of monopoly officials. It is still to be seen whether the young people recently recruited can free themselves of this atmosphere which can be regarded by no means advantageous.

Other merchants form a not too distinct or urban group of the society of agricultural towns, and their low origins are disguised by their petit bourgeois unity. They represent a truly provincial petite bourgeoisie which could find its place in a Western-type small town as well and would not enrich the traditions and cultural life of the town just as it does not in the Hungarian agricultural town. The members of this stratum do not know anything about the specific urban character of the agricultural town and if they have the opportunity, they unconsciously follow urban patterns. They long for town-life; they want asphalt pavement and street-lighting at night but even if all their dreams came true, this would not mean urban culture only an ill-matched urban civilization. They keep aloof from the peasantry thinking they are much more urban though the agricultural towns were built by peasants and not by petit bourgeois merchants. This petite bourgeoisie is also renowned for the fact that it lays claim to the leading position in the town and if its members cannot realize this desire then they try to achieve it through their children, though neither as regards culture, nor Hungarian ideals or agricultural town traditions do they promise anything which would amount to more than promised by those who hold power.

The commercial institutions of the agricultural town adapt themselves perfectly to the trading position of the town. Towns functioning as local markets are situated as hubs of local road systems and are connected with the capital city by a single route at most. All the towns of the Hajdúság and Nagykunság regions fall under this category: their road system does not link them to the capital town or a major town close to their regions but encompasses the town itself which therefore has not even an opportunity to break through the local trade circuit. Actually Hódmezővásárhely, too, is such a town and the main cause of its slow development is this road network. Export markets like Kiskunhalas, Kecskemét, Cegléd, Nagykőrös on the other hand maintain brisk traffic with far-away regions and the capital city. It should be noted that, despite disadvantageous road conditions, export markets could emerge at places where the producers and the merchants were fit for this role, for instance in Makó, Szentes or Orosháza.

The town of transit trade, however, became part of a road network with lively traffic and their rapid development is mainly due to this fact. Such towns are Szolnok, Nyíregyháza and Békéscsaba. Once again Szeged and Debrecen are exceptions since for instance Debrecen has no outstanding position as regards road network, nevertheless it could emerge as a significant trade centre, whereas Szeged, despite of its excellent geographical position, has remained a sleepier and more languid town than Debrecen.

As regards the internal structure of the town, commercial institutions have fully adapted themselves to the pattern of the agricultural town. In all agrarian towns the downtown district is at the same time the centre of trade as well and market-places, shopping streets and business offices have sprung into life according to the proportions of trade.

Shops and business offices have been concentrated in all agricultural towns in the downtown, the centre of a buoyant commercial activity; no such institutions can be found in any other districts of these towns. Together with the institutions of public administration, shops and offices, they fully occupy the city-like core of the town endowing it with the character of a Western-type town. In some small agricultural towns such cities consist of merely a square or, in addition to it, of a street running to the station, whereas in Debrecen, Szeged and Szolnok, and partly in Nyíregyháza and Békéscsaba they comprise a whole district, thus lending urban character to the town even at a cursory glance.

Geographical urban research, however, often claimed that agricultural towns are lacking an urban character. This view is based on the fact that even in agricultural towns like Kecskemét the fruit and other markets are on the main square, and this may seem to some observers somewhat country-like and Oriental. It is undeniable that with the exception of Szeged, Debrecen and Szolnok the markets are actually on the main squares in all agricultural towns but this is deemed rustic only by highly biased views doubting the very urban character of the agricultural towns. If the market is a commercial phenomenon just like the downtown shop—and from the point of view of the town it undoubtedly is—why could it not be located at the same place. The market is a commercial institution and therefore it has a justified place among the shops and offices.

Naturally there exist better technical facilities for commodity trade than an open space where carts and wagons stop in rain and mud leaving much litter and garbage; this, however, falls under the same category as the canalization of the town. Canalization is not a precondition of urban character but a condition of a lovely town and therefore it ought to be introduced in the agricultural towns, too.

The agrarian towns actually look for better facilities for holding markets. Wherever there are abundant funds there are some experiments with such facilities, however, these agricultural towns do not prove their urban character by this, it is only a proof of their good taste in town-planning. In Jánoshalma, for instance, the selling and buying of fruit proceeds in huge plank-halls, and this market is at the same time a veritable marketing organization as well. In Makó a so-called onion-hall has been built with the aim of selling onion there on the basis of samples. This latter experiment has failed but will be certainly followed by others. The success of such experiments is not a precondition of urban character but its result. In addition to the qualities of the agricultural town this urban character is sufficiently proved by the trade and institutions to be found in these towns.

5. WORKSHOPS

Agricultural towns are first and foremost residential towns of primary producers, secondly, administrative centres, and thirdly, trade centres. All these factors have more or less influenced the development of the towns and have left their marks on their present character. Industrial production, however, played no such role.

None of our agricultural towns had been an industrial town before it became an agricultural town and none of our towns became an industrial town after it had emerged as an agrarian town. This phenomenon can be explained by the simple fact that neither the population nor the natural endowments of our agricultural towns are suited for industrial development. This was the reason why no Western-type towns have developed in the Western parts of the Great Plain. The towns of the Great Plain have only raw materials and in the past even these were only beef-cattle and corn whose transport is so easy that their industrial processing takes place in the capital city or some other old industrial towns. Fruit, vegetables, poultry and industrial goods appeared masswise on the market only at a time when all industrial activity had already been concentrated in the capital city. Thus it happened that while large-scale export trade was created by the needs of local production, industry has been developed to a much smaller extent by this very local production though it would have been able to provide raw materials in abundant quantities for industrial processing.

Small-scale industrial production oriented towards the demands of local consumption is not worth mentioning since such production can be found in any village and this kind of industrial production never resulted in urban development. Only such industries can be regarded as city constituting factors as are oriented not only towards local needs but are linked by means of one of their factors of production or raw materials or by their finished product consumption to distant regions. The conditions of such an industry as well as of export trade are absolutely given in all the agricultural towns; there are locally produced raw materials the processing of which is the task of the local industries so that trade could transport the finished goods to far-away regions.

Such industries developed very slowly, and even today they are not sufficiently developed in order to characterize agricultural towns permanently by such industrial production.

The processing of beef-cattle has taken place for a long time in the workshops of handicraftsmen but such small-scale production and/or processing has been too unambitious and unorganized as to transform the industry into a significant branch of the economy. It is only now that the Szeged and Debrecen salami factories as well as some minor plants of the meat industry in Csaba and Gyula have become important factors of the economic life of the Great Plain and succeeded in turning out some brands of products representing considerable production standards.

The processing of cereals, the other ancient raw material, took place from the very beginning in large-scale enterprises, and this was the only branch of industry which was of considerable importance in our agricultural towns as early as the past century. Flour-mills are integral parts of every agricultural town, flour production is a factor of the industrial production of every agrarian town, but compared with the production of Budapest the significance of all the mills of the Great Plain tends to dwindle. Though the Vásárhely, Orosháza and Szeged mills producing high-quality flour have gained certain fame through their products the role of these mills in the economic life of their towns was not as important as this branch of production would have deserved. The overwhelming part of the crop was transported from the towns by the agricultural town corn-dealers and only a small percentage remained there for local processing though if the whole crop had been processed at its place of origin there could have developed a large-scale industrial production.

In recent times at least semi-processing of agricultural produce has started on a larger scale as a concomitant of the exports of small products of the Great Plain, but even this industrial production is merely a complementary factor of exports. The canneries of Kecskemét and Nagykőrös, the poultry slaughter-houses of Kiskunhalas, Szentes and Csaba process agricultural small products much in demand on foreign markets. However, with the exception of the Kecskemét, Nagykőrös and Cegléd canneries which turn out tinned food, only semi-finished products are produced.

The large-scale solution of the industrial tasks of the production plants of the Great Plain is a problem of the future when industrial production will become a decisive feature of the agricultural towns. At present, industrial production is but an accessory urban role in our agrarian towns though it is an established fact that only industrial production can bring about considerable urban development. We do not want to state thereby that it is only the lack of a large-scale industrial development which prevents our towns from becoming truly urban settlements. It should be emphasized only that the absence of this factor hinders the exploitation of all opportunities of urban development.

The relative insignificance of the industry is reflected by the employment statistics of our agricultural towns. Even in our most industrialized towns the ratio of industrial population does not exceed one-fourth of the population, whereas in the other towns this ratio considerably lags behind this proportion. Moreover, industry meeting local needs can certainly be discounted from this figure since such industry can be found in any village and is able to satisfy the demands of only subsidiary industrial needs.

The circumstance that industrial production is but an incidental factor of minor importance in the life of our agricultural towns is further supported by the spatial distribution of the industrial plants. Every agricultural town has its commercial and administrative districts but none of them have industrial districts. Both small-scale industrial plants and big factories are to be found absolutely haphazardly built all over the towns, and this once again proves that industrial production has not been regarded as highly important by either the leadership of the towns or their society as a whole. While the whole town becomes animated when a market is opened, or closed, the question whether an industrial plant should be settled in the town and if so where, does not arouse any interest whatsoever. Only one type of industrial establishment has received its due place in our agrarian towns: the brick works on the perimeter of the town as close as possible to the railroad. The flour mills for instance have occupied sites at discretion, in some places in the midst of the residential district, at other places in the village-like districts or on the outskirts of the towns. And similarly located are all the other industrial plants: there are settlements where the industrial plants are located amidst the houses next to the station since it is there that they are closest to the railway-line, whereas at other places the chimneys of the factories belch out their smoke right in the downtown district. Only Békéscsaba and Szolnok have their industrial districts primarily serving as sites of industry.

As regards small-scale industrial workshops, it is of much less importance that they should not be scattered all over the town and wedged in residential districts. However, the chaotic situation in our agricultural towns is much more the sign of carelessness than the result of the careful consideration of the needs of the population.

The disesteem of industrial activity is reflected by the social position of the industrial population as well. Persons employed in industry, i.e., the workers and the white-collar workers as well as the artisans, craftsmen and their journeymen constitute the least valued strata of the petite bourgeoisie and the working class. Only the prestige of the manufacturers and the entrepreneur bourgeois became accepted and this, too, following the example of the West, without striking deep roots in our agrarian towns.

The industrial working class is the most turbulent and restless stratum unceasingly demanding and malcontented prompting the dominating bourgeoisie as well as the petit bourgeois smallholder peasantry to stiff resistance. Both of these strata regard the organizing working class engaged in politics as a destructive and subversive stratum and therefore they try to reduce its role in the life of the town as much as possible. Yet, the restlessness of this working class is fully justified in a society which partly considers the significance of industrial production in an absolutely uncomprehending way, and—partly in defense of the interests of the bourgeoisie and the farmers—treats the working class rather parsimoniously. But even such strong resistance has proved unable to eliminate entirely the role of the working class. Despite its having been pushed into the background, it is the working class which, in contrast to the agricultural town society prone to sluggishness, represents the industrialized element in the life of the town; it is a rather necessary driving-force because of its class-conscious culture and its in many respects anti-agricultural endeavours. It is by no means a social stratum living in the atmosphere of the agricultural town but just because it stresses rather neglected points of view it is the most energetic driving-force of urban development. Though its way of thinking is alien to the concept of the agricultural town, in the long run it is not harmful to it since it demands general urbanization just like the peasantry which had founded the agricultural town.

Industrial employees and independent artisans are petit bourgeois to the core. They merge with the other strata of the petite bourgeoisie without reservations. This social status has but one factor granting them some kind of self-consciousness: the notion "craftsman" or "artisan" used to be in the post-war years (and to a certain extent is still) the desired form of production, the coveted social status in the view of the upward striving peasantry. In those years every ambitious peasant lad wanted to become a craftsman and every haughty peasant lass dreamed of marrying an artisan. This craftsman romanticism has come to an end, instead we witness the increasing prestige of jobs with old age pensions. Peasants try to get jobs with pensions—even if this means jobs as office messengers or janitors—just as it had taken to craftsmanship. However, craftsmen still preserve in their mind the high esteem of their vocations originating from earlier times and therefore they regard themselves as more valuable and creative people than either the peasants or traders. Incidentally, they are also petit bourgeois and they, too, long for such a kind of urban life as any other petit bourgeois. They also strive at achieving a higher status but in their case, compared with any other stratum at a similar level, this is the most justified by the work ethic of truly productive work and a career that should be much more respected.

From above, however, they get fairly little respect. Craftsmen—if this term does not mean industrial bourgeois of an industrialist type—are meant to be by and large identical with domestics or servants, and when bourgeois housewives complain to each other, they tend to mention, right after having finished with the domestics, the craftsmen who do not deliver the carpets in time, do not finish installating the bathroom and are cheeky enough to demand outrageous prices for repairing the kitchen range.

The only exception is the group of craftsmen who have reached a certain bourgeois standard of living and particularly that of some entrepreneurs regarded as industrialists. Though industrial occupations are not considered to be vocations worthy of gentlemen those craftsmen are held in high esteem who, despite the laborious character of the job demanding realistic calculations, are able to carry on their trade seemingly like gentlemen, not calculating and above all not working. Such career skills are attributed to the industrialist who is unanimously honoured by the society of the agricultural town though this very society has no sense whatsoever for any kind of serious industrial venture. Since the figure of the industrial entrepreneur has been idealized in such a distorted way and craftsmen working seriously and appearing in their true form are so much underrated, this society has actually no sense for industrial production. Thus it is the industrial organizations of the agricultural towns which are the most inadequate and most unworthy of all the other institutions of the town.

Technology as a peculiar local manifestation of industry and/or industrialization is a problem of outstanding interest of the society of agrarian town.

The urban organization of agricultural towns had emerged at a time when production was based on manual work and tractive power and the main means of transport had been the horse. Since then, this town has merged into a world of higher technology, production being based on machines and transport on steam and engines. Yet, as regards its way of thinking it has remained in the world of the old productive forces. The famous Hungarian poet Endre Ady has pointed out in Debrecen: "Listen you gents, already tomorrow there will be trouble, and no small one, human mind travels by means of locomotive today and Fata Morganas do not want to remain Fata Morganas". This, however, is true to a certain extent of all agricultural towns. At that time the ideas upon which the foundation of the agricultural city was based, used to be up-to-date and even ahead of their time but today the attitudes of society got alienated from these old ideas. What new vistas would open up for production and life as a whole if new ideas based on skillful dealing with machines and technologies bursted into this town organization like fresh gushes of wind! What a boom could be experienced in agricultural production, what a highly developed industrial production could emerge and what an obvious, natural way of traffic, transport and communication between farmsteads and town could be found if "human mind travelled by means of locomotive"! The achievement of developing such an urban organization is a reason for hoping for its future development as well. This can be realized only if industrial revolution touched "the Tartar brains" of the agricultural town and also townsfolk carried out its industrial revolution.

6. GARDENS

In ancient Hungarian language the term "garden" had meant an encircled plot and as such it had meant first and foremost the fenced courtyards of stock-breeding; only more recent usage extended the term to encircled places serving plant cultivation. Gardens—in both meanings of the term— had an important role since these two kinds of gardens are the institutions of agricultural porduction, which are able to provide an urban framework—in addition to the system of farmsteads—to the population of primary producers.

The garden for animal keeping divides the inner part of an agricultural settlement into two zones: living quarters and gardens with pens and this is actually identical with the outlay of the ancient inner or winter quarters which has been preserved in a great number of our stock-breeding villages even after the withering away of the old quarters system. This system has survived in historical continuity in quite a few of our settlements and up to this date there are live examples of the inner district zone system. At such places the core of the village is a narrow residential district consisting of winding streets where there are no outbuildings, whereas the outward zone consists of broad lots with stables and barnyards where manfolk come to work as in some kind of workshop every day.

Such a garden system is in itself able to transform an agricultural settlement into an agricultural town. At the time of their foundation and later under the Turkish occupation it had been this system which had created the Hajdú towns, and even more recently Mezőkövesd, too, could be regarded as a town due to this circumstance. The Hajdú towns, however, have developed into farmstead towns and their garden system has almost entirely withered away while in Mezőkövesd there has emerged no farmstead system and therefore with the decline of its garden system it has lost ist urban character. Prior to the development of the agricultural homesteads in every agricultural town of the northern region of the Great Plain there evolved the garden system for a time but it was rendered superfluous by the farmsteads, and today no traces of them can be found.

Though the garden system is no longer a living institution, its urban role and social influence can be reconstructed on the basis of its scattered remnants. In garden-towns there still can be found some gardens and also in the villages along the Danube particularly in Dunapataj, moreover in all the Hajdú towns the traces of the garden system can be clearly pointed out in the settlement structure of these towns.

The inner zone of the settlement is unequivocally residential district. Streets are only wide enough to allow traffic; plots are just spacious enough to build a house on them surrounded by a tiny flower-garden and the dwelling-house is nothing more than the mere residential building without any annex of economic character. In the past such a closely knit settlement was justified only by the requirements of the possibly closest social bounds and defence, whereas today this order is longingly thought of: how easy it would be to supply such a residential quarters with all public utilities! How uncomplicated and cheap it would be to build here canalization, water mains, pavement as well as gas and electricity networks.

The external zone, on the other hand, consisted of spacious and fenced pens and gardens with roads to the pastures between them which became wider and wider as they led from the town, so that the cattle-track should be as comfortable as possible. If there was no field work, men camped here all through the day and it was from here that they came back to their dwelling-house to eat and sleep—just as it were a workshop. Here they stockpiled the fodder and manure since it was from here that they could reach the ploughlands and pastures in the shortest time.

Today this system serves only as an historical example but as a very instructive one. It would be an excellent solution if the central areas of a town could not be relieved of farm-buildings and barnyards by means of homesteads. The rural districts of our agricultural town are still in need of such a solution.

The other garden, the intensively and carefully cultivated agricultural land has become an urban factor of the agricultural town only later on. The development of the farmstead system has driven production out of town for a time and there remained but some small vineyards and kitchen-gardens on the perimeters. In the course of time, however, these gardens along the perimeter of the town increased in area and when pastures were ploughed they began to extend to somewhat distant parts, too, and occasionally they reached as far as the farmsteads.

At the time of the renascence following the devastations of the Turkish occupation, i.e. at the beginning of the 18th century, every agricultural town had some small vineyards and kitchen-gardens but these developed in different directions and on different scales in each of these towns. The garden cultures of the present-day agricultural town are rooted in these gardens. It was here that the vegetable- and fruit-growing of Nagykőrös, the onion-growing of Makó, the paprika culture of Szeged and the fruit-growing of Kecskemét, Cegléd and Kiskunhalas had their origins. On sandy soils it was the vineyards and orchards which developed though potgardens were also preserved to cover local demands, whereas on harder grounds it was the production of vegetables, culinary plants and spices which came into prominence to the detriment of viniculture and fruit-growing.

When the pastures near to the towns were distributed it was an established garden culture which got chances for extension and a new upsurge. In Makó it was onion-growing, in Nagykőrös vegetable culture, in Szeged paprika-growing, in Kecskemét and Cegléd vineyards and orchards which became widespread. For covering local demands vineyards and vegetable-gardens were preserved but none of them increased their area. On the other hand, at all the places mentioned above the turnover of produce and products which have become gradually famous assumed ever greater dimensions. The Makó onion, the Szeged paprika, the Nagykőrös lettuce and gherkin, the Kecskemét apricot and grapes and the Cegléd grapes and fruit have gained national fame as early as the middle of the last century. And when production conquered ever newer areas, export trade was started to foreign markets so that the famous national produce became world-market brands at the turn of the century.

The garden production of the agricultural towns developed along these lines, and it is a problem of outstanding importance what its effects have been on the life of the towns.

Garden production is undoubtedly a force of urban development. It is possible that a town should emerge by means of market gardening since a primary producing population adequate in numbers and demands with those of the towns can gather together on an area of a village if it is well versed in such a production culture. It is also possible that an existing town should be further developed by the emergence and evolution of garden production. The urbanizing force of garden production manifests itself in two ways. Indirectly it necessitates an intensified trade activity thus increasing the commercial significance of the town and the number of those engaged in trading activity thereby contributing to the settlement's urban character, whereas directly it raises the primary producers of rustic-peasant character to a higher cultural level thus transforming them into more urbanized people.

In the fully developed agrarian town—which could be a trade centre or an administrative centre as well—urban primary producers appeared who acted as an urban factor even without the help of the homestead system. Though the settlement type of the gardening producers is of a rustic character—these people tend to live in the village-like districts of the agricultural towns and their gardens and orchards are in the zone surrounding the town and are cultivated just as in the villages—they constitute, similarly to the homestead farmers, an urban element of the population since they represent a higher level of production culture and their living standards by far exceed those of the village peasants.

Besides, influenced by their urban demands they resort to the homestead system—as far as it is permitted by the given branch of production—and production is concentrated just as on the farmsteads on their agricultural land and thus, their urban houses can be increasingly transformed into the actual scene of their urban lives. As soon as the vineyards have extended beyond the limits of the fenced plots along the perimeter of the town, farmsteads were built between the vine-stocks just as on the arable land. The function of such farmsteads was the same as that of the livestock keeping homestead on the arable land only its layout was somewhat modified according to the changed needs. Here, too, the ancient form fully corresponds to the ancient homestead, i.e., the heated stable. The homesteads in the vineyards were of a unicellular nature: in one of the corners there stood the kitchen stove and next to it there was the resting-place, whereas in the unseparated other part of the building the viticultural tools, the vine-props and other implements necessary for vintaging were kept. Thus, such farmsteads, too, were divided into temporary living quarters for those working in the gardens and another part serving the purposes of production but here the tools stored were not those for animal husbandry and tillage but were implements of viticulture.

The analogy is valid in another respect, too. At the homesteads in the fields the part with the stove of the farmstead has gradually become the permanent living quarters of the farm hands and has therefore been separated by a wall from the other parts of the house. Just in the same way there took root the vine-hoers at the homesteads in the vineyards and gradually they, too, detached their living quarters from the tool-shed.

The homestead system has struck roots in one form of the gardens, i.e. in the vineyards and thus this kind of garden production has become a fully urban factor not only because of its higher production culture but by means of its settlement organization as well. At places where vine-growing and fruit production have extended to the zone of the old plowland and farmsteads this twofold urban function has become a united one both theoretically and in terms of its spacial structure. This means that vineyards and orchards were planted in the neighbourhood or plowland farmsteads and therefore the maintaining of separate vineyards and vineyard farmsteads has become unnecessary since both could be located at a single place. This was the trend of development in all the vineyards and orchards of the region between the rivers Danube and Tisza, and in this way the plowland farmsteads of Szeged, Kiskunhalas, Jánoshalma, Kiskunfélegyháza, Kecskemét, Cegléd and Nagy-kőrös have become garden farmsteads as well, fully integrating viticulture and fruit-growing into their urban organization based on homesteads.

But even in regions where the production of vegetables has become acclimatized, farmers made use of the advantages of the homestead system. At the beginning such cultivated gardens, too, were only fenced plots along the perimeter of the town and only more recently did they extend to and displaced inner fallow pastures. Even if nothing like a homestead system had been established by these gardeners, their production would have assumed an urban character but at most places homestead-like quarters were built in these kitchen-gardens, too, patterned exactly after the plowland and vineyard farmsteads. In Makó, for instance, from the time on that they ventured out to distant fields with their kitchen-gardens, the onion-growers built huts and shanties of reed, planks or wickerwork both as living quarters and tool-sheds. Similar huts are to be found on the Nagykőrös vegetable fields and these, too, are adaptations of the homestead principle to actual needs. The development of vineyards in the direction of homesteads is still going on. In all the towns where vegetable-growing has been taken up by homestead farmers as well—in Szeged, Kecskemét and Nagykőrös but not in Makó—garden cultivation has extended to the area of the farmsteads, and the plowland homesteads or vineyard homesteads or possibly both of them have become also vegetable-growing farmsteads. Thus all the branches of agricultural town primary production, i.e. plowland and garden production together have entirely fitted into the homestead system.

The transformation of garden production into a homestead system has become a general phenomenon. However, in all the towns pursuing garden production only part of production has been transferred to the farmsteads and/or has brought about its specific kind of farmsteads. Part of it always remained within the bounds of the rural production system, that is some of the gardeners have not moved to work on the homesteads but tend to cultivate their gardens from their urban houses as centres of production. Even in that case—as it has been pointed out—such gardeners succeeded in becoming urban elements both as regards production and living standards. They have become urban primary producers because garden production is an urban factor even without the homestead system, and this is borne out by the fact that the peasantry was able to develop a significant garden culture only within the framework of an urban organization.

The garden cultures of the agrarian towns are not of a common origin in all of the towns and the level of their development, too, is rather different. Yet, they have a common feature: their development was made possible by the organization, social atmosphere and urban character of the agricultural town and at the same time, the garden culture has further enhanced the urban character, the social progress and emancipation of the agricultural town and has also shaped the outward appearance of the towns. In Szeged, Nagykőrös and Makó paprika, vegetable and onion culture are as natural formations as the agricultural town itself. Following the regeneration in all the three of these towns cotters had their tiny garden-plots along the perimeter of the town just as the farmers; they, too, grew all kinds of garden produce for their own household needs. Since the cotters were more dependent on the yield of their tiny garden plots than the farmers, they worked them more thoroughly. At some places it was paprika, at other places lettuce and cucumbers, and yet at other places onions which were deemed most valuable, and since it was just the produce in question which yielded the best results in their gardens, they kept on specializing themselves on the growing of it. There was also a great demand for specially produced goods and therefore the cotters soon limited their whole garden production to a single or a few plants. They went so far in tending special cultures that they began cutting our vine-stocks in order to replace them by onions, paprika and lettuce since there were no other suitable lands for increasing production when the inner pastures had been divided. The cotters who have strengthened as a result of this succeeded in obtaining the right that wherever pastures were divided, they also received a part of these, thus gaining ever newer and bigger lots — as compared to the previous situation — for their special production. And these pastures were everywhere the best soils partly for the kind of soil (around Szeged and Nagykőrös it was a uniform hard black soil as against the sandy soil of the distant homesteads), and partly as they were rich in dung owing to the long periods of grazing and animal husbandry. Production received a new impetus by these newly conquered lands and the town grew richer by a new produce, whereas part of the cotters succeeded in rising to the standard of the farmers.

Up to this date garden culture is mostly in the hands of the cotters and/or dwarf holders in these towns; farmers have only partly joined such production practices (mostly in Nagykőrös and Szeged, least at Makó).

Viticulture and fruit-growing have not developed with such inner momentum. Vine was grown by farmers and cotters alike, and in a uniform traditional way by both of them. The technique and tricks of viticulture as well as the value of production were learned in the course of ages, and wine and grapes were not produced for the market but for household needs. Thus there was no incentive which could have given the impetus to production. Similar was the situation with fruit-growing since fruit trees were planted in the majority of cases in the vineyards. Yet another reason for the less dynamic development of viniculture and fruit growing is that the farmers' produce was not of such an outstanding quality that it would have been able to arouse demand in faraway regions.

In order that viticulture and fruit-growing should assume more general importance an initiative from above was needed otherwise they were to remain on the level of producing for household needs. The initiative was actually taken first by Kecskemét and followed up by Cegléd where entrepreneur farmers partly of peasant and partly of upper middle-class and bourgeois origin started growing vine and fruit on the sandy soil with

257

tremendous energy, and by means of their skills and unswerving will they succeeded in gaining excellent results thereby setting an example to all the other producers of the region. But not only were they followed by others but by experiments they discovered or won such varieties of fruit and grape which became as much sought for as Makó onions, Szeged paprika or Nagykőrös lettuce, and their fame soon spread not only in the country but to overseas markets as well. Their example was followed first in their native towns, later on by Nagykőrös — incidentally there were some local initiatives there — and finally production gained momentum in Szeged and Kiskunhalas, too. Owing to ever newer initiatives, there developed a splendid viticulture and fruit-growing culture at all these places. It was the farmers, and primarily the upper middle-class and bourgeois landowners who were in the vanguard of this branch of production, while cotters joined in production only later on, and even at that time only partly. One of the reasons for this was the fact that they secured high wages by means of their vine and fruit-growing activities. Consequently, their living standards were much higher than before.

There are no uniform statistical data available as to what percentage of farmers and landless peasants and/or dwarf holders participate in garden cultivation in the individual agricultural towns. The census does not mention such gardeners separated and, in addition to that, many of them are not exclusively gardeners and therefore they come under the heading of ordinary tillers of the land as well. On the basis of partly indirect calculations and partly estimates, the situation can be characterized in the following way: in Makó the smaller part of the primary producers, particularly landless peasants and dwarf-holders are engaged in onion-growing and they are called by local residents "onion-gardeners". In Kecskemét, Nagykőrös and Szeged the majority of the primary producers is engaged in viticulture, fruit-growing and vegetable and paprika production (this majority is primarily made up of farmers), whereas in Cegléd and Kiskunhalas it is again the minority of primary producers who are engaged in viticulture and fruit-growing. In all the other towns a disproportionally small part of the primary producers is engaged in garden cultivation. Thus far nowhere has garden production become more developed than in the above-mentioned towns, although at some places initial steps are being made. Thus vegetable and fruit-growing of the market-gardening type is increasingly developing in Gyula, Békéscsaba and Orosháza, while in Nyíregyháza, or more exactly in the town's environs traditional apple-growing is widespread. At all these places, however, the ratio of those engaged in gardening scarcely approaches ten per cent of all primary producers.

The primary producers of the agricultural town can be by and large characterized as a stratum which is no longer peasant in the old sense of the word; by developing their specific urban pattern they have further ensured their emergence from the level of peasant existence. This is increasingly true of primary producers engaged in garden-production.

258

Wherever cotters reached the point of developing gardening culture by means of their own efforts, this stratum skipped the stage of becoming smallholders and became immediately small-scale entrepreneurs engaged in industrial-like production; it is they who from among all peasant strata preserve peasant traditions to the smallest extent. They maintain their high-level and mostly non-peasant type production on their own land if they are dwarf-holders or on leased land if they are landless peasants, and fit into the society of the town as a mobile, enterprising petit bourgeois and/or proletarian stratum the members of which are prone to all kinds of innovations. The onion-farmers of Makó, the paprika-farmers of Szeged, the truck-gardeners of Nagykőrös are individual social groups living according to their own traditions, and within such groups landless peasants, farmers and tenants tend to stick together much more than in other branches of production. They are all unbalanced farmer's economies for whom the soil does not have any mythical value but is a means of production with which they undertake ventures audaciously, and if some or other of their enterprises have failed in one year, they boldly live off their capital to maintain their living standards whereas in favourable years they buy back the land they had been obliged to sell. In general this is a group with rising living standards, its members being fully aware of the tangible possibility of rising to the status of landed farmers from the ranks of the landless peasants, and therefore they do not regard the farmer stratum as something being out of reach.

As regards their social life, they are well on their way towards embourgeoisement just as any other peasant stratum, and their aspirations and needs are of an absolutely urban character. They appreciate the good things of life and this means that they make use of the possibilities of the town to a much greater extent than peasant landowners. They spend all their income on meeting their needs and anything they acquire comes from the increased income of their production and not from capital withheld from consumption. In their attitudes there is no trace of peasant submissiveness; they are not loyal to the gentlemanly upper middle-class or the bourgeoisie; their political orientation is entirely dissident. It had been the so-called Independence Party which they had identified themselves with in the past; since then their votes are divided between the socialist and the party of small-holders.

The members of these groups are truly children of the agricultural towns and therefore they are the most loyal and progressive elements of the agrarian towns. They are fully aware of the fact that their existence depends on the urban organization and urban market and thus, all their efforts are aimed at the maintenance and development of the town. Their economic means are usually insufficient to develop their houses into totally urban mansions but anybody among them who has the opportunity and means does it much sooner than the homestead farmers. Under the present conditions they are the pioneers of urbanization in the agricultural towns and in the future they could become the leading force in the process of urban development.

The farmer-gardeners, i.e. the vine and fruit-growers of Kecskemét, Szeged, Cegléd, Kiskunhalas are farmers who dared to embark on garden production which seemed risky at first and meant by all means an innovation, and are therefore the outstanding representatives of this stratum. These gardeners are the elite of the farmers, and this fact is reflected not only by their produce but by their social life as a whole as well. Their life is to a certain extent more urbanized and they themselves are less peasants than the tillers of the farmsteads, and thus it was these farmers who have further developed the true spirit of the agricultural towns. They have a stronger and more intensively felt need for the town and, therefore, partly because of the markets and partly because of their social needs they come home from their homesteads more frequently than the plowmen, and they furnish their town dwellings sooner and in a more exacting way. Under all circumstances their children go to school from their town dwellings and if they are gifted they are sent to higher schools most often with the intention to direct them to other occupations but more frequently to have them trained as educated agriculturists. The specific and fast development of Kecskemét and to a certain extent of Cegléd was started by these farmers engaged in garden production, and the thriving and developing life and urban character of these two towns, and particularly of Kecskemét can be explained by the fact that the leadership is in the hands of such farmers. This leadership has achieved outstanding results because it is a leading stratum which has the best chances to be able to assimilate the professional officials of the town. In Kecskemét they have achieved striking results. Everybody is a vine-dresser there and this vine-grower spirit makes itself felt in the leadership of the town resulting in a higher quality and more fruitful administration than anywhere else.

The two types of gardener strata have settled in two zones of the town. The farmer-gardeners, partly in their capacity as homestead farmers tend to live in the residential streets of the town and of all the houses of agriculturists it is theirs which have assumed the most urban form. On the other hand, the cotter and dwarf-holder gardeners—who generally have no farmsteads—live in the rural districts of the town. The fact that even these rural districts are not entirely of a village character is explained by the fact that the primary producers living there are not rural plowmen but gardeners. The original nature of the settlement could not be changed by them but if the economic conditions of their development strengthen or are re-established, it will be the task of future development to totally urbanize these districts. The outlying districts of Makó and Nagykőrös, and the so-called "Lower City" district of Szeged are all such small gardeners' settlements, and this is the most appropriate place to start the urban reorganization of the rural districts of our agricultural towns by means of radical town-planning.

260

7. HOMESTEADS

According to census definitions people who were living at homesteads at the time of the census were registered under the heading "outskirts population". On the basis of such calculations 29.9 per cent of the population of the Great Plain lived on homesteads in 1930, and this average by and large corresponds to the average of the towns. As to the individual towns, Kecskemét had the highest percentage of population living at homesteads (56.2 per cent), whereas Makó, the Hajdú and Nagykun towns had the lowest percentages (below 20 per cent).

If we correlate these figures with the number of primary producers, we can conclude that a very high percentage of the primary producers live on farmsteads; in Kecskemét about three-quarters of the primary producers live on farmsteads and even in towns having the lowest ratio of outskirts population their number amounted roughly to at least one-third of all primary producers. It follows that on average the majority of agricultural town primary producers fall directly under the heading of the homestead production system, and if correct farmstead statistics were made, the figures might reflect an even higher percentage.

The significance of the homestead system is also conspicuous if calculations are made not on the basis of the population of the outskirts but on the basis of farmstead buildings; the number of farmstead buildings is compared with the number of houses to be found in the central areas.

Let us examine the relevant data of our country-towns:

Municipal boroughs authority

	Total number of houses	Houses in the central areas	Number of homestead buildings
Szeged	20,299	10,295	10,004
Debrecen	14,609	5,893	8,716
Kecskemét	14,252	4,887	9,365
Hódmezővásárhely	14,102	8,086	6,016
County towns			
Békéscsaba	8,332	5,722	2,610
Cegléd	8,967	5,645	3,332
Csongrád	5,880	3,647	2,233
Gyula	5,065	2,973	2,092
Hajdúböszörmény	6,837	5,302	1,535
Hajdúnánás	4,636	3,689	947
Hajdúszoboszló	3,922	3,022	900
Jászberény	6,851	4,647	2,204
Karcag	6,459	4,380	2,079

	Total number of houses	Houses in the central areas	Number of homestead buildings
Kiskunfélegyháza	7,474	3,512	3,962
Kiskunhalas	6,816	3,221	3,591
Kisújszállás	3,554	2,696	858
Makó	8,731	6,754	1,977
Mezőtúr	6,271	3,911	2,360
Nagykőrös	6,192	3,808	2,384
Nyíregyháza	7,390	4,291	3,639
Szentes	7,987	4,844	3,143
Szolnok	6,480	5,540	940
Túrkeve	3,520	2,651	896
Large villages			
Békés	6,775	4,164	2,611
Orosháza	5,924	3,213	2,711
Szarvas	5,654	2,689	2,965
Törökszentmiklós	5,640	3,465	2,179

The above statistics have omitted Mezőkövesd because having no farmsteads it is not an agricultural town; Hajdúhadház, Kalocsa and Gyoma were also omitted because the census does not indicate data on residential houses in the outskirts as the number of the farmsteads in these towns is below 500. In the case of Kalocsa the reason for this is that the outskirts with the farmsteads have been separated from the parent town and have become an independent village; in Hajdúhadház not all the gardens have settled as farmsteads as the precincts of the town are not large enough and finally, in Gyoma up till now the farmstead system has not struck roots because the precincts of the town are not large enough and for the same reason it is doubtful whether this settlement could be regarded as an agricultural town; if, however, Gyoma is considered an agricultural town, she is at the lowest limit of this category.

An interesting grouping can be detected among the towns mentioned. In part of them the number of dwelling houses of the downtowns and the outskirts are balanced reflecting a highly developed homestead system: every house in the town has its farmstead somewhere along the precincts. Such towns are Szeged, Hódmezővásárhely, Csongrád, Gyula, Kiskunfélegyháza, Kiskunhalas, Mezőtúr, Nagykőrös, Nyíregyháza, Szentes, Orosháza and Szarvas. However, it should be taken into account that quite a few of these towns have settlements which are not homesteads but outlying residential districts and/or villages. These settlements cannot be separated numerically from the real homesteads but they provide a basis for more accurate estimates. Thus, for instance, in Szeged and the Slovakian towns some of the homesteads are farmsteads which have developed into fragment-villages and some of them are residential areas. This correction is particularly significant in the case of Szeged, and when we take this into account Szeged is among the agricultural towns with fewer homesteads.

In the second group of towns there are significantly more dwelling houses and in such settlements the homestead system is less developed. Such towns are Békéscsaba, Cegléd, the Hajdú towns, Jászberény, Karcag, Makó, Szolnok, Túrkeve, Békés, Törökszentmiklós and some of the towns already mentioned like Hajdúhadház or Gyoma. There are a number of reasons why fewer homesteads are to be found in these towns. In the Hajdú towns which had been garden settlements for a long time the reason was simple: not all the gardens had been transformed into homesteads, and the same phenomenon can be witnessed in some of the towns of the Nagykun and the Jász regions, such as Karcag, Túrkeve and Jászberény. The reason for this development in Makó and Cegléd is that the vegetable fields and vineyards around the town have remained the centres of production, whereas in Szolnok and Békéscsaba the towns begin to lose their agrarian character owing to their role in industry and trade, and therefore the number of homesteads is fewer than that of the town houses.

The third group is made up of towns where the buildings in the outskirts by far outnumber those of the downtown districts. In these towns the homestead system has reached its highest stage of development though at a certain phase of their development these settlements have been garden towns. However, this conspicuous imbalance is actually the consequence of a process contrary to what created the homestead system. The population moved out to outlying residential areas and farmsteads having a fragment-village character. Kecskemét has quite a few of such villages and residential areas (Kadarfalva, Sikra, etc.). In Debrecen the outlying zones of the garden district are categorized as outskirts by the census, though these zones emerged on place of the old outskirts and gardens forming an integral unit with the town itself. If these outlying garden settlements of Debrecen and the outlying villages and colonies were left out of consideration, these towns, too, would come under the first category of towns and the number of their homestead buildings would equal that of their town buildings.

Yet another correction would be necessary regarding the number of homesteads. However, because of the present census system this is not possible. We should also mention regions where homesteads have lost all connections with the town house and have become independent settlements forming together not a homestead system but a fragment-village. Such regions are primarily the so-called tenants' farmsteads which are very common around Szeged. These farmsteads offer a permanent place of residence for persons working there since their economic strength is insufficient to maintain houses in the town as well. Though they cannot claim as their own the land they cultivate, they have become eternal homestead dwellers; they migrate from one strip of leased land to another, and are finally buried in a cemetry of one or another homestead centre.

A similar development toward villagehood is indicated by farmsteads—though not on leased but on owned lands—around Kiskunhalas, Kiskun-félegyháza, Kecskemét and Cegléd. In this region between the rivers Danube and Tisza viticulture and fruit-growing make it possible for farmers to make their living on small strips of land though they have not enough material means to maintain a town house as well. In the region east of the river Tisza there are fewer such settlements and regions. In the surroundings of Békés, more exactly in the districts across the river Körös there are some permanently settled homesteads, and a few can also be found around Törökszentmiklós and Jászberény. The Slovakian homesteads, particularly those around Nyíregyháza have almost completely taken this path of development.

With all these corrections an estimated 60 per cent of the population of agrarian towns is involved in homestead farming. It should be noted that this figure also includes those elderly people who had lived on farmsteads in their youth. In order to check these data a detailed statistical survey of the homesteads would be necessary; in this survey not only the population of the farmsteads but also its urban connections would be registered. By urban connections I mean the ownership of urban houses, independent sections of houses or paternal homes in which they will live in their old age. It would be instructive to find out the number of sections of homes at homesteads and compare these data with the number of town dwellings. In addition to this survey, in the central district it ought to be determined whether primary producers living there own any farmsteads. In the case of old people it is interesting to know whether they possessed a farmstead when they were of working age. A clear and exact picture on the present-day homestead situation could only be obtained on the basis of such data. On the basis of these data it could be exactly established where homesteads have become villages and have needs like villages. Until then we can do nothing better than accept approximative estimates and examine the homestead system on the basis of such evaluations.

Homestead buildings have the same ancestors as town buildings: the unicellular house which had been the shelter and home of both man and beast. The village and town houses had been changed and divided to such an extent that the ancient forms had become unidentifiable; a long time after this the ancient forms appeared on the homesteads and triggered off the development of a peculiar way of building.

The heatable stable or an identical type of housing had been common at the Cumanian dwellings from the time of the earliest settlement, and in the environs of the other agricultural towns from the age following the devastations by the Turks. This type of housing served as shelters for herdsmen. In some of these houses they lived all through the winter, too, others they inhabited only in summer but all served a single purpose: giving temporary shelter and protection to the more exacting cattle. The greater part of the building was the stall, while the hearth and the bunk of herdsmen occupied only a corner. Prior to the development of crop-producing homesteads it had been this form of farmsteads which had been the most widespread. Such kind of buildings were perfectly suited for cattle-breeding homesteads since neither did the herdsman live there permanently nor were his wife and children with him because every herdsman had his town dwelling, and his wife and children lived there. If the wife did move out to the homestead for some specific reason and established a "household" there, part of the stable was fenced off, an oven was built with an opening towards the stable and this space served as a room.

The situation changed when the cattle-breeding homesteads were transformed into farming ones, that is when there arose the need for a longer or even permanent stay at the farmstead. This change had an effect on the structure of homestead buildings, too: the separation of the room from the stable became a general feature, whereas the porch and the kitchen still formed a single unit with it. Here lived the farm hand with his household, and he also helped as a hired labourer in the field work; if there were no hired farm hands, then it was the able-bodied sons of the farmer, be they married or not, who helped. There were no bigger and more divided homestead buildings all through the 18th century. However, as the number of those living out on homesteads increased, i.e. as the family of the farmer's son living there proliferated, the homestead building was enlarged all the time. As a first step the hearth was again separated by a wall from the stable and thus the kitchen and the porch were created. In that case it was necessary to build a chimney as well and the building became very similar to the village or early town houses. If such a solution was chosen, doors opened from the porch into the living room and the stable; such patterns can still be found all over the Great Plain. When the quantity of food and the number of household utensils further increased, a pantry was built for stocking the produce as a second step, and this too, was separated from the stable. The stable and the dwelling were still under a common roof but the whole pattern of the dwelling has fully developed: a room, the porch, the kitchen and the pantry. The homestead building did not develop any further as a unit; if more spacious farm buildings became necessary, those were built separately. However, the standard homestead building had preserved this form until the middle of the past century. All the buildings needed for the increasing demands of farming were built as separate units. Thus, there were separate sheep-sheds, cattle-shed and stables, and where there were such separate sheds it was only the stables which remained inside the farm-house. For the keeping of pigs separate pigsties and pens were built everywhere; summer enclosures were also built for cattle. For storing agricultural implements sheds were built either as lean-tos at one end of the stables or as separate buildings in the form of stalls. For the storing of bread crops there were built first clamps, later on granaries, and barns for storing corn on the cob. By and by the homestead was turned into a settlement, however, the dwelling occupied no more than the single room separated from the stable as well as the necessary conveniences. Everything was made to serve the aims of production, and at a time when town houses were usually decorated already, the homesteads still consisted of plastered, white-walled buildings with reed-thatched roofs.

Well-to-do farmers whose families and farm hands lived on the homesteads needed more living space. Consequently they divided the old homogeneous building in two. The dwelling house was constructed according to the old order and the division was repeated as many times as many dwelling sections were needed. The stable, the cow-barn, and the sheep-shed were located in separate buildings. Larger homestead buildings were built in this way as early as the middle of the past century, and some of these were as big as a manor with the difference that they had no separate, ornate and comfortable dwellings.

These two types of farmsteads are still to be found in the world of scattered farms, and both of these types have undergone but little change in the past fifty years. Earth is still used as building material only the reed of the roof was replaced by tiles at many places; the end of the homestead was made of planks but nowhere was it ornamented as decoratively as the town houses. Walls are still whitewashed everywhere, only the rooms are painted in colour at some places at the very most. The kitchen has remained at the same place and has also retained its function, but it has become a single unit with the porch, and smoke-holes were built within the walls instead of the free-standing chimney. Homesteads with many rooms are still regarded as absolute rarities though farmsteads with two or more living quarters—where there are several families living together—are as frequent as they had been in the past.

The farmstead buildings and/or groups of buildings are located in the middle of the land irrespective of the siting of the neighbouring homestead. If a depression or some hillocks run through the land, the siting of the homestead is adapted to this circumstance. However, the homestead is only very rarely built right at the road. The so-called row or cluster homesteads of the regions inhabited by Slovakians are departures from this free siting.

The majority of the homesteads are treeless and bare, and particularly the homesteads of the Nagykunság region stand without any green patches nakedly on the plain. Beginning with the first decade of the century, however, the afforestation of the homesteads has become more or less a general feature on the Great Plain and the characteristic picture of various present-day farmstead-regions has developed together with the vegetation. Homesteads in the Nyírség region are tiny villages surrounded by slender acacias; homesteads are connected with each other by rows of trees and the limits of the estates are also marked by alleys. Homesteads in the Jászkun and Nagykun regions are lonely, treeless, not even lime-washed buildings

266

with reed-thatched roofs in the midst of the barren and dried-up plain, and peat is tacked up on the wide farm-yards. The homesteads of Szarvas are veritable streets flanked with tall acacia-trees whereas the roads leading towards the spire of the town along the farmsteads are lined by hedgerows or fences. The homesteads of Orosháza, Hódmezővásárhely and Makó form separate wooded islands on the black earth, lines of poplars leading from the cobweb-like patterned roads to the farmyards; only here and there do some tall Lombardy poplars rise above the dense foliage of the homestead. The old homesteads of the Kiskun region, or of Kecskemét and Szeged are without exception long, white buildings with thatched roofs, standing on the grass-grown banks of some pond and their white walls are reflected by the surface of the water. Some lonely trees stand at the corner of the building, storks are nesting on the chimney just as reported by the famous Hungarian poet of the past century, Sándor Petőfi. More recently built homesteads in the regions between the rivers Danube and Tisza are, however, of quite another quality. Bedded among orchards and vineyards almost nothing can be seen of the tile-roofed buildings and the farmyard is densely planted with trees. The homestead building is often surrounded by a veritable wood of acacia or fruit trees and therefore, a landscape with such homesteads seems to be rather an urban district in the green belt than a region on the Great Plain a mere twenty to thirty kilometres from the town.

Agricultural production on such homesteads is of the following pattern. Most of these farmsteads comprise the entire production activity of the owner. The farmer keeps his tools and implements here, his cattle are stabled here, all his fodder, manure and crop is stored here. Consequently, every act of his production takes place either within the farmyard and/or the farm buildings or in the fields surrounding the homestead. Naturally he has such a dwelling here where he can live both in summer and winter, he keeps all his household implements here. However, neither his holiday attire and more precious furniture nor his valuables—if he has any—are kept on the farmstead. As a rule these are kept in his town house which belongs either to the farmer or to his parents, and whenever he spends some time in town, he can use the house, moreover he can store all his valuable things there all over the year.

Farmers who have their own house in the town—often even those who have no such house—store the crop not on the homestead but in the shed of the town house. Wheat is brought here at the time of threshing and later on it is sold from here. Those who have a house of their own in the town maintain a perfectly equipped urban household whereas those who lodge in their parents' house have only a few furnishings at home. If children go to school at town from the town house everything they need is supplied from the homestead so that the grandparents should have as little trouble as possible.

Only work and supplementary activities are carried out on the homestead.

Weddings, baptizings, name days, feasts at pig-killing are all celebrated in the town, and expectant young mothers, too, move to the town dwelling so as not to give birth to their children on the farmstead. Old people do not live on homesteads anyway, and if anybody of working age falls ill he is immediately taken to the town dwelling. Therefore it happens only rarely that somebody should die on the homestead. But even if somebody happened to die there, the burial rite is held in the town.

The owner of the homestead farm lives like this until he is capable of work and his children have grown up. By that time his parents usually do not live anymore and the town house passes into his hands. If he had not inherited such a house, he buys one and spends his retirement in the town. To spend his old age on his farmstead is regarded as a disaster and humiliation by a homestead farmer, and even if there are a few who take this upon themselves of their own accord, they are looked on as fools and are constantly ridiculed.

The dwelling and the home being separated to such an extent from production there is an uninterrupted traffic between homestead and town. Those working on near-by homesteads go home to town three times a week, i.e. on Sundays and weekly market days, whereas from far-away homesteads only twice a week, and finally from very outlying homesteads and in winter only once, on Sundays. They start as a rule early in the morning and reach the town already at seven or eight o'clock, on market days even earlier, and as soon as they have unharnessed the horses they hurry to settle their affairs, or if they have nothing to arrange they simply have a good talk in the farmers' association or at the marketplace. Everybody has his lunch at home and immediately after having eaten they leave for the homesteads. From two o'clock in the afternoon long rows of carriages disappear homewards in clouds of dust just as they had headed for the town in the morning. Farmers who live permanently in town have a different schedule: they ride out to their homesteads only from time to time to give orders to and supervise the work of their farm hands. They, too, tend to ride out in the afternoon on market days, at other times, however, they start in the morning and return in the evening though all of them have quarters on the homesteads, too, where they can spend the night in case of emergency. These homestead farmers do not spend less time on the road, it is only that they spend more time in the town and less on the homesteads.

A more detailed examination of life on the homesteads shows quite clearly that—unlike an urban-rural system dividing people into townsmen and countrymen—the agricultural towns' urban society is not divided into homestead and towns-people. People living on detached farms are integral parts of urban society and their temporary living on homesteads does not result in some kind of social unity with the others living out there. It is only the next neighbour with whom there develops a neighbourly relationship since everybody frequently needs some kind of help and cattle, too, roams over to the neighbour's pasture. However, people on the homesteads have almost nothing in common with the third or fourth neighbour. The place of the homestead farmer in urban society is marked out according to his town dwelling irrespective of his homestead. He who lives in a street of the lower end of the town is a member of the low-end society and does not belong to those upper-end farmers whose homestead is next to his own. Though a considerable part of their lives is spent on their homesteads such farmers do not form some kind of separate homestead lobby but as townsmen fight for the fulfilling of their various public needs at the homesteads. Thus, living on the homesteads does not result in forming a social group and even less in establishing a community. Some groups of the urban community and urban society have specific interests related to homesteads but these are asserted not by reference to being the owners of homesteads but by belonging to a specific urban stratum.

It would be a grave mistake to indicate the interdependence or a feeling of community among the homestead people since everybody living on a farmstead is dependent on the town, has common interests with the town, and his interests meet only here in the town with those of other homestead people. And this throws a light on the true character of the homestead system: the homestead is not part of the countryside but that of the town; it lives as a district of the town under conditions which are naturally determined by the distance from the town and by the nature of agricultural production.

8. CULTURAL ACCOMPLISHMENTS

Whatever factors played a role in its foundation and whatever forces had participated in its further development each town has sooner or later become a centre of culture. This is demanded partly by the needs of a greater concentration of population, i.e. people want to receive cultural products locally, while on the other hand the higher institutions of culture and education are necessarily established in urban settlements. It may also occur that a town is called into being by culture itself if it is able to create institutions around which a town can grow later on. Such well-known examples are centres of learning or festival towns where it is of little importance whether other urban functions developed within their walls or not.

Among Hungarian agricultural towns there are two which had met the requirements of urban functions owing to their cultural institutions prior to their having become agricultural towns: Debrecen and Kalocsa. In Debrecen it was the Calvinist college and theology which have developed an intellectual centre around itself whereas in Kalocsa this function was performed by various Catholic shools and the theology. In addition, in both of these towns the public collections of the schools and/or bishoprics, too, have contributed to this evolution. Nevertheless, in neither of these towns have the schools had a key role. Though Kalocsa succeeded in maintaining and even developing all its schools it did not become a significant centre and it even lost its role as an agricultural town, whereas Debrecen is much more important as an agricultural town or administrative centre and even as traffic centre than as a seat of learning.

Though culture had not been a fundamental element or a factor of key importance in the history of our agricultural towns, sooner or later each of the agricultural towns became lesser or greater cultural centres and acquired or founded their various urban cultural institutions.

In this respect, too, two agricultural towns which have emerged as medium-sized towns, i.e. Szeged and Debrecen play an outstanding role since both of them are seats of universities and thus give home to the highest organs of education and scientific life. There follows as a close third Kecskemét with its law academy of university status. But here already ends the list of agricultural towns which can boast of higher institutions of education and scientific life. Besides, these towns are also regional centres and seats of high-level institutions of public administration. All the other agricultural towns are of a local character, that is all kinds of medium-level educational institutions are to be found there. Such, however, are in all other towns as well.

Every agricultural town has one or more junior high schools, mostly separately for boys and girls, and in the majority of the towns there are even several such schools for boys. In addition, all agricultural towns—with the sole exception of Orosháza—have their own grammar schools which play a significant role in the cultural life of urban society. For this reason it is the Great Plain from where more peasant youths succeed in becoming intellectuals than from any other region. Every agricultural town has at least either a teachers' training college or a secondary agricultural or commercial school, but frequently all the three or at least two types of these are to be found in a town. Of outstanding significance among these is the Szarvas Agricultural School partly because it has a considerable urbanizing effect on a town otherwise of minor importance and partly because the school had and still has a highly important role in the development of agricultural production on the Great Plain.

From among the agricultural towns Szeged has the greatest number of schools; 169 elementary and vocational schools, 17 secondary schools, one college and a university. Kecskemét is ranked third outrivalling all the towns of Transdanubia—with the sole exception of Pécs—with its 144 primary and vocational schools, 11 secondary schools and one college. There follow Békéscsaba, Nyíregyháza and Szolnok, whereas all the other agricultural towns having one or two secondary schools are at the bottom of the list.

Regarding public collections, museums of various nature, we get exactly the same result. First is Szeged with its public collection of 121,758 pieces, however, Debrecen occupies the first place concerning the attendance of its collections: though there are but 59,296 exhibits there, annual attendance comes to 270 thousand as against the 187,620 of Szeged (the above figures relate to the year 1935). These two towns are followed by Kecskemét the public collections of which are almost as substantial as those of Debrecen but attendance is a mere fraction of the above 3,361 persons. The public collections of the other towns are without exception small ones very similar to the private collections and their attendance is insignificant reaching not even thousand persons a year. Nevertheless the Hódmezővásárhely ethnographic collection, the Jászberény Jazygian museum and the Karcag Great Cumanian museum are worth being mentioned. In addition, Vásárhely can boast of a private collection which is unrivalled in the country both as regards its section of peasant art and its modern Hungarian paintings.

Considering public libraries, Debrecen is top-ranking its holdings being altogether 307,065 volumes, followed by Szeged with 141,681 volumes, however, the attendance of the Szeged libraries exceeds that of the Debrecen ones considerably. The third place is not occupied by some major and lively agricultural town but by Kalocsa with 70,730 volumes, though attendance here is by far less than that of smaller libraries in a number of greater agricultural towns.

As regards publications and printed matter, it is again Szeged and Debrecen which are leading the list, followed closely by Kecskemét and Gyoma, the latter ones both because of their nationally renowned and distinguished printing houses. The Kecskemét printing house is the publisher of the products of modern Hungarian literature; almost all the periodicals of the young avantgarde writers have been published here, e.g. the *Válasz,* the *Tanú,* the *Magyarságtudomány,* the *Apolló* as well one of our high-level special periodicals, the *Magyar Sakk-közlöny* (The Hungarian Chess Journal) well-known all over Europe. The overwhelming majority of the most beautiful Hungarian publications are printed in Gyoma.

If our agricultural towns are examined not on the basis of their cultural production but according to the number of their intellectuals it turns out that the ratio of intellectuals—including civil servants—is exceeding 10 per cent in Szeged, Debrecen and Szolnok, whereas in Kecskemét, Békéscsaba and Nyíregyháza their percentage is around five per cent, again with the exception of Kalocsa which, however after having been deprived of its outskirts has ceased to be a real agricultural town.

In all the agricultural towns intellectuals are regarded as bourgeois, and though some of them do not reach the bourgeois standards of living, considering their economic situation, they are raised to this level owing to the high prestige of intellectual occupations. However, only those ones among them belong to the leading group who are affiliated somehow with political movements, that is first of all lawyers and journalists. It is a tradition in agricultural towns that practicing law and being a journalist go hand in hand with engaging in politics, and there are but few exceptions to this rule. Such politics consists naturally in only advocating local interests and of paving the way for individual careers, but one element of it is nevertheless significant as regards the life of the towns. It is a recurring stock phrase of local politics that only such politicians should be elected deputies as are first of all members of the government party, secondly, influential personalities since it is only they who are able to help the town. Help is naturally understood as financial rehabilitation of the town or the construction of some magnificent public buildings. This, however, does not prevent the success of such slogans or catchphrases. These swaggerers naturally refer eagerly to the example of Szeged which was actually considerably helped by its ex-minister MP, or to that of Jánoshalma which is soon going to be raised to the level of agricultural town owing to the spectacular care of its MP, an active undersecretary of state. At the same time, contrary examples are also often mentioned. It is frequently pointed out that Hódmezővásárhely is a decaying town because it had always elected representatives of the Kossuth Party or socialists as MPs. On the other hand, the leaders of municipal politics are often experts in frequent machinations just to merit the goodwill of the government. A tangible example is a great agricultural town on the plain between the Danube and the Tisza: until the end of the world war it had always been the candidate of the Kossuth Party standing for independence who had been elected here, and when this trend came into power as a result of the October Revolution of 1918, Michael Károlyi was hurriedly elected honorary citizen of the town. After the crushing of the revolutions of 1918 and 1919, they took a stand against Nagyatádi, became fervent adherents of Sokorópátkai, later on they eagerly joined Gyula Gömbös. And all this only to court the favour of the government in power, for the sake of winning advantages for their town.

Whether this conformism is deemed good or bad it is by all means belated. Before the war all the agricultural towns had been steadfast supporters of the traditions of 1848, and at times when it had been really important what kind of candidate would be elected, they had always voted to the dissatisfaction of the government. Thus the possibilities for acquiring quite a few public buildings and schools were squandered. At that time the agricultural towns were regarded as unreliable and therefore all the new schools were built in ethnic areas, and the agricultural towns lost many significant means of education. And now, when it is attempted to make up for the losses this seems to be a hopeless effort since today there are no ethnic areas to be used as counterweights.

The other groups of bourgeois intellectuals are quiet and modest citizens of the town. Those who are more demanding but not rooted deep enough in the soil of the agricultural town are complaining and long to move to more buoyant and cultured regions. From the point of view of a formal cultural attitude they are right. In the agricultural town everything is still in the stage of elementary education and highbrow intellectuals have no feeling for crude cultural elements, and even less energy and fewer possibilities to embark on serious cultural development work. Thus every teacher in the agricultural towns keeps on repeating the complaints of the Nagykőrös poet János Arany and pines to escape from this world just as the night-insects try to break out from the dead darkness into the radiant halo of the lamp.

Though Szeged and Debrecen try hard to maintain a higher level of urban culture and the broader or narrower circles gathered around the academic, scientific life and arts attempt to uphold some kind of urban standards, it is keenly felt by everybody that the "puszta", i.e. the Hungarian plain is very near and higher-level culture rests on very few pillars. From among the smaller towns, Szolnok has an artists' colony and some artists cultivate the higher arts but they are interested mainly in the river Tisza, not in the society of the town or the harsh realities of the agricultural town.

If the agricultular towns are examined from the aspect of the consumer's side of culture, the picture is very much the same. Most hopeful and promising is the situation from the point of view of school education. All the secondary schools of the agricultural towns are well-attended; an increasing percentage of their pupils come from the peasantry, the ratio of pupils coming from the peasantry is by all means much higher than in any other parts of the country. This seems to be the most effective means for the peasantry to get a share in the leadership of Hungarian society. On the other hand, however, on the Great Plain the percentage of educated people is smaller than in other regions of Hungary. This can be explained by the fact that some towns have received secondary schools but recently, and partly by the fact that schools are still rare in our agrarian towns.

As regards the other fields of cultural consumption, i.e. the reading of books and newspapers, theatre-going and the buying of works of art, the towns of the Great Plain lag far behind Hungarian towns of a Western type. Considering such statistics it should be taken into account, however, that when a Western-type Hungarian town and an agricultural town are compared the elements are not of the same type since an agricultural town roughly equals a Western town plus its rural surroundings. If we compare such agricultural settlements with their environs, the settlements show a marked advantage. However, even if the results seem rather distressing, this should not be attributed to the agricultural towns but to the sorrowful state of Hungarian society. When all is said and done, the agricultural town is a step forward on the road leading towards the improvement of general conditions.

If the cultural achievements of agricultural towns as a whole is compared with similar urban units, i.e. Western-type Hungarian towns and their surroundings, the balance will show a definite advantage for the agricultural town.

The agricultural towns can even boast of works of art and outstanding cultural achievements. These settlements are even more important in creating the conditions for outstanding cultural achievements.

The society of agrarian towns has created towns out of the waste, it has raised masses of people otherwise doomed to rural or farmstead forlornness and impotence to the level of urban organization. And most significant of all, the peasantry of the agricultural towns has set out on the road to embourgeoisement much sooner and more successfully than the people of the villages in regions dominated by Western-type Hungarian towns. The agricultural town succeeded in opening up immensely new vistas by clearing the road for a general educational improvement. This type of settlement is only waiting for an activating movement and national development and consequently for schools and freedom to achieve the best and greatest results of the Hungarian people both in political, scientific and artistic life. Today all this is only in the phase of preparation and the general production of value lacks a number of other preconditions, nevertheless the agricultural towns can boast of such possibilities as no other Hungarian regions.

Yet it is true that of the results achieved in agricultural towns the multi-coloured and lavishly abundant works of peasant art are missing. The inhabitants of these settlements have been peasants in the genuine sense of the word for only a brief historical period. Thus works of peasant art could be created only for a very short time. Nevertheless the inhabitants' creativity has been reflected in earthenware, leather-work as well as in some melodies and ballads recalling the whistle of the winds on the Great Plain. But it would be no use and would make no sense to yearn for peasant art, since the peasantry of the Great Plain devoted its energies to other efforts; it created all the conditions for a higher-level culture which it was capable of creating under the given conditions.

However, there are a number of finished achievements within the walls of the towns which have emerged from the barren soil of the "puszta". Only creative spirits who have not looked for the safety of moderate sanctuaries but have been able to stand their man against the crude and bristle material and the biting chill of the air of the plains have been and are able to create anything in the agricultural towns. Only under such circumstances, in such an atmosphere could the works of Sámuel Tessedik, ... Vedres and the Debrecen herbalists come into being; their achievements have a due place in the highest spheres of learning and Hungarian culture. But still more outstanding examples can be cited: a great part of the lives and works of the poets Csokonai and Petőfi is related to the agricultural towns, and even today—following in their footsteps—the majority of literary works in the countryside are created in the agricultural towns of the Great Plain. It is true that the past and the future is spoken of more frequently than the present as regards achievements, but who dared to say that in the present state of our people and culture it is not times past and the far-away future which seem to be of greatest value?

9. SPIRES

There is but one agricultural town which owes its existence to the influence of the church, and this is Kalocsa, the seat of the archbishop, and even this was not an agricultural town for a long time. It had been built as a church centre, later it had become an agricultural town by means of the massing of the people of the surrounding villages. But later the town itself re-established its villages and once again became a church town without any other noteworthy urban functions.

There is no real agricultural town at the development of which the church played such a significant role. Perhaps Debrecen is a sole exception having been the centre and bishopric of Hungarian Calvinism for centuries owing much of its urban character to church life. Szeged has become an episcopal see but later and though it is a markedly ecclesiastical town today, this has become a characteristic feature but recently.

Incidentally, church life and church are not significant elements of urban development. The church is an accessory element of every rural settlement, and the lower-level organs of church life are able to perfectly fit into the structure of the village. The church is actually a characteristic mainly of the rural settlement, and only a few famous churches, first of all the administrative church centres, represent any city constituting force. No matter how great the attendance of the places of pilgrimage should be, these are chiefly villages, and almost no cases are known showing that towns have developed out of such places.

The urban function of the churches is reflected very interestingly on hand of the example of the agricultural town. Some of our towns, for instance Makó and Hódmezővásárhely, have only village churches. Here the population gathered together and settled down closely side by side, yet, as separated villages they immediately built up their own churches. And since people living together within one village were generally of one religion, every village built only a single church, whereas the inhabitants of the other village who were perhaps of another religion built up the church of their own denomination. Thus it happens that in the centres of the towns there is still no church but every village-like district has a church in its own centre. Similar is the situation in Szentes. But there the two settled villages were built so close to the roads leading to the rivers Kurca and Tisza respectively, that the two churches of the two villages were erected directly in the vicinity of each other and later on this place has become the centre of the town itself. Thus, these, too, are village churches though this character of theirs has become somewhat dimmed.

In all the other agricultural towns, i.e. in those ones which have a concentric structure the churches stand in the middle of the town and thus, they are located not in a village-like but urban way and have urban functions. All the towns of Cumania, the Hajdú towns as well as Debrecen and Kecskemét show a similar lay-out. In Kecskemét the churches are lined up in the core of the town like a thinly scattered forest, and the main square of the town sprawls in the shadow of the steeples. Later on churches were also built in distant parts of the town, but for a long time the total population of Kecskemét attended services and mass in the central churches; going to church was a significant aspect of urban life. After church service people could meet each other, and thus public social life has received support by religious ceremonies. In agricultural towns with village churches such an opportunity did not exist, moreover, going to church and meeting each other according to village affiliation after service did not increase the feeling of urban interdependence but on the contrary, strengthened rural seclusion. In Makó, for instance, the Calvinists of Szentlőrinc do not acknowledge the Catholics of Buják as their equals as urban citizens, and similarly, the Szentes upper-town folks do not take in the lower-town ones. In Hódmező-vásárhely the many village-like districts—just because of the separateness of their churches—adapt themselves to urban life by upholding their own consciousness up to this date.

Even in Szeged the Lower-town and Upper-town churches had been actually village churches and at the same time they had been separate centres of church life; though both of these had been Catholic churches they had not enhanced the feeling of urban community but rather separated the people. This tradition has struck such deep roots in Szeged that when at later times another church was built, this was built in a third village-like outskirts, i.e. in the Rókus district, and only after the world war has the so-called Votive Church been completed as the representative and central cathedral of the town.

In Debrecen, on the other hand, there had been the so-called Big Church in the shadow of which the town spread out and developed, whereas the outlying suburbs were granted churches but later when the number of their congregations has grown to such an extent that they were able to build a church of their own since the Big Church would have been too confined in space to hold them.

It would be a grave mistake, however, to state that this specific role of the church buildings has been defined by the churches and/or the denominational affiliation of the faithful. Kecskemét, for instance, is a Catholic town, yet its churches emerge in central places, though it is also true that the oldest body of the population is Calvanist and the so-called Old Church is still the main church of the town. Hódmezővásárhely, on the other hand, is a pure Calvinist town, nevertheless its churches are situated entirely like village churches; it is only the church of the Greek Orthodox community which occupies a central position although this denomination has no serious part in the life of the town. The situation of the churches therefore has been defined not by religious affiliation but by quite different factors of the settlement, first and foremost by the fact whether the town has developed as a result of the clustering of a great number of settlements, e.g. the villages of the southern part of the Great Plain, or as the outcome of a ringwise growth around an existing urban core as in the towns of the Hajdúság and in the Cumanian towns as well as in Debrecen and Kecskemét.

As regards the location of churches, the religious affiliation of the inhabitants of agricultural towns is not important. However, religious affiliation is important in terms of the other aspects of the settlements' life.

It is only astonishing at first sight that our agricultural towns are mainly Calvinist and that an unexpectedly great number of them have a Lutheran majority.

The overwhelming majority of the population is Calvinist in the following towns: Debrecen, Hódmezővásárhely, the four Hajdú towns, Karcag, Kisújszállás, Mezőtúr, Nagykőrös, Túrkeve, Békés and Gyoma, while Makó has a small Calvinist majority.

The inhabitants of the following towns, however, are mostly Catholics: Szeged, Kecskemét, Csongrád, Jászberény, Kiskunfélegyháza and Szolnok. Moreover, a minimal Catholic majority lives in Cegléd, Gyula, Kiskunhalas, Szeged and Törökszentmiklós. It should be added that in Szentes, Kiskunhalas and Gyula but even in the overwhelmingly Catholic Kecskemét, too, it is the Calvinists who are the oldest inhabitants of the agricultural towns; the Catholics have settled down later and they have become a majority. The Calvinists still occupy positions of key importance, and even in Kecskemét much complaint is heard to this effect.

Békéscsaba, Szarvas, Nyíregyháza and Orosháza have a Lutheran majority, of which Orosháza is a purely Hungarian settlement whereas the other three are of Slovakian origins.

Thus it turns out that 14 of our agricultural towns have a Calvinist majority, 11 have numerically a Catholic majority but out of these Calvinists have the leading part in Kiskunhalas, Gyula, Szentes and to a certain extent in Kecskemét. Of the towns with a Calvinist majority there is only a single one where the influence and percentage of the Catholics comes near to that of the Calvinists, and that is Makó. There are four towns with a Lutheran majority.

It would be a grave error to conclude from the above facts that the dogmatic differences of the two churches have some kind of direct effects. This would be as mistaken as to state that those regions where the one-child system is practised are mostly of a Calvinist majority because of the more liberal and lax articles of faith of the Calvinist church facilitate the "immorality" of their adherents to a higher degree than those of the Catholic church. Actually the explanation of this phenomenon can be partly found in historical reasons and partly in the nature of the Hungarian people.

A reason to be found in the nature of the Hungarian people is the fact that at the time of the Reformation the Calvinist church appeared as a generally liberating religion, and it was the most Hungarian regions which experi-

277

enced this liberation exactly as Hungarians, since this religion brought them the Holy Scripture and the preaching of the Gospel in their mother tongue. Thus it happened that Calvinism became the true Hungarian religion and when the landlords and princes tried to reconvert the converted Hungarians to Catholicism, people defended their Calvinist church as an integral part of their Hungarian national character and freedom.

This was the point where the Hungarian nation, the Hungarian demands of liberty and the Calvinist church were carried along into a common camp. Opposing princely tyranny as well as lordly despotism the insurrectionist Kuruts soldiers, the Calvinists and all the other Protestants found themselves in a common camp, and the agricultural towns, particularly Debrecen, became the bastions of this front of self-defence. It was only the Calvinist churches and particularly that of Debrecen where it could happen later on that the rebellious declaration of Hungary's independence was read out in 1849.

Also after the Austro-Hungarian compromise of 1867, it was the inhabitants of the agricultural towns following the Calvinist and Kuruts traditions which, opposing terror and pressure and bearing the risk of discrimination and oppression, sent members of the Independence Party to the Parliament. And one further point: higher standards and enhanced consciousness were brought to the peasantry by the church which preached them the Gospel in an intelligible language, on a rational basis and which did not proclaim humility as the foremost of all virtues. The Calvinist peasantry therefore attempted to rise from its state of peasant subordination much earlier and much more intensively than Catholic peasants, and one of the landmarks of these efforts was the emergence of the agrarian towns.

Even today, both as regards social consciousness and human dignity, the peasantry of the ancient and purely Catholic agricultural towns, such as Kiskunfélegyháza, Jászberény or Csongrád are more modest and flexible than for instance the peasants of the Calvinist towns of the region east of the river Tisza. Even the privileged Jazygians are more devout and docile than the Lutheran Hungarians of non-privileged Orosháza or the Calvinist peasants of Makó though these latter ones had been the serfs of the bishop of Csanád for a long time.

Thus, both the church and the churches of various denominations had their role in the development and urbanization of our agricultural towns, though this influence made itself felt but indirectly. The emergence of the agricultural towns was accompanied by social processes in the course of which the deeply felt conviction and the spiritual attitude of the people played a great role in preserving public liberties as well as the liberties of the feudal estates. At this point it became already important to which denomination one belonged and in which church one worshipped the Lord. Finally this effect asserted itself and the present situation when the majority of the agricultural towns is Calvinist can by no means be regarded as incidental though this situation was not brought about directly by the dogmatic differences of the two churches.

A direct urban factor, however, in the life of our agricultural towns is the settlement of the administrative institutions of the church since this means an everyday urban function which—just like public administration—is capable of linking the countryside to the town. Church institutions increase the number of town inhabitants having an urban occupation, and they also enrich the town with urban buildings.

Particularly two towns owe much to the church administration in this respect: Szeged and Debrecen. Debrecen had been a church centre prior to its becoming an agricultural town, whereas Szeged has become such a centre only later, but church functions have left indelible marks on both of these towns. Debrecen, however, is the centre not only of the Calvinist Church but one of Hungary's Jews as well and this has added to its urban functions. As regards its significance as a church centre, these two towns are closely followed by Nyíregyháza which is first of all a Catholic bishopric but at the same time the seat of the Lutheran bishop, too. In the other agrarian towns no church institutions of outstanding significance can be found, the administrative organs of the various dioceses and deaneries are merely clerical offices invested with a certain scope of authority without any particular administrative institution or a greater number of administrative and/or clerical population.

The outward appearance of our agricultural towns has been considerably moulded and urbanized by the buildings of the various church institutions; our oldest and most beautiful historic monuments can be found among them. The Debrecen Big Church with the college is the most monumental group of buildings of our agricultural towns; its beauty consists not only in its historical atmosphere, but its architectural style, too, enchants the spectator with attractive and well-proportioned forms. The Lower-town church and cloister as well as the Upper-town church similarly built together with a monastery are the warmest dashes of colour in Szeged which is otherwise a rather dreary and grey town. Both of these clerical blocks of buildings determine the character of the squares where they are to be found: the Lower-town clerical ensemble standing in the middle of a spacious square dominates the forms of its milieu, whereas the Upper-town group of buildings embraces a small square creating a friendly and urban atmosphere. A similar square is formed in Makó by the church, the parsonage and the schools of the Calvinist Church. All these are well-proportioned, white-walled buildings giving the plaster coated, unadorned brickwork the most beautiful forms of neoclassic provincial architecture and lending it an atmosphere which, though being of urban character, recalls the scent of the Great Plain. The unequalled grand sight of Kecskemét is created by the fact that the churches lined up side by side enhance and increase in proportions the urban beauty of the main square. Taken by themselves the churches are

279

not particularly beautiful and even the beauty of the town hall erected among them might be questionable, but together they are an attractive and fascinating picture.

One might continue by enumerating all our agrarian towns and the final result would be the same everywhere: the churches and the clerical buildings have all grown out from the soil of the agricultural town and have found a form more fortunate than that of any other buildings. This form is urban and at the same time reminding of the plain, thus reflecting most perfectly the very essence of the agricultural town. Even at places where it was most determinedly attempted to develop a Western-type townscape, and forms and materials were supplied absolutely arbitrarily—as for instance at the Dóm Square in Szeged—,the surroundings of the buildings destroy the effect of contrived outlandishness and the proud buildings do not breathe the same air as the model they were patterned upon. The Dóm Square of Szeged, too, has become a rather rustic countryside architectural ensemble, and though it has not been beautified completely, its forms embody an escape from the bleak, sandy plains of the environment. This escape is not successful; the whole architectural ensemble reflects the failure of an escape from the sandy plain.

10. COMPACT AND SCATTERED VILLAGES ALL AROUND

The settlement system of the agricultural towns is of such a nature that by means of it even the population of a whole country may settle in urban areas and villages could be eliminated. Examples of this exclusive agricultural town settlement system are the three major towns in the area between the rivers Danube and Tisza, as well as the regions of Debrecen and the Hajdú towns. In the other parts of the Great Plain, however, the agricultural town system could not survive as an exclusive pattern since the settlement of individuals and public institutions has brought about independent communities on the plains of the towns even if the towns themselves raised objections to it. Thus, Kiskundorozsma was settled on the Szeged plains despite the intermittent and vigorous protests of Szeged, and similarly, newly settled villages were built in the vicinity of other towns, too. So even in regions dominated by agricultural towns there emerged an increasing number of villages and though their density lagged far behind that of the Transdanubian villages they considerably changed the character of settlement.

But the principle of agricultural town settlement has become such a living tradition with the peasantry of the Great Plain that even at places where villages were settled down these started their existence within a much wider framework than the normal rural dimensions. And though they did not grow into towns they developed their own farmstead system opening boundless vistas for their development. Today there are a great number of communities among the villages of agricultural town regions with more than ten thousand souls and the territory of quite a few of them exceeds the twenty thousand "holds" (one "hold" equalling 0.57 hectares). In the region of the 29 agricultural towns there are 34 villages with such a numerous population and such a vast territory, and, in addition to that, they succeeded in developing their own homestead system as well.

These giant villages or more exactly, tiny agricultural towns are the following: Bácsalmás and Jánosháza in the County Bács-Bodrog, Endrőd, Füzesgyarmat, Mezőberény, Szeghalom, Tótkomlós and Vésztő in the County Békés, Berettyóújfalu and Sarkad in the County Bihar, Battonya in the County Csanád, Kiskundorozsma and Kistelek in the County Csongrád, Balmazújváros, Hajdúdorog, Nádudvar and Püspökladány in the County Hajdú, Dévaványa, Jászapáti, Jászárokszállás, Jászladány, Kunhegyes, Kunszentmárton, Tiszaföldvár in the County Nagykun-Szolnok, Abony, Fülöpszállás, Kiskőrös, Kiskunmajsa, Kecel, Kunszentmiklós, Nagykáta, Lajosmizse and Szabadszállás in the County Pest, Nagykálló and Újfehértó in the County Szabolcs.

With the exception of the three Cumanian settlements, i.e. Kunszentmiklós, Szabadszállás and Fülöpszállás as well as the one-time county seat Nagykálló all these villages have more than ten thousand inhabitants. It is justified to make an exception with these communities since all of them have extensive boundaries, highly developed homestead systems, moreover the past of all the four vast villages is identical with that of the agricultural towns.

Of the above communities all could develop into agrarian towns, and they have already reached a stage when most of them have become district seats, have district courts and revenue offices and in addition, all of them have junior high schools; some of them, for instance Jánoshalma, have even high schools and markets which render them fit to cope with urban functions. In Hajdúdorog there is a Greek Catholic bishopric. All of the villages with homesteads have road systems which turn these sprawling communities into centres of more or less extensive regions.

Apart from these communities which are well on the road of becoming agricultural towns and cannot be regarded as part of the environments of the other towns, there are smaller villages, too, in the area of the settlement with homesteads where there is no specific reason for such a pattern. The area of these villages is not so vast that it could not be cultivated within the bounds of the village system, and neither is the village so big that its inhabitants should be compelled to buy or to take homesteads on lease in the surroundings of other villages. Yet, they keep on building farmsteads since this has become a general and binding habit all over the region, and this is done without any direct need. Despite their homestead system, such smaller communities are villages which have become integral parts of the environs of one or another agricultural town. These areas are comparable to the villages without farmsteads in the neighbourhood of Western towns. These small villages may be not farther off the town than their homesteads but since they have been transformed into independent communities and their settlement pattern is of a village character, they constitute — besides the homesteads as their own areas — the outside surroundings of the towns. There are but a few such communities, incomparably fewer than in Transdanubia, nevertheless all agrarian towns have some of them.

In addition to such communities, the agricultural towns have other areas, too, within their own confines. Homesteads which had closely and organically belonged to the agricultural town became separated from the town in the course of time or because of the natural breaking up of lands or as a consequence of some settlement intervention, and these homesteads became elements of independent settlements. They became villages though houses did not take on the shape of compact formations, did not line up side by side as in regular compact villages; they rather resembled the villages of Western and Northern Europe. To mark out exactly the places of such villages detailed statistical surveys would be needed which would answer also the question whether one or another homestead still belonged to the town or has already broken away from it. On the basis of outside observations such homestead areas turning into villages are the Szeged homesteads, part of the Kecskemét and Cegléd homesteads, the areas along the river Tisza of the Nagykunság, the homesteads of Szabolcs County as well as the region of Békés County east of the river Körös.

The compact village settlements within the bounds of the agricultural towns occupy an intermediary position between the independently administered villages and the homesteads transforming into scattered villages. These are not independent administratively but together with the homesteads come directly under the jurisdiction of the municipal administration. Their settlement is, however, of a village character and their everyday life, too, is by and large similar to that of the villages. Such settlements are Röszke, Szentmihálytelek and Szatymaz, in the area of Szeged, Kupa in the area of Cegléd, Kadafalva and Szikra in the area of Kecskemét, and some outlying settlements in the area of Debrecen.

Examining one by one these three kinds of rural elements of the agricultural towns the following social relationships can be pointed out.

Homesteads transforming into villages are outwardly just like the real homesteads. The most apparent change in them is the fact that the overwhelming majority of them are fenced in, so that similarly to the rural houses, they begin to assume a home-like character. The shape of the buildings, too begins to assume the form of dwelling houses. At such places the back ends of the houses tend to be painted and ornamented and it is quite frequent to find homestead buildings holding two or three rooms. In the Szeged homestead villages exact copies of the Lower-town and

Upper-town houses are erected and, likewise, at the Slovakian farmsteads exact copies of the downtown type of houses of the nearby town are being built. As a matter of fact the traditions of Hungarian homestead building would demand a different practice, notably that urban houses cannot be transplanted to the homesteads since the farmstead building has other functions. At every homestead transformed into a dwelling-house afforestation, too, has assumed a rural character. In the fenced courtyards there are trees everywhere; in front of or behind the house there are orchards or kitchen pots whereas these are rather rarely to be found on real homesteads.

The internal life of such homesteads is also entirely different from that of the real homesteads. All the furnishing serves permanent habitation and people live accordingly. It is not only all their work which links them to the homestead building but they are returning here from all their trips, and even if the old ones had not been born on the farmstead, they will die there. When babies are born, the mothers cannot go anywhere in town from here; the midwife has to be brought out here or if necessary, the expectant mothers have to be taken to the doctor in the town or to some central hospital.

People go to town from the homesteads only if the need for some major sale or purchase arises or if they inevitably have to appear before court. Such settlements are certainly very far away from the town and often riding to town would take half a day. Arriving there, no home is awaiting them only the inn, and after having arranged their affairs they start for their homesteads not from their homes; they leave the town setting out for the gloomy solitude of their farmsteads. If the farmers settled on their farmstead recently, the awareness of belonging to the town is still alive. When going to town, they still say they are going home, yet this has become a mere catch phrase and reminiscence and not the expression of real adherence as in the case of genuine homestead dwellers.

These are the people depicted so immortally by such authors as István Tömörkény or Ferenc Móra. These people of the Great Plain, are rooted in the sandy soil; they are neither villagers nor townsmen. They are abandoned and solitary homeless people and all their lives are centered around the courtyard of a tiny house on the plains. On a very rare occasion does this life open up towards the nearest towns.

Naturally such homestead people need a homestead centre but such a centre should be called properly a village centre since its very structure resembles that of the Western scattered villages. These villages have some shops, some artisans, a public administrative institution, a veterinary surgeon and a physician, a school, a church and a cemetery. This centre represents the core for the people of the plains; once or twice a week they go there for shopping, to call on the blacksmith's or the cartwright's workshop and on Sundays they go to church. It is here that they baptize their children, get married and bury their deceased.

Even more laborious is the fate of those people of the plains who are permanently banished to homestead areas which do not belong to any major town but to some small community on the plain which has no downtown whatsoever. Orgovány and Jakabszállás are well-known scattered communities of this type. The lands of these communities are nothing but barren sand, and for people living there the town or the railway are as distant ideas as for the inhabitants of the Kirghiz steppes. Even production is totally paralyzed by the state of banishment since cultivating the barren sand would call for more means than owned by the poor dwarf-holders of the plains. Even if they succeed in wringing something from the sandy soil, they can transport their produce only with immense efforts to the market of a town. These are the areas where the difference between the real homestead system and the homestead villages can be seen most clearly. While the life of Jakabszállás is mere agony and drudgery on the plain, the neighbouring fields of Kecskemét abound in flourishing orchards and both men and goods are transported by narrow-gauge railway to the town. Actually the Bugac area of Kecskemét is even more removed from the town than Jakabszállás, yet, life there is on a higher standard and not so desolate as in the nearer Jakabszállás.

The life that developed in the not fully independent village communities on the fringes of the homestead areas of the towns is somewhat easier since more people live there together but no genuine community life could develop there for lack of administrative independence. Despite the fact that they fit into the administrative system of a town, their social life still shows the traces of rural independence. They are villagers who—if they are labourers—find work on the homesteads in the vicinity; if they happen to own some land, they have their little estates nearby and cultivate them from the rural settlement, i.e. by means of the village system. Their houses are therefore entirely built on the rural pattern. The courtyard serves as the yard for both the dwelling and the farm, and all the events of their lives take place here. Their links with the town are as developed as those of other communities which live under the same conditions but are independent administratively. They are foreigners in the town, tether their horses at the drive-ins, have their lunch in the inn and having settled their affairs hurry home again. They are in a worse situation than villagers because they do not dispose of their taxes and/or part of their taxes, and thus it depends on the goodwill of the town whether they receive new public institutions or not. As a rule they get a church and even independent parishes are founded—but whether they would get a physician or a fire brigade or any administrative organs depends entirely on the town. The more developed ones have already got such institutions but the others will have to wage a protracted and torturous fight for such institutions. The inhabitants of such settlements have ceased to be townspeople even in their manner of speaking or their memories, and only their registration certificates prove them to be, for

284

instance, citizens of Szeged. They themselves declare themselves to be inhabitants of Röszke and come to Szeged only as guests.

Independent villages in the area of agricultural towns are, however, similar to villages anywhere in Europe. Their life is a closed, independent circle which they cross only when going to the nearest town which is rather an infrequent event.

Production in villages is simpler, more primitive and undivided than that in the agrarian towns. In a rural house all the functions are undivided: it serves simultaneously as the home and shelter for man and beast, the storage-yard for fodder and manure, and traffic consists only of riding out to the fields daily to cart in all the produce and fodder and to cart out all the manure. Such traffic is naturally more than that of the farmstead people but its centre of gravity is entirely different. Villagers feel always at home, leave their house only for short times, and spend the night at home by all means. Such undivided farming implies a more tranquil way of life and a more measured and balanced view of life. Villagers look upon the world always from the same point, and though not regarding themselves townspeople they do not consider themselves farmstead people either. They live in close relatedness with similar people and living among their neighbours—incidentally, everybody is everybody's neighbour in a village—they never feel lonesome.

Such life is naturally restricted by the fact that in vain are villagers inside and at home, this means next to nothing since being a small community they can call into life but few public institutions. They have a community organization exacting taxes, keeping order in the village day and night, a church where they can go to say their prayers every day, a small marketplace where they can sell at the most some chickens or eggs if they are short of money. There is a grocer's in the next street where they can buy salt and kerosene, and if it is a somewhat larger village it also has a lawyer and a doctor, and perhaps a shop which would buy the bulkier produce of the farmers. But this is all. If villagers want to buy more serious goods or want to sell such, if they have to be taken to hospital or are in need of some special medical examination or if they have a lawsuit, they have to go to town. The only difference between them and the homestead people is that they can satisfy all their lesser needs in their village but for more serious needs they still have to go to town, whereas homestead people satisfy both their primitive and more sophisticated needs in town and sustain themselves on the farmstead only on the level needed for their work.

The life of the rural society is therefore quieter, less pretentious and tends to take place on a lower level. Schools are far away, and if a villager would want to have his children educated, he ought to send them to the nearest town which would mean mostly an unbearable financial burden for him. Villages have no newpapers of their own, those published in the towns arrive with a day's, but at least half a day's time lag. Thus, people have to

285

rely on each other and arrange their unpretentious lives so as to be occupied by trivial things for which townspeople would have no time at all. Their thoughts are occupied all the time by the weather, by the health of men and cattle and by the attitudes and behaviour of the other villagers as well as on returning from town by the discussion of strange things experienced there.

There is no denying that this kind of life is more placid and balanced than urban life but at the same time, it is of an unambitious and inert nature. The peasant living in a village is not at all similar to one dwelling in an agrarian town. He is easier to control, humbler and respects the masters much more; in brief, he is of a more peasant character than his equals in the agricultural town.

The town, on the other hand, even the agricultural town pays little attention to the village. It readily receives guests from the villages since such visits inevitably enrich the town, but beyond this purposeful hospitality it has nothing in common with them. Sometimes a village is only five kilometres away from the agricultural town, nevertheless the townsman knows less about it than about his own farmstead thirty kilometres away. And this is the heart of the matter. The administrative and settlement boundaries divide these two spheres of life and in one of them, though people live and work primitively and even lonely from time to time, there is still an urban atmosphere because such seclusion is only temporary and the rest of the time is filled by the town. However, in the other sphere of life people live in a warm human community all the time, yet, they are outcasts for their small community is not strong enough to establish the higher institutions of life.

The boundaries of the homestead-type settlements, i.e. those ones which cluster round agricultural town units are generally regarded as identical with the limits of the Great Plain. By and large this seems to be true but if the agricultural town area is more closely examined it turns out that it extends to both sides of the river Tisza beginning on the left bank from the Nyírség region right down to the border of Hungary and even beyond that to some regions of Torontál, while on the right bank it begins at the Jászság region and again it extends to the national border and beyond that to the Danube. It is in this area where the 29 agricultural towns, the urban character of which has been examined above, are to be found, and it is in this area where there are 34 homestead-type big communities the life of which is similar to that of the agricultural towns differing from them just in proportions and its lower standards. Finally, it is here that villages in the area of agricultural towns are to be found which, irrespectively whether they are within or without the administrative boundaries of these towns, come by all means under the influence of the agricultural towns.

On closer examination it will be found that the following regions are parts of the zone of agricultural towns and homesteads. With all their territories Békés, Bihar, Hajdú, Csongrád and Jász-Nagykun-Szolnok counties belong

286

to this zone and, in addition, the following areas can also be regarded as occupying parts of this zone: the town of Makó as well as the central and the Battonya districts of Csongrád County, the towns of district rank south of Cegléd in Pest County, as well as the Abony, Nagykáta, Dabas, Kiskunfélegyháza, Kiskőrös and Kunszentmiklós districts of this same county, Nyíregyháza and the Nagykálló districts of Szabolcs County, and finally, the Bácsalmás and Jánoshalma districts of Bács-Bodrog County.

The area of this territory is altogether 4,597,993 "holds" and according to the 1930 census its population came to 2,137,769. This means that the territory makes up 28.3 per cent of the national territory in 1930, whereas its population amounted to 24.6 per cent of Hungary's total population in 1930.

Of the 2,137,796 persons living in the settlement area of the agricultural towns 1,121,421 people, i.e. 52.4 per cent lived in the agricultural towns themselves. However, the remaining population is still not a real rural element since 417,289 of them live in small agricultural towns which comes to a further 19.5 per cent of the population living in that area. As a result, only 599,086 souls, i.e. a mere 28 per cent of the total population of this area can be considered rural population in the genuine sense of the word.

These ratios are beyond any comparison with the percentages of the Western settlement areas because the ratio of urban population and of those living in large villages is so much higher here. On the strength of more exact statistical data on the homesteads these figures ought to be modified by selecting and deducting those homestead areas which have been transformed into villages, but even after such due corrections the ratio would be of a similar value. The reason for these highly advantageous data is solely the urban principle as embodied in the homestead system and the agricultural towns. All what has been said about this system by relying on various sociological perspectives is summarily and emphatically expressed by these data.

VI

TOWN AND ITS ENVIRONS*

* The Hungarian original is to be found in Ferenc Erdei's *Összegyűjtött művei* (Collected Writings) *Településpolitika, közigazgatás, urbanizáció* (Settlement Policies, Public Administration, Urbanization), Akadémiai Kiadó, Budapest, 1977, pp. 531—545. The study was first published in *Társadalmi Szemle,* 1970, No. 10. pp. 25—35.

In the new series of "Discovery of Hungary" I undertook to explore and describe—under the title "Town and its Environs"—the phenomena of modern urbanization on the example of the town of Szeged and the county of Csongrád as they are evolving under our developing socialist conditions. I have based my book on an extensive and far-reaching collection of data; in addition to that, this is also my homeland so my personal experiences also date back half a century. I started this undertaking by raising more or less definite questions. Although that was not my set purpose, by the time I had finished my book, I could also draw certain generalizeable conclusions.

The method I followed was neither scientific nor political in the strict sense of the word, although both viewpoints are relied upon. My book is rather of literary character (it is very much like literary sociographic reports written before the war) thus, in fact, my concrete descriptions as well as my more or less generalizeable findings and conclusions have documentary validity. Having explained that much, I give here some of the major ideas of the introductory and concluding parts of my book, which will be published next year.

QUESTION AND ANSWERS

I am looking for the concrete answers to the general questions of our age in Szeged and its environs in 1970.

One of the most comprehensive all-encompassing phenomena of the social change of our age is the growth of the towns and the spread of urban characteristics, in short *urbanization*. This is the process, whose visible flood can be continuously traced everywhere; the process of urbanization also reflects its underlying causes: the technological progress, the extension of the division of labour and the transformation of interpersonal social relations.

Every civilization had towns: our European civilization also began with towns. Indeed, even our prehistory is connected with towns and civilizations named after them. We could say that the civilization is synonymous with the towns.

We have to see that only the minority of the population lived in the towns and, for a long time, in rather small towns; we also know that besides the civilized urban world a rural civilization also existed; this was an ethnographic culture which developed according to its own laws and had a contact with the urban world only through narrow or sometimes wider channels. Figuratively speaking: the towns were, in fact, peaks or islands in the sea of their rural environment.

By now this has changed. The towns kept growing and increasing in numbers; by the 1960s the majority of mankind lived in towns or settlements with a population of more than 10,000 people. From among these towns 1,500 have more than 100,000 inhabitants, and the number of those towns whose population is above one million exceeds one hundred; indeed, two of them (New York, Tokyo) have more than ten million inhabitants. Speaking figuratively again, by now there is no sea, no island, for the islands grew so big that the sea of yore became reduced to lakes. The change is so tremendous that even the metaphor has to be reversed: the advancing urbanization must be likened to the tide of the sea, where districts left out of urbanization for the time being became steadily eroding islands. And this tide has such an irresistible force that the towns are now shaping their district to their own image at an ever-increasing rate and pace, transforming villages and sporadic settlements, which once formed a separate world, to suburbs. This is the essence of the urbanization of our age.

The rapid growth of towns is an objective law of development which cannot be stopped and cannot be reversed. This could happen only in the case of a catastrophe of cataclysmic size. Be they socialist or capitalist societies, be the town on the European, the American, the Asian, the African or the Australian continent, the validity of this law does not change. The figures indicate that the extent of urbanization varies by various areas. Compared with the total population, the number of city-dwellers who lived in towns of 100,000 or more inhabitants was in round figures 62 per cent in North America, 47 per cent in Oceania, 28 per cent in Europe and the Soviet Union, 19 per cent in South America, 11 per cent in Asia and 10 per cent in Africa in 1966.

But what is that irresistible and irreversible force that drives this urbanization? This force is *the progress of the forces of production, and the scientific-technological revolution.* As a result of this revolution modern science obtains knowledge about animate and inanimate nature, which, when used as technology, can multiply the productive capacity. "Machines make man grow a thousand fold," this is said not without reason.

Urbanization is coupled with the accelerated global population growth. At present fertility levels mankind is likely to double its numbers every forty years. At the same time, the doubling time of the efficiency of human labour takes just about that long in the industrially developed countries, but much longer in the Third World. On the other hand, scientific knowledge doubles every ten years, in other words, scientific knowledge is largely replaced with new knowledge each decade.

This transformation of the life conditions of mankind is very promising. The chance of overcoming starvation and disease, ignorance and servitude, and of creating a new world based on justice is inherent in this explosion-like transformation. Yet, the very same conditions would also lead to the destruction of mankind. This is how a scientist would express this idea: "Will we succeed in eliminating the risk of war parallel with technological progress? If we won't, the life-time of technological civilization will be practically nil." Thus, the scientific-technological revolution intensifies the dilemma of choice between Good and Evil.

And the thing that will decide the dilemma is the way in which society assimilates the driving-power of its own progress, the development of the forces of production. This is the critical point.

Prying into the contradictions of the two cultures, C. P. Snow pointed out in 1962 that for him the industrial revolution means increasing utilization of machines, factory employment of men and women, and also that a large part of the population, which formerly made a living from agricultural work, became factory workers in England, or people engaged in the distribution of manufactured products... The industrial revolution matured the conditions of an other change, of a transformation very similar to the industrial revolution, but much more profoundly scientific, rapid, and as regards its achievements far more amazing... I think that the society of electronics, nuclear energy and automation today differs in its essential features from anything that existed until now. When in their full blossom, these new methods will transform the world much more thoroughly.

Transform, but into what?

Kindlers of the fire of the scientific-technological revolution are struggling with the thought rent with inner conflict. Some scientists contribute to the increase of destructive nuclear power, others protest against that. Many of them express their visions about the heartening and horrifying possibilities of the future in the genre of science fiction. Some are optimistic, while others are the opposite. Their majority, those who feel the responsibility most profoundly, keep warning us, anyhow: "How could man always rise a head above its million-times more powerful and more clever creature, the machine?" The following statements can also be heard from scientists: "It is our duty to show the alternatives of good and evil, and to incessantly look for the path leading to the improvement of the plight of mankind; the stakes are so big, the forecast is so uncertain, and the change is so sweeping that the whole of society must consciously undertake the responsibility for planning the future."

But the historic movement of society goes forward according to its own laws. In the capitalist world phenomena referred to by the notions of "industrial society" and the "consumer society" appear: the power of managers of the economic life and that of the military increases; manipulation of the masses through mass communication assumes frightening dimensions. All these processes are coupled with the steadily growing dependence of the less-developed countries.

The socialist countries are forced to compete with these processes. The economic and arms race forced the socialist nations to keep their positions in production and productivity, in the material standard of life and in the realization of the scientific-technological revolution; indeed, the need appeared to bridge the historically inherited development lag. At the same time, these nations also want to assert socialist ideas: the freedom of man and the humanity of various social organizations and communities. However, these ideas must be realized under the pressure of the coexistence and the competition of capitalism and socialism.

Therefore struggle takes place between the old and the new in the arenas of society. In addition to this conflict, we experience the explosion-like growth of the forces of production, which in itself is neither good nor bad, since it is capable of strengthening hopeful and terrible alternatives. Through the mass media we get information on the dual nature of technology every day.

Yet the fact that behind daily events we may observe the continuous historical change of society should not escape our attention. The unprecedented growth of the forces of production is the underlying factor of their historical change. Where is the growth of technology to be felt? The growth of technology is reflected by changing production methods and the transformation of life circumstances. The news we hear daily provide inadequate information of this process. Aspects of this process are usually analyzed under the inclusive notion of urbanization.

We are subjects of a radical transformation in terms of work conditions and in terms of the division of labour. New and still newer social work organizations are developing, and the conventional family work organizations are being forced back to a steadily narrowing area. Job and homes become separated in space and time, and while on the job a new sphere of human life is developing. Half of the best part of our life has to be spent conforming to the laws of rapidly developing technology: we have to earn a living working with machines, obeying the needs of rational administration, and also in a programmed cooperation with other persons. The world of work pushes all types of traditional human relations to the background: those between man and woman, husband and wife, mother and daughter, relatives and neighbours. There is a uniform rule here: we are all parts of a uniform organization with each participant having a special role. What could and what should be the nature of the world of work in order to be both efficient and bearable; in what way do various property relations influence efficiency and work satisfaction; how quickly and through which means could conventional work organizations be transformed into the necessary new ones. These are all questions still to be clarified. By now the development of society created enough empirically observable facts to give a generalizing answer to these questions. Yet, our experience in new work organizations is not yet extensive enough. Therefore, we have to carry on observing to give adequate answers.

There is also a radical transformation in terms of housing. Differences in housing conditions are more important than those to be found in the world of work, the reason being that the social nature of housing and settlements structures is more conservative, than that of the work organizations. Big and smaller towns, the various housing estates, and the even greater variety of suburban housing estates represent various solutions to the problems of transport between homes and work places and the relationship of persons and families with one another and the social services. Housing and settlement structures should ensure a life with dignity. Housing should consider the aspects efficient work, recreation, of sensibly spent leisure time. It should also ease the burdens of commuting. As regards these problems one can easily draw premature conclusions; however, this is even more risky than in the case of the world of work. The careful tracing of trends in housing policy is even more interesting than the long-run observation of work organizations.

After all, the question of questions is: *what kind of society are we building in the wake of the revolutionary progress of the forces of production?* The European workers' movement and Marxist socialism had faced this question well in advance, and formulated the conceptual answer more than a century ago. And it also began the test of practice more than half a century ago. The following factors are of crucial importance: the social ownership of means of production, the social planning of the economy, the political hegemony of the working class, the concentration of social responsibility in a single socialist workers' party, and the creation of a socialist state organization and institutional structure.

But history still left open many questions, and posed many new ones, while it also confirmed a number of unexpected solutions. This is the reason why the efforts aimed at the realization of the socialist idea also branched off in a number of directions and why those opposing socialism also gather renewed strength and start counter attacks on new and still newer fronts.

What is then the answer to the big question? A conceptual ideological answer can and must be given, and socialism takes the lead in that. But a practical answer, in which the everyday considerations of individual people are expressed, where the laws of competition assert themselves, also must be given. And this historic competition taking place in our age is open in the practice of ordinary life. And its openness is not only unavoidable, but also stimulating. Only the pressure of competition indicating the perspective of final victory makes our goal realistic: based on the immense growth of the forces of production, we should be capable of building the society which is the best hope of humanity. And because this process is lengthy, and not exempt from contradictions, we must pay never failing attention to the development of society. This is also the basis upon which generalizing conceptual-ideological answers concerning the questions posed by history can prove their viability.

In my book I am looking for concrete answers to the general questions of our age confining myself to a given geographic locality and to the present. I feel compelled, however, to add some explanatory remarks to this.

I am completely aware of the fact that the laws governing society are equally valid on the macro as well as on the micro levels. I am also convinced that Marxist science has already fundamentally clarified these issues: the historic development of society is determined by the objective law of the development of the forces of production. Social relations are shaped by the level of the forces of production not without resistance, but through class struggles and the conflicts of social institutions; history progresses according to the dialectics of this dual movement. But the social process is different in the macro and the micro spheres. The former sphere is the realm of the great forces: the macro sphere is the field of social stratification. In this sphere we encounter class struggles, the struggle for political power and dramatic social conflict. In the micro sphere, however, the continuously progressing development of society takes place: processes of elementary organization, the formation of fundamental social institutions, the development of villages and towns. Changes in the family structure, in the world of work and in consumption patterns also take place here. In the micro sphere the social process is less visible, this is the more conservative sphere of society.

The critical issues of our age appear primarily on the macro level. Opinions and conflicts divide the world as regards these problems. Most debates intend to clarify the effects and perspectives of the scientific-techno- logical revolution. The micro sphere is not so much debated. Conflicting views on the micro sphere are made less dramatic. These are problems treated by urbanistics, and in a narrower sense by sociology.

THE PURPOSE AND THE CONCLUSIONS
OF THE AUTHOR

What is the value of the word if it has no clear meaning? What is the message good for if is it not clear where it springs from and what it is aimed at? Let the author account for his purpose, let him admit openly what he wants.

Allow me to begin with saying that I began to paint an all-compressing picture about a part of our life, a part of our country, the region between the Danube and the Tisza a generation ago, with a young head and heart. My purpose then was to expose some concrete manifestations of objective social laws, and I did not disguise my subjective conviction that that world could not go on as it was: it had to change fundamentally. I made no mistake, the change did come.

296

Not only the world changed since then, however, but I also in it; four decades have passed since then.

I spent most of my life studying society. I learnt the methods and the professional jargon of some relevant branches of science, and I used them more or less successfully in exploring a historically changing society. What was the outcome of all this? The result was more or less knowledge on some sections of society, on the economy, on administration, on town and village life. I also dealt with homestead farming, the peasantry, cooperative farms and Hungary's place in the world. I guess I could even be satisfied, but I am not at all. It disturbs me that I still have no clear picture of the whole, and I am beginning to doubt whether it is at all possible to create a complete picture based on my findings and insights. In other words, every bit of knowledge in a special line of learning has a place, a role, and a certain utility, but all of them cannot substitute for an overall image on our age and society. One of my aims was to contribute to this with this work.

I spent half of my adult life in political struggles aimed at changing society. I started and ended up as a peasant politician, but in the meantime I fought at many fronts: in economic policy in creating the alliance of workers and peasants, I fought for socialism and I was assigned a lot of tasks in building socialism; I participated in the land-reform and in the reform of public administration. I could be satisfied in this respect also. I fought with enthusiasm and I contributed something to the whole of the work. Yet I am not entirely satisfied in this respect either: did principles and systems really get realized in practice the way we expected? I must say no, they did not, and we must also subject ourselves to the incessant second examination of history: ideas and reality, theory and practice must be continuously brought face to face. When writing this book, my other intention was to contribute to this something also.

The opportunity I grabbed is alluring and full of risks. Some of my younger friends (writers and scholars) joined forces in order to discover Hungary again, this time around the 25th anniversary of the new Hungary. I also joined their ranks, with the burden that already prior to the war I undertook the same task. And to make my endeavour mercilessly serious, I chose my own birthplace as test material: the place where I grew up, and to which I always returned. Here I have no excuse for erroneous information; here I am obliged to know everything. The intention, which guided me in writing this book, is obvious: in knowing society as well as in confronting ideas with reality I looked for the strictest control.

And ultimately what was that I wanted? Or, for the sake of easier understanding, what was that I did not want?

I did not intend to enumerate our achievements on the occasion of the anniversary. What we put into the balance sheet will not really give the measure of what we achieved in twenty-five years. Instead, we have to consider what we in fact did to influence the course of history. We have to consider our actual solutions to the major and minor social problems.

I did not aim at getting to general scientific or political conclusions; in fact, I rather tried to avoid theoretical generalizations. More precisely, I confined myself to posing questions openly and in their fullness, therefore, with the most general validity. However, I gave only concrete answers adequately reflecting historical reality.

How much authenticity could all that I have expressed with these intentions have on such foundations? I certainly do not verify my findings in a strictly scientific way. Although I used quite a few scientific methods and I also tried to verify my findings, the method I adopted was still not the kind that would by itself show the validity of my conclusions. In keeping with my intentions, I utilized both scientific and non-scientific methods of approach, but even these methods do not ensure authenticity. Could we speak then of the authenticity of the writer? In this instance that is no help either, for the matter in question is not the subjective approach of the writer, and the recording of something. What I considered the essence, and what I endeavoured to express was not recording, but the reflection of reality. When all is said and done, the authenticity of the work is reflected by the combination of the subjectivity of the author and his objective methods of examination.

First, I started to ask questions. Sometimes I received more than one answer. In the course of inquiry further questions also emerged and they were answered by my findings. I have no complaints: precisely at this historic moment Szeged and its environs gave many and enlightening answers to my questions. Based on my questions, it is possible to arrive at certain generalizable findings and conclusions. But these are not scientifically elaborated conclusions, because they can be obtained only through a scientific method. Neither are my conclusions political or ideological tenets, for those would have required a much greater commitment to political values. In the following the purpose is to sum up concrete observations of a documentary value. When judging the merits of my findings, this should not be forgotten. With more or less certainty I shall outline my major findings in the following:

1. *The historic moment* at which I explored urbanization in the city of Szeged and its environs was rather remarkable. 1969 and 1970 were the years, when two social factors proved to be influential, one of them being progress made in the development of our socialist institutions, the other the coming of the new industrial revolution. These two factors are well reflected in production, consumption, the world of work, housing, the development and functioning of our institutions. In short, change has come to influence all walks of life.

On closer look, we could say that these two factors reflect the intertwinement and relationship between the social relations of production and the productive forces. Be it capitalist or socialist society the sweeping progress of the forces of production did not come to a halt and its effect is universally felt. This progress is reflected by the sudden technological change penetrating certain fields. At present, the characteristic feature of our social relations is that our socialist institutions, developed on the basis of people's power achieved two decades ago, are in a process of modification conditioned by the intrinsic laws of institutions as well as by the effects of the productive forces. The new economic mechanism is both part and a stimulating force of this historic process. Obviously, the development of the forces of production and the change in the institutional system mutually influence each other.

This finding can surely be generalized to the whole of the country. Yet in Szeged and the County of Csongrád, the above processes are more visible because this region of the country was rather underdeveloped and industrialization took place at a stormy speed. The modernization of the social relations takes place against a historical background which is specific in many respects.

2. The characteristics of the present give a genuine reflection of the achievements of the Hungarian nation over the past twenty-five years. When considering the present, we become aware of the fact that social change was *complete,* radical and all-inclusive. Szeged and its environs show that all areas of the nation were affected by social change. In every town, village and in the homestead areas life changed radically, even if there is a great variety in the degree and quality of social transformation. Obviously, this can also be generalized when observing the settlements from County Zala to County Szabolcs, only the degree of variations is likely to increase.

But these changes were not even, and the present conditions show the effects of previous phases to such an extent that the phenomena of today often cannot even be comprehended without a knowledge of the historical past. In the County of Csongrád social change was in all probability faster than in other regions of the country.

In the past twenty-five years three distinct periods can be distinguished in the history of Szeged and the County of Csongrád. Between 1944 and 1949 the old social structure continued to exist, but with two essential changes. One was that the popular forces broke to the surface: the working class, hardened here through the traditions of working-class movement, and the peasantry, whose stratification changed in the wake of the land reform, became political factors. The political forces directed at the future shaping of society clashed with one another producing a political stalemate. A continuous open and sharp local class struggle was being fought in this region. The role of the middle class was especially great and this influenced the outcome of local struggles in a variety of ways.

Based on the outcome of the struggle for power, from 1949 to 1960 the socialist reorganization of society took place. In every field of life the development of social relations was defined by centrally controlled political actions. The socialist transformation, the socialist consolidation after the counter-revolution of 1956 as well as the socialist reorganization of the agriculture were not exempt from serious social conflicts.

Also in this region the real consolidation of the socialist system followed only after 1961, i.e. after the socialist reorganization of agriculture. The years after 1961 saw a rapid growth of agriculture, also in the county of Csongrád. However, there was one decisive local factor. This is the spectacular acceleration of industrialization. Coupled with the growth of local autonomy, then with the effects of the new economic mechanism of 1968, this opened a new era of general prosperity. This period is also the time of the scientific-technological revolution and the onslaught of urbanization.

Dividing the nation's history after 1945 into particular periods is a task for the historians. The development periods to be identified in Szeged and its environs might not be generalizable, but it may contribute to the historians' work.

3. However, in 1969—1970 the social conditions in Szeged and the County of Csongrád do not only show the consequences of the history of the recent past, but also the marks of the earlier historic development. In short, we may say that present-day social relations indicate that *even the most revolutionary transformation is realized on the basis of the earlier history*. In the course of my investigations I realized that very old historical traditions determine to a surprising extent not only the present social conditions of our settlements, but also the concrete form and functioning of the new, socialist institutions.

Perhaps the most striking manifestation of this is that settlements as well as institutions vary to a very great extent, and differences are even greater in the actual life of settlements. This is the situation in spite of the fact that the same socialist state holds them all together, and that our institutions rest on a common concept expressed in laws of general validity and in social norms. This is the most understandable in the instance of cooperative farms, for they are social organizations of the peasantry. But the same applies to industrial and commercial enterprises, and to various public institutions, and in particular to the concrete life circumstances of people.

Various development levels cannot give a full explanation for the differences among the settlements. In addition to that, there is also structural variation and there are also differences in character. The underlying cause of these differences is to be found in history, which in turn includes the totality of geographic, ethnic and other endowments as well. In terms of local social relations it seems completely obvious that the transformation of property relations, political change, and the various political actions affect a given historic and social world, therefore their influence gets modified.

4. In connection with the above we can speak of a generalizable historic

experience. *We have to see that for radical social change and the emergence of an adequate social structure a long period is necessary.* This time is longer than we expected in the period of planning. This is the most obvious in the case of cooperative farms. But the same applies to state farms, state and council-controlled industrial and trading enterprises as well as to various cooperatives and to social institutions. As regards the life circumstances and life styles we can say that it takes a long time for change to take place.

However, institutional change is amazing and newly founded institutions are capable of starting to operate in a short time. At a close look, however, it turns out that behind institutional change a continuous and organic development extending over a considerable time is taking place. An objective rule asserts itself in this process: this process is neither rapid, nor can it sidestep the time necessary for growth and development. At the most, we can find exceptions to this rule.

In the course of local inquiries one can almost always feel the particular phase of development the institution in question goes through, or the actual development level of life circumstances. And this is valid in respect of all kinds of cooperatives, enterprises, the introduction of new technologies, new consumer goods or the operation of any kind of organization. The same applies to the administrative organization of towns and villages. And it is also part of the objective laws of development that certain institutions are incapable of achieving development and wither away after a shorter or longer period, though before they lose their influence they fill a useful role. Certainly that is the situation with the machinery stations, some sparsely settled areas given independent administrative standing, a number of school types or some schools, and quite a few enterprise organizations.

5. It is a generally valid thesis that *conciousness follows the changes in the forces of production and in the production relations with a time-lag.* On the basis of local enquiries this can be undoubtedly proved. Yet the matter is still not that simple. A surprising variety in attitudes, in the ways of life was discovered in the social world of the city of Szeged and its environs. This variety is probably to be identified in all regions of the country.

However, the surprising variety is completely understandable, indeed, even necessary. We live in a new era, in which the remnants of the earlier era are still exerting their influence; life styles are affected by the various periods of the past 25 years. Last but not least our society is also influenced by developments taking place outside Hungary. What is most interesting and also the most understandable is that, compared to the given historic situation, there are plenty of ahistoric forms of consciousness that either lag behind or are ahead of the time.

In the following, I give a brief description of various life styles and attitudes to society:

— With some modifications the conventional peasant way of life and outlooks are still very much alive, the principal reason being that a large area

301

is settled by homestead holdings (the proportion of people living in sparsely populated homestead settlements is greatest in the County of Csongrád);

— There are already masses of cooperative peasants working on large-scale farms whose way of life and attitudes are no longer of peasant character;

— Petit bourgeois attitudes concentrating on obtaining additional income, and saving money for buying or building a privately-owned home or garden or a car as well as a selfish, family-centered behaviour are very common among all social strata. On the basis of my subjective impressions, I could not say how common these attitudes are among workers, the various white-collar groups, or cooperative peasants.

— Consumerism, aiming at the maximum enjoyment of the "good things of life" is becoming quite common. The changed conditions of life and the foreign influences are primarily responsible for this new attitude.

— There are more representatives of a life style emphasizing the human values of culture, appreciating science, literature, arts, music, and the culture of other peoples than ever before. In addition to the old types of these humanistic attitudes, also new ones developed.

— In addition to the above type, there are not only in the form of exceptional cases various other life styles and attitudes both in towns and villages; we may meet a variety of escapism and the advocates of various hobbies. Some hobbies strengthen social integration, while others are means of escape. There are persons obsessed with high-tech., whose only concern is technology both on the job and at home. There is a great variety of hobbies.

Be that as it may, there are certain meeting points, or general features, or tendencies. In this diverging multiplicity of life styles and attitudes there are certain trends. One such trend is that some attitudes are general in the majority of society. We can speak of two definitely existing social attitudes here: the first is value placed upon human equality realized in ambitions and expectations; the second is the appreciation of expertise and a high value attributed to getting a good training and an education. In the given historical-social situation there are two conflicts in the world of various attitudes. One is the conflict between consumerism and work ethic: consumerism is becoming more common to the detriment of the work ethic. The other conflict is between socialist values, mores and world outlook and the other non-socialist attitudes. Under the conditions of increasing industrialization, advancing urbanization and increasing standard of living, it is hard to see how these trends will develop.

6. Under the conditions of our socialist society the local examination of the city of Szeged and its environs was instructive also in respect of the laws, essence, and the special features of *urbanization itself*. Some generalizable findings and conclusions can be given in this respect too.

The first of these is that urbanization cannot be seen in terms of the growing numbers of city-dwellers. Neither can urbanization become the basis of some mystic, modern philosophy. Urbanization can be completely explored in terms of a Marxist interpretation of history and society. The main factor of urbanization is the development of the forces of production, more precisely the second industrial revolution. Urbanization can also be described as the concrete historic process of the "elimination of substantial differences between towns and villages".

The second point is that urbanization progresses in the fields of production, economy, and in respect of working conditions just as well as in consumption, in the environment and in general in the conditions of life, and even beyond that, in the organization and management of society. Yet in the progress of urbanization the most interesting and from the aspect of further development the most important problem is the issue of infrastructure. The problems of infrastructure are particularly highlighted in our society including housing, the supply of the community, transport, the organization of various services, and ultimately the development of the whole of the settlement network.

The third point to be made here is that urbanization is also a question of the relationship of town and rural districts. In terms of history, the relationship between town and village represents the relationship between centre and periphery. It is also a tie of super and subordination, and exploitation of rural districts by the towns. In our age, and particularly in socialism under the conditions of modern technology and a more highly developed division of labour, the sensible organization of town and country into a single unit, the regulation of bilateral relations on equal footing became a possibility.

7. Finally, the local examination of Szeged and its environs allows some conclusions to be drawn also *as regards the future*. A lot of phenomena indicate that urbanization affects the whole of our society and it starts processes whose consequences will fully develop only in the future. This applies both to industrial-technological progress and to the development of our socialist institutions. At the moment, our society is in the attractive and alluring early phase of industrialization and urbanization, when the dangers and social risks of these processes can hardly be seen.

In other words, this means that we are in the ascending phase of the era of prosperity; the processes aimed at achieving industrialization, a higher technological standard, more productive labour, a higher standard of living and a more urbanized life are going forward with objective force. However, two remarks should be made here.

One of them is that urbanization takes place in the micro-world of our society; it is a manifestation of trends in the social process and of the aspirations of people. The macro-structure of society, foreign and domestic policy, the national development of our institutions, in short, the principal political trends may either facilitate or hamper urbanization. Until now this macro-structure promoted, indeed, in essence it triggered the acceleration of progress. The most likely conclusion is that in the future, too it will promote prosperity and urbanization.

The other remark should be made on the consciousness of society and on social attitudes. Elements of both good and bad atmosphere are necessarily simultaneously present in our society. However, my observations in Szeged and the County Csongrád overwhelmingly prove the existence and spread of an optimistic, hopefully expectant atmosphere that encourages action. Individual careers, the actual realization of life ambitions, family, work and communal endeavours, all these can increasingly unfold. People and enterprises, towns and villages are planning, initiating and organizing bravely and ambitiously. These subjective factors are also telling signs of a coming prosperity and the further development and growth of our socialist society. This can be said in spite of the fact that there are still grave social problems which can only be eliminated with huge efforts only. "Good luck, nothing else," sighed once a poet of hard times. "More and better work, and a policy that serves that," — this is decisive and this has to be emphasized by a scholar of a more prosaic discipline.

VII

PROBLEMS OF THE REFORM OF PUBLIC ADMINISTRATION*

* The Hungarian original is to be found in Ferenc Erdei's *Összegyűjtött művei* (Collected Works), *Településpolitika, közigazgatás, urbanizáció* (Settlement Policy, Public Administration, Urbanization) Akadémiai Kiadó, Budapest 1977, pp. 381—391. The study was originally published in the periodical *Fórum,* 1946, No. 1., pp. 86—94.

The fact that the question of the administrative reform has been placed on the agenda is an event of yet immeasurable importance in the development of Hungarian democracy. The profound and radical transformation started by the political system of democracy is obviously transforming not only the whole of the social order of Hungary, but also the administrative organization of the state. The administrative reform has been historically timely since the liberation, and it was only for political reasons (the specific circumstances of political life) that it could not be started. By now, however, the time for the reform has arrived.

On our part we had already raised the question, when the reduction of the number of public servants was decided, stating that this purge could only be regarded as the first step in the transformation of administration and that it was necessary to continue with a second step: the organizational reform of public administration. A few months later the statement of the Left-Wing Block espoused the task and included the reorganization of the administration by the people into its programme. Finally all the four Parties of the coalition accepted the idea of the reform of public administration and an agreement was reached on the principle that the elaboration and implementation of reform of public administration had to be a part of the preparations for the municipal elections. By that agreement the issue of administrative reform became in practice part of the programme of the government, and by now the time has arrived to raise and solve all of the essential problems of this great reform work.

As soon as the plan became timely, the National Peasant Party submitted its recommendations concerning the administrative reform. These recommendations are the starting point of the administrative reform, since other similar reform plans are not yet known. This is justified by the circumstance that the draft in question is the result of lengthy preparatory work, and experts of public administration as well as the political forces have already approved its essential principles. Therefore, when elucidating the problems of the reform of public administration we take the major aspects of this draft as a basis.

What are the pivotal points of this reform recommendation? When the details are disregarded, the essence of the recommendation can be summed up in the following:

307

1. The units of the general municipal administration must be reorganized in accordance with actually existing social and economic units. Instead of small villages, large villages, county towns and boroughs uniform village and town organizations must be set up in such variations as demanded by the social and economic conditions of the settlements (municipality of detached farms, cluster of tiny villages etc.). And instead of counties and districts town-counties must be organized around the 60-80 regional urban centres of the country.

2. The specialized agencies of local administration have to be adjusted to the reorganized units of the general public administration in order to ensure that every administrative organization should organically fit into the actual social and economic structure of the country.

3. The central state administration has to be decentralized from the ministries to state district offices organized by regions. By that the ministries will be relieved of many tasks and they will be able to function as governing authorities, and the regional centres will become centres of major regions also administratively. Also the higher organizations of specialized agencies are to be grouped around these regional administrative institutions.

4. The new structure of public administration must be shaped in a way that the leading posts should be filled by elected laymen, but the public servants should be well-trained professionals.

5. Administrative processes must be simplified so that generally all issues can be settled by two administrative organs. Minor issues are to be settled by two self-governing organs, whereas more important issues have to be solved by one self-governing and one state organization. Only in exceptional cases should it be allowed to have a decision-making process of three levels.

The draft reform built on these principles raises a multitude of detail problems whose adequate solution demands even more innovation and rationalization. However, the problems of the reform can be discussed in merit even if the details are not thoroughly considered. We shall endeavour to elucidate the question from three aspects here: from the political, the administrative, and the social history aspect.

I

The fundamental political question of the reform of public administration is whether it is possible to realize a profound reform affecting all walks of life after the shocks of the war and in a period of reconstruction? We are firmly convinced that this is possible, indeed this is the period when we should begin the reform.

The reduction of the number of public servants has ended. This purge was so thorough that there have not been so few public servants for a long time. The present number of public servants will obviously be increased later in

308

several areas. It is logical to start the reform at this period, to ensure that those who will be employed later will fill the new organizational posts under the new conditions. The other consequence of the reduction of the number of public servants is that the transformation of public administration was only partly effected. True and complete reform will come only when we rebuild public administration replacing former officers and the old organization with new officers and new organizations.

Stabilization creates the possibility and necessity for the reform of public administration on two sides. One of them is that the balance of state finances requires the rehabilitation of the finances of municipalities. This is almost impossible in the present organizational framework. The revenues of various municipal budgets are disproportionate to an extraordinary extent. Adjusting them is not possible in any other way, but with government subsidies, or some other government interference. Under the given organizational circumstances, it is very difficult to start various municipal endeavours. The new organization that would be structured on the foundations of the draft would open new and profitable public works opportunities for almost every municipal budget. One of the difficult questions the new organization would solve is the serious problem that emerged after the land reform particularly in the agricultural towns and larger villages. On the other hand, stabilization makes possible the reform by creating the conditions for future calculations and for drawing up balanced budgets.

The administrative reform is made pressingly urgent by the reorganization of various specialized agencies of local administration and of the bodies of interest representation. Agricultural public administration must be fundamentally reorganized, and at the same time the development of a body representing agricultural interests is also under way. Both of these organizations almost founder on the disproportionate and irrealistic conditions of public administration. The question of whether these organizations should be based on the counties or on the districts is irresoluble, since neither of these units is suitable in essence, and the organizational unit that would be called for is something between the county and the district. The same applies to other branches of the specialized organs of municipal administration, but particularly to the administration of education and generally to the organization of schools, and also to industrial, commercial and financial administration. The reform is urgent on the part of each branch. If we do not lay the new foundations of public administration, then either separate frameworks have to be created for the various specialized organs, which is an immeasurably irrational and expensive solution or we must stick to the completely unsuitable framework of public administration to the detriment of special interests.

The most decisive argument is mentioned last. Holding municipal elections, in other words, the elimination of temporary measures at the municipal and county level is an unquestionable requirement of democracy. It is an even more imperative requirement of democracy that we reject the perpetuation of old, feudal and bureaucratic forms of the public administration in the same way as we have abolished the constitutional form of kingdom. The only solution is, therefore, to lay the final order of self-governing administration on the foundations of a radical administrative reform. Thus it is impossible to hold municipal elections without the reform. However, elections can really be not delayed for long, therefore the reform must be worked out without delay.

But the political aspects, which emerge as consequences of the reform are not less serious either. The points of view listed justify that the reform must be brought under roof now, and urgently. There are, however, some general political consequences of the reform, which generally favour the introduction of the reform now.

The reform would establish modern administration by the people instead of the old, feudal system. It would conclude the work, which the establishment of the republic began; it would establish the lower levels of administration worthy of the republic. In addition to the fact that our administration would improve by this and the executive work of the democratic executive power would at once become more efficient, the reform would yield even further political results. So many local opportunities and the solution of so many unsolved local problems would accompany the implementation of the reform that all this would be attributed to democracy in the eyes of the public, and the whole country would become aware of the fact that the political order of democracy can show real and great results.

The reform draft recommended is so deeply democratic that the new structure of public administration would forever guarantee the democratic organizational framework of Hungarian society. It is precisely its organizational form which makes the present system of public administration capable of suppressing and modifying government measures, while the recommended new public administration would be the broadest guarantee for the implementation of every democratic reform. It would be an organization of Hungarian society which would ensure democratic political and social development for a long-long time in every stratum of society and in every district of the nation.

The reform is bound to have a particularly noticeable influence on the life of the peasantry and on the development of villages and scattered homesteads. Our present organizations suppress the peasantry from the higher levels of political and cultural life and exclude them from the life of the towns almost institutionally. In contrast, the recommended reform would institutionally connect the villages and scattered homesteads with the life of towns, and, by way of self-government, it would institutionally ensure the peasantry's participation in the nation's life.

It would be extremely important for our democratic system to support a reform that affects and interests everybody; this reform would alter the old, feudal character of the nation in almost all walks of life; the whole system would become more democratic. The reform would win over strata otherwise distrustful of our new order to the cause of democracy. The implementation of the recommended reform would transform every school-book, every map, every railway time-table, and every administrative document into a propaganda document of democracy.

II

It cannot be doubted that Hungary's public administration is irretrievably bad. One could enumerate an endless list of objections the modern science of public administration or modern life could raise against it. This is not our intention for anyone could easily do so after having studied a textbook on administration or after having recalled his experience. We present only a few fundamental objections to the present system of public administration and we also show how the reform would remedy these shortcomings.

One of the cardinal troubles is at the top, i.e. in the highest central state organs of administration. Hungarian ministries are inundated with concrete matters concerning permits, allocations, revisions or decisions of the third degree reserved for the ministers. The outcome of this situation is that our ministries grew into vast organizations, dealing with issues distressingly slowly. Above all, these ministries are incapable of doing the work, for which they exist, i.e. governing the country in a comprehensive way. This cannot be remedied but by removing the burden of dealing with concrete issues from the shoulders of the ministries; a decentralization of government tasks would restore the original task of the ministries which should consist in governing. This will also bring about that statutory orders of the various ministries become concerted at the regional level. This would put an end to the system in which sub-prefects of the counties or the county recorders of the districts find themselves faced with the most contradictory government decrees issued by various ministries.

Today the special administrative agencies are interfering with the organizational processes of general administration through and through. Immeasurably much irregularity and controversy as well as much unnecessary trouble and annoyance for the people spring from this. Establishing harmony amongst these different administrative organizations, concentrating their institutions in one location, in the seats of their common town-county, would be an immediate achievement of the reform, which would considerably simplify transactions and considerably reduce costs.

Our municipal administration also has innumerable troubles, but the chief one of these is that the county administration is not self-governing. Once it used to be the self-governing body of the nobility, but it never

311

became that of the people. The present framework of the county is no longer holding together people having common problems and living in a community of interests, but a district comprised of territories falling apart; therefore it is not surprising that the municipal boards of the counties are impotent and inefficient bodies. Districts, the territorial sub-units of the counties impose their rule on the villages from above; thus they are far from being self-governing units. The only thing that could remedy this hopeless situation would be the establishment of higher-level self-governing bodies based on actually existing social and economic units; these are towns and urban centres and their environment. This is the only way of making the counties self-governing.

The other crying contradiction of our autonomous administrative organization is the complete separation of the towns from the villages, the counties and the districts. This is precisely the result of feudal development, even though in modern life every phenomenon of the society converges in the towns and the problems of the country can also be solved only through the towns. What follows from that? The conclusion that the towns and their environs must be placed in a common administrative framework, because that is the only way to ensure the good public administration of the nation. This is the only way to solve the problems of towns and villages. This is the basic idea of the reform of public administration.

III

Hungarian public administration is of a feudal character right to the bone. Feudal traits are characteristic of not only the bodies and processes which evolved under feudalism, but even of those institutions which developed after 1848 and after the Austro-Hungarian compromise of 1867. This is natural, since the Hungarian state organism and the political and economic structure of Hungarian society maintained their profoundly feudal character even after the liberal-bourgeois transformation on the surface. That is the explanation of the peculiar historic development that Hungarian public administration preserved its feudal features in spite of all changes.

Our municipal organization, special administrative agencies and central administrations can all take "pride" in that they preserved in an intact form their feudal institutions, and that the whole of their way of administering affairs preserved the character that it developed under feudalism. In this respect the county played a major role; the county is justifiably the target of the criticism of every democratic political endeavour, which desires to democratically transform our public administration. This is what happened in the reform age, and this is what is happening just now. Let us, therefore, consider the county, and some of its most marked features as representing feudal vestiges.

In essence the county is a unit of self-government, which provides general administration to a particular district in a self-governing framework. But even the first glance reveals something wrong about both territoriality and about self-government.

The borders of the counties gained their present shape in the course of a long historic development. This historic development did not originate from the people or its grass-roots organizations but from the landed nobility. The county has always developed as the municipality of landed noble families, and it has developed its borders as a certain unit of the estates of the nobility. This explains the territorial division provided by the counties. For the estates of the nobility and for the noble families the county was the smallest unit, where everybody knew everybody, and where the estates represented a direct community of interests. This territorial division has not emerged in order to serve the people; the county does not hold together the working classes, the towns and villages, the workshops and the small farms or the offices of administration in a genuine unit. The county is too big to become the direct territorial unit of the people of a given region, and too small to justify the establishment of a comprehensive public administration unit. Therefore, as a territorial unit, the county is an unreasonable traditional framework today, tolerated patiently by the tradition-bound people alongside with countless administrative hardships and other feudal traditions.

As a body of self-government the county has withered away. It used to be genuine self-government for the nobility of the county, and as such it filled its role excellently. However, when the county became the self-governing body of the whole people only in name, real self-government withered away by necessity, because the preconditions for self-government were not given. First of all, the territorial condition of self-government did not exist. The people of a county do not live in such a proximity and in such a community of interest that it could develop an actually functioning self-government. The county is too big for that; the various districts do not know the others. Therefore the counties are generally made up of several units, whose territory and people belong together closely and genuinely. However, the political conditions of self-government are also lacking. The municipal board of the county cannot become a body of the people even if its members are really representatives of the people, for they must make decisions on general issues and on personal issues, where the directness of self-government cannot assert itself. Electing county recorders for the districts is, for instance, a completely abstract political question at the county meetings even today, where the interests and view-points of the districts can in no way be asserted. The public servants of the counties are particularly hostile to self-government. Not only because some of the former county officials are still in office, but also because the very positions of the lord lieutenant and of the deputy-lieutenant entail hostile attitudes to self-government; in

313

addition to that, these posts are inadequate also in terms of central public administration. The lord lieutenant is both a government official and the head of self-government, from which it follows that he is rather an obstacle to self-government instead of leading or developing it. The deputy lieutenant is completely integrated into the organizational hierarchy of administration and, as the leading official of self-government, he is incapable of directing or even of serving it. The county recorders of the districts are in a completely impossible situation both in terms of self-government and central public administration.

The circumstance that the towns form separate bodies within the territory of the county is a conspicuously feudal characteristic of the county. The county of the nobles excluded the towns, and this state survived even when the modern administration was established. Towns enjoying municipality status are completely outside the county organizationally, while the county towns fit into the county rather unwillingly. This is a profound organic fault, and by now a nonsensical feudal vestige of public administration considering the fact that the life of modern society is structured by urban centres, and agriculture as well as the life of the peasantry also become economically and socially organized by the towns. This is an anachronism which a modern, democratic state can no longer maintain.

There is no need to enumerate examples and arguments in order to prove the untenableness of the old county structure, indeed of the whole of the old administrative system. Here, however, we have arrived at the great question, whether on the basis of rational considerations it is really possible to do away with an old and traditional organization, like the county. This is where most of the doubts arise from several sides. Therefore, we must by all means clarify certain issues.

In the first place we emphasize that, however revolutionary it appears, the draft submitted concerning the elimination of counties and the establishment of town-counties is not simply a utopian rational proposal. It is by no means the result of abstract theorizing but an organic development of Hungary's public and social organization, complying with the political principles of the people's democracy. Thus, the draft is revolutionary insofar as it deeply and consistently reaches the conclusions of democratic transformation, and traditional in that it intends to build a modern public administration precisely on the basis of Hungary's social development and an organically developed territoriality.

All this could, perhaps, be difficult to understand and not clear enough for those, who do not see clearly the development of the counties as social units and frameworks of organization. Therefore, it is necessary to outline the development of the counties in order to see the town-counties of the draft proposal in the right historic perspective.

Before proceeding with that, we should also mention the misgiving according to which it is not at all possible to modify, let alone substantially

314

change such permanent and historically lasting frameworks as the counties. Undoubtedly, the county organization is the organizational framework of not only the feudal order of society, but also a general and historically very durable organizational framework of Hungarian society; no social system can disregard that for the sake of any kind of innovation. We must accept that the county organization is the permanent organizational form of Hungarian society which is shaped by each historic period to its own image. However, no historical period can totally eliminate it. But we must also see clearly that this permanent or at least lasting form underwent essential changes. At present it needs such an essential change to suit the requirements of modern life and of a democratic public administration by the people based upon genuine self-government. After having given an outline of the counties' development, this misgiving will not be justified.

The starting-point is that the development of the Hungarian counties reached its present form after three great historical periods having substantially differing organizational forms. The ancient county before the rule of King Stephen, the St. Stephanian county and the county of the nobles in the age of feudalism were all entirely different from the "modern" county as we know it today. There is something in common in all of them, a common principle is embodied in each of its forms, but always according to the substantial economic social and political conditions of various periods.

The ancient counties before St. Stephen were the visible frameworks of the primitive feudal organization of Slav societies settled here before Hungarian tribes settled down here. Thus, the counties were not territorial units, but topographic forms of a feudal organization. The essence was that the feudal lords of certain castles or fortress-like settlements organized the neighbouring settlements under their leadership and levied taxes on working people. Thus the counties had no boundaries; counties extended as far as the overlord residing in the fortress was able to extend his feudal influence and landed interests. Therefore these counties were not administrative frameworks, but economic and political, therefore power organizations. They were the foundations of a feudal social structure.

The St. Stephanian counties developed more or less on the basis of these ancient counties. The centres of most of these counties were the old feudal seats of the ancient counties, around which the king organized his feudal estates. Even where there were no such ancient county foundations, St. Stephen organized royal counties in the same way. These royal counties were not simply administrative frameworks either. They were the economic and political power organizations of the feudal king, therefore the tribal society of the conquering Hungarians remained outside them. Thus the royal counties did not have boundaries in the sense as the modern counties have. Therefore, they were not territorial units, but units of economic and feudal power. They extended to where the seigniory of the kings was asserted, and did not include territories which had other landlords. What was, thus, the essence of the royal counties? They were organizations of the landed interests of the king organized around given estates, managed by land-stewards. But these county seats were not only the centres of the royal estates, but also military and ecclesiastical centres, i.e. they essentially played the role of towns. Therefore we can say that they were urban centres of a character developed and required by the given social order. They were also towns insofar that the gradually developing and specializing industrial trades as well as the markets settled also in these centres. In modern terms, therefore, the St. Stephenian country was based on the principle of holding together the town centres and the country organized around them.

The development of the county of the nobility substantially transformed the system of royal counties. First of all, the counties became territorial units with definite boundaries, and they also developed into administrative frameworks. This transformation occurred when the counties, from being royal estates, were transformed into frameworks of the self-government of nobles. In other words, the royal estate changed into an organization of the landlords of a particular district. This is what the transformation of the royal counties into the counties of the nobility means. In the course of this transformation the organizational principle of the counties of holding together a town centre and the district belonging to it became less pronounced. The county of several landlords and several noble families could no longer be as centralized as the single royal estate; as a result the county of the nobles became a rather decentralized unit. The seat of the county was often changed according to the residence of the deputy lieutenant or the Lord Lieutenant. But the county centre did not become completely insignificant. The old royal centre of the county, which became the royal centre of national administration through the Lord Lieutenant appointed by the king — or in some instances a hereditary office — continued to operate in most instances. With decentralization prevailing, the county ceased to develop centrally. The county became decentralized insofar that county life of the landed noble families shifted its centre from one estate to the other; in addition to that, the towns as industrial, trading and cultural centres developed outside the framework of the county of the nobles; they were directly under the supremacy of the king in accordance with the economic policy of the royal treasury. That made the separate development and the separate autonomous life of towns within territory of the counties possible. A further important feature of the county of the nobles was that not only the towns were excluded from it but all lands which remained royal estates. As separate privileged areas, these remained outside the county even territorially, as for example the Jászkunság district did.

316

The transformation of the county of the nobles into "modern" county meant first of all that they became exclusive territorial organizations. In other words, they annexed the privileged areas as well as most of the towns. Only those towns retained independence, which, as royal boroughs, became separate municipalities having the same legal status as the counties. The other consequence of the transformation was that the counties by now became principally administrative organizations whose authority extended to the whole territory of the county. There was yet another change: the county became more centralized again, since the county town became an important administrative centre, and as such it increased its own potential for urban growth. But the transformation did not change the fact that the separately developed towns also continued as separated centres of the county. This modern administrative centralization could not unite, for instance, the County of Csongrád into one body, for Szeged and Hód-mezővásárhely developed irretrievably as separate units with the surrounding areas. The development of the "modern" counties, therefore, created a territorial division, which did not take into account the economic and social progress that took place in the meantime, but simply confirmed the county framework as it developed under feudal conditions. This is the problem to which all the fundamental faults and absurdities of the present system of counties can be attributed.

After this description of the development of the counties, the plan of town-counties is obviously not the result of abstract reasoning. The plan is revolutionary insofar as it intends to liquidate the relations of the county of the nobles as they developed, but not for replacing them with some abstract, utopian organization, but to restore the genuine county framework. In other words, the plan of the town-counties embodies the same principles which emerged in the ancient counties, and in the St. Stephenian counties, or in a certain sense in the counties of the nobles, but suiting present-day economic and social relations. The misgiving that we want to abolish a traditional institution for the sake of a new one of uncertain future is unacceptable. Just the opposite is true. We want to realize a really proven and really permanent organizational principle in a modern way. We want to organize counties which fulfill the reason and the aim of the county organization. If this is a revolutionary innovation, then it is one, which realizes the reason and aim of the county system incomparably better than the "modern" county formed awkwardly and irrationally from the counties of the nobility. This recommendation thus organically follows from the development of the counties, and is most profoundly rooted in the traditions of Hungarian society.

Besides all that, the new town-counties will excellently serve the purpose of public administration; this is just one more argument favouring the implementation of the recommended reform.

Finally, we have to say a few words also about the future. What will the

317

institution of the town-county mean for social progress? Briefly speaking, it will mean the countrification of towns and the urbanization of the country. In other words, urban centres would be organically linked to their environs, and vice-versa, the districts to their towns. This would do away with the disproportionate situation that exists now between the town and its environs. This perspective precisely agrees with all the reform ideas and practical needs which emerge today concerning the future of the towns and their environs. And above all, it would provide an institutional and organizational framework for the peasantry to improve its place in social life.

VIII

SOME FEATURES OF THE HISTORIC DEVELOPMENT OF COOPERATIVE FARMS*

* The Hungarian original is to be found in Ferenc Erdei's *Válogatott írásai és beszédei* (Selected Writings and Speeches) Kossuth Könyvkiadó, Budapest, 1973. pp. 71—76. The study was originally published in *Párttörténeti Közlemények*. 1966. No. 1. pp. 25—41.

THE HISTORIC COURSE OF GRADUALITY

In the period of socialist reorganization the principle of graduality raised the question between what types of cooperatives the peasantry joining cooperative farms could choose, or what grades of cooperatives were justified in the various countries. However, this problem found solution everywhere, where the socialist reorganization came to a successful conclusion. In Hungary just as well as in other countries the so-called No. 3 type of cooperative farms became dominant, which in essence correspond to the Soviet "artel" type cooperative form. However, the decision itself did not take the principle of graduality off the agenda. What actually happened was that although the artel-type cooperative farms became dominant, the actual building of the large-scale socialist farms was possible only gradually; this graduality existed even within the same type. In addition to that, the existence and size of the household farms of the members of cooperative farms and their relation with the cooperative also assumed a form of graduality.

The development of Hungarian cooperative farms characterized the actual historic course of graduality in a particularly instructive way.

a) Cooperative farming is a special way of farming in which elements and remnants of the former small-scale farming by individuals or families become related to the new large-scale cooperative farming forms. The development of cooperatives has proved that uniting the individual small holdings in a large-scale farm in a gradual way was necessary. It became also clear that such a constantly developing combination was absolutely necessary for both production growth and for gaining the support of the members of the cooperatives. This also means that the agricultural structure that developed as the result of socialist reorganization cannot be regarded a "failure" or "a political-tactical concession". This is the necessary course of the socialist development of the agriculture; this is not just a short transition period, but it constitutes a long-lasting development period identical with the first phase of socialist agriculture. It was the achievement of Hungary's agrarian policy that this was recognized in time and the development of agriculture was based on this insight.

If the present farming conditions of the Hungarian cooperative farms and simpler farming associations are seen as a whole, then a great variety of the combination of large-scale cooperative farms with production on individual household plots and of the relations betwen the two are found. *A full range of graduality in this sense* could be compiled, and the point here is no longer so much the graduality of the various types of cooperation, but graduality within the legal and social framework of the cooperative farms, or as it is popularly called, within the cooperative farming sector.

In the present phase of development (for development is continuous, even if it is not rapid and not as conspicuous as it was in the period of socialist reorganization) the followingy *types* can be outlined:

— The simplest cooperative farm is the specialized farming cooperative, or the cooperative farming group, in which the overwhelming proportion of the production of members is carried out in their individual or family plots, and they contribute to the communal farm only certain specific work (e.g. ploughing, cereal harvesting), or take care of some parts of various branch activities (e.g. establishing plantations, animal husbandry.

— Specialized farming cooperatives and cooperative farming groups, in which several work phases or the bulk of the work of a branch of production is concentrated in the cooperative farm, including the development of adequate forms of collective arrangement and cooperative remuneration of labour, represent a more developed grade of cooperative farming.

— Some cooperative farms (few in numbers and only in some districts) are called "mixed cultivation" cooperatives, which means that the members carry on open-field plant production and animal husbandry—with the exception of the animals raised in their household farms—within the cooperative farm, but their vegetable and fruit production is done individually, and the cooperative farm in this respect provides only certain organizational, purchasing and marketing functions (besides establishing new, large-scale orchards in the communal farm, as it is being done already in most locations).

— Except household farming, the majority of cooperative farms extended communal farming to all branches of production and also established the large-scale system of organizing and remunerating collective labour, and of profit sharing. However, where manual labour is the decisive factor of production, the family cultivation of labour-intensive plants is relied upon and mechanized labour is provided by the cooperative, while the members do the manual labour of cultivation and cropping in return for a direct share of the crop.

— There are much fewer cooperative farms, where there is no family production of labour-intensive plants, but even these plants are grown on a large scale. However, also in these cooperatives household farming is as frequently found as in the other types. (This was the original form of the No. 3 type of cooperative farms.)

— There is only a small number of cooperatives, where not only family cultivation ceased, but the household farming of the members has almost perished.

322

— Joint enterprises of cooperative farms, where several cooperative farms establish jointly operated large-scale production in particular branches could be regarded as a higher level of the concentration of large-scale farming.

The situation reached in cooperative farming the course of development indicates also the future course of development. It is not at all likely that the proportions developed between the state and the cooperative sector would be substantially modified within the foreseeable future, but it is certain that—depending essentially on technological developments—the share of large-scale production will gradually increase within the cooperative sector, while the manual household, or family production that employs the labour of the families will remain considerable for a long time to come.

b) We obtained not less important historic experiences concerning the *household farms.* The most important of these are:

Firstly, that the justification and necessity of household farms will remain valid for an extended time. It follows that national and district economic policies as well as the management of the cooperative farms must not consider the household farms as a necessary evil to be tolerated for the time being, and to be deliberately "liquidated" as soon as possible. This would entail consequences that are difficult to foresee. Therefore the fundamental direction of our economic policy aimed at the maintenance of household production as long as it is indispensable for subsistence farming, for commodity production and in terms of investments and the labour force, is unconditionally right.

Secondly, it was proved that the relations between cooperatives and household farms substantially differ by various branches of production. Some branches, for instance wheat and cereal production, industrial plants and sheep-farming are already overwhelmingly concentrated in large-scale farms and the cooperatives are really capable of taking over their production. However, the simultaneous existence of large-scale and household farming in almost equal proportions is justified in the other sectors until an adequate technological level and the necessary investments are realized. Maize production, some sectors of the vegetable production, viniculture and breeding of cattle and pigs belong to these fields. Finally, there are some sectors, where the preponderance of household production will remain justified for a long time, such as the growing of various vegetables and berries and poultry farming.

Thirdly, precisely because of the above, it was also proved that the production of household farms cannot be disregarded by the socialist planned economy. Therefore the production of large-scale cooperative farms and of small-scale household farms has to be jointly planned both in the national economic, and on regional and cooperative levels.

Last but not least it must be unambiguously stated that the necessary acknowledgement and planned handling of the household farms does not mean any loss in the importance of cooperative farms. This is not a question of either-or, as it is preferably posed on the left as well as on the right. We face here a complex historical process of the development of socialist agriculture where our primary ambition is the maximal development of cooperatives. However, this is coupled with maintaining, assisting and in some sectors even developing household production simultaneously and in conjunction with large-scale farming so that production, investment and labour management factors are also taken into account.

THE DIRECTION OF DEVELOPMENT

Even this rather sketchy account of the historical course of development provides a basis for certain conclusions about the future.

The development tendency already apparent from the above has already gained definite, programme-like expression in the relevant resolution of the 22nd Congress of the Communist Party of the Soviet Union. The programme accepted by the CPSU included the following definitions:

"The kolkhozes and sovkhozes...are increasingly developing into enterprises of the communist type in respect of the character of labour, and the welfare and cultural standards of the workers.

As regards their economic conditions the kolkhozes are becoming similar to the publicly owned agricultural enterprises, transforming into highly developed, mechanized enterprises.

The remuneration of kolkhoz peasants will be similar to those enjoyed in the publicly owned enterprises."

These expressions unambiguously indicate that the trend is for cooperatives to develop into enterprises. But when the cooperative farms are seen from the side of practice and of economics, then they must already be regarded as enterprises even in their present phase and this approach must not be changed in the future.

The various disciplines dealing with cooperative farms had to recognize that the complicated problems of the management of cooperative farms could not be formulated, and a solution to the problems could not be found so long as cooperatives are not regarded as a specific economic organization. As long as we stick to the concept of *association of persons,* or *mass-organization,* or *cooperative society,* the responsibility and interests cannot be grasped either by the executives or the members, and even the aims of collective farming cannot be made clear. For that reason we must reach the conclusion that the cooperative farm must be regarded as a special *type* of the enterprise established on the basis of cooperative property (collective leadership, special character of the members as owners and workers etc.).

The ten to fifteen years development of Hungarian cooperative and state farms and the three to four decades of the large-scale socialist farms of the

324

Soviet Union provide a basis also for identifying further development trends. We can speak of the following major trends: increase in the size of the farms, development of features characteristic of enterprises, the emergence of internal organization, the development of actual employment relations, the simultaneous development of wages and profit sharing in both the cooperatives and the state farms, and a more developed division of labour in accordance with high level technology.

All these issues are still being debated. However, the number of unclarified issues declines and as regards major development trends agreement has almost been reached. However, we must be aware of the fact that further research as well as new historical experience are still necessary to get a comprehensive and clear picture of the historical development trends of cooperative farms.

IX

SOME SOCIAL QUESTIONS OF THE COOPERATIVE FARMS*

* The Hungarian original is to be found in Ferenc Erdei's *Összegyűjtött Művei* (Collected Works), *Szövetkezeti írások I* (Essays on Cooperatives I), Akadémiai Kiadó, Budapest, 1979, pp. 249—265. The essay was first published in *Valóság,* 1969/No. 2, pp. 74—89.

In the 1968 volume of *Valóság* some articles published on the social questions of cooperative farms deserve particular attention (Márkus, I.: Mezőgazdaságfejlesztés és helyi erőviszonyok (Agricultural development and local power relations), in No. 2., Kunszabó, F. A negyedik hullám (The fourth Wave) in No. 3., Gyenes, A. "Munkások" és "parasztok" a mezőgazdasági termelőszövetkezetekben ("Workers" and "Peasants" in the Cooperative Farms) in No. 4. But even in addition to these studies, various sociological surveys and the daily reports in the press, the radio and the television also provide interesting information on the change taking place in the peasant societies of the villages in general and in the cooperative farms in particular. Examination of these social processes in a number of connections and in a detailed way could, therefore, be considered as timely.

In this study I should like to elucidate the following social questions of the cooperative farms: 1. The start and the actual historic development, in other words the recognizable tendencies of development in the operation of cooperative farms. 2. The development of the social stratification of the membership of cooperatives. 3. The social bases of the leadership of cooperative farms.

THE FOUNDATION AND THE DEVELOPMENT
OF COOPERATIVES

From a historical perspective by now it is clear that the collectivization of agriculture took place in the course of actual historical development with substantial modifications. Naturally, this is by no means to be considered as a failure (only the failure of dogmatism), on the contrary, it could rather be seen as an example for the extraordinary viability of a socialist institution.

When Hungarian collectivization movement was started it was modelled on the Soviet kolkhoz movement and on the organization of kolkhozes as had developed by then. However, two important remarks must be added here. One of them is that the contemporary model of Soviet kolkhozes stood before us as a result of an already long and interesting development process. (History selected the kolkhoz form from a great variety of farm communes and cooperative type associations and the role of the machinery stations developed gradually etc.). The other one is that in Hungary there was a good number of deviations from the original model even at the beginning. (Cooperative farms of a lower type played a more important role; the household farms were much more common; in Hungary the principle of establishing only one cooperative in each village was not followed.)

Nevertheless, the conception we endeavoured to realize at the beginning was homogeneous and closed. Its theoretical background was the "cooperative plan" of Lenin, and its practical example the kolkhoz constitution of Stalin. It was a peculiar cooperative model. Lenin regarded the cooperative course as a digression from large-scale socialist agriculture: in his opinion cooperatives were to complete a long and strenuous course leading from small-scale producer peasant farms to the modern, large-scale socialist farms. His consistency in envisaging this development in the cooperative form is, however, of fundamental importance.

Thus a special cooperative form evolved, unknown in earlier history; the cooperative is a collective farm owned by the members of the cooperative, who became owners as well as workers of large-scale farms. When discussing the socialist transformation of the village, we practically speak of the colourful historic course of this cooperative institution.

In our days, twenty years after the start of Hungarian cooperative movement and forty years after the Soviet collectivization we have sufficient experience to review the far-reaching social processes triggered by the initial cooperative model as well as the modifications they caused in the organizational relations of cooperative farms and in the social situation of their members.

István Márkus considers the development of the relation between the peasant families and the cooperative community decisive in this process. He comes to the following conclusions: "It was assumed that the cooperative was to become a collective of families — independently of the fact whether one or more persons signed the enrolment form in the family. Leaving behind the small-scale obligations of individual farming, the families would have joined in the activities of the large-scale farms with the whole of their labour. After having become convinced of the higher performance and profitability of the large-scale farms, they would have regarded the common property as their own, and thus the establishment and consolidation of the common farm as well as its modern development—even at the cost of sacrifices—as their own direct interest. This was the idea, which, as it soon became evident, could not stand the test of reality." Setting out from this, he regards as the essence of the social development of cooperatives the conflicting interest of the families and of the cooperative community; he looks for the resolution of clashing interests, for the possibilities of the evolution of genuine cooperative communities on this basis. His opinion can be accepted in essence, but some points have to be clarified in order to get a more exact picture of this development.

The relations of the family and the cooperative farm are really fundamental. It is also true that after a relatively short transitional period according to the original concept the working communities of the families ought to have been absorbed in the communal organization of labour. In fact, things did not happen that way.

At the beginning we had the notion that families joined the cooperative farms (and became dissolved in it as a labour organization), and accordingly we keep records up to this very date of how many members the cooperative farms have and how many families joined forces with them. (The only exception is the German Democratic Republic, where the principle of individual membership was asserted in response to the social relations of a more industrialized society.) But what do the numbers show? In 1949 and 1950, that is at the start, there was an average of 1.5–1.6 members per cooperative families. And since 1960, (thus in the concluding period of collectivization) there are no more than 1.1 members per "cooperative farming family"! What is behind these figures?

These figures indicate that the families by no means joined the cooperatives in their entirety, which, viewed from the other side, means that they continued to remain significant social and economic units; however, they were transformed to suit the cooperative conditions. (István Márkus gives an interesting and adequate account of this process.) The process could be described by saying that the families joined the cooperative farms in a *representative way*. Someone of the family joined and took with him the land, that was to be taken, and the other means of production, but, owing to this, the family community did not disintegrate. (Generally the head of the family joined the cooperative, but in the case of those, who had regular employment elsewhere the wife did, or quite often some other member of the family or nobody from those families which owned the land but their tenants.)

The policy of collectivization partly tolerated and partly even encouraged this process. It tolerated it by being satisfied with representatives joining and with the contribution of the means of production. This process was encouraged by acknowledging the household farm and the concept of supporting membership, and also by the circumstance that from the start participation in the common work and the development of communal labour organizations was extremely liberally interpreted by the executives of the communal farms as well as the political and economic bodies.

Even the interpretation of cooperative membership has been rather uncertain and equivocal from the start. *Family membership?* Yes, inasmuch as land, economic rent and household farms were calculated by families, and the requirement that every able-bodied member of the family should be members of the cooperative was never asserted. ("Representative" mem-

330

bership of the family was regarded to be sufficient throughout the country, and the practice that wives and those of the grown-up children, who stayed in the agriculture, joined the cooperative separately developed only sporadically.) *Individual membership* was asserted, however, inasmuch as the obligation of working for the cooperative was limited to persons who joined the cooperative; and the general meetings of cooperatives only cooperative members had a voting right. Other members of the household were treated as "members of the family", who could decide whether and how often to participate in the common work. The new cooperative association law tilted the scales in favour of individual membership by recognizing the household farm as a right of the individual cooperative member.

The survival of the family working team and of the family plots also meant that the working organization of the communal farm had to be built up separately. And this could be achieved only with difficulty. The brigades and working teams originally served the objective of realizing the involvement of the labour of the families in the communal work, and at the same time the organization of collective labour based on participation in the profits according to the number of units worked. And that was what did not go so simply. And when the situation became critical, and the communal farms did not get enough labour from the families at many places, then a system of tilling the land by families within the communal farm developed. In other words, a compromise was reached between the family farms of cooperative members and the collective farms. By declaring the "organic unity of collective and household farms", the new cooperative association law sanctioned this process.

Another result of these developments was that *the cooperative membership failed to become identical with being employed*; and at the moment various types of employment exist in the cooperative farms. Of the total labour force (100 per cent) of the cooperative farms members account for 66.2 per cent, non-member family dependants 14.3 per cent, and employees 19.5 per cent (including 8.1 per cent permanent employees).

In order to complete the picture, however, it should also be considered that the proportion of non-working members is rather large, too: in round figures some 40 per cent of the full membership; most of them are retired and receive pension and/or land rent (about one-quarter of this group occasionally works for the cooperative farms), but the proportion of the other non-working members is also almost 10 per cent of the total membership.

There are yet some further characteristic data underlining the peculiar duality of the family and community farms. Until 1958 the proportion of members under the age of 20 (which approximately agrees with the participation in the work of family members working as members of the cooperatives), was 8–10 per cent of the total membership which changed to 4–5 per cent in 1959–1960, and to below 2 per cent since 1961. The

331

explanation is that in the early years family members also joined the cooperatives then mostly made up of the agrarian proletariat but later, as more small-holder families joined the cooperatives, fewer family members became members of the cooperatives.

And if the composition of the labour force of collective farms is given not by the number of the persons participating in the collective work, but by the number of working hours performed, then figures from 1967 give the following picture: of the total of working hours members (without pensioners) performed 69.4 per cent, pensioned members 6.2 per cent, family members 8.3 per cent, employees 16.1 per cent.

The above features of the social development of the cooperative farms arising in the wake of their establishment would, in any case, justify two conclusions. One of them is that compared to the original ideas, development took an unexpected course, while the other one is that coupled with gradualness, a certain regularity is recognizable in this development.

But what development periods can we speak about?

Ferenc Kunszabó distinguished the following periods:

— During the first wave (1949–1952) small and medium-size cooperative farms were organized; in that period the labour of the cooperative families performed cooperative work within the framework of brigades and working teams;

— During the second wave (1955–1959) the assertion of the system of wage incentives became dominant (owing to this the management of labour and profit sharing started to develop);

— The third wave (1960–1962) saw the completion of the cooperative reorganization based on the generalization of the experience of the earlier period;

— At present, the fourth development period is starting, in which the complete emergence of large-scale farming will be accomplished on the basis of up-to-date means of production.

Antal Gyenes, distinguished two "basic cooperative models":

— Cooperatives of moderate size, manageable with direct, democratic methods represent the first model. In these cooperatives the members have a full overview of the communal farm, therefore they can become their masters;

— The second model is that of the larger cooperatives, where the members cannot have a comprehensive understanding of the collective farming. These cooperatives are headed by professional executives, and individual members can follow two logical courses: they either retain "their status as farmers on the periphery of large-scale production adjusting to the changed conditions", or become wage labourers of the large-scale organization, without assuming responsibility for risk-taking but demanding fair wages for their work. "Historically, and particularly in terms of the national economy the first model belongs to the past, in fact it had never played a significant role."

332

Both of the above periodizations have a certain basis, but the phases of development can, in my opinion, be defined much more simply, rather obviously the following way:

— *In the early phase of cooperative reorganization* (1949–1956) forcing the original model by way of administrative means and coercive economic political measures was characteristic; this policy led to a series of crises, to the collapse of the alliance of workers and peasants, and to frequent change in the policy line;

— *in the concluding period of the reorganization* (1957–1961) the alliance of workers and peasants was strengthened again; in this period more flexible organizational forms became common coupled with the economic and political means of influencing. Cooperative self-government and material incentives were increasingly asserted and varying local methods of farm management were acknowledged; These elements provided the basis for the successful conclusion of collectivization;

— *the period of consolidation* (1962–1967) was a period in which the internal conditions and organizational framework of the cooperative farms became settled. In this period adequate forms of organization and management became general and consolidated in the cooperatives, while the principles of cooperative democracy and independent management were gradually asserted. This period of development also witnessed the necessary emergence of compromises; various local solutions were employed, including communal and household farming, and the various forms of management and wage policy;

— the period that began with 1968 can be regarded as the phase of *modern large-scale farming* marked by the mile-stones of the 1968 reform of economic management, a new law on cooperatives and the establishment of the associations of cooperative farms.

SOCIAL STRATIFICATION IN THE COOPERATIVE FARMS

The original idea of collectivization reckoned with the development of a "uniform class of cooperative peasants". In two respects this expectation can still be seen valid even today.

Firstly: in historic retrospect the peasantry, once divided into classes, can now be regarded as a uniform class insofar as its stratification is no longer determined by the size of private plots, but uniformly by the cooperative property and farming as well as the relation of the individual members and families to the collective farms and their position in them.

Secondly: in the further future, in principle uniform, factory-like large-scale conditions will develop in the collective cooperative farms; the role of the household farms will decrease, family farming will come to an end, and work relations similar to those prevailing in the industrial works or in the state farms will develop. In fact the only difference that will survive will be derived from *cooperative ownership*. Naturally, it is true that this is essential, and this (and only this) is precisely what justifies that the workers of cooperative farms, as a class of "cooperative peasants" be distinguished from those of state enterprises even in such a development period.

However, between these two periods of development there is a historical period we are experiencing just now. Also in the case of cooperative farms, it is impossible to omit this period which cannot be interpreted either in the perspective of the recent past or that of the distant future. Therefore, we must devote our attention to the present historical reality in order to clearly see present-day trends. This is the reason why the efforts of Antal Gyenes, István Márkus and Ferenc Kunszabó aimed at exploring the stratification and the "interest structure" within the cooperative farms must be welcome.

These three authors are unanimous in pointing out *a certain duality in the social stratification of the members of cooperative farms*. The essence of this is that part of the members remained in their peasant existence bound by the interests of their family farm; these members became fully adjusted to the needs of the cooperatives. The other group of the members became genuine workers of the large-scale collective estates adjusting to the labour organization and discipline of the large-scale collective farms, therefore their status as a stratum became similar to that of the labour force of industry. Recognition of this duality is not novel, it has been discussed—as Antal Gyenes pointed out—for quite a few years. However, the novel feature is that the articles of each of the three authors bring up the matter more pointedly. Antal Gyenes does this by finding a coexistence as he puts it symbolically of "workers" and "peasants" in the cooperative farms. And István Márkus and Ferenc Kunszabó underline this by considering peasant membership tied to family interest an obstacle to further progress.

None of them takes a definite stand concerning the actual size of one or the other group in the Hungarian cooperative farms. Antal Gyenes believes that "a relatively small proportion" of cooperative members belongs to the "peasants", while István Márkus and Ferenc Kunszabó talk about this type as if they represented the majority of cooperative members. In fact, it is really difficult to verify the proportion between the two groups, for no statistical data indicate this division. Some facts, however, offer essential proof. In 1967 about 20 per cent of the total labour force of cooperative farms worked as skilled workers and tractor drivers, and the proportion of employees was close to that figure. On the other hand, only those working in plant production can be considered as predominantly engaged also in family production; the ratio of this group is estimated at 30 per cent of the total labour force of the cooperative farms. Considering the various data of approximation, the most likely estimate is that about one-third of the labour force of the collective farms (independent of the fact whether they are members or employees) belong to the "worker" group; another third belongs to the "peasant" group, while the last one-third is of miscellaneous or intermediary character.

In order to decide how to judge the actual situation from the *aspect of development* we must subject this stratification to closer analysis.

There are no disputes on evaluating the reasons which gave rise to this stratification. At the end of the first phase of the socialist reorganization of agriculture we encountered a dilemma. One way was to continue to force the large-scale forms "envisaged", thereby hindering the consolidation of the new collective farms. The other way for action was to find a compromise solution between cooperative and family interests thereby contributing to the process of consolidation as well as to the growth of production. Hungarian agrarian policy decided in favour of the latter course, and rightly, as proven by the results.

István Márkus characterizes the motives of this decision and its effect on the cooperative community sharply, but acceptably: "We have drawn the negative lessons of the first period of collectivization by trying to couple the requirements of the operation of large-scale farms with family interests and consequently with the family organization of labour that directs and controls itself in a traditional way. On the one hand, we accomplished this partly by allowing household farming to grow vigorously. On the other hand, in compliance with the wishes of broad peasant strata, we have introduced the distribution of the more labour-intensive cultures to family production, and also the various alternatives of share-cropping." And he continued: "This, however, has legalized the duality, which the cooperative farming form intended to terminate not without good reasons. This duality meant that the large-scale farm with its own operational and development interests stood on the one side and the families on the other side so that while they also worked for the cooperative farm, they also retained, indeed they developed further their own autonomous world thereby representing their own interests, which were independent of or even conflicting with those of the large-scale farms. The result of that was that the village itself remained, at least for a considerable time, a stronger and more valid collective than the cooperative could become; in the instance of conflicting interests the village is a living community, and the cooperative farm a formal organization—the cooperative farm may give orders only by considering what the village really wants."

And András Gyenes characterizes the nature of this process from the aspect of the members of the cooperative farms: "The individual small-scale producer... had a logical choice between two alternatives in the cooperative farms... Either he tried to maintain his status as his own master on the periphery of large-scale production adapting to the changed conditions; in this case he remained a farming-peasant in the strictest sense of the word; he made the decisions, he sought for, and could also find the information necessary for farming decisions. He preserved his entrepreneurial independ-

335

ence, and in turn he accepted—as the most natural thing in the world—risk-taking. He could, however, choose the other alternative: he could become a worker in a large-scale organization, subjecting himself to discipline; in that case he renounced independence as an ideal of life; he put an end to being an independent farmer, accepting the way of life of a "worker" thereby rejecting any risk-taking... As soon as he can he achieves an employment status for himself; he would only be too glad to waive his membership rights which, he could not realize to a degree that he could have felt himself as a real farming peasant. But even if he were not an "employee", he would live and work with the same mentality as his employed colleagues."

However, there is a serious difference in evaluating a basically unequivocally interpreted situation. András Gyenes does not consider this duality as unfavourable for the progress of Hungarian cooperative farms. He emphasises the following: "I should like to seriously advise everybody not to regard the presence of the peasant in our agriculture as a disgrace of the socialist revolution. It is high time to dispel once and for all the illusion that in agriculture the transformation of small-scale commodity production into socialist large-scale production could be completed within a few years." Later on Gyenes adds: "The peasant exists, and we need him too."

István Márkus and Ferenc Kunszabó come to a different evaluation of the situation. István Márkus writes about the "monopoly situation of the membership" and that the members may make full use of that to the detriment of the interests of the collective farms. He comes to the following conclusion: "There may even develop a situation in which the majority of the village—by virtue of its monopoly position—would aim at preventing the strengthening and development of the large-scale farm." Therefore he comes to the conclusion that: "The compromise between the collective farms and the families as well as that between the labour organization of the large-scale farms and families, which strengthened the relative independence of the families, has to be gradually terminated. Naturally, this does not mean that we should eliminate the interest of families in performing the work of the large-scale farm, but that it should be realized in a new way so that it cannot come into conflict with the requirements of the cooperative farm."

And Ferenc Kunszabó emphasizes the following: "...the private interests of members of the cooperatives expressly prevent the development of a genuine, large-scale crop structure..."; "...the principal obstacle to reducing share cropping, which is both necessary and possible today, is the resistance of the members..." Based on the analysis of the Szekszárd district, he even comes to the conclusion that although the number of machines and the fertilizer consumption have doubled between 1963 and 1966, share-cropping has also grown by 30–40 per cent. Considering these figures, he makes a passionate call for the elimination of the remmants of peasant-family farming.

336

Undoubtedly, the conclusions of Ferenc Kunszabó and István Márkus are both one-sided and premature. This is at least indicated by opposing and also one-sided views expressed by executives of cooperative farms. According to these, "wage-worker attitudes" have become quite common among the members. This makes the management of collective farms even more difficult; Géza Pete's comment on István Márkus's article ("Peasant Monopoly or Cooperation" *Valóság*, No. 4.) also warns of one-sidedness when it points out the possibilities for the reconciliation of the interests of families (having a member in the cooperative) and collective farms also mentioning further possibilities of cooperation.

But whatever is our opinion about the situation as it developed, and whatever conclusion we reach, the articles quoted must undoubtedly be credited for the sharp light they throw on the social conditions of cooperative farms. It is to their credit that they characterize the social stratification of cooperative farms in an adequate way. These articles call attention to a field we neglected in the periods of the organization and consolidation of cooperatives. Then exact knowledge on stratification was substituted by hypotheses.

We must also add that these authors do not characterize the social conditions of cooperative farms merely in an abstract way but on the basis of concrete knowledge, or at least based on sociologically representative samples. And in doing so *they do not only call attention* to undoubtedly interesting and important phenomena, *but also contribute essential data to the information they have already had on the cooperatives.* It will be worth emphasizing at least one insight from each of the three authors' articles.

The point to be underlined in István Márkus's study is what he says about the transformation and the consolidation of the peasant family. He points out the following: "The rise of consumption, and by that of the standard of living, the competition for investments of consumption character and the by now rather competitive struggle for preparing the children for other careers is gradually extending to the whole of agrarian society. Each individual is trying to secure a better position in this for himself and for his family. And this is also the medium, in which almost all of the remnants of the old class and stratum differences become dissolved. Even class differences in opinion and in political loyalties, playing an important role during the decade after the war determining attitudes to the cooperative farms, become dissolved in this. In this competition for securing the future of the families and a favourable start in life for the children, the remnants of the old peasant possession as well as the social position, official position, or a financially rewarding job etc. acquired after the liberation may offer a positional advantage." And he continues: "The spread of consumerism, efforts made at building new private homes as well as educating children for non-agricultural careers contribute to the massive spread of attitudes indifferent to the development of the large-scale farms. The general rise of the standard of living and life circumstances becoming rather uniform, dissolve the village classes of yesterday and lead to the emergence of uniform political attitudes. In this situation the local social forces, which earlier, in the first and second phases of the cooperative movement worked actively in the organization of large-scale cooperatives and committed themselves to the cause of progress, give up their positive isolation. These social forces become like the majority; they put up with the already customary stagnation or slow development; they assimilate with the politically indifferent strata feeling impotent to take a stand against representatives of contrary interests."

What he says about the strata important in terms of modern large-scale farming and of a progress towards social relations corresponding to that also deserves particular attention: "However, in all the villages this small group of leaders could not by itself carry through the further development of large-scale farms if it could not rely on a broader, new stratum of the transforming agrarian society. This stratum is made up of mostly young peasants with varying qualification levels whose work, earnings, thus whole existence is already related to the technology of large-scale farming. Foremost among these are people, whose work is related to machines: tractor drivers, machine-shop workers, truck drivers, mechanics—qualified exponents of work of industrial character which became necessary and keeps growing in importance in the large-scale farms. Those who have been elevated above the average financially and in respect by the labour organization of the large-scale farm also belong to this stratum. They are intermediate and junior executives, heads of various departments, junior agronomists, technicians, brigade leaders, workshop foremen etc. The third group is that of white-collar workers (accountants, administrative clerks etc.) to whom the large-scale farm gives the opportunity of utilizing their training locally."

Ferenc Kunszabó gives particular emphasis to the social elements of industry-like agricultural production: "The stake, which we neglected in the fifties, became completely clear by the start of the third wave: to transform Hungarian agriculture into a system of large-scale farms capable of realizing inexpensive mass-production with the help of massively utilized modern technologies and the latest methods of farm and labour management. In other words, the point is industry-like agricultural production...General opinion tends to appreciate this as a sufficient degree of mechanization. But the matter has other components also, which are—when mechanization is already a fact, and only then—no less important." He continues then to sharply criticize traditional forms of labour management as well as the disruptive forces of family interests from this aspect.

Antal Gyenes throws a particularly penetrating light on the social relations of large-scale farms. What he says about "peasants" and "workers" is equally essential.

"The peasant is invariably a member of the cooperative, but he is on the

338

periphery of cooperative production, that is he does not fall in line with the large-scale labour organization of the cooperative farm. His relation with the collective large-scale farm is fundamentally no more than his participation in the communal plant production principally within the limits of "family cultivation", preferably for a "share". Accordingly, the work he does for the cooperative, which does not mean genuine participation in the labour organization of the large-scale farm, is not the sole basis of his existence, indeed, often not even the principal factor of his material existence. The peasants' essential source of income is the commodity producing household farming. His membership in the cooperative and the collective large-scale farm provide his living only insofar as they establish the conditions for the commodity producing household farming. Thus the peasant is a small-scale producer taking part in the cooperative farming in a special way. Naturally, he is not an independent small-scale producer in the old sense, but a peculiar figure of the Hungarian cooperative agriculture; the whole peasant stratum is part of the cooperative agrarian society." And he continues: "He did not trade his whole form of life for a new one, but adjusted it to the changed conditions. He is not an independent small-scale producer, yet he is still farming, venturing and thinking in the terms of the market." And still further: "The peasant is not a socialist producer, but he is no longer an individual small-scale producer in the old sense of the word either. He is a constituting element of the cooperative agriculture, into which he fitted himself in his own way. His activity is no longer antagonistic to socialism, indeed, this activity is still indispensable today in terms of the development of the socialist national economy. It would be a mistake to think that he is speculating. Producers engaged most extensively in household farming production do not sell their produce on the free market, but through the channels of cooperative trade: either through the agency of their own cooperative farm or directly. The peasant has no time to take his produce to the market, look for consumers, sell in retail; he is too much occupied by production. It is not worth going to the market because the time he devotes to producing pays better than that he would spend on going to the market."

Gyenes gives a similarly adequate description of the workers of cooperatives: In addition to the minority group of peasants, the other, sharply crystallized group within the large group of cooperative workers is that of the workers. In our opinion this group is by now far bigger than the one constituted of the peasants. Apart from ownership relations their work is characterized by the fact that they work full-time in a stable job the whole year through. Of the two basic types one "bargained for" an "employment status", therefore he has no membership rights, but he is not concerned about that. The other type is a member of the cooperative, but his attitudes are completely identical with those of the "employees". The first type usually has an auxiliary farm but that is used for the partial satisfaction of the food needed by the family and is often quite negligible. The other type has a household farm, but does not regard it as a primary means of living. Both types have accepted the labour organization and discipline of the large-scale farm, and submit to it as to a natural thing. They are neither farming, nor venturing, and their attitudes are almost completely identical with those of the workers of industry and the employees of state enterprises. They do not see the cooperative farm as the only possible place of employment; they pick and choose between cooperative and state farms according to the advantages they offer. They have preserved hardly anything of the traditional peasant order of values; both types have completely transformed their value orientation and radically changed their mode of life. But they did not do so in accordance with the expectations of the theory of collectivization. In fact they acted completely logically, almost "as it is written in the book". They gave something for something. Something, which was value to them for something else that is worth the exchange."

All these findings are new in many respects, and in any case important and interesting, yet they are *far from being sufficient for drawing unambiguous and suitably established conclusions*. These are valuable starting points, but we still must go much further: both science and politics must carry out comprehensive and thorough analyses in order to place economic political and social political decisions on a sufficiently firm basis.

Particularly the following problems have to be examined: 1. the quantitative features of the social stratification of cooperatives together with all of their recognizable variations; 2. the unravelling of the development tendencies; 3. all the factors which influence these social processes (technological progress, economic and social environment etc.); 4. and finally the unifying and differentiating factors affecting cooperative farms.

The social stratification developing in the cooperative farms and the prospects of the emergence of a homogeneous rural class can be safely evaluated only on the basis of such a comprehensive inquiry. We can already conclude that the originally envisaged peasant unity, as a homogeneous social formation did not so far materialize on the basis of the cooperative reorganization. On the contrary a differentiation took place that must be reckoned with in the next period of development. In order to predict how the cooperative farms will develop in the next period on the basis of modern, industry-like large-scale farms, or how the unity of the class of cooperative peasants will in fact emerge and what kind of conditions and consequences should be anticipated in the course of such development, we still need a number of comprehensive surveys.

THE SOCIAL BASES OF THE MANAGEMENT
OF COOPERATIVE FARMS

The articles in question also discuss the problems of management in cooperatives in a clear and concise way. On one issue all the three authors agree and in that respect it is impossible to contradict them. They see that *high-quality management and good managers are basic preconditions for the development of cooperatives.* However, the authors expressed this basic idea in different ways and they also come to different conclusions.

In evaluating the situation at Tiszaföldvár, István Márkus draws the following conclusion: "Every sign indicates, however, that the decisive factor is good management, pooling expertise in management, organization, technology from a number of fields. As we have already emphasized, these managers as experts in the development of large-scale farms were to a great extent able to overcome retrograde forces which were strong also here at the beginning." István Márkus's main conclusion is that the management of the cooperative farm should become independent of local and family interests.

Ferenc Kunszabó comes to a similar conclusion: "...if professional skill and business-like management formed one of the crucial issues of the strengthening of cooperatives even five years ago, then the ability of thinking in economic terms and expertise in management are becoming decisively important today and in the future." Ferenc Kunszabó's conclusion is very much like that of above-mentioned author. "We cannot expect the solution from the members"; therefore professional managers independent of the members and prepared to risk conflicts should be put in charge of the cooperative farms.

Antal Gyenes also emphasizes the role of "independent" executives; however, he does so in a different way: "...If the manager fails to raise many times above the simple member in professional skill and executive ability sooner or later he will have to be dismissed for his task is to lead, and that is why he is freed from doing ten to twelve hours of manual work. On the other hand, the man who, from morning till night often works almost two shifts of hard manual labour, cannot be expected to compete with the professional executive, whose job is to gather information, to work out optimal decisions and to guarantee expert management of the highest standard. The separation of professional management and of manual work contributes a great deal to the efficiency of economic organizations. Large economic organizations simply cannot operate without this kind of the division of labour." The conclusion Antal Gyenes arrives at is also different; the management of a cooperative is satisfactory only on the basis of cooperative democracy with the membership participating in decision-making. This is why I totally agree with him.

However, the evaluations of István Márkus and Ferenc Kunszabó prompt me to disagree because their conclusions are one-sided and premature. Nevertheless, it is not my contrary opinion that I wish to express, but I should like to speak of the *social background of the managers of cooperatives.*

My opinion on this issue had been published prior to the appearance of the three articles discussed here: "The executive collectives, which developed cooperative farms until now, and are capable of further developing them in the foreseeable future have already been forged together. Who are the people they are composed of? They are mostly peasants—some of them were agrarian proletarians formerly, others independent farmers with smaller or larger holdings—selected by the test of practice because of their natural disposition and readiness to learn. Besides them, however, qualified professional agriculturists have an increasing weight and role in the management of cooperative farms. Among managers we also find workers, and industrial experts, who joined them in the course of or after the reorganization. Still, when we want to define the character of the membership and the executive collective as a whole, it is found that the cooperative farms reached the present-day development level as a peasant institution" (Kritika, 1968. No. 2.).

However, this somewhat simplified statement has to be made more exact. At least the following issues must be discussed: 1. development trends in the management of cooperative farms; 2. the social composition of the managers of cooperative farms and relations within management; 3. the relations between management and the membership of cooperatives.

Profound changes have affected the management of cooperative farms. In the early as well as in the concluding phase of the organization of cooperatives political and social organization have been the principal issues. At that time, the majority of the executive cadres, who played key role in the cooperative farms, were workers and peasants and party secretaries. The technical experts, who gradually gained increasing role in the management of the large-scale farms, joined them during the period of consolidation. And under the conditions of the new economic mechanism started in 1968 executives of the manager type (chief accountants, marketing vice-presidents, head of production branches) became dominant in the executive teams.

In spite of all of these changes the central role of the presidents remained intact. However, their position as well as their relations to the membership and the environment underwent essential changes. Accordingly, the presidential position demanded varying abilities from the presidents in the course of time. Those who have been presidents for 15 or 20 years had to live up to ever more sophisticated tasks.

Substantial organizational and social changes have also taken place during the development of the management of the cooperatives. The number of educated professionals increased, and an increasing number of

342

the peasant and worker cadres, who became unsuitable for leadership due to lack of talent and education, fell by the wayside. Parallel with the growth of the cooperative farms leading teams composed of executives of various professional background evolved in the majority of cooperatives; and this also changed the proportion and situation of the representatives of the membership in the cooperative bodies. All of these aspects must also be taken into account, when considering the situation, suitability and the prospects of the management of cooperative farms.

Until now much public interest has been paid to two extensively debated problems concerning the social composition of the management of cooperatives. One of these is the relation of worker and peasant cadres and the trained professionals, and the other one (now in the wake of István Márkus's article) the difference between local executives having a relationship with the members and those recruited from elsewhere, who are less dependent on the membership. A third problem should also be mentioned: this is the danger of the bureaucratization of executives of cooperative farms resulting in their isolation from the membership.

The circumstances that mostly the will and confidence of the members were asserted in the election of presidents was also one of the factors of the success of the cooperative reorganization. Owing to that, *the majority of the presidents were peasants chosen from the membership.* The situation is essentially the same today with the difference that the number of presidents chosen from fellow uneducated peasants, who subsequently acquired some training, is increasing year after year. In 1968 12 per cent of the presidents of cooperative farms were graduates of universities or academies, and 57 per cent completed some kind of high-school education, even though their majority were worker or peasant cadres. A representative survey we conducted in some counties gives the following picture about the schooling levels of the presidents of cooperatives:

originally uneducated peasant	*52.7*
originally uneducated worker	*17.5*
graduate agricultural engineer	*17.5*
others	*12.5*

And when the five executive functions of the cooperative farms are considered (president, vice-president, party secretary, chief agronomist, chief accountant), then the percentage division according to the same representative survey is the following (even when the consolidated cooperatives showing good or mediocre management are separated from the unconsolidated ones of poor management):

343

	in good or medium cooperatives	in poor
peasant	*38.6*	*36.3*
worker-tradesman	*10.2*	*9.9*
agricultural engineer	*22.0*	*27.2*
other training background	*29.2*	*26.6*

The central question of one of the periodically renewed debate is *how long could peasant (and worker) cadres fill executive positions in the cooperative farms*; is not the time here to replace them with professional people of suitable qualifications? The express or unsaid opinion of professionals is: yes, it is. However, the unfoundedness of this view is supported not only by the subjective opinion of the other side, but also by at least the following objective facts:

— social relations between members and the executives continue to be important, and the circumstance that the members appoint someone from their own ranks plays a significant role;

— the management of cooperative farms is not just a professional task for which any kind of diploma gives qualification; it requires an ability to lead, experience in management and organization as well as continuous readiness to learn; the present executive teams of cooperative farms have already been selected by taking into account the above criteria;

— school training in itself qualifies people only for special tasks; general ability and qualification in several fields are more decisive for the executive functions, particularly for filling the position of general leadership and of presidency, therefore such executives grow up only on the basis of practice even among professionals;

— in order to understand the organizational and personal relations of a cooperative, one has got to work in it for a long time; therefore, even in the longer run, the principal way of the selection of executives can only take place by internal selection;

— finally there is yet another important consideration; in the opinion of the party and administrative executives of the counties some three-quarters of the present presidents of cooperative farms are even in the long run capable of managing the cooperatives and a further 10 per cent of them can still become suitable for their jobs.

The point of controversy raised by István Márkus is *whether local executives or others independent of local interests* are more capable of developing the communal farms? Underlining the experiences at Tiszaföldvár, Márkus gives the following summary: "It is essential that the new executive team was not attached to the local society by any ties of interest; the circumstance that they undertook a common task bound them together very closely... This independence and the complete agreement on the objectives formed one of the

344

conditions of the maximal assertion of professionalism in the management of the cooperatives. I think of professionalism in farming, in decision-making, in labour organization, in judging the members' work performance and professionalism—which is very rare in cooperative farms—in ensuring that people worked in situations that suited their abilities."

However, this conclusion is made more exact by the following statements: "It would lead to one-sided conclusions, if we emphasized the fact that only the executive team came from outside. It is at least as important that these executives had been living in the district for 10–15 years; they knew the problems and the people either as administrative executives or executives of machine stations or state farms, or as party workers. They joined the cooperative farm in question from the outside, but the cooperative farms of the district were already familiar to them, and the people also knew them. Before they took charge of their present functions, they had already commanded respect, or they had a good background for becoming the respected managers of the cooperatives." Later on Kunszabó emphasizes the following: "Although less frequently than the average, the adequate talent can also be acquired by teams predominantly composed of local people. Right here in the county of Szolnok there are some above average cooperative farms led by presidents, who rose from the local peasantry and where the majority of the executive team (generally with the exception of the chief agronomist) are also local people. But the best ones are different. And perhaps we could even draw the tentative conclusion that even under favourable conditions executive teams of local origin proved to be capable of producing extraordinary progress and the consolidation of the large-scale farms much faster than the average only on rare occasions."

But the situation is not as simple as that. First of all, we have an important historical experience; the fact that the cooperative farms themselves chose the executives mostly from their own ranks had played an important role in the success of the socialist reorganization and the subsequent consolidation. Furthermore, the division of good, and mediocre cooperative farms according to the origin of their executives still proves that the mediocre ones are not those, where the president is local. In 1967 we scrutinized 40 cooperative farms in County Szolnok from this aspect and found the following proportions:

	Total	Local president	Non-local president
Cooperative farms with bad performance	10	6	4
Mediocre cooperatives	18	15	3
Good cooperatives	12	9	3
total	40	30	10

Membership is generally made up of two groups. In the first group we find those predominantly old members who are dominated by the interests of family farming, therefore they belong to the retrograde interest alliance opposing the more rational concepts of the collective farm. In contrast with them most of the younger members demand a status at the large-scale farm (a permanent status) for themselves so much so that the management is now complaining about the "wage-worker" attitudes of younger members.

However, the development prospects are not so simple that a more goal-oriented, large-scale farming could develop which is more independent of the rank and file. Neither can at present an all-out offensive be launched against retrograde local and family interests, in the way as Ferenc Kunszabó recommends. Such a policy has also technological and economic obstacles.

There is, for instance, a very important branch of production, cattle breeding, where we have no generalizable large-scale technology, and even for the realization of something approaching that long-term investments of an immense size would be needed. Thus we must support household dairying with all possible resources no matter how adversely that may affect collective farming.

But even where there are modern technologies available, or already established in some districts, we cannot be sure that their rapid spread would be advantageous. Take poultry production, for instance. The timing of the general establishment of "poultry factories" is "only" a matter of an economic political decision, but it would again require such heavy investment and imports that we must not proceed with it while household poultry production can be managed by simpler means and more rationally and economically.

But a bolder management of the cooperative farms as urged by István Márkus and Ferenc Kunszabó is not free from risks for conceptual and political reasons either. We want to strengthen and not to reduce *cooperative democracy*. Therefore the management of the cooperative farms must by all means come to some sort of consensus with the membership. And it must also be realized that in addition to being rooted in selfishness and traditionalism the family interests of the members and the retrograde forces contain also rational elements useful in terms of the national economy. This is rightly emphasized by Antal Gyenes. In order to develop collective farms, we must fight against the retrograde forces. However, as Géza Pete, the practising agronomist pointed out in his contribution, a consensus is also a very important role in this fight. For this very reason cooperative leaders with local roots, standing closer to the interests of the members will not be at a disadvantage in the coming period either.

István Márkus's article does not neglect this side of the problem either. He gives a very interesting and instructive account of how these relations take shape by various settlement types. We also get a description of those groups or strata of the cooperatives which can be relied on by progressive

346

cooperative management. Yes, but the management of the cooperative has not only to win the cooperation of one or the other group of the members, but it has to rely on them, too. Thus the problem must be interpreted more broadly, and the matter that has to be examined will be *the social basis on which the leadership of the cooperative relies,* and the ability of this leadership to strengthen the community of interests in the face of disruptive and retrograde forces.

And when we view the issue from this side, then the situation is not so simple even as regards the "worker" type members whose interests coincide with those of developing the collective farm. Thus each member has his own individual and family interest, and the collective farm also has its own interests. And even if the two would ultimately coincide, that mutuality does not become automatically asserted. This mutuality can only be realized in the course of the resolution of minor conflicts. *This is the reason why the nature of the operation of cooperative bodies and the assertion of cooperative democracy are of decisive importance.* And the crux of the matter here is not only how well the executives "keep busy" the elected bodies, no matter how advantageous it is what István Márkus writes of Tiszaföldvár: "In both cooperative farms it is worth noticing how much attention is paid by this respected management to keep the elected bodies of the cooperatives as busy as possible: management involves the elected leadership as well as the committees in the decision-making process. Furthermore, the hierarchy of the cooperative, the organizations of middle and lower-level management, also operate as advisory bodies. The requirements of the operation and further development of the cooperative are not only represented by the supreme management of the cooperative alone, but by a broader stratum of leaders including the elected leadership, or the board of directors as well as medium-level and lower-level management. By way of regularly increasing the income of the members and of consistently asserting the requirements, management has gained the confidence of the majority of the members. Members consider as their own interest to support the development plans of management."

We also have to see that the specific "workers' interests" of members submitting themselves to the discipline of large-scale farms also arise. The management of the farm must come to terms with these interests even in the case of lasting or recurring conflicts. In state or capitalist enterprises the two parties which negotiate in the case of conflict are management and the trade-union. However, there is no trade union in the cooperative farms, therefore the *general meeting and the management themselves have to be two-faced to deal with conflict resolution.* Naturally, this is very difficult, and it is quite predictable that sooner or later the establishment of some kind of "labour dispute" organization will be necessary in the cooperative farms. (Participants of the debate carried on in the columns of *Társadalmi Szemle* discussed this problem from several aspects.)

347

Thus, the organizational and social relations between management and the members of the cooperative farms may involve the element of conflict. This applies not only to the "retrograde peasants". Precisely for that reason the third social problem that emerges in connection with the cooperative leadership must also be voiced. We must mention *the danger of the bureaucratization of the management of cooperatives creating barriers between management and membership*. Although this danger has by no means assumed serious proportion, signs of it are already apparent; therefore, we must discuss it.

Leaders of Hungary's cooperative farms merited imperishable historic credit for the way they organized and strengthened cooperative farms and defended and are still defending the collective farms against every internal and external disruptive force. This honourable endeavour is also the prime reason why they sometimes defend the collective interests rather sharply, indeed even in a bureaucratic way and occasionally even in opposition to the membership. We find quite a few presidents who are not friends of the household farms. Instead of endeavouring to realize the organic unity of cooperative and household farming under the given conditions and for the benefit of the cooperative, they try to find means to restrict household farming. In some cooperatives, old members are coldly treated and annuities are only regarded as superfluous expenses.

The motives of some other phenomena are less than respectable. These problems originate from the fact that the duality of cooperative membership (being a co-owner and a worker) is disregarded. The attitude of some leaders interpreting cooperative democracy in such a way that nobody, neither members nor outsiders should interfere with the management of the cooperative, arises from this. And so does the other, rather widespread opinion that the accounts of the cooperative should be scrutinized only when the leaders of the cooperative request it, and the handling of disciplinary and labour disputes should not be interfered in from outside. It should be mentioned here that in many cooperatives the Control Committee does not function in the way as the law stipulates.

Executives of cooperative farms enjoy considerable and growing social appreciation and most of them deserve this appreciation. However, even if they work with courage and devotion, the presidents and professional executives also have their weak sides. There are objective factors: remnants of the earlier system of management, independence granted by the new economic mechanism, and last but not least the general tendency of bureaucratization. These factors contribute to the spread of bureaucratic phenomena. Bureaucratization is a real danger and the spirit of struggling against it must be kept awake. Science and politics must deal comprehensively with bureaucratization in the interest of a successful further progress.

I endeavoured to elucidate two debated issues related to the social bases of the leadership of cooperative farms, and I called attention to a third one.

However, there are still other social issues related to cooperatives that merit attention. In order to illustrate this, and to document how much alive these problems are in circles directly affected by them, I quote here *a summary of a survey we carried out in December 1967 among party, council and cooperative executives in the county of Szolnok.*

The endeavour to ensure *collective leadership in the cooperative farms,* and the legal stipulations which define the respective authority of management bodies and of the various officials fundamentally comply with the requirements of life, and so does our policy on the cooperatives. This, however, does not mean that there do not exist various degrees to which collective leadership is actually asserted. Based on our experience in the county of Szolnok the following can be said:

— No matter in what form these qualities assert themselves, a strong, leader-type personality, rich in ideas and ready to take the initiative is a precondition for the management of cooperative farms, for the management of the cooperative is impotent, where such qualities are lacking. Cooperatives with weak performance usually do not have such a strong leading personality.

— If the tone-setting executive is not such an active man, ready to come up with initiatives, but a manager disregarding the members' opinion, then cooperative life stagnates or even declines. This type of manager belongs to the second type of leaders. The first type and this second type account only for 8–10 per cent of the county's cooperatives.

— The typical, well-working cooperative farm is the one, where there is at least one leading personality with initiative who can assert this quality in the collective also by making the decision-making process more adequate. In the implementation of the decision the president of that type relies not on himself, but on the collective decision even if the contribution of the collective to the initial concepts was not really creative or controlling. Management of this kind is appearing in a growing majority of the cooperative farms.

Even without having their own clear initiative the respected peasant leaders generally draw up plans together with the body of management. These presidents would like the executive group to make its own decision. Once a decision has been made, these leaders will consistently represent it. Under the conditions of relatively small cooperative farms management of this kind is still able to work well.

The actual development of the management style of a cooperative is also influenced by the field the president or perhaps some other official came from. If the manager comes from a field where the method of individual leadership is customary (the army, state farm etc.), he is likely to continue that management style even in the cooperative. If the leader comes from a collective body of leadership (party, council etc.), then he is likely to advocate collective management. The peasant executives elected by the

349

membership keep in pace with progress proportionately with their ability of educating and training themselves.

Often too much confidence is given to those leading personalities who are able to take the initiative and cooperate with the management. This circumstance may reduce the participation and control of both management and the members.

This unambiguous experience is that independent of the actual management style or the origin of the executives, only those leaders can lead the cooperative farm actively and efficiently who are capable of developing their own qualifications. Not only expertise in agriculture, but also many other factors are necessary here. As far as the future is concerned, university training obtained either on full-time or part-time basis will be a general requirement for executives.

Another condition of successful management is that the executive collective's human qualities and professional training should form a complete whole, because the county always looks for professionals, who happen to be missing from the team, when executive teams are refreshed.

The composition of the executive teams of cooperative farms is very variable, but definite tendencies are also evident.

The role of professionals and the demand for them are growing rapidly, so much so that the cooperatives are willing to seek acknowledged, proven, good experts in any corner of the land, and to offer good salaries to them. Those, who have qualifications and also thoroughly know the internal relations of the cooperative because they grew up locally are appreciated and relied upon to the greatest extent in executive teams. Young graduates' careers heavily depend on their ability to fit into the perspective of the cooperative; thus they take into account the future and do not regard the cooperative only as a source of income. Some of the old, less-qualified executives are dismissed, but those who learn and develop finally succeed.

The professionals find their place in the executive team according to their attitudes to the cooperative farm. The employed professionals, who show indifference will not strike roots, but those who become members enjoy much appreciation in the cooperative farms.

A number of problems is caused by the way the schools send their graduate students home. From this aspects Karcag, where contacts with practice, links with the cooperative farms are the best in the academic training stands out in a positive sense. The problem of training junior executives, that is the course that leads from the school to responsible positions as professional leader is not at all solved. This is also a national problem, but the county makes serious efforts to find a solution to the problem. In the county of Szolnok top management is most often in the hands of the "quintet" (president, party secretary, chief agronomist, chief zootechnician, chief accountant) who have regular meetings mainly preparing decision-making.

350

Brigade leaders and heads of departments constitute a critical level of management. These positions are filled by former peasants, able to cope with their tasks within certain limits. These persons fail to keep abreast with technological progress and higher standard farming; in practice, therefore, they do not participate in the management of the cooperative farm. And progress is not easy in this respect. Nevertheless, brigade leaders, who successfully work for higher qualification are just as capable of meeting the requirements of their growing tasks as the presidents capable of development.

In connection with the acitivities of *presidents* the phenomenon that it is becoming increasingly difficult to persuade cooperatives to elect outsiders for president deserves particular attention. Succession nowadays is decided within the cooperatives; most often they choose one of the departmental heads, or brigade leaders, a former peasant who succeeded in getting a degree. But professionals, who fitted themselves adequately into the perspective of the cooperative are also frequently elected to the presidential post.

The majority of the executive teams of the cooperative farms have a definite, well-developed social basis on which they can rely, and this also influences the leadership in a variety of ways. In this the following factors play various roles:

— the circumstances under which the cooperative was founded (the background of the founders);

— the branch of production on which the success of the cooperative farm depends, since members working in that branch have greater importance in terms of both the cooperative and management;

— there is a new tendency that the management is increasingly seeking the support of those, who work as machinists representing the new agro-technology.

Owing to the influence of these factors, the following types of cooperative farms are to be found in the County Szolnok:

— Cooperatives relying on the old core of former agrarian proletarians; this type is predominant in the towns, and interestingly, the young skilled workers, mostly children of the founders, belong there to the same basis; therefore management relies on worker-type members there.

— The social basis providing the support of management is made up of the founding members also in the Jász and Kun districts. In these districts there are also numerous cooperatives founded by peasants previously owning moderate-size land.

— Where, due to the circumstances of formation or to production profile, no such grouping supporting management has emerged, the executives themselves endeavoured to encourage the development of some supporting group. If they succeeded in doing so they could also consolidate the situation. Where these attempts were unsuccessful management lacks support even today.

351

— The situation of cooperative farms based on detached farms, where the members are tied to the cooperative farm by virtue of these lands constitutes a different case. In such cooperatives management relies only on peasants working in animal husbandry or those permanently employed.

Considering the above, we get an explanation for the way *presidential elections take place.* It is evident that these elections cause fewer difficulties nowadays since an increasing number of cooperatives have talented potential candidates. However, in the weak cooperative farms presidential elections cause crises even today. These cooperatives do not have talented executives and an adequate social basis management could rely upon; frequent mergers and poor management can make the situation even worse. Nevertheless, the majority of the cooperative farms either elects one of their own members to the presidential position, or they find the right person somewhere else.

From all of the facts outlined in the above *certain conclusions on the future development of cooperative management can and must de drawn.* But these can neither be as definite nor as one-sided as the conclusions of István Márkus and Ferenc Kunszabó. Only the following trends are really traceable:

— in the coming period in the course of the development of modern, industry-like farming, the role of experts using developed technologies and familiar with rational thinking will increase;

— the cooperative character of the cooperative farms and the nature of collective farming will, however, remain decisive in the relation of management and membership; therefore a management which is isolated from the membership will not be able to do well in the coming years;

— the conclusion that professional experts less dependent on the members should as soon as possible replace the present local peasant executives cannot be justified either as an objective tendency, or as a subjective requirement; this could not be realized without damaging both economic progress and cooperative democracy;

— the course of progress will continue to be gradual transformation, and the better part of the present peasant (and worker) executives are expected to be able to keep pace with the requirements of progress, indeed, there will even be a new generation of this type of executives, even though the role of the professionals will also increase.

X

LAYING THE MODERN, SCIENTIFIC FOUNDATIONS OF SOCIAL MANAGEMENT IN SOCIALISM*

*The Hungarian original is to be found in Ferenc Erdei's *Összegyűjtött Művei* (Collected Works) *Tudománypolitikai, kutatásirányítási és szervezéstudományi tanulmányok* (Studies on Science Policies, Research Management and Organizational Science), Akadémiai Kiadó, Budapest, 1980, pp. 459—471.

Part of text was originally published in *Valóság,* 1965, No. 4. pp. 20—30. The concluding part of the article is identical with the text published on pp. 25—27. (pp. 483—485 of the above-quoted volume) of the study *A mezőgazdasági szervezéstudomány néhány elméleti kérdése* (Some Theoretical Questions of the Science of Agricultural Management).

This article is an attempt to give a general outline of organizational science. Due to the nature of the subject, this article is rather sketchy and does not include the consistent discussion of relevant professional literature on the detailed elucidation of the questions raised. A report of the Scientific Management Commission of the Hungarian Academy of Sciences: *Laying the Modern, Scientific Foundations of Management and Administration and the Training of Managers* (Budapest, June 1964. pp. 256.) should be regarded as the documentary basis of the issues explained in this study.

*

The problems of raising the standards of management, the training of leaders and the selection of managers, and generally the up-to-dateness and control of management emerge with urgency and in several fields in the present phase of our socialist development. The demands are particularly urgent in economic management, but they can also be felt in the general social management and particularly in public administration. Responding to urgent needs, a few years ago scientific inquiries began in every socialist country. Theoretical literature on this field keeps increasing; various courses in management and administration were started and the subject of management became part of the curriculum of numerous university faculties (economics, engineering, public administration etc.).

Scientific management and administration emerged in the developed capitalist countries a long time ago primarily in the economy. Research is being carried on in many branches of science (sociology, psychology, law etc.); the relevant professional literature is already filling libraries and a vast network of management training developed. New technology and the application of new and still newer mathematical methods have given a particularly great impetus to scientific and practical activities. The practical experiences as well as the results of investigations became generally known also in the socialist countries, indeed some results have already been utilized or become parts of various surveys.

Thus when laying the modern, scientific foundations of social management was put on the agenda in Hungary, we could rely on extensive research results and practical experience in addition to the experience of the workers' movement, the party and the first period of socialist construction. There is, however, one aspect, where we cannot count on any assistance; thus far in the laying of the scientific foundations of social management no generally accepted theoretical bases have developed; we cannot yet speak of a uniform discipline. This did not happen even in the most developed capitalist countries. One could rather speak of the many-sidedness of approach and the almost irreconcilable variety of attitudes. May it suffice to refer to the variations, one could almost say the confusion of the terminology.

What can we do, then? We should learn and utilize as much as possible from the foreign experiences and research results (whether they come from socialist or capitalist countries), and endeavour to contribute to the systematization of the extremely diverging and rapidly expanding knowledge also on the basis of our own experience and investigations. This is, naturally, an almost hopelessly vast task, therefore we must consider even the most modest starting point or contribution as useful.

Let us start with the premise that when we talk about management, administration, and control in the terms of everyday language, the concepts are rather unambiguously defined. In this sense we can speak clearly of the up-to-dateness, the sociological and psychological problems, the technological standard of management and the selection and training of the leaders etc. Discussing these issues in that way the differences in the conditions of management and control as well as the various functions of management can be ignored or neglected. Thus we can speak of the problems of management so that it is understandable to the president of a village council or the minister, to a foreman or the manager, to a brigade leader or the president of the cooperative farm, to a military commander or the head of a research institute. But the knowledge of management one could discuss in that way would be rather superficial and either too general or too detailed.

The situation changes when the matter in question is the laying of scientific foundations of management, the science concerned with management. Both in capitalist and socialist countries there is a trend which aims at systemizing knowledge on management under the label of *management science* comprising sociological, psychological or complex knowledge as well as the information on the technological means and organizational methods of management and administration. In contrast to this, we may also find the notion which conceives of management not in itself, but in the framework of the organization, or more generally of the system in which the organization exerts its activities. This concept seeks to lay the modern scientific foundations of management not under the heading of *scientific management* but under that of *organizational science*. In my opinion there is a fundamental error here, and this is primarily the issue that has to be clarified. The present article is dedicated to this crucial issue.

356

1. MANAGEMENT AS A FUNCTION WITHIN THE SYSTEM

The common interpretation of the social leadership, of management and administration is that someone organizes, manages the activities of other people to achieve certain objectives (the person exerting the function of leadership induces others to carry out certain operations in a predetermined order, to deal with activities organized and coordinated to suit the objective to be achieved). From this view it also follows that we must regard management and administration as primary and more general; it is management which organizes the attitudes and activities of people; therefore the process and the result of organization are secondary. Is this concept right? I hold that it is not, and offer the following to support my view.

There are a number of possible types of the function of leadership: we can differentiate at least the following types:—a leading body controls the activities of subordinate bodies or institutions (this type includes the councils of ministers, the central committees of parties, the presidia of academies and supreme controlling bodies of the general meeting type);— the leader of a given social organization manages the operations of the given organization (from the point of view of the management model it is immaterial whether the body in question is a ministry, an enterprise or a scientific institution;—the man in charge (plant manager, brigade or team leader, foreman or master-tradesman) directs the work of his subordinates to perform their definite duties;—a government institution or functionary (an authority competent to deal with certain matters, a judge or a traffic policeman) controls and directs the attitudes of citizens within the scope of limited authority.

It is easy to recognize that the vast majority of the functions of management belong to the first three types whose striking common feature is that the organizations, or persons in charge do not determine the activity of the subordinated organizations or individuals; they only bring them into operation and set concrete objectives, since a definite social organization is concerned in each and every instance (party, or government institution, enterprise, sub-units of enterprises, plants, workshops etc.), where both the leading and the subordinate organizations have definite functions. *Therefore the function of management does not create a kind of organizational framework, but it simply fills its role within the limits of a given organization.* (This role includes some organization also, but only within the given institutional organization and determined by the objective framework of laws, statutes, ownership relations and the division of labour.)

We are left, however, with the fourth type, the typical instance of which is the control function of the traffic policeman. Obviously, the traffic policeman does not fill his own role within a definite organization, for the vehicles and pedestrians in the streets are not parts of a given social organization. This is true, yet it is *still not the traffic policeman, who organizes the traffic.* Traffic is also subject to a given organization (the rules of the road, the system of road signs), and people are obliged to observe this. What is, therefore, the function of the traffic policeman? He sees to it that the rules are observed, and also fills a definite function of the system of signals (which otherwise can be partially filled also by traffic lights or some other technical equipment). Therefore, we must see that even when management and administration do not operate within a definite social organization, *they still fill their functions within a definite system.*

I think all that is sufficient to support the opinion that *management must be seen as a function within a system, and scientific knowledge related to management must be based on the knowledge of the systems within which the management operates* (in the case of social management fundamentally on those of social organizations).

Going beyond social management we should approach the problem of management more generally. It is well known that certain control and "management functions" operate both in the system of automatic machines as well as in the regulative system of the living organism which causes the whole system to function. And it is worthy of attention that this control and "management function" turn out of the context of the system has never even emerged in the technical and biological sciences (or in mathematics, a mutually cooperative co-science of these). The obvious explanation for this is that the system itself is always primary in terms of both cognition and the structure, and the control function cannot even be approached without a thorough knowledge of system.

And once the relation of management and system is seen in such a general manner, i.e. extended equally to social organizations, living organisms and the automatic systems of machines we find ourselves in the very heart of cybernetics. Let us take a source closest to us, the work of Rezső Tarján (*Kibernetika*, Cybernetics, Budapest, Gondolat Könyvkiadó, 1964). What is cybernetics in his words? "Cybernetics is a new, complex scientific discipline which studies the structure and behaviour of complicated, highly organized systems with the strict methods of the natural sciences, primarily relying on theoretical methods, but also on experimental ones wherever that is possible". Naturally, cybernetics is not simply the science of organization, and particularly not in terms of the social sciences, since it sets out from the logical examination of machine systems and endeavours to explore analogies with the living organisms. Rezső Tarján throws a precise light also on this: "... cybernetics is the first conscious attempt in the history of sciences to apply (practically and in a technological way) those organizational principles which are observable in the most sophisticated organized systems, that is in living organisms".

In spite of all of these, the analogies of cybernetics can be utilized for laying the scientific foundations of social management and for exploring the connections between management and social organizations as systems;

358

these analogies are also very convincing. Cybernetics has explored organizational and operational principles which, in the form of a most generally formulated model, can be more or less applied also to the structure and operation of social organizations. Thus cybernetics is an important science for the science of social organization.

2. THE VARIOUS MEANINGS OF ORGANIZATION AND MANAGEMENT

If we accept that social management is a function within the system, we must look for laying the scientific foundations of management within an organizational science, which examines development, structural principles and operation of social organizations and generally of social systems, and within that the role of management by relying on a dialectic concept of the historic development of society. And here we no longer tread an unknown territory. The Marxist science of history, political economy and the philosophy of Marxism—Leninism provide a good basis for obtaining scientific knowledge on social organizations and on the development and functioning of management. We should see that the disciplines of Marxist social science do not coincide with the science of organization. (These disciplines cannot be regarded identical with sociology or even with economics).

However, before discussing the science of organization more closely we must make the meaning of organization more definite. Up till now we spoke of organization and organism as if we meant exactly and unambiguosly defined concepts by them. This, however, is not the case even if we are discussing social organizations and social organisms only. This term is used in a number of meanings even in this sense. (The circumstance that the Latin word *organisatio* and its English, Russian, French or German equivalents denote the process as well as the result of organization makes the exact use of words even more difficult.)

In everyday usage the meaning of the word is almost limitless. Generally it can be used to denote any activity aimed at linking and arranging the various motives of action (human attitudes, time, objects). Thus we may organize a programme, a meeting, accommodation, meals, leisure work processes, the delivery of materials, energy supply, transport, purchase and sales. An enterprise, an office, a scientific institute and within these workshops, departments, workshops can also be organized.

If we want to narrow down the meanings in order to get a more precise definition of social organization and the function of management, we must make the following distinctions: (1) *organization as the creation of organizations and organisms* (whether they are government organizations and organisms or economic, party or general social organizations); (2) *organization, as the operation of the given organization* (ensuring the definition of objectives and the conditions of operation); (3) *organization aimed at the planning, construction and subsequent operation of machines, systems of machines;* (4) *organization, as the devising and setting up of technological processes* (linking capital equipment, object of work, and the remuneration of knowhow in order to produce a product or some other achievement).

The essential difference between the four types of organizations is obvious. The first two interpretations can only be used in connection with social organisms, because a state of organization in the living organism is independent of human organization. In this respect the only thing that society can do is to obtain knowledge on the living organism's functioning; within certain limits we are also capable of influencing the organism ensuring the conditions of its existence and the "healing" of its malfunctions. The operation of technological systems is concerned with the interrelation of objects and their relation to people, while the first two types of organization in question take place in the interpersonal social sphere.

The third and fourth interpretations specifically refer to technology, since the living organisms and their functioning as well as the social organizations and their functioning develop historically, according to the laws of biology or to social-economic laws. Even if it presupposes a given socio-historical development level, organization interpreted in the third and fourth ways can be relatively freely changed in accordance with the results of the natural sciences.

Once we accept this difference, we obtain an essential criterion of distinction. We must distinguish social organization in the stricter sense from the organization of technology. And once we do that the sphere of social organization will be limited to the structure and functioning of social organisms, and it is here that we can look for the place, conditions and the rules of the functioning of social management. This is the way we can arrive at laying the firm and scientific foundations of management and administration.

A further very essential delimitation is still necessary, however, before actually starting to discuss organizational science. The meaning of management and administration is manifold, and this is particularly observable in economic life. When we talk of improving the methods of economic management and administration in general, the issue at stake is the development of our economic management mechanism.

But what do we mean by economic mechanism? By economic mechanism we mean the sum of those factors which decisively influence production distribution, consumption, in fact the filling of demands. The term includes prices, wages, planning methods, the system of investments, the order of material management, financing, and the rules of the market as well. Considering the foregoing, it is obvious that the development of socialist planned economy means a different kind of management and administration than the establishment and operation of social organizations. Undoubtedly, in this case, too, the point in question is the operation of a given social organization (the socialist national economy and its enterprises). However, these "management and administration" methods are not of organizational nature, but they are of a purely material and economic character, and they act "automatically". Compared with the "pure" content of management and administration, this difference emerges with particular clarity in economic life. In principle the content and aim of management and economic influencing play similarly different roles, for instance, in public administration or in scientific institutes, but there they do not determine so decisively the operation of the organizations as in the case of economic organizations, enterprises.

We must, therefore, distinguish the *organizational interpretation of management and administration* (the building up of organizations and their operation) from the *application of the means of material-economic influencing*. Naturally, this distinction cannot be sharp, because, for instance, the planning system includes both organizational and material incentives. We must also keep in mind that the management of any social organization must use both ideological and economic incentives even if the role of these two incentives is less important in non-economic organizations.

3. THE CHAPTERS OF ORGANIZATIONAL SCIENCE

If management is regarded as a function within the system, and organization is interpreted as the process of establishing and operating social organizations (or more generally speaking, systems) then we have defined the subject of *organizational science* within which we can explore the characteristics of management. However, in the sphere defined in this way, we find rather complex problems of organizing, organization, management, control and administration which call for systematization in order to identify the various elements and to shed light on their interrelations.

The first and most general aspect of systematization is to approach the structure and operation of the social organizations either abstractly and with a claim to generality extending to all of sectors, or by examining the separate fields such as public administration, economic organization and military organization etc. Since both of these approaches are justified and necessary, we must separate the *general part* of organizational science, which discusses principles of organization and functioning as regards the whole of society, and the *particular part* which examines the historical development and problems of organization by the various sectors of society.

As a matter of fact, this approach is by no means new since ever since organization and management have been a general subject of scientific investigation, there has been a general organizational science and the disciplines concerned with the various walks of society have had, even if unawares, an organizational chapter for a long time. What is perhaps novel is the endeavour aimed at the conscious linking and separation of these two perspectives. (This endeavour itself springs precisely from the circumstance that in the economic organization one invariably comes to face general organizational issues of both the national economy and the companies.)

However, in an independent organizational science it would not make much sense if each special social field had a separate chapter. It is far more reasonable and fruitful to show caution and conservatism in this respect saying that this chapter should stay where it is now, i. e. in the relevant discipline. The organizational chapters of the respective disciplines do anyhow need the help, or at least the control of general organizational science. (I am sure of this in respect of economic organization, sectoral economics, and business management, and probably this applies also to public administration.) There is something else, however, that must be firmly recommended: namely that each field of the social sciences possibly concerned should make conscious efforts at developing its own chapter of organizational science; without that it cannot even systematize its own knowledge and for lack of such knowledge on organization it could fall victim to organizational illusions treating also its own organizational problems one-sidedly.

The *general organizational science* is developing, only it is not labelled as such in many instances, or it is given the name *management science*. So long as we consistently regard it as organizational science on the basis of the foregoing, we can outline at least its major chapters with logical necessity.

Its *first chapter* must, in any case, deal with the *social organizations*. Only the careful and systematic study of the origins, development, establishment, structure and various types of the social organizations can produce reliable knowledge, on the basis of which the organizational and operational principles and among others the position and conditions of management can be explored. This is essential whether the studies concern economic organizations (enterprises, sub-units of enterprises, organizations exercising control over enterprises), or organizations of government administration, or some other social organization. The size and importance of the tasks of this chapter are best demonstrated with reference to the well-known problems, such as centralization and decentralization, the organizational levels, the assertion of independent responsibility on the various levels of the organizational hierarchy, and the adequate or inadequate functioning of a particular organization.

The point is not that we do not have an extensive and important knowledge on the social organizations. The science of history asserting the point of view of historical materialism as well as political economics explored fundamental knowledge concerning organizations, but bourgeois sociology also accumulated valuable research findings. But this body of knowledge did not yet become an exact and systemized science which could treat the organizational and operational principles of social organizations with the exactitude the relevant sciences achieved in exploring engineering systems or living organisms. Nevertheless, there is a lively demand for this, and it is becoming increasingly more realistic to develop a really mature organizational science. It must be emphasized that such knowledge is of equally great importance both in terms of gaining knowledge on society and in terms of shaping it.

Naturally, knowledge on the structure, growth and development of social organizations is important both in capitalism and in socialism. It is unnecessary to prove the particular significance of organizational science in the socialist society, since new social institutions, organizations have been developed in socialism. By now, we have decades of experience and the practical tasks of the development of organizations are also evident. In such a situation it is impossible not to have a discipline that methodically collects and processes this knowledge. Therefore it is totally natural that the organizational chapter of organizational science must be initiated by the students and decision-makers of socialist society. These students and decision-makers have an urgent need for organization knowledge and they also have the available material for study. During the time of socialist reorganization and the decades of socialist construction we have acquired knowledge both on the old abolished institutions and organizations and on the new socialist institutions and organizations founded by ourselves; this proved to be a unique historical possibility. We have the historical material to point out the general organizational and operational principles of social organizations, and also to compare the principles and trends of socialist and capitalist societies.

The second chapter of organizational science could deal with the function, contents and operational principles *of management* and the organizational methods of the operation of organizations. This is approximately the material of knowledge discussed by *business management,* but not exactly. Namely when the function of management is jointly treated with the psychological and "self-administration" problems of managers and of corporations, then both the cognition of the reality of management and the clear evaluation of the psychological and social factors of people filling executive functions and of corporations will be more difficult. Thus this chapter of organizational science must objectively analyze the management function (independent of the fact whether it is exercised by an individual or a corporation) and also the psychology of individuals or corporations.

Once we approach the management function with such an objective point of view, and treat it as the principal (starting and initiating) factor of the operation of the relevant organization, everything will be clearer. Let us start with the grouping of management functions.

There is a number of known ways of grouping *management functions* (customarily also called "tasks"), but classifying them into a group of four or

363

seven is the most frequent. One of the versions of the type identifying four management tasks is the following: planning, organizing, operative direction and control; the other type is: evaluation of the situation, setting the objective to be achieved, organizing the elements of work and control. The most common enumeration of the functions of management identifying seven tasks is the so-called POSDCORB "formula": planning, organizing, staffing, directing, coordinating, reporting, budgeting.

If we take out from this list that, which concerns the person, who fills the management function, and also what pertains to the establishment of organizations and not to the operation of a given organization, then the issues can be simplified and the objective functions of operative management can be divided into five groups: (1) *information and the evaluation of the situation* (evaluation of the condition, institutional organization, economic and social environment and the past and possible future performance of the organization); (2) *decision-making* (definition of objectives and tasks, thus planning which is in fact the setting of objectives, including the preparatory activities) (3) *operative organization* (organizing the division of labour, personnel conditions, and budgeting of the given task; this activity is not identical with the establishment of the given organization, since that is already given together with its operational principles; management brings into operation an already given system; operative organization is aimed at additional organizational work within the already existing framework of an organization; (4) *giving orders* (issuing instructions, rulings, work schedules); *controlling* (controlling the operation of the whole of the organization by way of specific enquiries, occasional checking and reports; accounting and statistics also fall into this group). It is worth being noted that the issue of higher military orders is essentially regulated in the same way.

Thus when the function of management is seen as an objective operative activity, orientation becomes immediately easier, and knowledge related to it can also be more easily obtained (according to organizational levels and special departments etc.). This is what gives justification to this chapter.

The problems of *executives and the bodies of management* could be the subject of the *third chapter*. The reason why this chapter takes the third place only is that the psychological and social problems of the executives can be adequately clarified only after having obtained knowledge on the organization and the characteristics of its management functions.

This chapter includes the following subjects: the problem of personal or collective leadership, the selection, professional qualification and general abilities of executives; the human-social relations between executives and subordinates and the organization of the management activity. Problems of management training (the levels and forms of training, the selection for training courses and the material of such courses) are also to be discussed in this chapter. Putting it simply: this is the place of almost all of the problems customarily discussed under the label of *management science,* if it is interpreted not as an independent science, but as a chapter of the general science of organization.

The *fourth chapter* is perhaps best described as the *methods and technological means of management-organization.* Everything concerning programmed and *ad hoc* decisions, the methods and means of information, accounting and statistics, traditional and modern management organization processes, mechanized or manual methods of office management and the use of computers and other technological tools falls under this heading. The reason why it is not right to call this field *management technology* is that not only the organizational methods and technological means of executives and management are discussed here but also the technological means of the operation of the entire organization.

It is completely obvious that the systemization outlined above cannot be lasting even if it were basically acceptable now. The actual functioning of organizations and the progress of scientific research bring up new problems and new approaches take shape. As a result, organizational science develops new fields. It is also certain that the fields of organizational science will develop differently in socialist and in capitalist countries. However, under our own specific conditions, I believe that the above systematization of the fields of organizational science may provide a starting-point for further research and the actual improvement of management.

4. THE INSTRUCTIVE EXAMPLE OF AGRICULTURAL BUSINESS MANAGEMENT

The author's special field, agricultural business management provided the impetus to the attempt of systemization outlined in the foregoing. It was necessary for me to use general management science considerations in order to solve the problems of business management of agriculture; the cooperative farms—these most interesting and instructive organizations of our socialist society—provided ample opportunity for making a number of observations, the experimental or even theoretical study of which would have been inconceivable without the existence and progress of our cooperative farms. It will be useful for the reader to become acquainted with at least the major features of my observations.

Right from the start, agricultural business management developed as the science of business management. However, the problems of this type of business organization did not practically emerge in capitalist business management, and even in socialism they gained importance only gradually.

The business management of *capitalist agriculture* discusses in detail the problems of production conditions (ownership, property, labour relations) and productive forces (their nature, proportions, interrelations according to various branches) as well as the economic problems of the input-output ratios. But all of these issues are examined there in relation to the farm, as the fundamental unit of production; thus management appears in terms of planning, decision-making and achieving the maximum profits for the owner or entrepreneur and not in terms of the structure of the farm. (The business management of capitalist agriculture takes as its basic model the "family farm" and not the large-scale farm employing several hundreds of workers.)

The business management of *socialist agriculture* deals partly with the same problems as its western counterpart (even the economic problems of input-output ratios lost importance only temporarily); however, in addition to these problems it must also face the business-organizational problems of the structure of the organization, because it has to deal with the business management of large-scale, socially owned farms employing several hundred persons.

This gains expression in the Soviet definition of the objective of this discipline: "The organizational science of socialist farms is a science, which explores the laws of the rational organization and management of production practised in the kolkhozes and sovkhozes." (Kolesnev). However, this programme-like definition has not resulted yet in the emergence of the field of business management that could be defined as the *structure and operation of the business organization.*

The situation is further aggravated by the circumstance that the constitution of cooperative farms, as political documents, failed to give a clear definition of the structure and divisions of the cooperative farms as a business organization; the management functions of the managing bodies of the farms were not clearly defined either. (This is understandable, since then and for practical purposes the most important issues were to unambiguously record the property relations and to set up the simplest frameworks for collective activities.)

Nevertheless, as the years pass, the cooperative farms are managed in a more and more clearly and business-like way; thus the fundamental issues of their business organization and management came to the fore. The science of agricultural management was, however, not at all prepared for defining and solving these problems. Under such conditions we struggled almost hopelessly with defining the tasks of the "organizational consolidation and development" of the cooperative farms and with the scientific foundations of their solution.

First we sought help in industrial management, in industrial business management, for we rightly assumed that the more developed organizational circumstances of both capitalist and socialist industry could provide some orientation. It turned out that the management and organizational structure of industrial enterprises have been organic parts of industrial and industrial business management for a long time. On the basis of the

366

experience of large-scale industrial concerns certain basic organizational principles concerning the structure of factory organization have developed in industrial business management, and a relatively firm framework of the organizational hierarchy has also developed. We had therefore the help of the following *basic organizational principles: the principle of dividing production* into various fields each unit having responsibility for a specific field of production; *the principle of coordination* (the need for coordinating functions); *the principle of dependence* (the hierarchy of various organizational levels; *the principle of functionally defining the tasks of various spheres* (distinction of the various spheres of activity); and *the proportions of centralization and decentralization*. The *organizational grades* (levels) developed in industry were also instructive for us: the *enterprise* is an independent legal unit making its own balance sheet; the *factory, or factory division* is a unit of the enterprise operating with a measure of independence; the *plant* is a production unit carrying out a definite production function; the *workshop* is a production unit within the plant doing certain processes or groups of processes.

All these principles have proved to be useful. However, as regards management, we did not get new insights. Namely, to our greatest surprise, in industrial economics organization is regarded to be a means of management; company structure and the assertion of organizational principles are conceived of as functions of management. (Interestingly, our colleagues in the state farms did not find this surprising; indeed, they accepted this view as obvious. However, when dealing with the problems of cooperative farms, we just cannot reconcile ourselves to this view). This is how the question emerged for us: now the cooperative farms are facts of reality; we have created these institutions which function on the basis of a certain type of ownership relation and according to socio-political rules. It is within this framework that their organizational structure and development have to be realistically asserted. This proved to be a rather instructive challenge.

XI

SOCIALISM AND THE STANDARD OF LIVING*

* The Hungarian original is to be found in Ferenc Erdei's *Művekkel élő társadalom* (Essays on Literature and Society), Budapest, 1978. pp. 165—181. Originally published in *Kritika,* 1963, No. 1. pp. 4—16.

The dispute that recently took place in the columns of Hungarian literary journals about the rise of the standard of living and the cultural, moral and political issues that it involves gave expression to three subjective standpoints according to the summary of the editorial of *Új Írás* (Aug. 1962), which closed the dispute:

— there is no real problem about this, since the standard of living of most people is not high enough to warrant worrying about it;

— we are witnessing a threatening "petit-bourgeois tendency", and "the petit bourgeois mentality is again inundating our country with the visible signs of material affluence";

— the rise of the standard of living "should not instil fear about socialism, for it does not imply the danger of petit bourgeois development, but it is a healthy consequence of the right development of socialist construction".

The debate between these subjective views led to no conclusion, and the editorial epilogue in "Új Írás" did not solve the contradictions either. The result was inescapable, for nobody explored the *objective historic reality* of the disputed situation in the course of the debate. This is what I am attempting to do in the following and I should like to revive the dispute on this basis.

1

The economic policy of socialism has two fundamental basic principles of unquestioned conceptual validity and in fact asserted since the 20th Congress of the Communist Party of Soviet Union: one of them is the requirement of continual rise of the standard of living, the other one is the principle of material interest.

a) The fundamental aim of socialism, that is *the accomplishment of material well-being for everyone* has been unambiguous even in the pre-Marxian labour movements and the Utopian theories. The scientific socialism of Marx and Engels was also built on this foundation, which did not become obscure in Lenin's theoretical precepts or the life and death struggle he prosecuted for Soviet power.

It is a historical fact, however, that the tangible rise of the standard of living could not be realized in the Soviet Union during the civil war because of the war conditions, and in the period of the reconstruction of the national economy for economic reasons. After that the faster rise of the standard of living was hindered by the objective economic needs of the defence of the socialist country and by the subjective motives of the voluntarist economic policy.

The turn occurred at the 20th Congress. This is what the resolution of the Congress stated: "The growth of industrial and agricultural production established realistic conditions for the continual increase of the material well-being of the Soviet people." This economic political basic principle was broadened in the programme passed by the 22nd Congress in two directions. On the one hand: "A higher standard of living must be attained in the Soviet Union than in any of the capitalist countries". On the other hand: "The aim of communist production is to ensure the incessant progress of society and to provide material and cultural goods to each member of society according to their growing needs, individual requirements and taste." We know the practical assertion of these economic political endeavours.

With some differences in detail the historic course of the rise of the standard of living was the same in Hungary too since the beginning of the building of socialism. And the principal characteristic of the present situation is precisely that the original and fundamental aim of socialism is beginning to be realized now when we achieved for the first time in our history the actual and relatively rapid rise in the standard of most people's lives in this formerly backward country. And we also know that Hungary is not one of the laggards in this respect.

The first conclusion concerning the subjective stands taken in the dispute can be drawn from this simple and obvious, yet epoch-making fact: the standard of living increased and continues to increase on a grand scale and in massive proportions, and this necessarily raises new and profound social, cultural and moral, and ultimately political problems. This happens completely independently of personal likes or dislikes, approvals or disapprovals, whether some considers it a sign of progress or smells danger in it. And it is just as inevitable that these problems can and must only be solved in the coming phase of the rise of the standard of living, and that reversing the course of progress is impossible unless an emergency situation demands it.

b) The other basic principle of the economic policy is the acknowledgement and assertion of the principle of *material interest*. This also has a history.

Lenin said in the first years of the Soviet power: "Every important sector of the national economy must be built on personal interest". He initiated the introduction of semi-independence for the business units, of progressive efficiency wages and generally of the application of material incentives. And those were really revolutionary years, and nobody understood and represented better the revolutionary spirit, and the revolutionary momentum of the masses of people than Lenin.

And yet this principle was pushed into the background in later years, and it was attempted to substitute this driving force with various management methods. The 20ths Congress returned to the footsteps of Lenin in this respect, too.

It is commonly known too that this principle is extensively and generally asserted in practice in the Soviet Union as well as in Hungary and in the other socialist countries, and that the growing economic achievements of recent years are largely due to that. This justifies the cardinal conclusion that material interest is an indispensable motive of the building of socialism and even that of communism.

c) The economic policy of socialism has, however, yet another element partly linked with the above two basic principles, partly derived from other sources. This is the acknowledgement, respect for and support of *personal possessions* and the *individual-family sphere of household economic activities.*

This sphere will considerably narrow at a higher stage of socialism but will not wither away within the foreseeable future, indeed, it will not lose its not-negligeable significance either. The programme passed by the 22nd Congress indicates that "to the extent we approach communism, individual needs will be increasingly met from social bases, the growth rate of the latter will be faster than the rate of increase of personal wages on the amount of work performed". Allowing for that, the proportion of individual and family household-economic activities will obviously decrease even further. Putting the matter into the perspective of historic progress, the programme stipulates that *"about half of the total real income of the people"* will be derived *"from social consumption at the end of the twenty-year period",* and includes such items in the category of social provisions as homes, transport, public catering etc.

The same principles and tendencies assert themselves in Hungary too with some modifications. Thus we must reckon with not only a rather wide sphere of personal possessions, but also with a rather extensive—though progressively narrowing—sphere of individual and family household-economic activities for a relatively long historic period, for at least one generation. And we must add again that this does not depend either on this or that subjective judgement, the "conceptual" standpoint of minor or major groups, but goes hand-in-hand with the building of the socialist society under the given historic conditions by objective necessity. In more simple terms: as long as the socially organized production and distribution is not capable of meeting every need of every member of society, the family home, the garden, the household farms of members of farming cooperatives and other "household labour" will not only be unavoidable, but also necessary. Personal possessions, the possession of consumer and utility commodities, their accumulation and increase, and personal and family life with them will be an element of the standard of living attained at a higher stage of socialism too, and the programme of communism did not propose doing away with them.

2

Calling to mind some relevant principles of the economic policy of socialism and the tendency of their objective historic realization, let us approach the disputed subject from *the aspect of socialist morale* also.

Let us set out from the most general precept of the programme of the Communist Party of the Soviet Union on this matter. "The communist morals include the major general moral rules developed by the masses of people in the course of thousands of years in the struggle waged against social repression and moral shortcomings. The revolutionary morals of the working class have a particularly great importance in the moral development of society. The communist morals gain new principles and new contents at the time of socialist and communist building work."

The historic view must be especially emphasized in this formulation. The point is not a set of eternal and unchanged rules, but general moral norms developed in the course of thousands of years of struggle of humanity, to which the revolutionary practice of the labour movement added something new and essential, and which is still gaining new elements in the practice of socialist building work. This also means that we, the present generation of socialist building work must also add our own contribution and formulate new moral rules as new social situations develop in the course of historic progress.

But what are the principal norms of socialist morals as expressed today?

When the programme summarily mentions this it underlines three major characteristics:

"… distinguished communist consciousness, love of work and workshop discipline, commitment to social values…"

And when it comes to detailing fundamental moral principles as if embodying them in a code of morals it sums them up in 12 paragraphs. It is easy to trace the "historic layers" of the moral norms in this list.

A few moral norms express the continuing validity and survival of the most beautiful moral endeavours of previous eras:

— humane relations and mutual respect among people…;
— honesty and justice, moral purity, simplicity and modesty in social and private life;
— mutual respect in the family, taking care of the upbringing of children.

The next group of moral principles is an achievement of the struggles of the working class and expresses the moral obligations of struggle against exploitation and solidarity amongst peoples:

— devotion to the cause of communism…;
— taking care of the protection and enrichment of social property;
— friendship and brotherhood towards every people of the Soviet Union; rejection of national and racial hostilities;
— brotherly solidarity with the workers of every country, with all peoples.

And finally another group of the moral principles expresses the most special norms of the socialist society—those which are most important in terms of the problems debated:

— conscientious work performed for the benefit of society...;
— a high sense of social duty, relentlessness towards those, who harm the interests of society;
— collective spirit and comradly mutuality...;
— inflexibility towards injustice, laziness, dishonesty.

The paramount and most general of them must be given special emphasis in this group of moral principles: the fundamental socialist principle of the attitude to work. (The comparison is obvious: just as socialist economics is based on the theory of value of labour, so is the attitude to work the principal pillar of socialist morals.) The programme itself devotes a separate paragraph to this, and when pondering the point it almost overflows the framework of the party programme: "The party places the objective of developing the socialist attitude to work in each of its members in the centre of its educational work. Work done for the benefit of society is the sacred duty of everybody. Honour and respect are due to any work (manual or intellectual) done for the benefit of society. Every worker must be educated by way of the best examples of work, the best patterns of social management. Work is the creator of everything that is necessary for human life, the development of man. Therefore everybody must take part in the production of the means necessary for his life and activity, for the prosperity of society. A person, who would receive some goods from society without duly sharing in the work would be a parasite living to the detriment of others."

Naturally, in all of their elements the socialist morals are also a fighting standpoint against opposing principles and practices whether they concern work, or the struggle against exploitation, or attitudes and standpoints opposing international solidarity. The programme underlines the following battle fronts: "The party regards the struggle conducted against manifestations of the bourgeois ideology and morals, the vestiges of the spirit of private ownership, and the struggle against superstitions and prejudices as an organic part of communist educational work."

It is also natural that the recognition and the expression of the validity of the development of socialist morals proceeds in Hungary on a course similar to that of the Soviet Union. Allow me to quote here a few details that are particularly deserving attention. The resolution of the 8th Congress emphasized the "assertion of the norms of socialist morals in public and private life and a consistent ideological struggle against the bourgeois and petit bourgeois ideologies." The resolution expecially underlines the role of socialist brigades, which "express the socialist consciousness and the leading role of the working class in shaping socialist work and the socialist mode of life and morals." Finally and in close connection with the debate in question a point concerning the interpretation of the party-mindedness of literature and art was raised in the closing address: "We talk of party-mindedness here in the sense that when the socialist and the capitalist systems clash over a question, then we should stand on the side of the socialist society."

The practice of the actual social assertion of the moral principles outlined cannot, however, be characterized as simply as the implementation of the principles of economic policy. We have to see that the latter can be asserted by the means of the state's economic policy, therefore it is easy to trace them, while the socialist morals gain (or fail to gain) expression in various situations of social life, thus their tracing requires a far greater amount of information with particular respect to economic policy and the rise of the standard of living.

3

Once we insist upon a more precise definition and are not satisfied with such general and hazy terms as "culture and mode of life", the essence of the recent dispute could be expressed in this: how is the standard of living developing in Hungarian society, what trends can be observed, what cultural, moral and political problems have to be coped with.

The problems which emerge in the present phase of our development are numerous and varied. If we pick out only the most disputed ones, we must discuss the following:

— the rise of the standard of living and its sources;
— the subjective side of the standard of living;
— the assertion of socialist morals;
— and finally: the rise of the standard of living and the question of political development.

a) *The rise of the standard of living* is evidenced in Hungary by statistical averages, the observations of foreign observers, but also and obviously in the directly known life circumstances of everybody's own relatives and acquaintances. Thanks to the increase of travelling abroad, many people also have a basis to compare the Hungarian standard of living with that in other socialist countries and with that of various capitalist countries. And that comparison is generally not really unfavourable.

Before we would argue about the worries felt about the rise of the standard of living it will be useful to examine the objective features of the Hungarian standard of living a bit more closely.

The real income of the population calculated either per worker, or per capita has been steadily and significantly increasing in recent years, even if not at a very fast rate. Although there is no actual figure about the subsistence level, empiric observation suggests that only a very small proportion of the people of Hungary is blighted with problems of elementary existence or suffers need in meeting these. And behind most of such cases one would find special personal, family or geographical reasons. And similarly, the stratum of the Hungarian society, which can easily afford to spend on luxuries, is also vary narrow—it is perhaps even narrower than the formerly mentioned stratum.

Most people in Hungarian society live at a "relatively satisfactory" standard. If there are more children in the family they have to spread their income more thinly, if a family spends a little more on food and clothing then they have little or nothing left for other necessities, and those, who are determined to effect some major investment, to build a house or to buy a car must do so at the expense of cutting down on everything else. And those, who want to attain a relatively higher standard of living at any cost, must work very hard, and make sure that each able-bodied member of their family works hard, too.

How should we appraise the standard attained? We must see in it the greatest achievement of the socialist building work, for it means in essence that extreme poverty has ceased to exist in Hungary and everyone can make a decent living with honest work. Yet even if we find the progress so far pleasing, we must not be satisfied with it. We have made a great advance in food and clothing provision, but we should think about how much work, investment and effort are still needed before everybody will have a modern home, and how far the national income must still be increased to ensure that the public utilities and amenities reduce the everyday problems of the household chores to a desirable level. And we should particularly think about how much more the standard of living must rise to ensure the satisfaction of the higher grade cultural needs!

But let us have a look at *the sources* of the rise of the standard of living.

We often forget that the standard of living already attained is to a considerable degree due to *social sources,* perhaps because we are used to this and consider it natural. Participation in the national income beyond the extent of the pay-envelop is also important for the reason that it is general, and because in this connection worries about the rise of the standard of living do not even occur.

There are many and varied sources of social income:

— there is a reasonably broad sphere of completely free social services, such as the major part of the public health services, basic level education, most of the trade courses, the duty-free availability of most of the administrative procedures, the free use of public institutions etc.;

— nominal fees are charged for a considerable part of the services, therefore those, who avail themselves of them receive social contribution; these include publicly owned homes, mass-transport, canteen meals, organized holidays, the majority of cultural services etc.;

— and there is also a great variety of special allowances, such as additional bonuses and favours due to people doing work that involves above-average risk to health, maternity allowances, old-age pensions etc.

Amongst the *individual sources* of the standard of living the main one is

377

naturally what people derive from their principal employment. The supplementary sources of income in addition to people's basic earnings also play a considerable role. Everyone knows that these have a great variety:

— payment for additional quantity or quality work in the form of overtime payment and bonuses;

— rewards for inventions and innovations;

— household farm allowance to members of cooperative farms;

— second jobs, part-time jobs and special assignments;

— finally the possibility of winning at recognized games of chance.

(According to the representative survey of the Central Statistical Institute in 1960, the various supplementary and occasional incomes amounted to 18.2 per cent of the total income in worker and white-collar worker families, and to 11.9 per cent if pensions, family allowances, education allowances and scholarships are excluded.)

These sources together enable the overwhelming majority of members of our society to live decently on what they earn with their principal job; and a smaller stratum of the population is able to attain an above-average standard of living either with overtime or with extra work, with outstanding individual diligence or ability—disregarding now the really exceptional cases of gains by trickery and at games of chance.

b) The participants of the debate had, however, misgivings about the *subjective aspects* of the standard of living, and this was quite justified. The question is how do the general possibility for and actual attainment of a higher standard of living appear in the minds of people; in other words, would this not give rise to the dominance of the "petit bourgeois view of life" morally as well as culturally?

The question is justified and the answer is unambiguous: the rise of the standard of living does inevitably produce this danger, therefore we must fight against this danger with all our power. The essence of the question is *how*?

Let us take the *cultural danger* first. Not that this is the lesser, but because it is milder in form and easier to tolerate considering the vital interests of socialist society.

As regards the cultural danger, this has a side that must be regarded as an infantile disorder of the rise of the standard of living, therefore we must be patient with it. People who can for the first time buy some better furniture, some pictures, books, go to the theatre, get a television set, travel etc. cannot be expected to have the cultural standard and the taste to unfailingly distinguish between genuine beauty and kitsch, the inherently fine and the cheap imitation, the higher standard and the lower one.

Furthermore, these are not the sort of simple questions for which it would be easy to define the right decisions and generally applicable yardsticks in social dimensions or at the level of the leading bodies.

It is necessary, though, to fight against the evident dangers and to fight

378

even more as the standard of living rises, for the possibility of putting a curb on the rise of the standard of living must in any case be excluded. Fortunately, there is already a particularly effective means, which evolved in the socialist countries and can be used under all sorts of circumstances: making people acquainted with the classic works of the national cultures and world culture. This surely is the heaviest and most effective weapon against the possible dominance of shallow pseudo-culture, kitsch, and the "petit-bourgeois taste". Appreciation of peasant folk culture, the cultivation of its traditions, is another important element of the cultural policy of the socialist countries. (Unfortunately, some elements of our cultural policy increase this danger, yet they are neither the most important, nor the durable ones.)

The *moral problem* is greater, however. The danger that the pursuit of higher earnings and the endeavour to acquire and accumulate material goods become dominant or permanent even under the social conditions of socialism is made realistic by the rise of the standard of living in general and by the various sources of a rising living standard.

Since this danger is very real, and overcoming it is a vital issue of socialism, we must use careful circumspection when approaching this problem to be sure that nothing that belongs to the essence of the matter is overlooked.

First we should ask: what are the things on which people cannot spend the income they earned under the conditions of our socialist society. They are the means of production, more precisely such means of production as would make the exploitation of other people's labour possible. This is a fundamental difference from capitalism, limiting the pursuit of income, the making of money-making one's dominant purpose in life with material force. Nevertheless, this has a negative side-effect also: it does not encourage savings, indeed it opens the way for irresponsible management of incomes and goods, which often leads to exaggerated claims for social assistance.

Secondly: is there a limit to individual incomes and to goods obtainable by them? The limit set in the constitution is the major means of production, the operation of which requires the labour of two or more people. Within this limit, however, society approves the spending of earnings and incomes on a family house, or a privately owned flat, a holiday or week-end house, garden, car, boat, home furnishing, cultural investments, and savings book. Incomes or making money beyond these or even enabling one to accumulate a greater number of goods provokes social protest, which is an obvious sign that socialism is in the making not only in the objective production relations, but also in people's minds. And let us add that similar social protest is evident when the earnings of some strata or groups stay below the socially necessary minimum for objective reasons.

Thirdly: the income conditions of the great majority are still well within the limit where they could pass the extent of acquisition permissible in socialist society. Indeed, incomes must still rise very much to permit a general access to the basic standard demanded by a higher standard of living. (According to the 1960 representative survey of the Central Statistical Office, the total of average per capita income—including earners and dependants—is below 1,000 Ft per month for 73–6 per cent of the population, betwen 1,000–2,000 Ft for 24.9 per cent, and above 2,000 Ft for 1.5 per cent.)

Fourthly: what is the actual spending-pattern of those, who have money left after they covered their fundamental needs? The variations could be grouped as follows:

— some people "live up" the surplus: they spend it on food, drinks, clothing, amenities, entertainment, travel etc.;

— others would spend it to satisfy their higher cultural needs: books, music, collecting works of art, fine furniture, higher education of children etc.;

— and finally some accumulate or invest the surplus in major items: a house, a privately owned flat, block of land, holiday home, car etc.

The question is what actual tendencies assert themselves in these alternatives and what social policy trends could be traced in this respect? This is not an easy problem, since each of these tendencies is typical in reality, and both valuable, progressive socialist values and selfish, individualistic bourgeois–petit-bourgeois deviations contrary to social interests are found in them. Perhaps the fairest way to find the general yardstick is to view the standard of life not only from the material side, but equally from the material and cultural aspect as the 22nd Congress did. Considering it this way, the "living it up" and "accumulation" can be approved or condemned depending on whether it furthers cultural progress or not. And going beyond that, the issue should be approached from socialist morals. It should be considered whether these attitudes serve a selfish, individualistic aim in life and personal affluence contrary to social interests, or the purpose of higher culture, increased qualifications, ultimately the furthering of social progress in harmony with the social interests?

Fifthly: in meeting their needs how far are people dependent of *finding the means while "paddling their own canoe"* under the current social conditions? Health services and education at the basic level are almost completely financed from social funds, but the proportion of individual contributions is also considerable. In the earlier period rent and higher education were also financed from the social account, but by now the better part of these must be met through individual efforts. And there is also a tendency that people should satisfy their needs concerning transport, holidays, travelling abroad, and cultural services from individual and family sources in a growing measure.

After summing up what has been said in the above, we find the following picture:

— a certain part of the fundamental needs (health services, basic level

380

education etc.) is already *generally provided by society* at the present stage of our socialist building work, while the greater part of these needs (home, transport, higher education etc.) must be financed *from individual efforts, personal and family sources*;

— endeavouring to secure higher incomes is a justified, objective necessity for this reason too;

— the laws and social evaluation of socialist society limit the increase of incomes and the acquisition of material possessions only in definite and extreme instances (acquisition of the means of production which could provide a possibility for exploitation, incomes without work, blatantly luxurious mode of living etc.);

— and last but not least the problems of the upper limit of the acquisition of incomes are confined to a narrow stratum of our society, while the principal problem of the great majority of this society is to meet the fundamental needs.

Well, the social problems of the rise of the standard of living, amongst them notably also the moral dangers it holds should be considered with attention paid to these circumstances, too. And once we set out from this, then a conclusion that the rise of the standard of living should be condemned, or even limited, or that the social, cultural, moral and political problems emerging in the wake of a rising standard of living could be considered a sort of decline, social malady, let alone condemnation of the policy asserted in our country cannot be supported by anything. Nothing justifies such standpoints. On the contrary, we must consider these symptoms as inevitable concomitants of a healthy and right progress and even if we must condemn and fight some of the phenomena, the whole of the social process itself can only be approved.

Let us see the major dangers.

First let us take the one, which has the deepest roots in history: *the attitudes of the private proprietor,* the danger of the revival, strengthening or even spreading of the bourgeois–petit-bourgeois mentality. Such a danger exists, and it is not a minor one. Indeed, this danger is so real that we must fight against it with the greatest vigour in every possible way. But how? The simplest way would be to eliminate the objective opportunities of this process. But that would be tantamount to the discontinuation of all individual retail and trade activity as well as the prohibition of household farming of the members of cooperative farms, and individual plots in the communal farms, strong limitation of patent and copyrights, the discontinu-ation of semi-private restaurants etc. This is not only historically impossible, but would also cause immeasurable political and economic damage, therefore fighting in this way against the otherwise obvious dangers is simply out of the question. The struggle against the growth of such tendencies must be waged under the existing conditions. Undoubtedly, this is the harder way, but the only realistic one. It is also certain that the struggle will be long and difficult, yet there is no way to avoid it. Each of the seven heads of the dragon must be struck off, it is not enough to keep the dragon out of the garden.

The other frequent symptom is the proliferation of *selfish individualism,* the pursuit of personal prosperity. This tendency is not exceptional, it is evident in all walks of life, not infrequently amongst executives and leaders in various positions. "Bonus-centredness", enterprise chauvinism, the enchantment of having a car or a business entertainment account at one's disposal, manipulation with sham results, the hideous criticism of rivals are variations of this theme. The objective exclusion of these dangers is beyond the dreams of imagination. There is no effective law or resolution that would preclude the possibility of such dangers. Efficient fight against them is limited to organized and individually pointed social action, encouragement of good examples and condemnation of the bad ones. And there is one other matter we must not forget: this danger is real and threatening not only when the standard of living is rising, and not only under social conditions established by a more democratic policy but also when the situation is just the opposite, when only its forms differ.

Thus, provided we weigh both the objective and the subjective sides of the rise of the standard of living, and compare the two seriously, we cannot fail to arrive at a very clear conclusion: we must fully approve the socialist economic policy which gave rise to the standard of living, and solve the problems that emerge in the wake of this rise not by the reversal of this economic policy, but by its further development simultaneously with the strengthening of the general socialist social policy.

Therefore, the unmistakable expression of socialist morals and the patient, many-sided, stable and consistent fight for its general assertion in society play decisive roles.

c) In contrast to the misgivings expressed in the dispute, *the social assertion of socialist morals* is the great question to which we must find the answer in order to highlight the prospects and tasks of progress.

However, one cannot step off the map of history in this respect either. We face here a very lengthy and toilsome historic process, in which the surviving vestiges of earlier eras, ideas about the future, influences of the outer world and most of all the consequences of material and economic progress are intertwined. Should we disregard these, our deliberations on the matter would be empty moralizing, an aimless verbiage of an empty moral sermon.

Therefore, let us consider first present-day social morals in the various strata; we should point out to what extent the old traditional views of life are still living realities, and to what extent they have been replaced by a new set of values. Detailed sociographic surveys are just beginning to explore the relevant data, but certain estimates are also possible on the basis of subjective observations.

Perhaps the most general finding is that the morals, views of life of every

382

old class of our society still live on in some form, although naturally some are withering away and others became component parts of the new moral rules of the socialist society to greatly varying degrees.

Understandably, it is the moral traditions of the *old classes* which have been preserved to the smallest extent. Yet they do not perish without a trace. They continue to live not only in the declassed underworld, the upsurge of which was evident during the periods of counter-revolution, but their general influence upon broad strata is also manifest. One of these, to be sure, is the *contempt for manual work*. However odd it is, in the socio-political system of socialism, when the worker–peasant alliance holds the power, broad strata of society believe that "getting rid of" manual work is tantamount to a rise on the social ladder; and there is a general tendency of fleeing from manual work. Undoubtedly, other factors also play a role in this, but the survival of the old "gentlemanly" attitudes to life has to be taken into account, too.

The capitalist bourgeois class did not disappear without a trace from the stage of history either. Assessing individuals and families on the basis of their money income, boasting of above average incomes, showing off and attempts to influence people with money are all remnants of the past.

The survival of the moral attitudes of *petit-bourgeois strata* is understandably far more extensive. The attitudes of the private entrepreneur, the elevation of hoarding to a life goal, the selfish chauvinism of personal affluence contradicting social interests are all social characteristics developed in the petit-bourgeois class situation; these attitudes have not ceased to have an impact on broad strata of society.

Peasant morals are a separate question. The class situation of the small-scale producer peasant is naturally of petit-bourgeois character and the social consciousness and moral attitudes developed on that basis are also similar. However, there is a substantial difference consisting in a moral attitude to work. While in the petit-bourgeois consciousness work is a necessary evil and a means of getting ahead, and breaking free from it as soon as possible brings social appreciation, in the traditional peasant attitudes well-done work is the general yardstick of human integrity; those who do not work may win social distinction, yet they lose some human respectability.

Work was the central motive, the fundamental yardstick in the attitudes, customs and moral rules of the peasantry manifested in various ways depending on class situation. Naturally, these features of peasant society evolved in the feudal era, and originally they were intertwined with its exploited class situation, and underwent modification under capitalist conditions according to the fact whether the peasants owned any land or they were landless poor. In the post-war years and in the course of the socialist transformation, however, the general moral attitudes including work ethic changed simultaneously with the radical change in the class structure. Today the old peasant work morals (unlimited working time, acceptance of hard working conditions, lack of aversion to manual work etc.) are mostly characteristic of the older generations. The younger generations increasingly insist on fixed working time, more civilized working conditions, standard wages, freedom from hard manual work and on undisturbed free time.

In *the working class* the moral rules that had evolved in productive work and political activity continue to dominate and in fact became the foundation of generally accepted moral norms of our socialist society. The surviving elements of this system, however, are not simply a continuation of the old motives; there has been a substantial change in attitudes. Readiness to take part in politics, the acceptance of technological progress and pride in workmanship continued also as traditions, but there are also new motives: a higher grade of social consciousness and political responsibility mark changes in the right direction, while the spread of petit-bourgeois attitudes to material prosperity and "easy living" signify adverse changes.

The traditions of *the professional classes and white-collar workers* also deserve attention. While the intertwinement of the old professional classes with the bourgeoisie and the remnants of the feudal privileged classes was general, a certain special professional culture and morals still developed in numerous professional and white-collar occupations where expertise made certain standards obligatory. In the various professional and white-collar fields these did not wither away, and are still indispensable constituting elements of professional training and responsibility.

Even the conclusion can be drawn from this cursory review that old moral traditions give a very considerable impetus to the general development of the new socialist morals. We saw that they are very much alive and assert their influence; therefore their valuable elements must be consciously relied upon also in socialism having a higher standard of living. The old moral traditions of the working class but also substantial elements of the morality of the peasantry and the professional classes have a valuable influence. At the same time, we must fight more vigorously against the survival of a great number of feudal, bourgeois and petit-bourgeois moral attitudes.

But where is the most important section of the front, where is the decisive battle to be waged and where can victory be achieved against the vestiges of the old world as well as the influence of the present capitalist world? Undoubtedly, we have to fight against the old morality in the sphere of work; the pivotal question of socialist morality is a deep-going change in the work ethic.

The fundamental moral norm of socialist work ethic and the highest human dimension of man to be achieved in his relation to work was accurately described by Marx, and this was enriched by further ideas in the programme of the 22nd congress of the CPSU. In *The Critique of the Gotha Programme* Marx pointed out that communism will be realized, when labour will be not

384

only the means of livelihood, but also the principal necessity of life. And this basic precept was further elaborated in the programme passed by the 22nd congress of the CPSU: "... owing to the change of the character of labour, the development of technology and on a high level of consciousness an inner necessity develops in each member of society to work voluntarily and according to talents for the benefit of society... work will not be a mere means of life, it will be transformed into a genuine creative activity from which happiness springs forth."

The joy of creative work, the reason and the objective of human life realized in work is naturally not an invention of communists. This principle had already been realized frequently in the history of civilized mankind and in the lives of some people, and the secrets, excitement, noble human pains and joys of such a life were also manifested in various ways by scientists, writers and artists let alone the fact that workers, craftsmen, peasants and intellectual workers have lived such lives for generations. *Yet this yardstick has never before become a law of society* and an objective of life dominant in the minds of people. It was socialism, communism, which for the first time set this as a realistic aim for mankind.

Thus this human-social programme as the expression of the objective of individual human lives and the reason of social progress is new in history, and the laying of its socio-economic foundations appeared on the stage of history also with the emergence of socialism. The religions (Jewish, Christian, and Mohammedan alike) set a sharply opposite picture of the world to their followers: man lost the happiness of Paradise, freedom from work, and since then he must earn his living with the sweat of his brow; but man should find solace in the life to come, where the faithful will again win the happiness of life without work.

And what was and still is the moral law of the capitalist world, the capitalist ideal that dominates the minds of the masses there? It is achieving richness, getting rid of the necessity of work, making other people work and the enjoyment of the "happiness" of consumerism and living from one's capital and its profits.

This attitude to life was replaced by socialism, by the prospect that men can be really human and happy only in its work; the socio-economic conditions of this higher-level life can be achieved in the period of historic progress that faces us.

The science of historical materialism also recognized that the acceptance of these morals and the realization of its general social assertion cannot be achieved without struggle. This can only be won by the masses of working people, workers and peasants by overthrowing the power of the exploiting classes and by giving statutory effect to their own morals and world outlook, forcing back the morals of the old world step by step.

A great variety of weapons can and must be used in the battle for giving statutory effect to socialist morals and for forcing back the morals of the old

385

world, but it must be kept in mind that this war will be very long, and the forces of socialism must fight from their entrenched positions in order to occasionally launch successful attacks. While the overthrow of the capitalist power and the socialization of the means of production can be linked to splendid historic dates, the victory of the socialist work ethic and the transformation of the minds can only be achieved through long struggles in which every weekday, every Sunday, every job situation and every opportunity outside work are all very important.

Let us review some of the major sections of the front and a few of their characteristics as examples.

First we should consider *school education*. Workshop practice at school is one of the essential means of educating children to work and through work. Anyone believing that this in itself is already sufficient for the acquisition of the socialist work ethic would make a grave mistake. Many methodical questions of pedagogy must still be solved to make the education of young people really effective.

As a second field we must consider *literature and the arts*. Do we already have works, which explore the greatest human-social problem of the necessity and freedom of work also presenting new solutions? Personally, I know only a very few. And I am convinced that the decisive features of the literature and art of socialism are not manifested in the artistic forms, but the representation of a new world outlook.

We must also mention the world of work. Members of our society spend the overwhelming part of their lives on the job; this is the concrete world, where the people's attitude to work and to life is essentially decided. We should ask ourselves to what extent we are aware of this and we should also consider our perspective to change the world of work. The role and significance of the socialist brigades are recognized. However, working conditions and their sociological, administrative, work-psychological and health aspects are still largely unexplored. We still need very much research in order to make realistic and efficient steps in the world of work. We must devote new energies to the scientific research of work because all over the capitalist world the human factors of work are the subject of thorough research, albeit research is being carried on in the interest of capitalism.

Finally let us have a look at people's *free time*. People spend half of their life away from work, and their free time also shapes their attitude to work and it is also the decisive factor of their whole view of life. What opportunities are offered to people to spend their lesure time? We can already organize recreation in many ways, and mostly rather well. But what are we offering as the purpose of free time? Our social conditions are still raw and rudimentary in this field. Thus far the social norms of social gatherings, "cultured entertainment", or refined pastime activities have not developed yet, and what is worse, this development does not even have trends. Under the existing circumstances, unfortunately, the vestiges of the

386

old world and the fashions coming from the capitalist world determine the way people's leisure time is being spent. Most leisure time activities are contrary to the socialist work ethic and binding people to old ideals.

The uneasiness and worry of the debaters about these issues is completely justified. But those, who would prefer to stop or slow down the rise of the standard of living are wrong and not following a progressive line. The same applies to those who would like to forget the principle of material incentives and limit the assertion of individual initiative. On the other hand, the impatience of those, who urge cultural activity and the rational development of social activities in addition to an actually asserted and right economic policy, is fully justified.

4

Finally we should also discuss, summing up the issue in a way, whether the momentum of socialist building work would or would not necessarily fall in the wake of rising living standards. The question was not put straight in the literary debate, but uneasiness on this point is very often expressed in discussions, and quite a few people answer the question in the affirmative.

It is, however, impossible to deal with the question in such a summary way, and neither is it possible to arrive at such an unambiguous answer. Such a danger undoubtedly exists, but that is a concomitant of development which is necessarily coupled with the welcome and on the whole approvable rise in the standard of living. The issue can be approached from several aspects. However, the only policy that must not be considered is the reversal of progress. That is what we expounded in the foregoing.

Nevertheless, the question has another side also. What has actually furthered social progress and the building of socialism better: is it propaganda organized from the top and managed by way of slogans and administrative means, or a less spectacular policy which also took into account the initiative of various strata, individuals and groups paying due attention to their views and interests? Undoubtedly, we have achieved lasting results, the actual solution of social problems and a profound development much better by way of the latter method. Indeed, this latter method was not so spectacular, not so "well-disciplined", nevertheless it meant more than that because it shaped actual social progress influencing both interpersonal relations and the people's attitudes. For that very reason, this latter method has a much more lasting effect.

Let me give just one example from the field I know the best. In the previous period of the organization of the cooperative farms, and the socialist large-scale agricultural units we almost completely ignored the members' attitudes making a genuine cooperation impossible with them. What were the consequences of this policy? We achieved a real consolidation in the organization of farming and in the adjustment of the members to the common work only with great difficulty and in fact only at a few places. In the next period, however, having relied also on the membership and the leaders elected by them, socialist agriculture was built more quickly and far more extensively. Although the "compromises" ouf our agricultural policy are resented by many people, the building proceeded on better and firmer foundations and most of all in such a way that more and more people became committed to the cooperatives, because they had a say in their organization.

Is that not a momentum? I believe it is; indeed, this is the genuine one, which did not get realized according to some far-fetched idea but by a conscious policy and the mobilization of the masses. It is true enough that there are still many phenomena against which we have to fight quite fiercely. However, this fight must not be carried on in a way that we turn back the rise of the standard of living itself, and the endeavours and initiatives of individual people, but rather by fighting against various dangers in the course of a healthy progress achieving socialism step by step, in the way Attila József, Hungary's famous poet put it:

"Until our beautiful ability,
order comes to light,
by which the mind conceives
the finite infinite,
the forces of production out there
and the instincts in here..."

FERENC ERDEI —
PORTRAIT OF A SOCIOLOGIST

BY TIBOR HUSZÁR

Ferenc Erdei was born in Makó in 1910. His parents were burgher-peasants. He graduated at the law faculty of the István Tisza University in the city of Szeged.

His career has been irregular in all respects. He joined the movements of the progressive intellectuals and already at the age of twenty-two had become one of their most influential personalities. He published a number of monographs between 1936 and 1944 (excerpts of these can be found in this volume) though from 1938 on, despite his being a Doctor of Law, he made his living as a farmer in a small village on the island of Csepel in order to uphold his intellectual independence.

After World War II, he was elected member of the Provisional National Government as the representative of his native town. From December 1944 he had an important role in the implementation of the land reform and the reorganization of public administration as the Minister of the Interior of the first democratic government. In the autumn of 1945 he left the government but retained a leading post in the National Peasant Party. Following the socialist change and the elimination of the multi-party system between 1948 and 1956, he held various offices as minister: he has been minister without portfolio, head of a number of departments and for a short time he even worked as deputy prime minister. In these years, particularly between 1949 and 1953, he published very little and he was less visible as a scholar.

The stormy events of 1956 induced Ferenc Erdei to reevaluate critically his past career.

In the spring of 1957 he travelled all alone in the country for some months visiting mainly the country-towns of the Great Plain which had inspired his works of early youth. He decided to face the painful consequences of a policy which he had endorsed, particularly in the field of agrarian policy, not only because of considerations of *Realpolitik*. Many of the consequences of this policy were against his wishes and theoretical ideas. For Erdei who wanted to serve first of all the improvement of the conditions of the Hungarian peasantry both as a scientist and politician this roaming over the country must certainly have been a veritable descent to hell. However, he went through this painful exercise because he believed in the possibility of renewal.

Though he has been one of the crucial personalities in the policy of alliance — which had such an outstanding importance in the strategy of the Hungarian Socialist Workers' Party (HSWP) following 1956 at the time of consolidation—he mostly devoted his energies to research and to the organizing of research activities. The scope of problems he was engaged in seems to be astoundingly broad. By his research work he wanted to serve the practice of the agrarian policy of the HSWP, the development of a new model of cooperatives based on the specific Hungarian conditions and at the same time overcoming the sectarian errors of the past. This model successfully combined the possibilities of the peasants' expertise, the household plots, entrepreneurial skill and the large-scale cooperative farms which have become the dominant feature of the sixties. The theoretical works and practical activities of Ferenc Erdei have greatly contributed to the elaboration of this model of economic policy. He was one of the foremost inspirers, and contributors to the new-type and practically tested agrarian policy.

It seems clear from the above that although he held important positions in public life over these years, too, the scientific aspects became more pronounced in his activity. He was elected Corresponding Member of the Hungarian Academy of Sciences in 1948, and Member of the Academy in 1951. From 1958 on right until his death he was—with some short interruptions—the Secretary General of the Academy as well.

This short epilogue cannot attempt to give a comprehensive evaluation of the whole oeuvre and especially of the activities of Ferenc Erdei as a politician. We are going to try to help the adequate interpretation of the excerpts taken from monographies and studies by tracing the evolution of the ideas on society, the views on science and the methodological principles of Erdei the sociologist.

*

Even if only roughly outlined, a picture of the career of Erdei the sociologist can only be authentic and comprehensible for foreign readers as well if the antecedents of Sociology in Hungary are briefly outlined first. Sociology has developed in Hungary later than in Western Europe or the United States and its first significant representatives were leaders of opposition movements of the intelligentsia.

Apart from the reform experiments of the conservative social politicians, it was in the works of legal scientists where the problems of sociology have first been scientifically posed. Professors of the Budapest University, first Ágost Pulszky and following in his footsteps Gyula J. Pikler broke with the dominant ideas of the philosophy of law of those times and popularized at the university the achievements of evolutionist sociology. A similar course was followed at the Kolozsvár law-school by Bódog Somló, a young and at that time fairly unknown professor of the philosophy of law. Their views were rejected by official academic circles but became the political creed for the scientific argumentation of the radical middle-class intellectual youth. Due to the historical peculiarities of Hungarian social structure, the scientific impulse did not result in the institutionalization of sociology but it stimulated a theoretical discourse of bourgeois radical character. To further the elaboration of *scientific* policy, this movement regarded as its prime task the stimulation of debates, the call for social political measures, the systematical study of social illnesses, "the discovery of Hungary"—as defined by Oszkár Jászi, the outstanding representative of this movement.[1]

The *theoretical* results of the movement are highly significant. These results had a

---

[1] Oszkár Jászi: "Tíz év" (Ten Years) In: *A szociológia első magyar műhelye* (The First Workshop of Hungarian Sociology). Two Volumes. Gondolat, Budapest 1973, Vol. I., pp. 94—107.

392

considerable role in making the public aware that the economic and political positions of the traditional feudal ruling stratum had been only partly restricted by bourgeois social development in Hungary and as a consequence, both the economic structure and the political system could be defined only as the symbiosis of feudalism and capitalism combining feudal and bourgeois values in a peculiar way. Despite their declared liberalism, the historical-traditional leading strata of Hungary did not promote fully the development of bourgeois democracy, i.e. the extension of suffrage, the secrecy of ballot, the settling of the problems of national and ethnic minorities on the basis of a general consensus, the democratization of public education, etc.

Empirical surveys, too, were conducted by the middle-class radical sociologists: Robert Braun took part in the comparative survey of W. I. Thomas studying the psychology of villages; the significant social characteristics of the working class were analyzed by Jenő Varga and those of the lawyers by Pál Szende on the basis of socio-statistical data.[2]

The movement was not homogeneous, its members belonged to different schools of thought. However, the radicalization of all its representatives inevitably accelerated with the sharpening of contradictions, and all of those who had remained faithful to the ideas and tenets of bourgeois radicalism at the beginning of World War I, took leading roles in the revolution of October 1918 and the most radical ones in the Hungarian Councils' Republic of 1919. Following the victory of the counter-revolution many of them were driven into exile. (Oszkár Jászi and Károly Polányi continued their scientific activities in the United States, Pál Szende in Austria, Jenő Varga and Elek Bolgár in the Soviet Union.)

From the point of view of the history of sociology in Hungary, or more specifically of the historical conditions of the start of Erdei's career these events were significant in two respects. Since the first theoreticians of Hungarian sociology were among the leading personalities of the two revolutions, for the counter-revolutionary regime sociology itself has compromised itself. Overrating the assumed or real points of contact of politics and science the regime either traced a direct relationship between them or disregarding the essential differences it approached all those scientific schools of thought which attributed similar characteristics to social and physical laws in a similar way. Thus in rather a strange way both positivism and Marxism were disapproved of and branded as *materialistic* theories. To counterbalance this, the establishment supported the schools of thought based on the *history of ideas* and the historiographical and ethnographical schools which justified and reinforced the demands to claim back former Hungarian territories, which were lost after the Trianon Peace Treaty. Not independently of this judgement, the historically obviously differing trends—reflecting different class contents—of liberalism, radicalism, socialism and communism were also treated in a uniform way, as official spokesmen pointed out time and again: liberalism had cleared the way for

[2] Róbert Braun: "A falu lélektana" (The Psychology of the Village) In: *A szociológia első magyar műhelye,* Gondolat, Budapest 1973, pp. 277—352; E. Varga: "Die Lage des industriellen Proletariats in Ungarn" *Die Neue Zeit,* 1918, Vol. II, pp. 305—317; Pál Szende: "A magyar ügyvédség válsága" (The Crisis of Hungary's Lawyers) In: *Értelmiségszociológiai írások Magyarországon* (Studies in the Sociology of Intellectuals in Hungary), Gondolat, Budapest, 1983, pp. 262—289.

radicalism, it had become the trail-blazer of socialism, whereas the latter has legitimized "communism". This explains the fact that of all the opposition movements the political regime granted a legal scope of activity only to the right-wing, so-called national radical trends, and at the same time it legitimized in its political ideology the leading role of various neo-conservative, autocratic-conservative trends.

This explains why sociology was unable to become institutionalized in the decades between the two World Wars and/or why it could achieve but temporary acceptance only in some special fields regarded as marginal ones at that time. Thus it got established in jurisprudence, in research areas related to the study of the effectiveness of legal norms, to updating public administration as well in the activities of some of the representatives of historical scholarship who rejected the theory of the history of ideas. It should be mentioned but briefly that Barna Horváth—an outstanding scholar of the sociology of law—was the professor of Ferenc Erdei at Szeged University. At the end of the thirties in the Institute for Regional and Ethnographical Research Erdei had established personal relationship with Zoltán Magyary directing the first empirical studies in Hungary on the problems of efficient public administration. He also had close creative connections with István Hajnal, professor and head of department at the Budapest University at the turn of the thirties and forties who worked on the problems of relationship between history and sociology.

At the same time, some more open-minded leaders and intellectual exponents of the counterrevolutionary regime were fully aware that the social contradictions which had led to the revolutionary events of 1918 and 1919 were still unsolved. Moreover, following the years of the Peace Treaty of Trianon, as a result of which the country had lost two-thirds of its former territory, these social tensions continued to be even more serious problems. A partial land reform leaving the economic positions of the big estates virtually intact had not essentially altered the plight of the agrarian labourers and smallholders whose number was unparalleled even by East-Central European standards. (There were 4.6 million people engaged in agriculture who had no land at all or had less than five acres, and they made up 67.4 per cent of the peasant population of the country.)

Owing to the structural conditions of the country, the land reform was rightly considered the central question but at the same time, the ruling classes jealously guarding their prerogatives did not undertake anything to solve this problem *in merito*. Moreover in the years of the great depression—i.e. at the time when Ferenc Erdei started out on his career—the conditions of the above-mentioned peasant strata deteriorated markedly: owing to low prices and high taxes almost half of all agricultural holdings (in the case of farms under 5 acres the figure amounted to 53 per cent) were tottering under the burden of debts.

Official policy propagating the revision of the national borders of Hungary as a panacea was well aware of the fact that the social situation of the village and particularly of the peasants constituted potential dynamite and therefore it was compelled to work out an ideological alternative for the young intelligentsia susceptible to radical ideas. The stylization of peasant life, the overstressing of the traditionalist function of the peasantry, the strengthening of the ethnographical approach, and—where it was considered justified—the organization of rural communal activities were the main components of such ideology.

The government—guided by such values—gave extensive support to the rural sociologist and village study groups of university students. Erdei could closely observe the problems of peasant life in his early youth; no wonder that he had written his first major paper as an essay submitted to the competition *Off to the village!* advertised by the Bartha Miklós Society. He was twenty-three and wrote about the social conditions of Királyhegyes, the village where his maternal grandparents lived.[3] During his university years he also joined the "Gábor Bethlen agrarian community movement".

These movements, however, did not develop according to the intentions of the government. Due to the world-wide economic recession, social contradictions and conflicts became more accentuated, and the young intellectuals—faced with unemployment—became increasingly radical minded. In contrast to conservative folklore, it was sociography which gained prominence and became *the decisive form and genre of empirical social studies* between 1934 and 1938.

Sociography has not been an exclusively Hungarian "genre": the Romanian school of thought led by Gusti had several Hungarian followers, while some other sociographical team-works showed definite affinity with the American community studies. Nevertheless, Hungarian sociography between the two World Wars was of a very peculiar nature: the most outstanding works of sociography—written in a variety of style—were closely connected with the progressive political *movements of the intelligentsia,* and they became sort of programme documents of that movement.

The representative works of sociography were stylistically varied. There were some so-called *literary sociographies* of classical value which can be definitely traced to the *fact literature* of that period. Most well-known of these has been *The People of the Plains* by Gyula Illyés. There were no traces of literary fiction in these works; the authors regarded the description of social facts as their task tackling, however, facts not conceptually but depicting sociologically relevant types and life-like situations in a highly sophisticated and intuitive way.

The other characteristic form of Hungarian sociography of that period is a variety of *reporting.* These works are sociographies because they are based on historical and statistical preliminary studies and also because facts observed personally fall into a monographic pattern. At the same time, stresses are often shifted in these works according to political objectives; exacting conceptual care, the strict control of the hypothesis cannot be considered a genre characteristics of these works. Nevertheless the representative books of this type—e.g. *Stormy Corner* by Géza Féja or *Silent Revolution* by Imre Kovács—should be regarded on good grounds as parts of the progressive traditions: owing to their suggestively and subjectively perceived and described factual material, they become *political indictments* of the ruling strata of Horthy-Hungary upholding many feudal requisites.

The so-called *scientific sociographies*[4] by Ferenc Erdei and Zoltán Szabó are of quite another genre. Their works are characterized first of all by sociological

[3] Ferenc Erdei: "Királyhegyes művelődés-gazdasági és társadalmi rajza" (The Cultural, Economic and Social Picture of Királyhegyes) *Századunk,* 1931, No. 1.

[4] Gyula Illyés: *Puszták népe* (People of the Puszta), Budapest, 1936; Géza Féja: *Viharsarok* (Stormy Corner), Budapest, 1937; Imre Kovács: *Néma forradalom* (Silent Revolution), Budapest, 1937; Zoltán Szabó: *A tardi helyzet* (The Situation at Tard), Budapest, 1937; Ferenc Erdei: *Futóhomok* (Drift Sand), Budapest, 1937; Zoltán Szabó: *Cifra nyomorú-ság* (Penury Disguised Under a Superficial Show of Wealth) Budapest, 1938; Ferenc Erdei: *Parasztok* (Peasants), Budapest, 1938.

learning, conceptual culture, a strict internal coordination of the monographies, and it is these features which distinguish them from the studies stimulating political ferment and social movements between the years 1936—1938.

The course followed by Erdei—considering only genre characteristics—reflects some different characteristics in other respects, too. In interpreting the studies in the present volume, I should like to point out but two aspects. Following 1938, the critical sociographical activities of the movement of populist writers became impossible. The democratic and anti-fascist March Front which had been founded on March 15, 1937, disintegrated. This front was a grouping of left-wing populist writers and communist students assuming the character of a popular front. The most influential personalities of the movement had been right from the beginning Imre Kovács, Gyula Illyés and Ferenc Erdei. Another impeding momentum was the fact that the two series publishing the best sociographical monographies: *The Discovery of Hungary* and *Service and Writing* closed down. It was virtually Ferenc Erdei who continued to cultivate and bring to perfection this genre although—as will be seen later on—his course, too, has undergone some modifications.

The declining significance of critical sociographies can be explained mainly by two political-historical facts. First, with the support of Germany and Italy the Peace Treaty of Trianon was partially revised in 1938—1939 and as a result, the positions of the right-wing parties strengthened dramatically. Second, Hungary's entry into the war on the side of the Axis Powers resulted in a political atmosphere in which any social criticism "undermining the unity of the fighting nation" was branded defeatism by the ruling elite which plunged the country into war and pushed it to the edge of a historical abyss.

The impact of such historical events on the development of social sciences cannot be restricted to a single chain of events, but we may mention the disintegration of the March Front and the termination of publishing critical sociographical works. However, the career of Erdei as a philosopher is irregular in this respect, too. As it can be traced in the studies published in this volume, from the very beginning he was aware that in social research, abstract social history, descriptive sociography and analytical social theory should be separated from the questions of basic political needs and attitudes.

During the first critical period of his career—i.e. following the low tide in the wake of the revolutionary upswing in the early thirties and/or the coming into power of Hitler in Germany and Gyula Gömbös in Hungary—an orthodox interpretation of value-free research can be observed. In one of his entries written after his study trip abroad in 1935 there appears a new emphasis in his works. In this respect the facing of the conditions of fascist Germany and the studying of the living conditions of the middle-class peasantry of Western Europe—their up-to-date farms, their status based on equality before law, the urbanization of villages—are of equal importance. Erdei also observes that even under such modern conditions of existence the agrarian strata are in many countries the reserves of the conservative political forces.

The political and scientific aspirations were simultaneously present in the works of Ferenc Erdei from the very beginning. At the middle of the thirties—partly under the influence of the foreign experiences and inspired by the strengthening popular movement—he rejected the thesis of "value-freedom" which was alien to his character anyway, and like many of his comrades he, too, wanted to put critical

396

sociography into the service of the movement of populist writers. His book *Futóhomok* (Drift Sand)—some excerpts of which can be read in this volume, too—was written under such inspirations.[5]

The hermeneutical-epistemological training of Erdei explains only partially why the author of *Futóhomok* was so unique in the school of Hungarian sociography. Erdei's relationship to Marxism should also be taken into account. It should be mentioned here but briefly—we are coming back to this question later in connection with other problems—that in the course of his sojourn in Western Europe he got the opportunity to study the works of Lenin on the peasant problem—as an irony of fate in the library of the Berlin University, only some hundred yards from the *Reichstag*. Although as a result of his readings he outlined for himself a peculiarly messianistic image of Lenin, the analyses on the internal structuring of the peasantry and the development of capitalism in Russia had a considerable influence on his ideas. The originally and individually interpreted image of Lenin had helped Erdei to discover the leading force of the radical reform—regarded as unavoidable by Erdei—in some dynamically developing strata of the peasantry. At the same time, Erdei got an impetus to examine the local societies as segments of society as a whole.

As a result of these influences, a peculiar dualism can be observed in his works. We may observe a claim to the scholarly character of his studies, more particularly an attempt to apply the achievements of the theory of social formations. We also see the intention to justify by means of facts and data collected also with the help of fine intuition the merits of his political programme, his hypothesis regarding the role of the burgher-peasants of the country towns. For this reason in *Futóhomok*—a book rightly to be regarded as the representative work of the scientific sociographies—exact scientific descriptions and authentic statements of facts are blended with utopistic improvisations and idealized characterizations of the agricultural cities of the Great Plain.

After the events of 1938, Erdei published his monography *Parasztok* (Peasants)[6] and following the decline of the movement he set out on new sociographical ventures. However, the contradiction mentioned above had only been solved gradually.[7] The year 1941/42 represents to a certain extent another turning-point. By making use of his continued studies of Marx's works and/or of the socio-historical research of István Hajnal, Erdei seems to have succeeded in accomplishing a higher level synthesis of political commitment and the strict criteria of scientific analysis. From among these works, this volume includes the fragmentary, unfinished *Magyar paraszttársadalom* (Hungarian Peasant Society) and *A magyar társadalom a két világháború között* (Hungarian Society Between the Two World Wars) which are of an outstanding documentary value.[8]

*

[5] For more details cf. Tibor Huszár: "A tudós és politikus Erdei Ferenc műhelyében" (In the Workshop of Ferenc Erdei, the Scientist and Politician) In: *Történelem és szociológia* (History and Sociology), Budapest, 1983.

[6] Ferenc Erdei: *Parasztok* (Peasants), Budapest, 1938.

[7] In this period Erdei publishes his sociographical studies, and two monographs summing up his theoretical studies: *Magyar város* (Hungarian Town), Budapest, 1939; *Magyar falu* (Hungarian Village), Budapest, 1940.

[8] Ferenc Erdei: *A magyar társadalomról* (Erdei's Writings on Hungarian Society), Budapest, Akadémiai Kiadó, 1980.

Without assuming a direct relationship, the influence of radical bourgeois sociology including primarily the problems defined by Oszkár Jászi can be seen in Erdei's ideas as well. A basic perception of Jászi has been the following: "It is but natural that we who have been studying the sociology and socialism of the end of the 19th and the beginning of the 20th centuries have identified ourselves as regards our ideas with those who lead the vanguard struggles of the great Western democracies. It is but natural that our interest, attention and longings are directed first and foremost towards the most advanced social formations.

On the other hand, the tasks our nation is currently faced with are not identical with the present-day tasks of the great Western democracies. There the problem of the transition from a bourgeois democracy to a workers' democracy has become an increasingly timely task, whereas in our country we first have to create a bourgeois democracy. Thus, we have to fight in the future for the advent of something the transitionary character of which we are convinced of, for something the spiritual and economic shortcomings of which we are well acquainted with from Western experiences."[9]

In the early works of Erdei the problems of the co-existence of feudalism and capitalism, of the superposition of these antagonisms was explored in connection with the relative sovereignty and/or disintegration of peasant societies. This can be seen from the more and more sophisticated typology of the "traditionalist", the "feudal" versus "burgher-minded" peasants or regions.

In *Futóhomok* the questions of social formation, i.e. the simultaneous articulation of feudal and capitalist production relations and scales of values is explored on the basis of preliminary historical studies and field work at the characteristic settlements of the region between the Danube and the Tisza.

In *Magyar falu* the situation of the Hungarian village and in it that of the peasantry is more directly related to the structural contradictions of Hungarian society as a whole. This work is of monographical pretensions: historical facts and data, local historical studies and field work are blended here in a refined way containing a number of hypothetical elements.

Spatial social contradictions, the relationship of town and village come to play a great part in this work. Incidentally Erdei thinks that the form of existence, the relationships and value judgements of the rural population (i.e. those of not only of the peasantry but of the so-called gentlemanly middle-class, thus of the rural intelligentsia, too) are to be explained by the dual—feudal and/or bourgeois—structure which can be pointed out in the spatial structure as well. Contrary to the bourgeois societies which as a whole represent "a single sphere of action" and where "in the inter-class relationships identical processes take place" and "these various classes take part in them according to their roles", in Hungarian society the different classes and regional groups not only represent different social roles but at the same time, they represent "independent spheres of action where leadership, control and in general all underlying elements of social life are made up of separate circles".[10] "And not only society as a whole is divided into a separate upper middle-class,

---

[9] Oszkár Jászi: "Új Magyarország felé" (Towards a New Hungary) In: *A szociológia első magyar műhelye* (The First Workshop of Hungarian Sociology).

[10] Ferenc Erdei: *A magyar falu* (Hungarian Village) Akadémiai Kiadó, Budapest, 1974, p. 159; in this volume p. 121.

398

peasant and bourgeois circles but towns and villages, too, represent separate spheres of action."[11]

This is why the rural way of life is so markedly separated from the urban way of life. It might seem that the village is "a society of simple organization squeezed within narrow bounds." At the same time the way of life of the different strata is of a closed type within the bounds of which everybody is in the possession of detailed information. This organization, however, is only seemingly simple. As a matter of fact, the village fits into society as a whole in a way that "it is a social sphere in itself having separate and specific active components of its own". At the same time, "every village is connected in some way or other with a town constituting a characteristic town-and-its–hinterland sphere of action". Moreover, the strata constituting the village belong according to their groups to separate stratum or class formations: "…that is the upper-class, the peasantry or bourgeoisie."[12]

The picture becomes even more complex when Erdei introduces the historical dimension into his analysis. The ideal types of the feudal and burgher villages differ according to the merits of their character and can be described separately simply and clearly. The majority of the Hungarian villages seem to be irregular cases in this respect, too: "Since bourgeois transformation has not taken place yet feudal and bourgeois stratification continue to exist side by side." Rural society is structured by both systems of stratification: "In addition to these two aspects of stratification, the rich variety of our village types should also be considered leading us to the conclusion that rural stratification in Hungary is far from being simple. Some of our villages are still entirely stratified in terms of a feudal structure, others have already been transformed alongside bourgeois stratification and between these two extremes we may find an infinite variety of village types."[13]

In *Magyar paraszttársadalom* (Hungarian Peasant Society) the problem is formulated as a component of a greater historical perspective: the disturbances of social organization are connected by Erdei with the fact that Hungarian social development as a whole has been delayed and belated. He links the specific character of development to the institutions of feudalism and the social structure of feudal Hungary, both of which were formed by external influence and processes controlled from above. This had been necessary in that given era from the historical point of view but at the same time the "short-circuited development stages" have given neither space nor time to "spontaneous movements" and "mature organizations". Erdei believes that it is the result of the "copying of Western evolution" that in the Hungarian society "feudal forms evolved less profusely and with less variety" than in Western Europe where "following the disintegration of the ancient forms" the evolution of society commenced "with a totally new start and by taking autonomous forms."[14]

At the same time, certain elements of nomadic society have survived even in the new social formation of feudalism. The development of feudalism was peculiarly

---

[11] Ibid. p. 159; in this volume p. 121.

[12] Ibid. pp. 159—160; in this volume p. 121.

[13] Ibid. p. 146; in this volume p. 110.

[14] Ferenc Erdei: "Magyar paraszttársadalom" (Hungarian Peasant Society) In: *A magyar társadalomról* (Erdei's Writings on Hungarian Society), Budapest, Akadémiai Kiadó, 1980. p. 32; in this volume p. 157.

influenced by this fact. This peculiar kind of social development has been important from the point of view of Hungarian peasantry as well since as a consequence, "the peasantry was not shaped within the body of Hungarian society but outside, so to speak under it. In a nomadic society the servants and conquered people had not been members of society; they were just subjected elements of a society structured within itself; similarly, in the society of noblemen the peasantry developed like a sub-social world presenting the clan units and traditions. This peculiar relationship survived even at the time of the full development of feudalism and the organization of the countries of the nobility."[15]

Historical analysis is not of a chronological character in the works of Erdei. He concentrates strictly on socio-historical correlations analyzing them in terms of the change of the social structure. Historical introduction thus serves the substantiating of the problems: by what structural reasons is it to be explained that Hungarian bourgeois development, too, has been delayed. At this point it becomes clear why Erdei went back to the very origins: the inhibiting factors—which are inseparable from the external conditions—were connected with the characteristics of the development outlined, first of all with "the over-development of the nobility" and the "peasantry becoming a too closed stratum".[16] This over-development was reflected by the fact that the dominant power positions of the "broad class of the nobility" were preserved by the countries of the nobility, i.e. by its territorial and corporate self-governing bodies. Irrespective of its ethnic origins this legal system identified the nation with the nobility excluding all other social strata from the *Natio Hungarica*. Thus, all these factors also hampered the emergence of a *bourgeois* nation.

The "over-petrification" of the peasant class, has been connected with these historically developed conditions, though this belatedness is explained by the cataclysms of political history as well, more precisely by the fact that following the peasant revolt led by Dózsa in 1514 and the Turkish occupation of the country lasting hundred and fifty years, Hungarian society "underwent a belated re-development". The hegemony of Austria beginning in the 18th century in this region as well as the peripherical situation of the region also impeded industrialization and urbanization.

From the perspectives of social history and structural changes the consequences can be summarized as follows: the agrarian surplus-population could be absorbed only to a minor degree by towns and industry and as a result, "bourgeois society" has become feeble. The supreme factors of bourgeois transformation, of national evolution, of creating a national culture were the so-called historical classes, i.e. the strata of the nobility. As Erdei put it, thus, "postformation" had become an important characteristics of *bourgeois* social development.

The most important privileges of the nobility and the institution of serfdom were abolished by the revolution of 1848, nevertheless "feudal social forms" have survived in many a field. The heirs of the former strata of noblemen, i.e. the class of great landowners and the so-called upper middle-class had a significant part in preserving these forms. These circumstances go far to explain the sociological status of the peasantry: not only the period of serfdom had been longer for the Hungarian

---

[15] Ibid. p. 33; in this volume p. 158.
[16] Ibid. pp. 35; in this volume p. 159.

peasantry than for its counterparts in Western societies but feudal characteristics have survived in the stage of free peasantry as well.

Thus, the problems outlined in *Magyar falu* (Hungarian Village) have been summarized at a higher level of abstraction in this book and have been based on solid historical facts. "In the West, both the development of feudalism and the bourgeois transformation had been complete: by now feudal forms have withered away or have entirely perished. Society as a whole, farmers included, has assumed a homogeneous bourgeois character and structure. In the West the former serfs have ceased to be peasants and have become agrarian bourgeois, petit bourgeois and workers occupying their social positions according to the bourgeois class structure. There are still to be found some memories of their peasant past, e.g. apparel, etc., however these are no longer rigid forms of everyday life but mere symbols."[17] As it could be seen from the above, in Hungarian society "in general the bourgeois economic organization has emerged. The technological framework of everyday life has been transformed and the intellectual atmosphere has changed, nevertheless feudal forms have not been entirely eliminated."[18]

The typology outlined in *Magyar paraszttársadalom* (Hungarian Peasant Society) captures the consequences of this specific social development. In the decades between the two World Wars the peasantry was simultaneously stratified and divided by relations based on capitalism and by the feudal elements present in the life conditions and the order of values. At the same time, the stratifying role of the various types of settlements was considerable. A great part of the peasantry did not live in villages and/or villages themselves belonged to different regions. Thus farmhands living on big manors, homestead farmers or peasant burghers living in the so-called agricultural towns where there was no industry — all these strata constituted integral parts of the peasantry, while the disintegration of the traditional peasantry was accelerated by the differences of the various types of the settlements.

Erdei has indicated already in *Magyar paraszttársadalom*: he has undergone a marked switch-over from the so-called scientific sociography to sociology. As reflected by a letter dated 1942 he thought it to be an insurmountable limitation of sociographies that they offer large scope to intuition while often substituting metaphores for scientific notions. The sociographer always runs the risk of getting stuck on the surface and he possibly generalizes his personal experiences.[19]

This severe value judgement was not quite unjustified in the case of Erdei as well: he was inclined — especially in his early papers — to over-generalize the behavioural patterns of the rich peasants of his native town, and/or of the traditional peasants of his maternal grandparents. However, this evaluation has been too severe as it can be seen from the excerpts in this volume and — hopefully — from this afterword: even in his sociographical works Erdei could avoid simple description owing to his sociological-epistemological studies and his historical approach. As a result, intuition and experience collected by him as a "participating observer" and "active sociographer" were not limitations in his carefully elaborated monographs contain-

---

[17] Ibid. p. 37; in this volume pp. 160—161.
[18] Ibid. p. 16; in this volume p. 160.
[19] Ferenc Erdei: *Levél Püski Sándorhoz* (Letter to Sándor Püski). ELTE Szociológiai Intézet Archivuma. (Archives of the Dep. of Sociology of Budapest University).

ing also sociographical elements. On the contrary, these sociographical elements richly coloured Erdei's theoretical argumentations.

Given the knowledge of his full oeuvre, however, we may state: though he did not have to bring about a total change in his approach, the demand of a partial correction seemed to be justified. In this respect, however, it is not the change itself which seems significant but the theoretical advance. In the monographs cited even in *Magyar város* (Hungarian Town), the individual social strata—though the social segments analyzed are depicted as parts of society as a whole—are analyzed primarily in terms of the role they play in the disintegration of peasant society. And similarly, when Erdei characterizes the towns, the subordination of the villages (though he writes about other functions as well) and/or the part they could have as integrating centres in modernizing rural settlements is a decisive factor.

It is an undeniable fact that the disintegration of the peasantry was a decisive process in modern Hungarian society. Yet, Erdei was right in showing dissatisfaction with his works in one respect: as it can be clearly seen from his works cited the presence of capitalist structures was regarded to be beyond question by Erdei. In his works it is stressed that the transformation of the peasantry and the villages is moulded by these capitalist structures. However, he failed to characterize the life and functions of the urban middle-class and the industrial working class and for this very reason in his early works the structural outline of Hungarian society is more simplified than that of the villages. His paper *a Magyar társadalom a két világháború között* (Hungarian Society Between the Two World Wars) was an attempt to overcome this one-sidedness.[20]

Parallel with this he commenced a broader empirical survey with some of his young colleagues, István Márkus and Jolán Majlát, who was to become his wife. They wanted to elaborate the formative changes of the society of Nagykőrös on the basis of archive source-materials, systematic social observation and data registration.[21]

Only a few chapters of *A magyar társadalom* (Hungarian Society) had been completed, whereas the monographs by Majlát and Márkus on the history of Nagykőrös were published in the pre-war years. The manuscripts of Erdei's two monographs on Nagykőrös were lost during the war. Nevertheless it is of symbolic significance that Erdei regarded his "switch-over to sociology" as a development of the theoretical basis and at the same time as an empirical verification of hypotheses.

The fragment entitled *Magyar társadalom a két világháború között* (Hungarian Society Between the Two World Wars) published first in the monthly *Valóság* in 1976 is to our mind one of the most significant works of Erdei despite its fragmented nature. The excerpts published in this volume summarize the earlier theoretical achievements of Erdei. Erdei once again adopted the theory of social formations in this more comprehensive attempt but here he has distinguished between the more universal notion of socio-economic formation and its concrete historical formations

[20] Ferenc Erdei: "Magyar társadalom a két világháború között" (Hungarian Society between the two World Wars) In: *A magyar társadalomról* (Erdei's Writings on Hungarian Society), Akadémiai Kiadó, Budapest 1980.

[21] Jolán Majlát and István Márkus: *Nagykőrös beilleszkedése a magyar rendi társadalomba a XVIII. században* (The place of Nagykőrös in the Hungarian Feudal Society of the 18th Century). Budapest, 1943.

which can be examined by means of sociological methods. One of the most original—though not adequately elaborated—elements of this paper has been the hypothesis of the simultaneous homogeneity and heterogeneity of the economic and social structures regarded as the specific product of the historical development of this region. As a matter of fact, in "the capitalist societies of Eastern Europe" it has been just the result of this development process that "the economy being of a basically capitalist character is one question and the social structure which is partly a feudal formation and partly a colonial-type formation is another."[22] The definition-colonial-type formation does not seem to be quite an exact one, however, it indicates an essential circumstance, i.e. the fact that in peripheral countries far removed from the centres of economic development both industry and modern credit systems are established by foreign or freshly settled capitalist entrepreneurs. As regards Hungarian social evolution, according to Erdei, "… Hungarian society is a characteristic example of the East European societies where capitalist transformation has been achieved from outside; therefore also the development of Hungarian society significantly reflects the peculiar dualism of production relations and the structure of society. (…) Thus Hungarian society between the two World Wars ought to be examined according to the above viewpoints if our aim is to comprehend empirical reality."[23]

This partly means that "class stratification of our society should be defined unambiguously according to its production relations; at the same time, the specific development of the social structure, which has to a great extent developed separately has to be thoroughly analyzed as well."[24]

Thus problems which were already posed in the early works of Erdei were transplanted into methodologically deliberate framework of interpretation. The specific dual structure of the Hungarian village—similarly to the whole history of the Austro-Hungarian Monarchy—is explained by a multiple complex structure. "Thus it was not bourgeois society but the compound of a bourgeois society developed together with the capitalist transformation and a feudal social structure which continued to exist in the course of capitalist development as well."[25] Therefore as a result of the specific social development, in Hungary "entirely independent structures became interlinked with each other within the framework of Hungarian society. Although these occupy the class positions of the very same economic structure, they are still parallel and separately viable social forms which are interconnected, interrelated and associated, nevertheless they have not merged into homogeneous bourgeois society even at that time."[26]

In contemporary sociology in the study of the Third World this emphasis on a multiple, complex and heterogeneous social structure, as possible indicator of discrepancy of social position and status may seem somewhat conventional but we may regard Erdei's way of posing the question in 1942 as something unique.

[22] Ferenc Erdei: "Magyar társadalom a két világháború között" (Hungarian Society between the two World Wars) In: A magyar társadalomról (Erdei's Writings on Hungarian Society), Akadémiai Kiadó, Budapest, 1980. p. 294; in this volume p. 10.

[23] Ibid. p. 295 in this volume p. 11. and 12.

[24] Ibid. p. 295; in this volume p. 12.

[25] Ibid. p. 295; in this volume ibid.

[26] Ibid. p. 295; in this volume ibid.

This conceptual construction was naturally not unprecedented. Let it be mentioned just as an example that in the analyses of Lenin or Max Weber—though with different perspectives and conclusions—similar ideas were formulated and they may have influenced Erdei, too. However, the assumption that in addition to the *coherent block* of modernized social groups preserving feudal elements we may also find the fully developed forms of the historical structures of modern bourgeois society (these structures have their proper roles in industry, trade and modern urban intellectual life) contained quite a few insights and starting points for further research.

Erdei draws an exact sociological picture of the components of the "historical-national society" (i.e. of the state, the churches, the great estates, the aristocracy, the so-called historical middle-class, the national petite bourgeoisie, then he proceeds to outline the productive situations, roles and strata comprising modern bourgeois society (capitalist venture, bourgeois aristocracy, bourgeois middle-class, petite bourgeoisie and working class).[27] These thoughts can be regarded as the antecedents of the later insight of Erdei according to which the full realization of the bourgeois democratic revolution in Hungary is an indispensable precondition of socialist transformation and that at the same time—just owing to the structure of society—this process is going to deepen into socialist transformation.[28]

*

Throughout his career Ferenc Erdei was attracted by both politics and science. However, due to social conditions and personal decisions Erdei could not always play both of these roles simultaneously. While he acted primarily as a scholar between 1938 and 1945, the public and political role became dominant in his life between 1945 and 1957.

The most important stages of the political career of Ferenc Erdei have already been briefly outlined in the introductory part of this study. Recalling the history of those years be it enough to point out as regards Erdei the sociologist: between 1945 and 1948—this being a separate stage in the history of the post-war years—Erdei hoped that sociology would be emancipated and institutionalized by the new, democratic society.

From this aspect it seems to be significant that Ferenc Erdei was invited to give the opening lecture at the first session of the re-established Society of Social Sciences. The paper *A magyar agrárdemokrácia lehetőségei* (The Chances of Hungarian Agrarian Democracy) is a written variant of this lecture.[29] As regards its literary genre it is rather a political essay than a sociological study, nevertheless it is a significant programmatic document of the renascent post-war sociology in Hungary.

The Budapest Péter Pázmány University of Arts and Sciences decided in the spring of the year 1945 to establish a Department of Sociology and Erdei was invited

[27] Ibid. pp. 324—346; in this volume pp. 58—93.
[28] Ferenc Erdei: "A magyar társadalom" (Hungarian Society—A Lecture delivered at Szárszó) In: *A magyar társadalomról* (Erdei's Writings on Hungarian Society) Akadémiai Kiadó, Budapest, 1980., pp. 347—372.
[29] Ferenc Erdei: "A magyar agrárdemokrácia lehetőségei" (The Possibilities of Hungarian Agrarian Democracy), Published by György Gyarmati, *Valóság*, 1980, April.

to lead the department. Since Erdei considered this to be incompatible with his function as a member of the government he rejected the invitation of the faculty. However, he supported the establishment of the Department.

During the post-war years a comprehensive movement of "people's colleges" was started to help and support the continuation of studies of children with working-class and peasant backgrounds. An academy was organized for the leaders of this movement. Erdei gave several lectures on the significance of sociological culture and on the main sociological characteristics of the structural changes.

However, his hopes were frustrated and came to nothing: beginning with 1948 the process of the institutionalization of sociology slowed down and soon practically all sociological activities were discriminated again: the sociology department—which was headed by Professor Sándor Szalai—was dissolved, the movement of people's colleges and its Academy of the Study of Society were wound up, the periodicals publishing sociological or sociographical papers—thus, the well-known monthly *Fórum*—were suppressed.[30]

For Erdei this process meant an individual tragedy as well since his outstanding monographs sank into oblivion. In the years of dogmatism the suppression of sociology was inevitable: in an over-centralized society the attempt to control the veracity of truths declared to be undeniable facts was branded as iconoclasm, whereas feed-back was regarded as a useless waste of time.

*

The revival of sociology in Hungary and the development of its institutional system has accelerated at the middle of the sixties parallel with the preparations of economic reforms. Erdei, at that time as Secretary General of the Hungarian Academy of Sciences, helped directly and stimulated this process. He undertook to write an explicitly sociological-sociographical work only shortly before his death, though the scientist's role had once again become the decisive element of his career from 1957 on.

Incidentally he came forward with a monograph again in 1959. His book entitled *Mezőgazdaság és szövetkezet* (Agriculture and Cooperative) clearly indicated the interests of an expert-specialist. More precisely, he wished to treat the problem of the modernization of the village and/or agriculture primarily from the aspect of agricultural economics, not separating this process from the broader problem of socialist transformation.[31] The research projects of the Institute of Agrarian Economics headed by him and also his personal research were built on the theoretical basis outlined in this book.

At the turn of the fifties and sixties the cooperative form of property had become dominant in the Hungarian villages. Though he did not do any empirical research on that problem, Erdei, too, was interested in the sociological consequences of this historical turn of events. His writings originating from this period reflect that he was fully aware of the fact that changes in the property forms and the industrialization of

---

[30] Ferenc Erdei: "Paraszti jövendő" (The Future of Hungarian Peasantry) *Fórum*, July, 1948.

[31] Ferenc Erdei: *Mezőgazdaság és szövetkezet* (Agriculture and Cooperatives), Budapest, Akadémiai Kiadó, 1959.

the country considerably affected the occupational structure, as well. Urbanization had an enormous influence also on class stratification. These processes were to determine the pace of rural modernization.

The recurring idea of his articles written at that time is that the evolution of the socialist village is a process which should not be considered finished. On the contrary, one of the chief characteristics of the sixties "is change itself, the period of transition".[32] At the same time, despite of all its transitional, temporary and differentiated nature, the general and characteristic feature of present-day Hungarian village "is the disintegration of the traditional unity of settlement, agriculture and peasantry".[33]

It was just the fact of "incompletion" that resulted in the possibility of various development alternatives. One possible alternative is linked with the reform of the economic management system of the national economy. It assumes "the development of theoretically uniform mechanized large-scale farming conditions on the basis of industrialized agriculture, that is the adoption of up-to-date technologies and biochemical methods as well as a more active market activity, the development of private household plots, the enlargement of auxiliary cooperative factories, the propagation and spreading of various forms of joint ventures, enterprise organization and wage systems and finally the strengthening of the forms of interest assertion, i.e. the association of farmers' cooperatives".[34] Ferenc Erdei has committed himself unambiguously—as it can be seen from his works—to this alternative.

Erdei's other field in agrarian economics was linked with the utilization of the results of organizational development with highly significant sociological results. As a matter of fact, Erdei's interest was not confined to the organizational problems of agricultural cooperatives and state farms, and to the problems of branch or sectoral control but it also covered public administration.[35]

In order to further the exact analysis of the problem, Erdei initiated empirical research already in the early sixties: in the district of Szolnok and the town of Karcag in all the cooperatives, and state as well as cooperative social organs. Erdei and his associates examined (on the basis of representative samples) "the inter-organizational relationships, particularly taking into account the initiatives of farmers' cooperatives as well as proposals submitted to the cooperatives".[36]

In the sixties sociographical research, too, was revived. A new forum was called into being where such books could be published: the publication of the series *Magyarország felfedezése* (The Discovery of Hungary) was resumed. This venture was supported by Erdei from the very beginning. He became member of its editorial board, and later on—as he explained in a conversation to the author of this epilogue—as a first step towards the synthesis of his sociological research he, too, embarked on some sociographical field work: returning to the wider region of his

---

[32] Ferenc Erdei: "Az átalakuló magyar falu" (Hungarian Village in a Process of Transformation) *Társadalmi Szemle,* 1969/12.

[33] Ferenc Erdei: ibid.

[34] Ferenc Erdei: ibid.

[35] Ferenc Erdei: "A termelőszövetkezeti gazdaságok állami irányítása" (The State Management of Agricultural Cooperatives) *Közgazdasági Szemle,* 1984, No. 4.

[36] Ferenc Erdei: ibid.

native town he wrote a monograph entitled *Város és vidéke* (Town and its Environs).[37]

This work analyzes the relationship between the town and the urbanized village, more precisely the satellite system which has sprung into being between towns and villages of various functions and of various orders of magnitude on the one hand, and between villages and farmsteads which have remained without any function on the other.

Erdei's work focusses on the social microsphere. Although change in the social structure and in power relations influences the social micro-sphere, the developments of basic social institutions (the family, trends in consumption and production and the development of towns and villages change in these latter spheres is slower and less perceptible: "these are more conservative sections of society."[38]

Let me stress but one question in this work, a problem which is felt to be particularly topical in Eastern Europe in terms of sociological research. Summarizing the experiences of his field work Erdei emphasizes among others: "In 1969—1970 the social conditions in Szeged and the County of Csongrád do not only show the consequences of the history of the recent past, but also the marks of the earlier historic development. In short, we may say that present-day social relations indicate that *even the most revolutionary transformation is realized on the basis of the earlier history*. In the course of my investigations I realized that very old historical traditions determine to a surprising extent not only the present social conditions of our settlements, but also the concrete form and functioning of the new, socialist institutions.

Various development levels cannot give a full explanation for the differences among the settlements. In addition to that, there is also structural variation and there are also differences in character. The underlying cause of these differences is to be found in history, which in turn includes the totality of geographic, ethnic and other endowments as well. In terms of local social relations it seems completely obvious that the transformation of property relations, political change, and the various political actions affect a given historic and social world, therefore their influence gets modified.

In connection with the above we can speak of a generalizable historic experience. *We have to see that for radical social change and the emergence of an adequate social structure a long period is necessary."*[39]

Erdei endeavoured to further summarize in a comprehensive theoretical way the correlations between these historical and present-day structural and/or functional processes when writing *Város és vidéke* (Town and its Environs). However, this work which might have been so important from the point of view of summing up his oeuvre has remained unfinished, the fatal disease has carried him off unexpectedly at the age of 61. Though his drafts have remained unwritten his life-work is of epoch-making significance. Ferenc Erdei is regarded with good reason as a classical author of Hungarian sociology.

[37] Ferenc Erdei: *Város és vidéke* (Town and its Environs), Szépirodalmi, Budapest, 1971.
[38] Ibid, p. 14; in this volume p. 296.
[39] Ibid, p. 441; in this volume pp. 300—301.